# 38 LONDRES STREET

Also by Philippe Sands

BOOKS

*The Last Colony*
*The Ratline*
*East West Street*
*City of Lions* (with Josef Wittlin)
*The Grey Zone* (ed.)
*Torture Team*
*Lawless World*
*Principles of International Environmental Law*
*Justice for Crimes Against Humanity* (ed.)
*From Nuremberg to The Hague* (ed.)
*Bowett's Law of International Institutions*

FILM

*My Nazi Legacy*

PODCAST/RADIO

*The Ratline*
*La Filière*

PERFORMANCE

*East West Street: A Song of Good and Evil*
*The Last Colony*

# 38 LONDRES STREET

*On* IMPUNITY, PINOCHET *in* ENGLAND *and a* NAZI *in* PATAGONIA

## PHILIPPE SANDS

WEIDENFELD & NICOLSON

First published in Great Britain in 2025 by Weidenfeld & Nicolson,
an imprint of The Orion Publishing Group Ltd
Carmelite House, 50 Victoria Embankment
London EC4Y 0DZ

An Hachette UK Company

The authorised representative in the EEA is Hachette Ireland,
8 Castlecourt Centre, Dublin 15, D15 XTP3,
Ireland (email: info@hbgi.ie)

1 3 5 7 9 10 8 6 4 2

A CIP catalogue record for this book is
available from the British Library.

ISBN (Hardback) 978 1 4746 2074 1
ISBN (Export Trade Paperback) 978 1 4746 2075 8
ISBN (Ebook) 978 1 4746 2077 2
ISBN (Audio) 978 1 4746 2078 9

Typeset by Input Data Services Ltd, Bridgwater, Somerset

Printed in Great Britain by Clays Ltd, Elcograf, S.p.A.

MIX
Paper | Supporting
responsible forestry
FSC® C104740

www.weidenfeldandnicolson.co.uk
www.orionbooks.co.uk

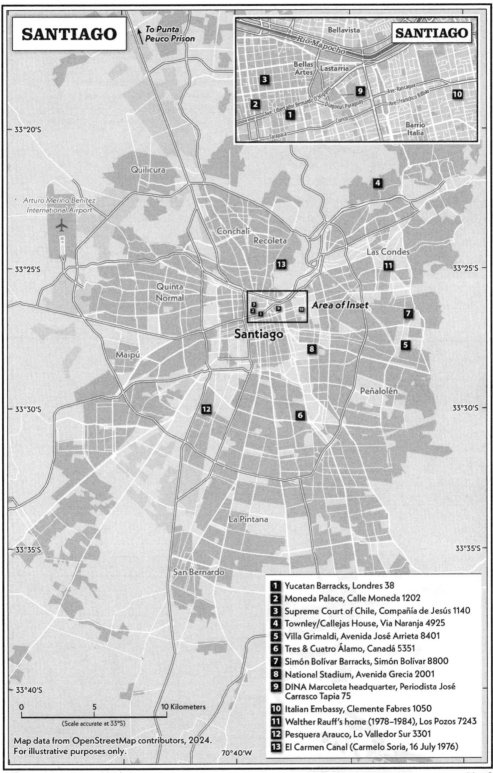

# SANTIAGO

To Punta
Peuco Prison

## SANTIAGO

Río Mapocho

Bellavista

Bellas Artes    Lastarria

**3**

**9** Ave. Rancagua

Diagonal Paraguay    Ave. Francisco Bilbao

**10**

**2**

**1**

Ave. Libertador Bernardo O'Higgins

Curicó

Tarapacá

Barrio Italia

33°20'S

Quilicura

Arturo Merino Benítez International Airport

Conchalí    Recoleta

**4**

33°25'S    **13**    Las Condes    **11**    33°25'S

Quinta Normal

Area of Inset    **3** **1** **9** **10**

**7**

Santiago

**8**    **5**

Maipú

Peñalolén

33°30'S    **12**    **6**    33°30'S

La Pintana

33°35'S    33°35'S

San Bernardo

0    5    10 Kilometers

(Scale accurate at 33°S)

| 1 | Yucatan Barracks, Londres 38 |
| 2 | Moneda Palace, Calle Moneda 1202 |
| 3 | Supreme Court of Chile, Compañía de Jesús 1140 |
| 4 | Townley/Callejas House, Via Naranja 4925 |
| 5 | Villa Grimaldi, Avenida José Arrieta 8401 |
| 6 | Tres & Cuatro Álamo, Canadá 5351 |
| 7 | Simón Bolívar Barracks, Simón Bolívar 8800 |
| 8 | National Stadium, Avenida Grecia 2001 |
| 9 | DINA Marcoleta headquarter, Periodista José Carrasco Tapia 75 |
| 10 | Italian Embassy, Clemente Fabres 1050 |
| 11 | Walther Rauff's home (1978–1984), Los Pozos 7243 |
| 12 | Pesquera Arauco, Lo Valledor Sur 3301 |
| 13 | El Carmen Canal (Carmelo Soria, 16 July 1976) |

33°40'S

Map data from OpenStreetMap contributors, 2024.
For illustrative purposes only.

70°40'W

Map 2

Map 1

# CONTENTS

*For Natalia*

There is not any thing
that hath bred greater troubles
than the libertie which is giuen to the wicked
to offend with all impunitie.

Jean Bodin, 1577

I am a monument

Walther Rauff, 1979

I am an angel

Augusto Pinochet, 2003

# CONTENTS

## Note to the Reader

I played a minor role in the unprecedented and historic legal proceedings that followed the arrest of Augusto Pinochet in London, on the evening of 16 October 1998. It offered a front-row seat in one of the most important international criminal cases since Nuremberg. Time has passed, but I have not forgotten the experience, the stories or the characters.

Many years after the arrest and the events that followed, I was researching a book about the Ratline, the route used by a Nazi to escape from the city of Lviv and Europe to South America. In the archive of an Austrian family, I came across a letter written by a former Nazi leader named Walther Rauff. Hunted for crimes against humanity and genocide, the SS man offered advice to an old comrade. A decade later, I learned, the author of the letter moved to Patagonia, in southern Chile, where he would manage a cannery that packed the flesh of king crabs into small tins.

It had not occurred to me that Pinochet and Rauff might be linked, but it turned out that the lives of the two men were deeply intertwined. This is the story of a journey to uncover their connection and its consequences, one that touches on matters of history, law, politics and literature. It also evokes ideas about memory, and the line that is said to separate fact and fiction, truth and myth.

On the lives of these two men, I have sought to describe fairly what I have learned, relying on documents, archives, testimonies and conversations. The account is not a complete version, or the only version. On such matters, where so many individuals are involved, there will be many perspectives and recollections. We know from daily life that two people who experience the same moment may see things differently, that memories are fluid and that what happened may be open to interpretation.

This is my interpretation, based on what I have seen, heard or read. It is a personal journey. It is about justice and memory and impunity, across time and place, about the threads that weave together our strange lives, in which questions and coincidences so often arise.

Philippe Sands
London and Bonnieux, November 2024

# Principal Characters

*Augusto Pinochet Ugarte*, b. 1915, Valparaíso; Chilean Army, President of Military Junta and Chile, 1973–1990
*Lucía Hiriart*, b. 1923, his wife

*Walther Rauff*, b. 1906, Köthen, Germany; German Navy; SS and Gestapo; manager, *Pesquera Camelio*
*Edith Rauff*, b. 1898, his second wife
*Walther Rauff II*, b. 1940, his son
*Walther Rauff III*, b. 1967, his grandson

## CHILE

*Carlos Basso*, b. 1972, journalist and university teacher

*Sergio Bitar*, b. 1940, government minister, economist, Dawson Island detainee

*José Camelio*, b. 1907, founder of *Pesquera Camelio*
*José (Porotin) Camelio*, b. 1932, son, *Pesquera Camelio*
*Humberto Camelio*, b. 1934, son, *Pesquera Camelio*
*Eduardo Camelio*, b. 1960, grandson
*Mariana Camelio*, b. 1996, great-granddaughter, poet

*Alfonso Chanfreau*, b. 1950, student, Londres 38 detainee, husband of Erika Hennings

*Manuel Contreras*, b. 1929, Army, DINA Director

*Hernán Felipe Errázuriz*, b. 1945, lawyer and diplomat

*Pedro Espinoza*, b. 1932, Army, DINA Deputy Director

*Eduardo Frei*, b. 1942, President (1994–2000)

*Samuel Fuenzalida*, b. 1956, Army and DINA conscript

*León Gómez*, b. 1953, history teacher, Londres 38 detainee

*Erika Hennings*, b. 1951, director of the Londres 38 organisation, detainee, wife of Alfonso Chanfreau

*José Miguel Insulza*, b. 1943, Minister of Foreign Affairs and Secretary-General

*Ricardo Izurieta*, b. 1943, Army, Commander-in-Chief

*Miguel Krassnoff*, b. 1946, Army, DINA

*Ricardo Lagos*, b. 1938, lawyer, economist, President (2000–2006)

*Miguel Lawner*, b. 1928, architect, Dawson Island detainee

*Orlando Letelier*, b. 1932, economist, government minister, Dawson Island detainee

*Osvaldo (Guatón) Romo*, b. 1938, torturer

*Miguel Schweitzer Speisky*, b. 1908, law professor, government minister
*Miguel Schweitzer Walters*, b. 1940, his son, lawyer, ambassador, government minister

*Carmelo Soria*, b. 1921, UN diplomat
*Laura González-Vera*, b. 1932, medical doctor
*Carmen Soria*, b. 1960, journalist

*Cristián Toloza*, b. 1958, psychologist and civil servant

*Jorgelino Vergara (El Mocito)*, b. 1960, 'junior waiter' to Manuel Contreras

# GERMANY

*Gerd Heidemann*, b. 1931, journalist, *Stern* magazine

*Karl Wolff*, b. 1900, Supreme SS and Police Leader

# SPAIN

*José María Aznar*, b. 1953, Prime Minister (1996–2004)

*Carlos Castresana*, b. 1957, prosecutor

*Juan Garcés*, b. 1944, lawyer, Allende adviser

*Manuel García-Castellón*, b. 1952, judge, Court No. 6, Audiencia Nacional

*Baltasar Garzón*, b. 1955, investigating judge, Court No. 5, Audiencia Nacional

# UNITED KINGDOM

*Thomas Bingham*, b. 1933, judge

*Tony Blair*, b. 1953, Prime Minister (1997–2007)

*Nico Browne-Wilkinson*, b. 1930, judge, Appellate Committee, House of Lords

*James Cameron*, b. 1961, barrister, counsel to General Pinochet

*Michael Caplan*, b. 1953, partner, Kingsley Napley law firm, solicitors to General Pinochet

*Leonard Hoffmann*, b. 1934, judge, Appellate Committee, House of Lords

*David Hope*, b. 1938, judge, Appellate Committee, House of Lords

*Alun Jones*, b. 1949, barrister, counsel to Crown Prosecution Service

*Jean Pateras*, b. 1948, interpreter, Metropolitan Police, Scotland Yard

*Jonathan Powell*, b. 1956, Chief of Staff to Tony Blair (1997–2007)

*Gordon Slynn*, b. 1930, judge, Appellate Committee, House of Lords

*Jack Straw*, b. 1946, Home Secretary (1997–2001)

*James Vallance White*, b. 1938, Fourth Clerk at the Table, House of Lords

# PROLOGUE

## Santiago, August 1974

A Chevrolet refrigerated van trundled along La Alameda, which connected the Moneda Palace to the University. Near the ancient Church of San Francisco it turned right, to enter the Barrio París-Londres, constructed around the intersection of two streets, Calle Londres and Calle París. The neighbourhood, once the garden of an ancient hermitage, was home to poets, writers and artists.

The van moved over the cobblestones before coming to a stop before a low grey stone building, number 38. Referred to simply as Londres, elsewhere the street might have been Londonstrasse, or Rue de Londres, or Londres Street.

Men in civilian clothing opened the van's rear doors and a group of men and women in blindfolds tumbled out and entered number 38. One was a twenty-year-old student of history, arrested for subversion. He wasn't sure where he was, but through a gap in the blindfold he glimpsed the black and white floor tiles that marked the entrance. A chessboard, the headquarters of the Socialist Party.

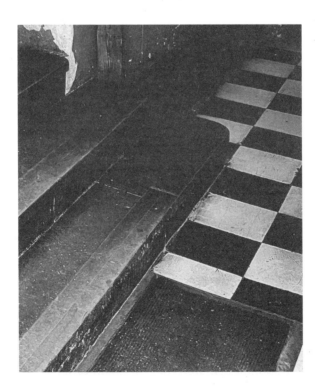

He was led up a few stone steps and into the building, separated from his companions and taken to a side room where he was instructed to sit. Another person, a woman, sat next to him.

'My name is León.'

'My name is Hedy,' the woman replied.

They waited. After a while, he was escorted to a staircase that wound up the back of the building, to the first floor. In another room, a guard ordered him to remove his clothing. Naked, he was made to lie on his back on the frame of an old bed, metal and cold. His wrists and ankles were tied to the frame. He was splayed, like a pig on a spit.

He heard low voices, and wondered if one had a German accent. As he lay, he made out the shape of an old typewriter, tall, elegant. He heard other voices and noticed a scent, cheap and familiar. The sounds approached, the scent sharpened. *Flaño*, a perfume that would come to induce a sense of anxiety and fear.

Later, when he was back in the room on the ground floor, a young man was carried in and deposited on the floor, in a heap. Alfonso, someone whispered, a philosophy student, in a dreadful condition. Shortly, a young woman was brought to him, another detainee. The two spoke a few words before the philosophy student was bundled out of the building, put in the back of a refrigerated van, and driven away.

He was never seen again.

## London, October 1998

Twenty-four years later.

Four police officers gathered outside Room 801, on the eighth floor of a medical clinic on a street in the centre of London. An interpreter was present, late on that Friday evening in October. They entered the room, where an eighty-two-year-old man lay in bed, recovering from an operation on his back. Augusto Pinochet.

The interpreter, a lady with bouffant hair, informed him in Spanish that he was under arrest and told him his rights. 'You are charged with murder,' she said, 'by a Spanish judge who wishes to extradite you to Madrid to be put on trial for a genocide you perpetrated in Chile, for torturing people and making them disappear.'

Three weeks later, in Paris, I greeted my wife at the large wooden gates that marked the entrance to the Pantin cemetery, on the outskirts of the city. This was where my grandfather was buried. We embraced. 'I've just received an approach from Augusto Pinochet's lawyers,' I told her. 'They would like me to argue that he is immune from the jurisdiction of the English courts and could not be extradited to Spain, for genocide or any other crimes.'

'Will you do it?' she asked in a firm voice. I reminded her of the 'cab-rank principle', the rule that required barristers to act like taxi drivers, to take every fare, to turn down none because of politics or personality.

'Will you do it?' she asked again.

You know the rule, so yes, that was my inclination.

'Fine,' she said in a tone that was both irritated and sweet, 'but if you do it, I will divorce you.'


## Hagenberg, Austria, June 2015

Seventeen years later.

I was on the upper floor of an ancient and dilapidated castle in northern Austria, making my way through the family archive of a long-dead Austrian couple. I found an old letter, written after the war, sent to Otto Wächter, on the run in Rome. The writer was a man named Walther Rauff, dispensing advice from Damascus in Syria:

> Maintain an unshakable toughness, don't be shy about the work
> you do, and don't spend time harking back to better times. Accept
> the current situation and you can achieve a lot and climb back
> up the ladder . . . The main thing is to get out of Europe . . . and
> focus on the 'reassembling of good forces for a later operation'.

Go to South America, Rauff told Wächter, who had once overseen the extermination of hundreds of thousands of Jews and Poles in Lviv, and then added: 'I will pursue things along these lines.'

I learned that the writer of the letter was also an SS man on the run. He was notorious for his role in overseeing the policy to use vans to gas Jews and others to their deaths, and then to kill hundreds of thousands of people across Europe, to make them disappear. Indicted for these acts of mass killing, Herr Rauff avoided capture and made his way onto the Ratline. Years later, he ended up at the end of the world, in Patagonia in southern Chile, the manager of a king-crab cannery.

Rumours about his past followed him. So did rumours about his connection to General Pinochet. 'Everybody knows,' said a taxi driver in downtown Santiago.

# PART I

## ARREST

*The certainty that there is no place on earth where crimes will go unpunished may be an effective means of preventing them.*
Cesare Beccaria, 1764

# LONDON, OCTOBER 1998

## 1

It was 17 October 1998, a Saturday afternoon, when I heard the news on the radio, waiting for the football results. It was my thirty-eighth birthday. The former Chilean dictator, General Augusto Pinochet, has been arrested in London, the BBC reported, at the request of a Spanish judge. This was interesting, as it wasn't every day that a former head of state was detained. The details were sketchy, but it was said that the extradition request alleged crimes of genocide, torture and disappearances committed during his years in power, from the day of the Coup that brought him to power on 11 September 1973 until he stepped down, in March 1990.

News of the arrest gave rise to anger, delight and disbelief. The Chilean government protested that Pinochet was a former President and Senator-for-Life with complete immunity. 'A transgression of international norms,' his son told a crowd throwing eggs at the British ambassador's residence in Santiago. 'An act of cowardice,' claimed the Pinochet Foundation, guardian of his legacy. 'He was sleeping when police arrived at his room in the clinic.'

Pinochet's opponents, on the other hand, were thrilled. Finally, he can be questioned on the fate of our loved ones, said the president of the Families of the Disappeared. A 'unique opportunity' to answer for his regime's human rights violations, said María Isabel Allende, daughter of President Salvador Allende, who died on the day of the Coup.

'An earthquake,' wrote Roberto Bolaño, a Chilean novelist living near Barcelona.

A matter for the courts, said the British government. 'The idea that a brutal dictator should claim diplomatic immunity would be pretty gut-wrenching stuff' for most people, said Peter Mandelson, a minister.

Former Prime Minister Margaret Thatcher declared the arrest to be outrageous, unlawful and inhumane, carried out 'at dead of night' on a sedated Pinochet. It put all former leaders at risk, inhibiting decisions that might cause a leader to 'appear before a foreign court to answer for it'. Those who wield 'absolute power' would be less likely to relinquish it, 'for fear of ending their days in a Spanish prison'. She was supported by Norman Lamont, a former Conservative minister who considered Pinochet to be a 'good, brave and honourable soldier'.

I was a teenager at the time of the Coup and knew little about Pinochet. Over the next years, I didn't visit Chile and the Chileans I came to know were mainly law students who took my classes, or academics exiled to Europe. I did, however, read books and see films about those times. In 1991 I saw a performance of Ariel Dorfman's play *Death and the Maiden* at the Royal Court Theatre in London and I have not forgotten Juliet Stevenson's portrayal of a woman who recognises her torturer, a memory she describes to her husband:

'Weren't you blindfolded and sick?' [*says the husband*]
'I can be sick and recognise a voice.'
'A vague memory of someone's voice is not proof of anything.'
'It's his voice. I recognised it as soon as he came in here last night. The way he laughs. Certain phrases he uses.'

Around that time I came to know a Chilean law professor, Francisco Orrego Vicuña, with whom I later worked on environmental issues. I was not aware he'd served as Pinochet's ambassador in London, until that detail emerged and scuppered his election to become a judge at the International Court of Justice. He was in decent company: the writer Jorge Luis Borges was said to have lost his chance of a Nobel Prize for Literature because of the admiration he expressed for Pinochet.

## 2

Augusto Pinochet Ugarte was born in 1915 in Valparaíso, of Breton and Basque heritage. He joined the military and made his way up through the ranks. On the way, he taught in military academies in

Chile and Ecuador, where he lived in the mid-1950s with his wife Lucía Hiriart. In 1970, Salvador Allende, the newly elected socialist President, appointed Pinochet as General Chief of Staff of the Army, serving under Carlos Prats, his friend and Commander-in-Chief. On 23 August 1973, after Prats resigned, Allende promoted Pinochet to Commander-in-Chief. Eighteen days later, on 11 September, Pinochet played a leading role in the Coup that toppled Allende, who committed suicide in the Moneda Palace, the home of the presidency. The events are portrayed in Patricio Guzmán's *The Battle of Chile*, a trilogy of remarkable documentary films.

Pinochet, a virulent anti-communist and Germanophile, was anointed as head of a four-man Military Junta, and later President of Chile. He was supported by large sections of the Chilean population and, in the United States, by President Nixon and Henry Kissinger, who became Secretary of State a week after the Coup. They welcomed Pinochet's government as a bulwark against Soviet influence and a means to promote free-market principles inspired by the ideas of the economist Milton Friedman and the 'Chicago Boys'.

The Junta legislated to 'remove Marxism from Chile', dissolving leftist political parties and expropriating their assets. The Socialist Party building at Londres 38, in the heart of Santiago, was acquired and turned into a secret interrogation and torture centre, known as the Yucatan Barracks. Here, to avoid drawing attention, interrogators and guards dressed as civilians, uniformed personnel were prohibited and unmarked vans and other regular vehicles moved prisoners in and out. The Junta took over private companies to operate and finance its secret activities and repression.

The Junta established a secret police force, the *Dirección de Inteligencia Nacional*, the DINA, to rein in opponents and run Londres 38 and other such places of torture and killing. As director, Pinochet appointed Manuel Contreras, a trusted Army man from the School of Engineers in Tejas Verdes near San Antonio, west of Santiago on the Pacific coast, giving him unlimited powers to destroy leftists. Every morning, Contreras reported to Pinochet who, he claimed, personally approved each DINA operation. Pinochet himself was protected by the *boinas negras*, the black berets, an elite military group.

For four years the DINA detained, interrogated and tortured tens of thousands of Pinochet's opponents. Many were killed, and by September 1977, when the DINA was dissolved, more than fifteen hundred people had disappeared. Imprisonment and assassination became routine in Chile, and also abroad. 'A country occupied by the dictatorship, which was directly in line with the thinking of the Nazi's,' thought the poet Raúl Zurita.

Within a day of the Coup, Salvador Allende's former ministers were sent to a newly constructed concentration camp on Dawson Island, in the Straits of Magellan, near Punta Arenas, in the south of the country.

Within a month, a Chilean Army death squad was engaged in a countrywide tour of assassinations. Ninety-seven people were killed in the operation that came to be known as the 'Caravan of Death'.

Within a year, the DINA was operating dozens of detention centres. At Londres 38, on average one prisoner disappeared every day. Nearby detention centres included the National Stadium; the Villa Grimaldi; the clandestine cells at Cuatro Álamos, part of the regular facilities at Tres Álamos; and the secret Simón Bolívar Barracks, operated by the DINA's Lautaro Brigade. The DINA acquired a house on the Vía Naranja, in a wealthy suburb of Santiago, where chemists produced sarin gas in the basement as literary salons were held on the upper floor.

The DINA operated centres around the entire country. In San Antonio there was the Tejas Verdes barracks and a little further south the torture facilities at Santo Domingo. In the far south, in Punta Arenas, the Old Naval Hospital was taken over and came to be known as the 'Palacio de las Sonrisas' ('Palace of Smiles').

A year after the Coup, the Pinochet government and the DINA acted to commit murder outside Chile. In September 1974, General Prats was assassinated in Buenos Aires. A 'most capable man,' said Pinochet on hearing about the death of his old friend and predecessor as Commander-in-Chief. 'I always felt affection for him.'

In October 1975, the exiled Christian Democrat leader Bernardo Leighton was the target of a failed assassination attempt, in Rome.

In November 1975, on Pinochet's sixtieth birthday, the DINA established Operation Condor, a joint project with Argentina, Bolivia, Chile, Paraguay and Uruguay. It would target leftist leaders and democrats across South America.

In July 1976, Carmelo Soria, a United Nations official with full immunity under international law, was abducted on a central

Santiago street. Two days later, the body of the dual Chilean and Spanish national was found in the city's Canal del Carmen.

In September 1976, Orlando Letelier, Allende's former ambassador to the United States and then Minister of Defence, was assassinated in downtown Washington DC.

On it went, for years, generating opposition. In September 1986, Pinochet's motorcade was ambushed and five soldiers were killed and many others injured. The President, who narrowly avoided death, ordered a series of reprisal killings.

Two years later, in October 1988, Chileans voted 'No' in a referendum that Pinochet organised to continue as President. Instead, they voted for a return to democratic rule, and in March 1990, after seventeen years in power, Pinochet stepped down, staying on as Commander-in-Chief of the Army.

A democratically elected government took office, a coalition known as the *Concertación*, supported by Christian Democrats and Socialists. President Patricio Aylwin established a National Commission for Truth and Reconciliation, chaired by Raul Rettig, which reported in 1991. The Rettig Report found that Pinochet's leadership caused over 40,000 people to be illegally detained or tortured, and more than 3,000 to be murdered or disappeared. Many put the numbers even higher.

In March 1998, Pinochet stepped down as Commander-in-Chief of the Army. He accepted the appointment of Senator-for-Life, which gave him complete immunity, as a parliamentarian, from legal proceedings in Chile.

By now, however, the cases in relation to the crimes of his government, and his own role, were stacking up. By October 1998, Juan Guzmán, a prosecutor in Santiago, was investigating Pinochet's personal role in allegedly authorising the 'Caravan of Death' operation. As with other investigations, it could not proceed to trial, because the Amnesty Law signed by Pinochet in 1978 precluded almost all prosecutions and trials for the crimes committed by the government he headed over seventeen years.

This was how things stood in Chile when Pinochet flew to London, a city he loved and where he felt himself to be welcomed, not least for his role in assisting the British in the Falklands/Malvinas war with Argentina, back in 1982.

## 3

The truth is that Pinochet felt himself to be above the law, and he had no regrets about his actions. I am a soldier, he liked to say, my Coup saved Chile from communism, leftist agitators and a Cuban future. In terms of style, he was not an intellectual or a thinker – unlike Carlos Prats, whom he feared for that reason – but something of a fox.

He liked *Star Wars* films and books about Napoleon Bonaparte, and enjoyed the company of military veterans, especially if they were old Nazis like Hans-Ulrich Rudel. 'Hitler's only mistake was to lose the war,' the Luftwaffe ace once told him. Pinochet admired his anti-communist stance, and was sceptical about the extent of Nazi crimes. He once asked a visiting West German government minister whether he was sure that six million Jews had really died. Wasn't it only four million?

Pinochet was proud of his personal library, with books on guerrilla insurgencies, the writings of Antonio Gramsci and other Marxist theorists, and accounts of communist crimes. He had an original copy of the sixteenth-century epic poem *La Araucana*, written by the Spanish soldier and poet Alonso de Ercilla y Zúñiga, and was seemingly untroubled by its lyrical account of colonial Spain's brutal response to the insurrection of Araucanian Indians in Chile. 'Brute, unparalleled malevolence has polluted our invasion,' the poet recorded.

Pinochet's appreciation of literature and brutality did not extend to lawyers, who made him wary. He appointed judges who would look after him, and lawyers who could protect him. He passed a law to immunise himself from risks of prosecution; the 1978 Amnesty Law gave him total protection.

The Amnesty Law was prompted by the response to Pinochet's decision to have Orlando Letelier killed in Washington two years before. This was a story I knew something about, as my father-in-law, André Schiffrin, published an account, *Assassination on Embassy Row*, and he and Letelier had been working on a book proposal at the time of his murder. 'Letelier came for lunch, a few days before the assassination,' my wife Natalia once told me. 'He said I had lovely freckles, a twelve-year-old girl remembers things like that.'

Letelier was murdered two months after US Secretary of State Henry Kissinger visited Pinochet in Chile, to offer support to the regime. Jimmy Carter had just won the Ohio Democratic primary, and Paul McCartney and Wings topped the music charts with 'Silly Love Songs'. The Kissinger visit coincided with the ending of the ban on political parties in Spain, imposed in 1939 after General Franco's Nationalists prevailed in the Spanish Civil War. Pinochet greatly admired Franco, who died a few months before Kissinger's visit, and was one of the few foreign leaders to attend the funeral.

During their June 1976 meeting at La Moneda, Pinochet and Kissinger worried that communism was 'springing up' again in Spain, and agreed that Chile's Coup was merely a 'further stage' of the conflict that caused the Spanish Civil War. I am 'very sympathetic' to your efforts in Chile, Kissinger assured Pinochet. 'We wish your government well,' the official transcript recorded.

Kissinger spoke the words in full knowledge of the massive human rights abuses being perpetrated in Chile, and efforts in the US Congress to block arms sales to that country. I want progress on human rights, he said, including constitutional limits on unlawful detentions. Only four hundred are still detained, Pinochet assured him, which wasn't true, but Kissinger seemed uninterested in the numbers. 'You did a great service to the West in overthrowing Allende.'

Of greater concern to Pinochet were the actions of Chileans abroad, and Letelier in particular. He's spreading 'false information', he told Kissinger. At that moment, in Washington, Letelier was indeed complaining about his treatment by Pinochet as a 'nightmare'. Letelier had been detained for a year after the Coup, including eight months on Dawson Island. 'How can the world permit something so brutal and immoral, in this century?' he asked. Is it true that a German in Chile planned the camp, a journalist asked. 'Walther Rauff,' Letelier replied, that's the rumour. 'I have not seen Mr. Rauff, and do not know him to be the planner of this camp, but I have read many reports on it being so.'

Kissinger's time in Santiago must have reassured Pinochet. Within a month of his visit, in July 1976, the UN diplomat Carmelo Soria was murdered in the capital and Pinochet instructed Contreras and Pedro Espinoza, his deputy at the DINA, to deal with Letelier. The pair instructed Michael Townley 'to execute the assassination'.

The thirty-three-year-old American, recruited by the DINA two years earlier, was married to Mariana Callejas, a Chilean writer recently awarded a literary prize by *El Mercurio,* a newspaper that strongly supported Pinochet. The DINA gave the couple a house on the Vía Naranja, in Santiago's wealthy Lo Curro district.

The initial plan was to kill Letelier with sarin gas, hidden in a bottle of Chanel No. 5 perfume. Instead, on 21 September 1976, on Sheridan Circle, in the heart of Washington's Embassy Row, Letelier's Chevrolet was blown up, killing the former minister and Ronni Karpen Moffitt, a colleague at the Institute of Policy Studies.

Pinochet was delighted by the news of his nemesis's demise, which was received as he prepared to receive Jorge Luis Borges at the Palacio de La Moneda. 'An excellent man,' the Argentine writer said of Chile's President, a 'gentleman' of 'warmth and goodness', words that thrilled Pinochet and extinguished any hope of a Nobel Prize for Borges. In the United States, Letelier's killing caused an outcry. Pinochet blamed political opponents and denied any involvement.

## 4

Letelier's assassination would have serious consequences. The criminal investigations that followed would lead to the DINA and Contreras, and pose a serious threat to Pinochet. The episode alerted him to the dangers posed by foreign prosecutors, and the need to take protective measures. Within a year, under pressure from the United States, Pinochet was replacing the DINA with a new Central Nacional de Informaciones or CNI. Losing his position as director, Contreras destroyed the DINA's documents, evidence of four years of criminality, but knew the power he held over the President. 'I'm not with him, he's with me,' he would say of Pinochet, who promoted Contreras to Brigadier-General, hoping to keep him quiet.

Pinochet sent a high-level delegation to Washington, including a trusted young lawyer, Miguel Schweitzer Walters, whose father was Minister of Justice in Chile. The US Justice Department's investigation was homing in on Townley, who confessed to Chilean investigators that he was involved, instructed by Contreras and Espinoza.

Pinochet refused a US request for Townley to be extradited, but forced Contreras to resign from the Army, and cut a deal with

Espinoza, who confessed his role and signed an affidavit exonerating Pinochet (he'd later recant, claiming duress). Espinoza was dispatched to Punta Arenas as head of the Army's Pudeto Regiment. There, it was said, he helped Contreras ship incriminating documents to Hamburg, to be able to reveal them if necessary.

In April 1978, acting through Schweitzer, Pinochet cut a deal with the Americans: Townley would be expelled to the US, the Americans would not investigate Pinochet or other DINA activities. The agreement was never made public. Instead, the two governments issued a joint statement, to the effect that Townley and other rogue agents killed Letelier, and Pinochet had played no role.

Transported to Miami in handcuffs and weeping, Townley insisted to US prosecutors that the DINA and Contreras were to blame for the crimes committed. Under pressure, Contreras privately admitted his role and threatened to implicate Pinochet, to save himself. I always acted 'on direct orders from him', was his line. Pinochet insisted he only gave Contreras general instructions on the mission, not details or the means.

In August 1978, a US Grand Jury indicted Townley, along with Contreras and Espinoza, and five Cuban exiles. The American request that Contreras and Espinoza be extradited to the US created a major crisis in Santiago. As US criminal investigators concluded that Pinochet was involved in the cover-up of Letelier's killing, if not the crime, the CIA reported that he was 'deeply troubled', drinking and aggressive. The CIA worried that the US government was now at risk of becoming entangled.

Fearing a raft of extradition requests, Pinochet and Contreras cut a deal, on the basis of a lie and a *quid pro quo*: they agreed that Townley was on a frolic of his own, and Contreras would protect Pinochet provided he himself wasn't extradited to the United States.

Pinochet duly took steps to prevent the Chilean courts from acceding to a US request to extradite Contreras or Espinoza. He ordered the Supreme Court's President to rule that the two men could not be extradited, which Judge Israel Borquez duly confirmed.

The Borquez ruling was appealed to the full Supreme Court, so Pinochet intervened once more, to toughen up the draft judgement in order to extinguish any risk of extradition. 'The language was changed to comply with Pinochet's order,' the CIA reported. On 1 October 1979 the Supreme Court confirmed Borquez's ruling, allowing Contreras and Espinoza to be released from detention.

Pinochet had saved himself, learned much about courts and extradition, and the power of Washington DC. He opened numerous bank accounts in the United States under various names, into which moneys were deposited, in amounts that could not have come from his modest presidential salary.

Townley now cut a deal of his own with US prosecutors. He pleaded guilty to the killing of Letelier, and agreed to be a witness for the prosecution, against his Cuban helpers. I obtained a first-hand account from Lucy Reed, an American lawyer with whom I sat as an arbitrator in international disputes. 'I remember the Townley case well,' Lucy told me, to my surprise, 'as I was the judge's law clerk during the case.' One exchange stood out for her. Do you regret your actions, the prosecutor asked Townley. 'No sir, Letelier was a soldier and so was I,' Townley replied, 'I received an order and carried it out to the best of my ability.' He said he did regret the death of Ronni Moffitt.

Townley took care not to implicate Pinochet. He said nothing about the DINA's role in the killings of Carlos Prats and Carmelo Soria, honouring the secret agreement negotiated by Miguel Schweitzer and the Americans. 'I don't think the judge was aware of that agreement,' said Lucy Reed, when I described it to her.

The judge sentenced Townley to ten years in prison. He was paroled after forty months, and on release entered a witness-protection programme in the United States. To this day his identity and location are secret, and the US has consistently refused to extradite him to Chile, to face charges for other crimes.

Pinochet had bought himself ten more years as President. Only after he stepped down in March 1990 did the Chilean courts investigate, prosecute, convict and imprison Contreras and Espinoza, for the murders of Letelier and Moffitt, the Supreme Court having ruled that the Amnesty Law didn't apply to crimes committed abroad.

As Pinochet prepared to travel to London in October 1998, no senior figure had been convicted by the Chilean courts for the crimes of his regime. His role in the 'Caravan of Death' case was being investigated by Judge Guzmán, but the Amnesty Law and parliamentary immunity protected him at home, and the rules of diplomatic immunity applicable to a former head of state would protect him abroad.

That is not to say he wasn't warned about the risks of foreign travel. There was a growing recognition of the principle of universal jurisdiction, which allowed the courts of any country to prosecute crimes against humanity and genocide wherever – and by whoever – they were committed. On 11 September, shortly before he travelled to London, Chile signed the Statute of the International Criminal Court, recently adopted in Rome.

Pinochet knew too that human rights groups had tried to have him arrested in the past. The efforts failed, but senior Army figures counselled against the trip. Britain has a new Labour government and Prime Minister, Tony Blair, he was told, much less sympathetic than Margaret Thatcher and the Conservatives.

Pinochet ignored the advice. He bore no responsibility for any excesses during his years in power, he was protected. He had a clear conscience, the British were a decent lot, and the Letelier affair happened long ago.

'I am an angel,' he would say, and truly believed it.


# 5


Eighty-two years old, on a vague mission to purchase weapons for his country, Pinochet travelled with his wife Lucía. The couple dined with friends in fancy restaurants. 'I love London!' he told Thatcher over tea. The couple went shopping – a coat from Burberry's, a book on Napoleon from Hatchards on Piccadilly – and he prepared for a minor operation on his back.

He found time to give an interview to the *New Yorker* magazine. Jon Lee Anderson arrived at his hotel with a photographer, for a shoot at the nearby Grosvenor House Hotel, in a room filled with white cupids. Pinochet found the décor to be unsuitable – 'Too gay!' Anderson told me – and wanted something more dignified.

'I was only an *aspirante* dictator,' Pinochet joked over tea, while repeatedly banging his fist on the table if a question irritated him. 'It was the closest that Pinochet ever came to showing me his fear,' said Anderson.

I want a gesture of reconciliation, Pinochet told him. Meaning? 'An end to the lawsuits!' Although protected by his Amnesty Law and immunities, nine criminal lawsuits were pending against him

in Chile, a development he did not like. The allegations included
charges of genocide and illegal expropriation of property, filed by
Gladys Marín, Secretary-General of Chile's Communist Party
(whose husband Jorge Muñoz was disappeared in 1976). Mere
talk of such matters agitated Pinochet. 'An end to the lawsuits!'
He repeated the words, banged once more on the table. More
than eight hundred lawsuits, he complained, some closed, others
reopened. 'They always go back to the same thing, the same
thing.'

A few days later, Pinochet checked into The London Clinic in
Marylebone and the *New Yorker* published its article, 'The Dictator', by Anderson. A photograph portrayed Pinochet as serene,
powerful and untouchable, a civilian in a pale-blue tie to match
his eyes.

The medical operation went smoothly.

As he recuperated, on the evening of Friday, 16 October, and
looked forward to going home, there was a knock on the door. A
police officer from Scotland Yard entered room 801, with a lady as

an interpreter. Within a few minutes, he understood he had lost his freedom.

Detained in London, said shocked friends.

Arrested for genocide and crimes against humanity, said the newspapers.

**6**

Two decades passed before I came to know of the events that led to that momentous evening in London. I first heard the details from Juan Garcés, a Spanish lawyer I'd come to know in the context of a case brought by Victor Pey, his Chilean client. Pey's newspaper *El Clarín* was closed by Pinochet on the day of the Coup, and he wanted compensation. I wasn't able to assist Garcés, but it allowed us to meet, in November 2018, at his home in Madrid.

Quiet and scholarly, with a gentle face dominated by a grey, walrus moustache, he has sparkly eyes and a soft and philosophical voice. In September 1973 he was a twenty-nine-year-old Spaniard working as a political adviser to President Allende. On the day of the Coup, as the Moneda Palace was being bombed by British-made Chilean Air Force Hawker Hunter jet fighters, Allende instructed him to leave. 'Someone has to recount what happened here, and only you can do it.' Garcés didn't forget the instruction.

He went to Paris to study for a doctorate in law, returning to Spain only after General Franco died in 1975. Garcés opened a law office in Madrid, handled cases on narco-trafficking and extradition, and in the mid-1990s, Chilean exiles sought him out. With the collapse of the Soviet Union and the Cold War on hold, the United Nations created international tribunals for crimes committed in Rwanda and the former Yugoslavia, the first such bodies since Nuremberg (1945–6) and Tokyo (1946–8), and negotiations were underway to create an International Criminal Court.

Ideas about international justice were springing into life and seeping into public consciousness. After fifty years of quietude, genocide and crimes against humanity were back on the agenda.

In Spain, as in other countries, ideas were floated. Could Pinochet be indicted before Spanish courts for international crimes, on the basis of universal jurisdiction? This was a matter of honour and justice, not revenge, Garcés believed, a nod towards justice and international cooperation. 'Victims and their families came to me, to ask about cases.' They did so because he was President of the Salvador Allende Foundation, which dealt with torture and disappearances in Chile.

Garcés gathered together people's stories. One was shared by the widow of the United Nations official abducted, tortured and killed in July 1976. His name was Carmelo Soria, and his wife Laura wanted to target Pinochet in the Spanish courts, as there was no justice for him in Chile. Garcés gathered evidence, talked to lawyers, met prosecutors.

When we first met, he mentioned Soria, but the name didn't resonate. Three years later, in February 2021, a prosecutor in Madrid with whom Garcés had contact wrote to me. His name was Carlos Castresana, and he'd read an interview in *El País* on the Spanish edition of my book *The Ratline*. The article mentioned that I was writing on the Pinochet case in London. I can tell you how the case really started, Castresana told me.

# 7

Carlos Castresana and I first spoke over Zoom in May 2021. He took me back to the spring of 1996, when he worked at Spain's anti-corruption unit and was a member of the Union of Progressive Prosecutors. Newspapers were writing about the twentieth anniversary of the military dictatorship in Argentina, and two decades was a significant moment in Spain, the time limit under the country's statute of limitations for bringing a case for crimes committed abroad.

Cases were underway in Argentina, as well as in France, Germany and Italy, Castresana told me. In Spain, however, despite the presence of many Argentine exiles, nothing was happening. 'I wanted to find a way to act on behalf of Spanish victims, on the basis of universal jurisdiction.'

Castresana returned to the origins of modern international criminal law. 'I loved the Nuremberg precedent, a victory for justice, done with a sense of fair play, a trial that was also a truth commission,' he said. 'I enjoyed very much your book *East West Street*, how personal, historical and legal issues came together.' He saw Nuremberg as a form of storytelling, and was curious about how the crimes were defined and the defendants chosen.

He delved into bringing a case, under Spanish laws, old or new. He worked out that Spanish courts could exercise universal jurisdiction over three international crimes committed in Argentina: terrorism, torture and genocide. 'The idea that the victim is not an individual with a particular nationality, but humanity as a whole, was significant for me.'

Terrorism was introduced as a crime in Spain in the 1970s, with a broad definition. 'General Franco considered terrorism to be almost anything,' Castresana said wryly. Curiously, he also introduced the crime of genocide into Spanish law. 'Franco took care not to ratify the Genocide Convention until 1969, thirty years after the end of the Spanish Civil War, and introduced it into the criminal code only in 1971.' Franco's legislators did not, however, follow the language of the 1948 Convention on the Prevention and Punishment of Genocide, which defined 'genocide' as certain acts committed 'with intent to destroy, in whole or in part, a national ethnical, racial or religious group, as such'. Instead, Franco's version mentioned 'national, ethnic, social or religious' groups: it omitted racial groups altogether, merged national and ethnic groups into one category, and introduced the notion of social groups.

Unwittingly, Franco's lawyers introduced another significant change: they left out the last two words of the definition in the 1948 Convention: 'as such'. The redaction meant that a Spanish prosecutor didn't have to prove that the act was motivated by a focus on those groups. 'By removing those two words,' Castresana realised, 'you define genocide like crimes against humanity, so you only have to prove that the attacks on certain groups occurred, not that they were motivated by an intention to destroy those groups as such.' In short, Franco unintentionally made it easier to prosecute genocide – adding 'social groups' and removing the 'as such' requirement lowered the bar. Ironically, Franco's legislation opened the door to the prosecution of Pinochet in Spain, for genocide perpetrated in Chile.

Franco's definition remained in force until 1983, when it was amended to follow the language of the 1948 Convention. This meant that the 1971 definition applied in September 1973, at the time of the Chilean Coup, and for the next ten years.

So the Franco definition covered Pinochet's crimes in that period?

'Correct,' Castresana replied. 'I was the first to think about using Franco's law on genocide.'

To reach Pinochet?

'Absolutely! In a humble way, I hoped to create a legal precedent, without knowing exactly what the consequences would be.'

Castresana gathered evidence on crimes committed in Argentina against Spaniards and others. Working with exiles, in March 1996, he filed a first case before the Audiencia Nacional, Spain's National Court. 'It was for international crimes committed in Argentina by General Jorge Videla (who seized power in 1976), against Spanish victims. I knew my colleagues, conservative Spanish magistrates, would be less likely to run a case with no Spanish victims.'

He persuaded Carlos Granados, the Spanish Attorney General, not to object. 'Most prosecutors were against the initiative, but Granados was decent, a Christian, honest, with a sense of history.' We must not be remembered as prosecutors who abandoned Spanish victims, Granados told him. Spanish victims were necessary to persuade conservative judges and the press. Without opposition from the top, the Argentine case took off. At the Audiencia Nacional in Madrid, it was assigned to Court No. 5 and the investigating judge Baltasar Garzón, who accepted the complaint.

Castresana now focused on Chile. 'Around 20 April 1996, I received a visit from the lawyer Juan Garcés. He said to me: "I have waited twenty years for what you have done with Videla and Argentina, please do the same thing with Pinochet."'

Castresana enquired about Spanish victims. Garcés proposed several names, including Carmelo Soria, who had worked for the UN's Latin American and Caribbean Demographic Centre in Santiago. He disappeared on 14 July 1976, and two days later, his mutilated body was found in a canal, near his car, in the capital. As a diplomat with Spanish nationality, his death caused a stir in Spain.

'The Soria case was notorious,' Castresana recalled. 'He was well-known, with a street in Madrid named after his grandfather, Arturo Soria' (an engineer who, at the end of the nineteenth century, proposed the idea of 'La Ciudad Lineal', the linear city arranged with buildings on either side of a single wide central avenue). Soria's murder gained broader attention when the European Parliament passed a resolution to deplore Chile's failure to find the perpetrators.

'I had a clear idea that the Pinochet case in Spain must be built around Carmelo Soria,' said Castresana.

He faced two obstacles. First, criminal proceedings in Chile were still pending on the Soria case, so he had to await a final ruling before starting a case in Spain. Second, the limit for bringing a case in Spain under its statute of limitations was 14 July 1996, the twentieth anniversary of the murder. 'I could only start proceedings in Spain if the Chilean courts closed the case before that date.'

He monitored the proceedings in Chile and prepared a lawsuit. On 4 June 1996, Chile's Supreme Court ended the Soria case, because of the Amnesty Law. To save himself in Chile, Pinochet unwittingly opened the door to a case in Spain. A month later, Castresana filed the case in Valencia, in relation to Soria and a dozen other victims. He named Pinochet and three other Junta members as defendants.

Simultaneously, the sister of Antonio Llido, a disappeared Spanish priest, filed a complaint, as did the Salvador Allende Foundation, on behalf of more victims. The Valencia court transferred the cases to the Audiencia Nacional, where they were assigned to Judge Manuel García-Castellón, in Court No. 6. 'In this way, Carmelo Soria's murder was the starting point for the case against Pinochet,' said Castresana. 'At the time we didn't think about immunity, because we never imagined he would be arrested!'

Much later, I met with Castresana and Garcés. We talked of the legitimacy of Spain addressing crimes in Chile, when it hadn't addressed its own Civil War crimes, and those of the entire Franco era.

'I have always been clear that the case against Pinochet in Chile was about exorcising the ghost of Franco in Spain,' said Castresana.

'We wanted to do to Pinochet what we weren't able to do to Franco,' said Garcés.

# 8

During that first conversation, Castresana was in Madrid and I was in Totnes, a small town in Devon in the south-west of England. I was visiting my mother-in-law Leina, who was born in Spain shortly before the Civil War. Her father, Federico de la Iglesia, a Republican army colonel, opposed Franco, so the family had fled to England. In

1940 they were given refuge by Leonard and Dorothy Elmhirst, at
Dartington Hall, in Devon.

Eighty years later, over lunch, I told Leina what Castresana had
told me. She listened attentively, as she is always interested in stories
with a half-decent human element.

'What was the name of the Spanish victim who got the case going
in Madrid?' she asked.

'Soria, Carmelo Soria.'

She stopped eating, looked at me and said, 'Ah yes, now I remember, Cousin Carmelo!'

Cousin Carmelo?

'Yes, Carmelo Soria, a distant family member who got caught
up in the Pinochet story. I remember, there was talk about it in the
family.'

In Spain, family is an extended experience, so Leina valiantly
sought to explain the relationship. Her family – by marriage now
also my Spanish and Chilean family – was convoluted to the point of
incomprehensibility. She drew a family tree. Her mother was Laura
Keller, whose brother Manolo married Marita Soria, and Marita
was Carmelo's first cousin. In this way, Carmelo was a cousin at one
or more removes.

'And now,' said Leina, 'he's your cousin too!'

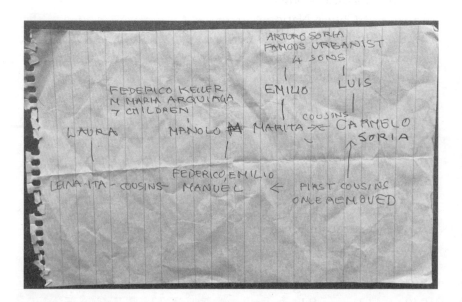

## 9

The death of Carmelo Soria, in July 1976, generated considerable pain and angst in his family. Spanish newspapers reported the story as an accident, while the Pinochet-controlled Chilean media suggested Soria was having an affair. This was fake news, the truth more brutal: the Pinochet regime ordered Soria to be eliminated for his leftist sympathies.

Leina introduced me to members of the Keller family in Madrid, who connected me to one of Soria's three children. Carmen engaged openly – after all, I was family now – and spoke of decades seeking justice for her father's murder. You should speak to my mother Laura González-Vera. 'She ran the legal proceedings in Spain, I focused on Chile.'

In Santiago a few months later, I sat with mother and daughter in the living room of the Soria home, surrounded by books, objects and memories. Two open women, strong, warm, smart and remarkable. Laura, eighty-eight, wore a patterned white shirt and a colourful skirt. A retired medical doctor, she was intelligent and lively, and weary. In a voice stripped of emotion, she described a brutal experience.

Laura was born in Santiago into a politically active family. When she was a medical student, her father José – writer, anarchist and recipient of Chile's National Prize for Literature – introduced her to friends in his circle. Arturo Soria, the grandson of a renowned engineer, arrived in Chile after the Spanish Civil War and founded *Cruz del Sur*, a literary publishing house whose authors included Pablo Neruda. 'Arturo was a bit anti-communist,' Laura said with a smile, 'but he had some communist friends, including Neruda and a brother.'

In the 1950s, when the Chilean Communist Party was outlawed, and Neruda fled the country, he asked Arturo Soria to look after Villa Michoacán, his home on Avenida Lynch Norte in Santiago. Neruda shared it with his second wife, Delia del Carril, known as *La Hormiga*, the ant, 'because she was always so busy'. Arturo recruited his younger brother Carmelo, who arrived in Chile in 1946, to guard Neruda's extensive library.

'Carmelo was living in the Villa Michoacán when I met him, in 1949,' said Laura. 'He was a strange character who'd invite me to a café frequented by people from Andalucía.' The memories were vivid. 'I loved his tales, about Spain and family life there, and the stories made me fall in love with this quiet gentleman who tried so hard to make me like him. He charmed me into loving him and it worked. We married in 1956. I was a doctor, paid to do what I loved. He worked for the United Nations. We had three children.'

The couple were politically engaged and supportive of Allende: Carmelo became involved with the *Quimanta* publishing house, established by the Popular Unity government to make popular books more widely available.

'My mother taught English and philosophy at the first co-educational school in Chile,' said Laura. 'She was a communist who worked for Allende's presidential campaign in 1952, and I met him in the second campaign, in 1958. He was kind: when my mum told him I was at medical school, he sent me little presents. "For the future doctor," Allende wrote. We stayed in touch, even when he was President. My father was a close friend of *La Tencha*, Allende's wife, Hortensia, who was very fond of him.'

The couple were at home with the children on the day of the Coup, 11 September 1973. 'We woke early, around 6.30am, heard the news on the radio.' They went to work, she to the Hospital San Borja Arriarán, he to the UN office in Providencia. 'I wanted to be at work, as the right-wing doctors were on strike. Carmelo had faith in his immunity, as a diplomat. We weren't fearful, didn't want to abandon our obligations.'

The Coup did not surprise her. 'A week earlier, at a meeting with Allende, he warned it could happen and, if it did, he would pay with his life. He knew what was coming, talked about it with Pinochet, the head of the Army.'

At the end of the day, one of the few to escape from La Moneda came to Laura's hospital. 'Doctor Quiroga told us that Allende was dead.'

Killed, or suicide?

'He killed himself,' said Laura. 'One of the doctors, Patricio Guijón, saw Allende's body, said it was suicide. He ended up at Dawson Island.' This was the camp where Allende's ministers were held, in Patagonia, near Punta Arenas.

Three years on, Carmelo and Laura didn't worry about safety. 'Carmelo trusted the protection of the UN, and spoke openly of the regime's abuses. "They are murdering people." He told an Argentine visitor to say what was really happening in Chile.'

Carmelo knew of the disappearances, torture and killings, even of one UN employee said to be associated with the MIR (*Movimiento de Izquierda Revolucionaria*, the Revolutionary Left Movement). 'One day, DINA agents came to the UN and noticed the nameplate on Carmelo's office,' Laura recalled. 'They made derogatory references to Carmelo, who was warned about his safety. He mentioned it to me. "They know where to find me now," he said.'

On 14 July 1976 they found him:

He always called as he left the office for home. He rang at seven, told the maid he had a headache, was coming home early. He never arrived. At about ten in the evening, I began to worry. I called hospital emergency rooms and friends. No sign. I went to bed and, remarkably, slept. I woke at six, he still wasn't there, so again I started to call around. A friend came over, we went to the police station to make a statement. They took a note, told us to wait forty-eight hours. Later, the La Piramide police station called and said a body was found, and a car. My daughters went to get more information, I went to find a lawyer, as I was sure he'd been kidnapped.

Laura stopped, briefly:

They spent all day looking for the car in a canal in the centre of the city, a narrow canal, just a couple of metres wide, a metre deep. They found the car, took it out of the canal, with a crane. No body. The next day they found the body, in the canal, a kilometre away, near a bridge.

They had to wait to perform the autopsy, because they were so busy with all the disappeared. I reached out to Miguel Schweitzer, Pinochet's Minister of Justice. I knew the Schweitzer family, because my father knew the Minister's brother, Daniel Schweitzer.

She paused. 'The Minister was the father of Miguel Ángel Schweitzer, who was Pinochet's lawyer. I knew Miguel Ángel, the son, when we were children, we swam together.'

Yes, I said, I knew Schweitzer the son. He acted for Pinochet on the Letelier case, and then in London. 'I rang Minister Schweitzer's office,' Laura continued, 'and said to the secretary: "Tell him that *Bisagra*, my nickname, wants to talk to him." I spoke to him. He knew something was going on, as Minister of Justice he must have been warned. I went there and told him he should resign, as Carmelo was murdered. He said, "But how, Bisagra?" He said he knew nothing of this, he'd make enquiries. He gave me his brother Daniel's phone number and I called him and said the DINA killed Carmelo.'

An autopsy had to be performed. Laura went to the hospital to observe the process, to see exactly what they had done, what caused her husband to die: .

At medical school I liked anatomy. I was interested in Sherlock Holmes and police novels, so I just went to the place where they did autopsies. Dr Fernández, the military doctor, met me. I knew him from university. He said a wife could not attend the autopsy of her husband. Miguel Schweitzer Speisky, the Minister, intervened personally, authorising me to attend. When Dr Fernández still refused, a person from the Ministry said I must be allowed in, because the Minister wanted to know everything.

Laura González-Vera observed Dr Fernández perform her husband's autopsy. He wanted to conclude that Carmelo Soria had drowned, but she objected:

> I asked Dr Fernández why was Carmelo's neck broken? Maybe an accident, he said. Why are his ribs broken? It was said that he was drunk and lost control of the car, Dr Fernández said. I said no. There was no water in his lungs, there were contra-indications of drowning. Besides, Carmelo's jaw would sometimes dislocate, and he knew how to put it back to its normal position. Here, his jaw was dislocated. I noticed his eye was out of place, I noticed the injuries to his head.

Was there evidence he was poisoned?

Laura shook her head. 'At that point, the use of gas had not occurred to me, we only learned about that later on.' The sarin rumours began to circulate when it emerged that Soria was held at Michael Townley's house on the Vía Naranja, where gas was being developed by Eugenio Berríos, a Chilean biochemist who was later murdered in Uruguay.

Laura knew her husband had been murdered by the DINA. She was well connected, and she learned of Pinochet's reaction. 'Mamo really screwed up,' he told a meeting of the Junta, using Contreras's nickname. 'Now the UN will come down on us.' Pinochet had his own ideas on the silencing of Carmelo Soria. 'Mamo should have found witnesses who'd say Soria molested a woman, so the DINA acted to defend her honour.'

Two months after the murder, threats caused Laura to flee to Madrid with the children. There she remained for forty years, returning to Chile for a few weeks each year, from March to May. 'I wanted to stay in touch with Santiago, and be back in Spain for spring.'

As the years passed, Laura fought for accountability, encouraged by her brother-in-law Arturo. 'He studied law, but never practised it,' she said, 'and he introduced me to people who were interested, who said they'd help.' Supporters included academics, exiles, journalists, and some who were close to Felipe González, Spain's Prime Minister from December 1982 to May 1996. Laura's statement for the United Nations circulated widely. Nicolas Sánchez-Albornoz, a

Spanish historian back from exile in Argentina, a friend of Carmelo's, organised a meeting in Madrid. One of the attendees
was Juan Garcés, who'd known Carmelo and Laura in Santiago.
'Carmelo knew and trusted him, he once ate at our house,' Laura
recalled. She also liked Garcés and trusted him.

'He offered to bring a case. I thought about it, then agreed. Garcés was persistent, and faithful to Allende.' Garcés introduced Laura
to a prosecutor in Madrid. 'The case started with Carlos Castresana, a wonderful jurist, a man who believed that crimes against
humanity should be punished even where the people affected were
long dead. That was how it happened.'

Did Laura imagine that her husband's case might be the catalyst
that led to the arrest of Pinochet in London?

'Yes,' she said with a smile. 'Well, I didn't know it then, but I
know it now.'

As our conversation came to a close, Laura showed me papers
from those days. We went over her diary for July 1996. 'That was
when it happened, when the judge in Valencia accepted the case.'

## 10

Carmen Soria is the younger daughter of Carmelo and Laura. She has warm eyes, long dark hair and colourful clothes, and smokes. 'I was sixteen when it happened. I saw my father the morning he disappeared, but we didn't kiss goodbye, as usual, because we'd had a fight. That evening he didn't come home. My mother assumed he was detained.'

Carmen spoke in a matter-of-fact voice, yet it was plain she was profoundly marked by her father's death, which changed her life, and later that of her three children. 'The story was horrible for them, because of all the comings and goings, the changes of country and school, the fact that I was harassed and targeted.'

Carmen's quest for justice – 'the eternal struggle of an ethical gaze', the writer Pedro Lemebel called it – began the day her father disappeared. She remembered the call, that he was detained at a police station, that she should attend. 'My sister went, I stayed behind, to gather papers, his passport and money, in case we needed to bail him.' When she arrived at the station her sister was seated outside. Carmelo wasn't there. The police said there'd been a car crash at the *El Carmen* Canal, that they'd found his wallet and scarf. 'I wrapped the scarf around me, it was July, winter in Chile.'

The police took the girls to the canal, where they were each given a long bamboo stick to prod the shallow water to try and find the body. The car was found, with a front seat and radio missing, and a bottle of pisco. No body. As they left, an ambulance turned up and word soon arrived that the police had something. 'I don't remember much, I fainted,' said Carmen. Many people were home. She remembered her eleven-year-old brother lying on the ground, banging the floor.

The phone rang constantly. 'Strangers called to abuse us, to say we were communists.' People shouted threats outside the house, banged on shutters. Frightened, Carmen slept that night surrounded by glass bottles, to protect herself. 'It was all organised by the DINA,' she said. 'To us, it was obviously an assassination, our mother didn't need to tell us that.' These were dangerous times. Two relatives were detained, then disappeared. Going out for errands, Carmen was chased. After someone tried to abduct her, the family left for Spain.

'First my brother, then me and my sister, on 11 September 1976, then my mother.'

Four years later, Carmen returned to Chile. There was often trouble. A professor was killed. Her grandmother warned her not to come home, the police were waiting. Working as a journalist, she was harassed and arrested. Once, at the cinema to see the film *Paris, Texas*, her camera and notebooks were taken.

The situation only changed in 1989, after Pinochet lost the referendum and the Rettig Commission held hearings. Slowly they learned more about what happened to Carmelo. 'I know who killed Carmen Soria's father,' Luz Arce, a DINA informant, testified. The Rettig Report confirmed that Soria was killed by DINA agents.

The family became actively engaged in legal proceedings. Laura took the lead in Spain, Carmen in Chile. Both were single-minded. 'My brother and sister thought I behaved like a tyrant,' said Carmen, 'that I didn't report enough to them.' She wanted to be generous to them, but it wasn't easy. She felt alone, each sibling dealt with the situation in their own way.

A criminal case was started in Santiago in 1976, the year of Soria's murder, but nothing came of it. After 1990, when Pinochet left office, a new criminal investigation was started, in which Carmen got involved and required police protection. 'My mother was terrified something would happen to me, but I had to do this, for my father.'

The investigating judge was Violeta Guzmán, at the Santiago Court of Appeals. 'I had high expectations, as she was known to be a fighter, but I also suspected that she was fearful,' Carmen said. 'Guzmán ruled she had no jurisdiction, because of the Amnesty Law.' The case was transferred to the Military Court, then to the Chilean Supreme Court. 'The legal proceedings became emblematic, because we had the support of the UN and the Spanish government.' In June 1996, the Supreme Court recognised the killing of Carmelo Soria as aggravated homicide, and named the perpetrators, including one of Pinochet's guards. 'That is what made the case so delicate, it went all the way up to Pinochet.' But the Supreme Court went no further because of the Amnesty Law. The ruling opened the door through which Carlos Castresana passed.

Carmen Soria did not give up. She lobbied to prevent the promotion of Brigadier Jaime Lepe, one of those identified as being involved in her father's murder. She filed a complaint with the Inter-American Commission on Human Rights. She agitated for an end to the Amnesty Law.

'I wanted to know every detail about what happened to my father,' she said. It took years for the facts to emerge, that he was abducted on a street, then taken to Townley's house. 'They crushed his ribs with heavy tyres. They electrocuted him. They may have used sarin gas on him, because he had convulsions, but that is not proven.

They put his head on a step, twisted and broke it. My father died on the Vía Naranja, at the house of Michael Townley and the writer Mariana Callejas.'

Carmen Soria took a long drag on a cigarette, exhaling slowly. 'Pinochet travelled to London in a time of impotence and impunity.' She said this with sharp anger. 'Over the years, my deep mistrust in the state and government did not diminish. It grew and it still grows.'

## 11

The case against Pinochet that Castresana filed in Valencia in July 1996 was dealt with expeditiously and followed the usual course. Having satisfied himself that procedural requirements were met, the Valencia judge transferred the case to the Audiencia Nacional in Madrid, the country's National Court. It went to Court No. 6 and Judge Miguel Moreiras, who was filling in for Judge García-Castellón.

Moreiras passed the Pinochet case to Javier Balaguer, the prosecutor attached to Court No. 6. He recognised its significance and, in two short lines, recommended that it proceed. 'I don't know how deeply he shared the ideas on torture and genocide, but he admitted the case,' said Castresana. Balaguer's decision was not appealed, so the Pinochet case was now live.

The next stage was to gather witness statements and other evidence. For two years Castresana worked with victims, and with *La Vicaria de la Solidaridad*, which the Archbishop of Santiago set up in 1976 to gather evidence on detentions, torture and disappearances. *La Vicaria* played a vital role in accountability and justice in Chile. Castresana's Pinochet case was assisted by a decision of President Clinton's Attorney General to respond positively to a request for assistance from the Audiencia Nacional, providing evidence available in the United States. This was 'a green light' for other governments, Garcés believed, a signal from 'big brother' that it was OK to open the door. Stories ran in the Spanish media, on the Soria and Letelier cases, but without much traction.

The Chilean case was proceeding in parallel to Castresana's Argentina case, before Court No. 5 and Judge Garzón. Castresana sensed Garzón was the more active judge, managing the case with an 'iron hand'. He established a link between the two cases, one that would become crucial: Pinochet's Operation Condor targeted opponents in Argentina, which meant Garzón's jurisdiction to investigate a killing in Argentina allowed him to follow the trail to Chile.

General Pinochet, as Commander-in-Chief of the Chilean Army, was alert to the cases and the legal risks. His concerns increased exponentially in February 1997 when Garzón issued an arrest warrant for the former Argentine President, General Galtieri. Pinochet sent General Torres Silva – his favourite prosecutor, and later Army auditor-general – to Madrid, where he persuaded the new chief prosecutor at the Audiencia Nacional, Eduardo Fungairiño, to try to stop both cases.

General Silva's visit was clandestine, but it caused Fungairiño to submit a confidential report to the council of public prosecutors. He argued there was no Coup in Chile, merely a temporary suspension of the constitutional order. News of the report leaked, causing a scandal. Fungairiño changed tack, replacing Balaguer, a progressive prosecutor, with the more conservative Jesús Peláez, said to be a member of *Opus Dei*, a conservative Catholic group. Fungairiño now encouraged Peláez to challenge the jurisdiction of the investigating judges in Courts No. 5 and 6, and to appeal to the full Criminal Chamber of the Audiencia Nacional.

Peláez was 'absolutely against us,' Garcés recalled.

He was 'a pro-Franco fascist,' said Castresana.

Eduardo Fungairiño started a case before the Audiencia Nacional to challenge the jurisdiction of the Spanish courts to investigate Pinochet and Argentina's General Galtieri. It was 1998. The hearing was set for the end of October.

As the case was pending, someone contacted Juan Garcés in Madrid and everything changed.

## 12

'It was sometime around Thursday, 8 October,' recalled Garcés. 'I think it may have been my friend Victor Pey who first alerted me, a small article in the Chilean press that Pinochet was in England for a medical intervention.' Human-rights organisations, including Amnesty International, who wanted Pinochet arrested, were also in touch.

Garcés had to move quickly. Over the weekend – Saturday, 10 and Sunday, 11 October 1998 – he prepared a document for Judge García-Castellón, in Court No. 6, the more cautious judge, who had the Chilean case. Garcés had already filed evidence supporting Pinochet's role in genocide, terrorism and torture. He now prepared a simple request to be allowed to question Pinochet in London about these crimes. The process was known as 'auto de procesamiento'.

Garcés worked alone at home. 'I had all the papers I needed.' As he drafted the request, he received a phone call from London from an unknown person, who confirmed the urgency. 'Pinochet is in London. We can't get him arrested by the UK authorities. The only chance to arrest him is an order from a Spanish judge.' The caller, he would learn, was Andy McEntee, the chair of trustees of Amnesty International UK.

Garcés contacted Oscar Soto, President Allende's personal doctor, to see how long he thought Pinochet would remain in hospital. Dr Soto doubted Pinochet would be able to travel immediately. Garcés was relieved, as Monday, 12 October was National Day in Spain and the courts were closed.

On Tuesday, 13 October, first thing in the morning, Garcés went to the Audiencia Nacional. He met with Judge García-Castellón and asked him to request the authorities in London to allow him to question Pinochet. García-Castellón wasn't closed to the idea, but he

wouldn't say he'd act on it, so Garcés worried he would do nothing.
'I knew his temperament so I wasn't sure he'd send the request.
He'd moved matters forward, allowed much evidence to be gathered,
but he was under pressure from the Spanish legal establishment.'
Castresana and Garcés expected that Chief Prosecutor Fungairiño
would do all he could to stop the Chilean case. 'I worried the con-
fluence of pressures would put the brakes on,' said Garcés. 'So I
prepared an alternative route, in case García-Castellón did nothing.'

This involved Judge Garzón in Court No. 5, who was investigating
crimes in Argentina. Garcés knew that Operation Condor offered a
link between Argentina, Chile and Pinochet. 'I didn't really know
Judge Garzón, but I'd attended a lecture he gave on crimes in Argentina, including *Condor*, so I knew his approach.' Garzón seemed
more likely to act.

A few months earlier, Garcés had filed another case before Judge
Garzón, about a 1976 killing in Argentina, part of Operation
Condor. Edgardo Enríquez Espinoza, a Chilean, was arrested in
Buenos Aires, then tortured and disappeared. (Espinoza's brother
Miguel, the founder of MIR, was killed by the DINA in 1974.) 'I
approached Judge Garzón on this case, in relation to his investigation of Operation Condor.' Garcés had witness testimony and other
evidence of links between the Chilean and Argentine intelligence
services, and he hoped this might nudge Garzón towards Pinochet.

'I went to see Garzón on Wednesday, 14 October. I spoke in a
very direct way, told him that Pinochet was in England, that I'd done
the preparatory work to allow him to intervene, and this was the
moment to act.' The political situation in Britain was ripe, Garcés
explained to him. There was a Labour government and an engaged
Foreign Secretary, Robin Cook, committed to an 'ethical foreign
policy', one with human rights at its heart.

'I said to Garzón: "Please send a request for letters rogatory, to
question Pinochet about his role in Operation Condor in Argentina."' (Letters rogatory is a formal request from a court in one
country to seek judicial assistance from a court in another country,
for example on matters of evidence – it was used by US authorities
in the Townley case.) Garzón suggested he was open to the idea, but
would only act if he received a formal, written request.

## 13

Baltasar Garzón was in his eleventh year as investigating judge on Court No. 5 of the Audiencia Nacional when Garcés visited him on Wednesday, 14 October. A square man, with a shock of strong hair and a piercing gaze, Garzón had a record as a fearless investigator of high-profile drug and terror cases. When I first paid him a visit many years later, he remembered meeting Garcés. It was on the Wednesday, and Judge García-Castellón may have been absent.

'I had spent five years investigating Operation Condor and crimes committed in Argentina,' Garzón told me. He knew that there were Chilean victims of Pinochet in Argentina, but also that Judge García-Castellón in Court No. 6 had the lead in investigating these matters. Garzón didn't want to tread on his colleague's toes. 'I accepted the new request from Garcés, but wanted to focus on the Argentine aspect, not Pinochet,' he recalled. 'But of course I knew that the case Garcés brought concerned Chilean aspects of *Condor*, so it came within my jurisdiction on killings in Argentina.'

'That day, I arrived at my office at the usual time,' Garzón told me, 'about half past eight in the morning. Juan Garcés arrived at ten. He asked to see me, I agreed. He came into my room and said very simply: "Pinochet is in London."' He brought a short document that set out allegations against Pinochet, 'one of the persons most responsible' for the crimes of Operation Condor. This was enough to allow Garzón to act, and Garcés gave him the document that described Pinochet's role in creating the DINA, with information on the killings of Orlando Letelier and Carmelo Soria. Garcés also had Contreras's testimony, implicating Pinochet as directly involved in authorising DINA's actions in Argentina, under Operation Condor.

'I want to take a statement in person from Augusto Pinochet as soon as he has recovered from his medical intervention,' Garcés told Garzón. Garcés asked him to request the British authorities to allow this, and to make sure they didn't let Pinochet leave before he'd been questioned about his role in Operation Condor.

Garzón hesitated. 'The real Pinochet case is before the Judge in Court No. 6, not my Court,' he told Garcés. 'Ask García-Castellón to make the request, as I only have a small part of the Pinochet case.' This was courteous and collegial.

'Why not suggest to García-Castellón that if he doesn't want to act then I will,' said Garzón, using Operation Condor as the motive. 'If you tell him I have jurisdiction to act, I am sure that he will give you the order you want.' In the meantime, Garzón added, he'd prepare a draft of the request that Garcés hoped for.

Garcés had another concern: that García-Castellón would want Scotland Yard to confirm that Pinochet really was in London. This was the catalytic moment for Garzón, who thought that with any delay Pinochet might be gone. I have 'the means and the capacity to take on this issue,' he said to himself, and decided to act.

That afternoon, Wednesday, 14 October, Garzón prepared a short note to be sent to London, via Interpol. Is Pinochet in Britain, and if so where? How is Pinochet's health? Please allow me, he said, to take a statement on his role in Operation Condor, and please 'guarantee that Sr. Pinochet Ugarte will remain on British soil until the moment of his statement'.

Initially, Scotland Yard brushed away the request in a fax. 'We don't understand why you need to know, or why you are asking this,' Garzón recalled their response. 'We are not required to answer your questions.' The dismissive tone spurred him to go further.

Fortuitously, or perhaps otherwise, at this very moment, Garzón received a phone call out of the blue. 'John Dew called me, from the British embassy.' The senior diplomat had come to know Garzón on a money-laundering matter in Gibraltar, the enclave in southern Spain that has caused much friction with Britain. Over a friendly lunch at Las Reses, an old-fashioned restaurant in Madrid known for tripe and colourful posters of bullfights, Garzón suggested ways of enhancing cooperation on Gibraltar. He liked Dew. 'Typical English. Very formal. Tall. Tie. Correct.'

On Garzón's account, Dew called to let him know he was aware of Scotland Yard's rebuff, and this would not be the final word. 'You will receive a new answer from Scotland Yard,' Garzón recalled Dew saying, as you are seen as a friend of Britain. 'Everything will be fine, as we have a very positive cooperation,' Dew said he told Garzón, recalling the conversation when we met in his garden in Oxford (he is retired, producing naïve landscapes and rather fine drawings of his times in Havana, Bogota and north Oxford). Garzón assumed that someone higher up must have authorised the call, as British diplomats tended not to go off on frolics of their own.

Later that same day, on the Wednesday, Garzón received a second fax from Scotland Yard, with a more cooperative tone. 'It confirmed that Pinochet was in a clinic in central London, and asked: "What do you really want from us?"' Garzón didn't yet know the answer to the question, so he waited until the next morning to reply. By now, Juan Garcés had provided draft requests for letters rogatory: one copy went to Judge García-Castellón, on crimes linked to Chile; the other went to Judge Garzón, on crimes committed in Argentina that were linked to Operation Condor and Pinochet.

With a written request from Garcés, Garzón believed he had the authority to act. On the morning of Thursday, 15 October, he wrote to Scotland Yard to say that he would issue letters rogatory, to be allowed to interview Pinochet about his role in Operation Condor.

Scotland Yard responded as Garzón hoped, with details of Pinochet's location at a clinic in central London. Garzón said he would travel to London on Monday, 19 October. 'To interview Pinochet.'

British newspapers were reporting that Pinochet was in London, and that Garzón was interested in speaking to him. 'I have not made a decision,' the *Guardian* quoted Garzón as having said. 'I shall be studying the position in the next few days,' he added, having been asked to request a rogatory commission. The newspaper suggested that there was 'no question' of seeking Pinochet's extradition to Spain.

The next morning, Friday, 16 October, *El País* reported García-Castellón's negative response to a query as to whether he planned to arrest Pinochet: 'I know that would be a very spectacular action, but I am not like this. I must have strong evidence in front of me, so far I do not have it.'

Early that Friday afternoon, in his office in Madrid at about a quarter to two, Garzón received word that Pinochet might leave London as early as the following day, Saturday, 17 October, and return to Chile.

Did Scotland Yard give you that information?

Yes, Garzón told me, by fax. 'Basically, they told me that Pinochet would leave on Saturday, the next day, so there was no point in coming to London on the Monday, as I intended. We cannot detain him, they said, tell us what to do.'

Until that moment, Garzón intended only to send a list of the questions he wished to put to Pinochet. The fax from Scotland Yard, with its new information, prompted an instant change in direction.

He decided then and there, on his own, without consultation or much reflection, to issue an arrest warrant. 'With questions alone, I wouldn't have any way to make him stay, to prevent him from leaving.' Hence his request for arrest and extradition, and to stop Pinochet from leaving. Garzón acted on instinct.

The fax from Scotland Yard caused you to change your mind?

'Yes.'

And that information was a direct consequence of the earlier conversation with John Dew?

'Yes. Why did I change my mind? When I was told this guy was leaving, I could have said, OK, there is nothing I can do, and García-Castellón won't do anything. But that would have gone against everything I was doing on universal jurisdiction. It was easier to do nothing, but instead I decided to jump into the vacuum.'

It was Friday afternoon in Spain, when most people were heading off for the weekend. Garcés had visited earlier that day, with a list of questions that Garzón could include in the request for the letters rogatory. The only employee still around was Jesús Sánchez, an assistant clerk. Garzón asked him to stay – 'it always happens to me, I'm always the last one!' Sánchez complained – to gather the files on the Operation Condor case. They were locked away, Sánchez told him, not available.

Garzón pondered what he could do without files. 'I went to my office and shut the door, to be alone, to think about what to do. One option was to just . . .'

Forget about it and go home?

'Impossible!' Garzón snapped. 'Option A was just to ignore the matter and leave the office. Option B was to write to Scotland Yard, thank them for their cooperation, and tell them it was now too late to do anything.' There was a third option: 'Here was a real chance to arrest Pinochet. So, I decided to change direction, to write an arrest warrant, and send it to London. I thought I would never forgive myself . . .'

If you did nothing?

Garzón nodded. 'I assumed the effort could fail, but I had to try. So I just started to write . . .'

On a typewriter?

'By hand, on a sheet of paper, with a pen. I did everything from memory.'

What were the crimes?

'I focused on state terrorism, torture and genocide. I wrote in the name of one of the victims, Edgardo Enríquez Espinosa, who was kidnapped in Chile on 10 April 1976, and mentioned seventy-nine other cases of Chileans who had been disappeared . . .' Garzón's voice trailed off.

As we spoke, we had before us a copy of the request for the arrest and extradition of Pinochet, which Garzón had drafted in Spanish. It laid out the facts, succinctly and starkly. As head of state, Garzón wrote, Pinochet was directly involved in the physical elimination, disappearance, kidnapping and torture of thousands of individuals. He relied on the Rettig Report, describing the roles played by Pinochet and the DINA, and Operation Condor.

The killed included Carmelo Soria, the UN diplomat.

The disappeared included a twenty-three-year-old philosophy student, a dual Chilean/French national called Alfonso Chanfreau.


## 14


By October 1998, when the matter reached Garzón, the story of Alfonso Chanfreau was well known across Chile. His widow, Erika Hennings, shared with me a more personal account, in a voice and spirit that were pained, gentle and committed, but not sad or broken.

'After fifty years, my struggle has changed but not the principles or emotions.' Alfonso's disappearance was profoundly unjust, impunity made real. 'What gives me my voice is to fight for justice and for truth.'

Erika Hennings was born in 1951, in Santiago, into a militant family, a Catholic father and a mother from a communist family. 'In the 1960s, when society was politicised, I became a militant communist, for a time.' During schooldays she and a friend visited another school, to offer support during a teachers' strike. 'That was where I met Alfonso, the *jefe de la toma*, the head of the occupation of the school. He was tall, wore a nice white shirt, was cleaning the tables in a classroom. We danced. I thought he was handsome, ahhhh, so handsome!'

They married in October 1972, at the age of twenty-one, and their daughter Natalia was born a few months later. They were university students. 'He studied philosophy, was a leader of MIR at the university, more a militant than a student,' she said. 'I was with the communists.'

The young couple didn't expect the Coup. 'We couldn't really imagine such a thing, on a day of fear,' Hennings said. 'There were arrests, including my uncle, and military trucks started to collect people, the disappearances came later.' Death was all around. 'We saw bodies in the Maipo River, in the centre of Santiago.'

'Alfonso was taken on the night of 30 July 1974, the next day they came for me.' Their daughter was with her parents. 'We were taken to Londres 38. Others were there, including León Gómez, who arrived a few days later.' They spent fourteen days there, together. 'What do I remember? The loud music and the perfume, when I think of it I smell it, the *Flaño*.'

On 13 August 1974, Alfonso was taken away. 'That was the day he disappeared. I saw him in the morning. We spoke. One of the torturers, Guatón Romo, took me to Alfonso and told him he should say goodbye to me. We talked about France, where we hoped to go, where his parents and sister and brother were. "Wait for me, don't learn French without me!" we said to each other. We could have left before, but Alfonso wanted to stay, to resist. That morning, we were able to say goodbye.'

Hennings was transferred to other camps, to Tres Álamos and

Cuatro Álamos in the south of Santiago. Given Chanfreau's dual Chilean/French nationality, the French government intervened, and Pinochet agreed to liberate seven arrested French nationals. Hennings assumed Alfonso was among them, but only when she was released did she learn that he was missing. 'When I saw he was not on the list of seven, I thought he must be dead. I hoped he could still be arrested, but deep down I knew. Straightaway I knew.'

Hennings went to the French Embassy. Having acquired French nationality by marriage to Alfonso, she was protected, up to a point. 'A French parliamentarian, Jacques Marette, on the right, came to Chile, learned about the disappearances, helped us.' She has always been grateful to him. She filed a legal case in the Chilean courts, which went nowhere. 'I was expelled, went to France, that was in 1974.'

Nine years passed before she returned. 'By 1984, the DINA was gone, replaced by the CNI, it was a society governed by fear. There were protests, and I became involved straight away.' The *Vicariá de Solidaridad*, a church organisation, was active, and the families of the disappeared organised themselves through the *Comite Pro Paz*. 'We were mostly women, mothers, there were a few men, we were under surveillance, often questioned by the police,' Hennings recalled. 'It didn't stop us. Londres 38 was already known to have been a place of detention and torture, so we focused on that place. In 1984 we put posters on the walls and daubed it with red paint.'

In 1986 she returned to France, to complete a course in teacher training. 'Since that second time I have loved France,' Hennings said, 'but not to live there . . .!' Three years later she returned once more to Chile. 'I arrived during the referendum campaign, working with *Médecins du Monde*.' She became active in the search for the disappeared, working with her friend Viviana Uribe (whose sister Barbara Uribe and husband Edwin Van Yurick were held at Londres 38, then disappeared).

At the end of 1989, with other family members, Hennings started a new case in Chile. She went to Londres 38, which had become the Instituto O'Higginiano a decade earlier, by a Decree personally signed by Pinochet. 'I visited, they let us in, we didn't say who we were.' In the autumn of 1992, she returned with Judge Gloria Olivares, and with other former detainees, including Viviana Uribe, León Gómez, Miguel Ángel Rebolledo, Hedy Navarro and Luz Arce.

They went to identify their torturers: Miguel Krassnoff, Gerardo Godoy and Basclay Zapata (known as *El Troglo*, said to be 'very sadistic'). Krassnoff annoyed the judge by wearing a military uniform, which he never did when he worked at Londres 38, and carrying a pistol.

The former detainees testified that Londres 38 was where they had been detained and tortured, and identified the three men as their torturers. 'Krassnoff said he only analysed information,' Miguel Ángel Rebolledo would recall, 'and *El Troglo* said he was only a driver.' The newspaper reported the visit, with photographs taken outside, including of León Gómez, with glasses and cigarette, alongside Luz Arce. In the court files I read a verbatim record of the testimony, a precise account of what happened on 29 September 1992.

We were ten witnesses, Erika Hennings recalled. 'As the widow, I was allowed to accompany everyone around the building,' she said. 'Krassnoff offered me his hand, and although my nature is to be polite, I did not offer mine. "I am gentleman," he said. A cold man, totally convinced ideologically by what he did.'

The visit brought attention to the Chanfreau case, although it went nowhere because of the Amnesty Law. Around this time, Hennings identified Guatón Romo as one of the main torturers at Londres 38. She later travelled to Brazil with Viviane Uribe to get him extradited to Chile, and would come face to face with him at Santiago's central police station. 'It was terrible, he recognised me, and remembered he had taken me to say goodbye to Alfonso. *Un mec ignoble.*' A terrible man.

'This was when I really started to engage with Londres 38,' said Hennings, wanting to create a place of national memory. She gathered evidence, much of which ended up in the files that Judge Garzón would use to request Pinochet's extradition from England.

## 15

On the afternoon of Friday, 16 October 1998, Baltasar Garzón, of Court No. 5 in the Audiencia Nacional in Madrid, put the finishing touches to his extradition request. By hand, he wrote:

I ORDER: The pre-trial detention of AUGUSTO PINOCHET

UGARTE for the crimes of genocide and terrorism, issuing international search and capture orders to permit his extradition. The urgent issuance of an international arrest warrant for execution by the British judicial authorities.

He signed the document and asked his assistant to type it up. 'Jesús Sánchez came back a minute later,' Garzón said. '"Don Baltasar, are you sure you want to do this? Do you understand the consequences?" I said to him: "Shut your mouth, type!"' Garzón reviewed the final document, approved it, and instructed Sánchez to take it to the Audiencia Nacional's registrar. She read it. 'This is crazy!' she exclaimed, then signed it.

There remained one formality, a box to be ticked. 'I had a legal duty to notify the prosecutor,' Garzón explained, 'but didn't fully trust him to do the right thing.' Garzón knew that Eduardo Fungairiño would withhold authorisation – the conservative chief prosecutor had warned a senior official from the Chilean Navy not to visit Spain, to avoid legal difficulties, and asked the Audiencia Nacional to declare that Garzón had no jurisdiction to investigate Pinochet.

'I decided to work around Fungairiño,' he said. 'It was Friday afternoon, I knew he might leave early, before the office closed at three. I waited until 2.58 p.m., then sent Jesús Sánchez to knock on his door. No answer. I asked the Registrar's secretary to record that we took steps to notify Prosecutor Fungairiño, but were not able to find him.'

The warrant for the arrest of Augusto Pinochet was finalised and ready to go, first to the Spanish police, then to Interpol in Madrid, then to London. Did you worry about immunity, I asked Garzón?

'I did not. It was clear that there was no immunity, as Pinochet was only a former head of state. In Spain, in other cases, like Berlusconi in Italy, it was understood you only had immunity as a serving head, while you were in office, not after.' One worry, however, was that the Spanish police might alert a senior politician, who'd intervene to stop the process. 'I called a policeman I knew, and said to him: "I am sending you an arrest warrant, it is totally secret, please do not report it to your superiors." The policeman said: "Judge, your verbal instruction is enough, it will be placed in the record, I need nothing else."'

In this way, a little after three o'clock in the afternoon of Friday, 16 October 1998 in Madrid, a warrant for the arrest of Augusto Pinochet was fed into a fax machine at the Audiencia Nacional. Garzón called John Dew to let him know what he was doing. Dew said: 'Thank you very much, your Honour, we will inform you what happens.'

The entire process, from drafting to transmission, was completed in less than a hundred minutes. By four thirty, Garzón was on his way to the Jaen bullring in Andalucía, 350 kilometres south of Madrid, to watch Curro Romero, his favourite bullfighter. On the road, he received a call from John Dew to confirm Scotland Yard had received the arrest warrant and was evaluating it. (Garzón told me he was the only judge at the Audiencia Nacional with a mobile phone at that time, an ancient Motorola version he called 'the gondola', due to its size and shape.) Dew called him again, while Garzón was at the bullring. 'Scotland Yard is taking the arrest warrant to a judge, to be signed,' he said.

# 16

Garzón's request for the arrest and extradition of Augusto Pinochet arrived at Scotland Yard a little after three o'clock London time. What happened next followed the requirements of international law and English law.

Spain and Britain were parties to the European Convention on Extradition, a treaty signed in 1957. This required Britain, on receiving the request for extradition, to surrender Pinochet to Spain, provided that the conditions set out in the Convention were met. The conditions included a requirement that an 'extraditable offence' must have been committed, an act that was a crime in both Spain and Britain and that was punishable by at least one year in prison. On its face, Garzón's request met the conditions.

The European Convention had been implemented into English law by the Extradition Act of 1989. This set out the procedures to be followed in London. The first step was for a magistrate to issue a 'provisional arrest warrant', to allow the police to detain Pinochet. Next, the Home Secretary could issue an 'Authority to Proceed', unless it was determined that an order for the return of Pinochet to

Spain could not lawfully be made. Third, Pinochet would appear in court – 'as soon as practicable' – to confirm that the offence was an 'extradition crime', and there was sufficient evidence, and to decide on conditions of custody or bail. Finally, the Home Secretary had to decide whether to send Pinochet to Spain. For each of these four steps, the 1989 Act set out specific procedures and conditions. It did not, however, address all aspects: it was silent on the question of Pinochet's immunity.

The first step was the provisional arrest warrant. By the time Garzón's request arrived in London, the courts were closed, so the request went to a Metropolitan Stipendiary Magistrate, on after-hours duty. That evening, the magistrate was Nicholas Evans, who lived in Hampstead, in north London. Scotland Yard prepared a draft provisional arrest warrant, which officers from the Extradition Squad would take to his home. Evans would review it, fill in gaps and, if all was in order, sign it. His signature would allow Augusto Pinochet to be arrested.

Many years later, Nicholas Evans gave me a first-hand account. This was a generous, neighbourly act: we happened to live next door to each other, our gardens divided by a narrow path, two fences, and a persistently aggressive bamboo plant.

I visited him on a Sunday in October. Tall and well-built, with a mop of grey hair and a generously ruddy complexion, he had much experience dealing with extradition requests, although none quite so momentous. That autumn morning, he greeted me in brown corduroy trousers and a blue jumper, inviting me to the first floor, a living room-cum-office, with a comfortable red sofa into which he settled, hands clasped across his chest. As we talked, the door opened and Diana, his wife, poked her head in. 'Coffee? Or something stronger?'

'It was Friday, 16 October 1998, exactly eighteen years ago to this day,' he mused. After a day in court, at Bow Street Magistrates, in central London, he returned home at about six o'clock. 'I happened to be on call', so Scotland Yard could turn up at any moment. 'You might well get a visit at midnight.' It was treated as an emergency. 'I was told that travel arrangements had been made by or on behalf of Senator Pinochet, for him to leave the UK the next day.'

Anything notable about the day?

'Nothing, it was just a day.' He reflected. 'Well, there may have been some talk, that an arrest warrant might be needed in the evening. I heard something about traffic between Spain and England.' He and his wife had an early supper and at about half past seven the telephone rang. 'It was Scotland Yard, to say they'd be around within the hour, and they were.'

Four officers arrived a little after eight o'clock, with an extradition request from Madrid and a draft provisional warrant for Pinochet's arrest. 'They stayed for about an hour, till nine. An inspector from the extradition squad, and an officer I knew. Can't remember the name.' Andrew Hewett, I suggested. 'And there was Lizzie Frayne, the clerk at Bow Street, very knowledgeable on extradition matters. She was helpful, she'd looked at the paperwork.'

Did he offer them a cup of tea?

'It's possible, probably not, just got on with it.'

Nicholas had prepared a little, between the phone call and their arrival. 'I think the name Pinochet was mentioned. I had heard it, but didn't really have a very clear understanding about any of the history, or precisely what was involved. Anyway, they said it may never happen, so I didn't spend much time thinking about it.' Nevertheless, he sensed it was unusual. 'I was beginning to realise this may be something out of the ordinary, so I went on to my computer and looked up the name. Pinochet. I read a bit about it, to have a better idea of the background. I didn't really know too much about it.'

I expressed surprise he didn't know more. 'I knew he was a Chilean dictator. I knew there was a lot of fuss about the way in which he conducted himself. But I didn't really have . . .' Nicholas drifted into a gentle silence, which became a thought, then a question.

'When did he come to power?'

'11 September 1973.'

'Well, I was called to the Bar in 1971. In 1973, I would have been running around magistrates' courts, busying myself with criminal work. I wasn't closely following foreign developments, I don't remember being exercised by what was going on in Chile.'

'It was long before the idea of international criminal law had really taken off,' I suggested, 'and far away.'

'Exactly,' he responded, briskly. There was no reason he should pay particular attention to other developments in 1998, like the creation of the International Criminal Court, that summer, or talk of indicting Serbian President Slobodan Milošević in The Hague.

'Pinochet was the first such arrest warrant for a former head of state, for international crimes,' I said.

'I had no knowledge of those other matters,' he said.

None?

Nicholas thought about this. 'If I'd been skipping through *The Times*, there may have been some reference to them, but generally speaking I would have passed on. I had all kinds of interesting work to do, it wasn't all prostitutes and beggars and things, you know! I had a diet of interesting work to occupy me.'

He brought the conversation back to the evening with the four officers. 'They arrived with an "Information"', the document which set out the basic facts and possible legal charges. They told him Pinochet might leave as early as the following morning on a private jet. The matter was urgent.

'Inspector Hewett brought an extradition request from a court in Spain, signed by Garzón. It provided Information on Pinochet's conduct, from which it was for me to see whether there were any suitable extradition crimes. It probably gave the Spanish offences, but they weren't terribly relevant.'

As the Magistrate on duty, Nicholas was required to go through an intellectual exercise of his own, not merely sign on the dotted line.

'You had to work out what offence under English law might have been committed, and satisfy yourself it was an extraditable offence?' I said.

'Yes, that's it. The process took rather longer than normal.'

He couldn't remember the length or detail of Garzón's document. 'Probably there was quite a lot in it, because it gave some history about the accusations against him. It was talking about the murders of thousands of people, of torture, of hostage-taking . . .'

'And genocide.'

'Can't remember that,' Nicholas said sharply, and continued:

There was a lot of material there, and I had to frame an extradition offence, something that is called 'The Charge'. My job was to come up with an appropriate Charge. Usually that's fairly straightforward, but this one wasn't, so there was a bit of discussion between us. I knew nothing about torture. Torture! Today I am familiar with the term, but back then was the first time I had come across torture as a potential crime.

He smiled, a big warm, decent, neighbourly smile:

> I could cope with burglary, theft, murder, but this was different. I wasn't happy about drafting some sort of torture charge. We went backwards and forwards, Lizzie trying to help me find an appropriate charge. Actually, there was potential for twenty or thirty charges, but all I needed was a single extradition offence that would satisfy the requirement to get him arrested. I plumped for murder, because I thought murder was straightforward. I thought it was fine, and I said 'Well, we don't have to worry about torture, if he's killed somebody – or he's accused of that – we can focus on murder, that's good enough.'

The group went round in circles in the quest for an appropriate extraditable offence under English law. They settled on murder. At one point, Evans said to himself: 'This is ridiculous, let's keep it simple.'

Did he give any thought to the consequences of his signature?

'No. I didn't have that sense then. I knew there might be a lot of fuss. I think I asked whether the Home Office or Foreign Office were aware of what was going on? I was told "Yes", so I didn't ask any more questions.'

Did he or the team from Scotland Yard turn their minds to the possibility that Pinochet might be able to claim immunity, as a former head of state?

'Probably, but it wasn't something I'd ever dealt with before. It was the first time the issue had ever come up.'

He was right. This was entirely new. There was no precedent for this, not in Britain, not anywhere. No former head of state had ever been arrested in another country for an international crime. A former head of state had been tried by another country for regular crimes connected to the other country – in 1992 Manuel Noriega of Panama was tried and convicted in the United States on charges of drug trafficking, money laundering and racketeering – but never before for an international crime, committed far away and long ago.

So you had no hesitation, on that score, on the issue of immunity of a former head of state?

'I suppose I thought simplistically, he's an ordinary Joe now, not a head of state anymore.'

A provisional arrest warrant is a formal document. It is addressed 'To each and all of the Constables of the Metropolitan Police', and empowers them to arrest the person named as the accused. Nicholas Evans proceeded to write:

Augusto Pinochet Ugarte . . . between the 11th September 1973 and the 31st December 1983 within the jurisdiction of the Fifth Central Magistrates' Court of the National Court of Madrid did murder Spanish Citizens in Chile, within the jurisdiction of the Government of Spain.

He signed it, and the Bow Street clerk, Elizabeth Franey, witnessed the signature. EF.

After the officers left, Nicholas told Diana what had passed – 'not a meaningful conversation' – and the couple retired for the night.

Did the name Pinochet give you any pause?

'No. I just started the process, something which I didn't appreciate might have the effect it did. I don't think I can take any credit. I was just doing my job. I didn't sign a warrant because this was my opportunity to change the world, certainly not. It was just another case. I signed the arrest warrant. Without it they couldn't do anything.'

The conversation meandered to an end. Nicholas stood and went to the window that overlooked the street. 'See that window there?' he said, in a tone of utter gentleness. 'The one with a light on.'

I nodded.

'That's John le Carré's study, that's where he writes. Funny thing, eh?'

## 17

As the four officers returned to Scotland Yard from Hampstead, with the signed provisional arrest warrant, their minds turned to practical matters. Pinochet, in a private room at The London Clinic, on the corner of Devonshire Place and Marylebone Road, spoke no English, so an interpreter was needed. They opted for Jean Pateras, highly regarded, with two decades of experience working with the Metropolitan Police.

Many years later I met Jean, who was happy to share what happened on that memorable evening. We  spoke first by telephone, then talked in her comfortable apartment, overlooking Sloane Square, drinking tea, close to boxes of papers from the Pinochet case. Comfortably ensconced in an armchair, surrounded by books and family photographs, a copy of the *Daily Mail* splayed across the carpet, she wore a cream-coloured top and matching trousers, offset by shiny, gold moccasins. Jean was a serious person, one who does her work with great professionalism. She is also one of life's fabulous characters, energetic and engaging, with abundant hair arranged in a style that reminded me of that moment in the late 1990s. Born in Costa Rica, her father was an Anglo-Argentine who had trained at Sandhurst, her mother born in Chile of English parents. She spent part of her childhood in Chile, where her grandfather ran a fruit farm.

With impeccable Spanish, Jean Pateras began to interpret for the Metropolitan Police in the 1980s, introduced to the work by a friend. '"Do you speak Spanish?" a visiting policeman asked. I said "Yes", and that was it. My first case was a bar of soap stolen from Boots the Chemist!' A companion to my own first case as a young barrister, I said, of shoplifting from Marks & Spencer. Jean loved the police work, mostly local matters before the English courts. Occasionally there might be a big war-crimes case, but Pinochet was on another scale. 'Genocide, torture and other horrors? All that was new to me.'

With gusto Jean recalled the evening of Friday, 16 October 1998. 'Scotland Yard called at about five in the afternoon. I was just back from court, relaxing. "Are you free, Jean?"' Exhausted after a long day, she said yes, if it was interesting. 'Oh yes, they said, this was interesting, but wouldn't say on the phone what it was about, just that they were about to get an arrest warrant for the person.'

Her interest piqued, Jean accepted and drove to Scotland Yard. 'What's going on?' she asked a detective sergeant in the lift. 'The DS said: "We are going to arrest General Pinochet". I said: "What? Sounds like a Woody Allen movie!"' We laughed at the oddness of the reaction.

On the fourth floor of Scotland Yard, Inspector Hewett briefed her, then headed off to Hampstead to get the arrest warrant signed. Jean knew Nicholas Evans, as she'd interpreted in his court. 'Go home, wait for us to call,' Hewett instructed her. She had supper with her husband, then waited. The call came at nine p.m., to report to Marylebone police station. From there, she, Hewett and three other officers left for The London Clinic. It was about eleven o'clock.

'We turned up out of the blue,' Jean said, 'no warning.' The officers showed their identity cards and explained their purpose. They were ushered to a lift, up to the eighth floor. Outside Room 801, guarded by two Chilean security men, a nurse told them Pinochet was asleep. His wife Lucía wasn't there.

Jean continued: 'Someone said, "Well, go and wake him up so he doesn't get a shock and have a heart attack." Probably me who said that, as I am so bossy!' So the nurse knocked, opened the door, went in, switched on the light. Jean listened to Pinochet being woken up. 'I went in after a few minutes with two detectives. It was just the three of us. He was sitting up in bed, in pyjamas, the lights on, two Chilean guards in the room, his private bodyguards. They didn't speak a word of English.'

Hewett spoke, then Jean interpreted:

I said, 'Buenas noches, my name is Jean Pateras, and please listen to what the police officer is going to say to you. I will repeat what he says in Spanish.' The Detective Sergeant read out the order for his arrest, and told Pinochet of his rights. You don't have to say anything, it may harm your defence if you do so, blah blah blah. Then I said: 'You are under arrest for murder.'

Pinochet listened. It was nearly midnight.

How did he react?

'He digested what was being said.'

What was his immediate reaction?

He said: 'I know the fucker who's behind this, it's that communist Garcés, Juan Garcés.' He was furious. Furious! 'Juan Garcés' was the first thing he said. I translated. He said he'd come on a secret mission, had a diplomatic passport and immunity. I told him, 'Your guards have to leave, because you are under the protection of the British Police.' I can't remember what happened then. All sorts of things.

Initially, the Chilean guards refused to leave, Jean said. 'One of them said, "No, I'm not leaving." I told him, "If you don't leave, you will be forcibly removed, go outside."' Two uniformed police officers came in and escorted them out. One would recall Pinochet as 'arrogant and unhelpful' and 'totally aghast that this was happening to him'.

Sensing Pinochet's anxiety, Jean sought to calm him. 'I said to him, "Look, I'm sure your ambassador is on the way, and you can speak to him when he gets here, and sort this out."' Not long after, the ambassador duly arrived. 'The ambassador came down with us in the lift. He said, "Don't think that I'm a friend of this man, my family had to leave the country because of him."'

Jean spent about an hour at The London Clinic. 'There was a lot to sort out. I was just hanging around while the police were doing this and that, signing things, making sure he knew what was going to happen.' It was after midnight when she left. Outside, on the street, the two Chilean security men lingered, not knowing what to do. 'They were just standing there, in the rain, across from the Clinic, the two of them. Standing and staring. Quite extraordinary. Huge devotion.'

At home in a state of excitement, Jean called her sister in Paris, where her husband was Costa Rica's ambassador to France:

It was about two o'clock in the morning, I said to her, 'Guess what I've just done! I've just arrested General Pinochet!' She said, 'Oh, come on!' I said, 'Yes, you'll read about it tomorrow.' My sister was thrilled, she thought Pinochet was a monster.

Jean Pateras was still energised talking about it twenty years later. 'It was so exciting, I can't tell you!' That night, she didn't realise this was not the last time she would be with Augusto Pinochet.

'I've got a whole load of the extradition papers, perhaps you'd like to have them?' It was not an offer to refuse. We exchanged farewells. I left with several large plastic boxes, filled with documents, hundreds of pages of Pinochet papers. Garzón's request was there, with excruciating and terrible details of the crimes that had led to Pinochet's arrest, including Carmelo Soria and Alfonso Chanfreau.

As I headed off, Jean mentioned the call she made the next day, to her mother, who was in Dorset, England:

'Guess what I did last night, Mummy!' Her response? She did guess, and said: 'I think it's absolutely disgraceful, the man's an absolute marvel, Chile was wonderful under him.' I said, 'Mummy, do you realise what this man has done?' 'It's all nonsense, darling, it's all nonsense.'

# NIGHTS IN CHILE

## 18

The arrest of Augusto Pinochet caused a shock across Chile, for supporters and opponents, and in literary circles. Roberto Bolaño welcomed the news, evoking Pinochet's impact on cultural life in Chile, on the 'mediocrities on right and left' who cavorted with the dictator.

At the time of Pinochet's arrest, Bolaño was gathering ideas for a new novel. *Nocturno de Chile* (*By Night in Chile*) was published while Pinochet was in London. The main character was Father Sebastián Urrutia Lacroix, an elderly Jesuit priest with rambling memories of the Pinochet years.

The novel garnered much attention and renown for the author, introducing a range of characters encountered by the priest. One was 'a middle-aged man, of average height, neither skinny nor slim, with a nondescript face'. Bolaño called him Mr Raef. He was a man who wore 'a light-coloured suit and a most elegant hat', the manager of a fish cannery that packed clams tightly into small tins for export to Germany and France. 'We're mainly an import-export firm,' Raef told the priest, 'but we are branching out into other areas.'

One day, Mr Raef approached Father Urrutia Lacroix. The manager of the fish cannery wished to speak privately about a sensitive matter, one that required 'extraordinarily absolute discretion and secrecy'. The priest accepted the condition, allowing Mr Raef to explain the confidential mission: he asked the priest if he would give classes on Marxism to Augusto Pinochet and other members of the Junta, including General Mendoza, the head of the police.

The priest accepted the mission. The classes began. Pinochet turned out to be a decent student, a regular attendee with a desire to study and learn, a man who delighted in reading and writing. The heart of Pinochet's desire, the priest observed, was to learn about

Marxism, 'to understand Chile's enemies, to find out how they think, to get an idea of how far they are prepared to go'.

The fictional character of Mr Raef the cannery manager was based on Walther Rauff, a senior Nazi and SS officer who fled Europe and fetched up in southern Chile, where he managed a king-crab cannery that exported crabmeat to Europe. In 1963, a photograph of him was published widely in Chilean newspapers, seated in the back of  a car wearing a light-coloured suit. The image left an impression on Bolaño, who noted the hat. The photograph left an impression on others too, I would learn.

Walther Rauff also inspired a character in an earlier Bolaño novel, *Nazi Literature in the Americas*, published shortly before Pinochet was arrested in London. A work of satire, involving a diverse cast of characters, a chapter on 'Two Germans at the End of the World' introduced readers to a place the author called 'Colonia Renacer'. The Colony of Rebirth (for that is the translation) was an estate in central Chile inhabited by residents who were, in the author's imagination, 'without exception, German'.

'Colonia Renacer' was based on Colonia Dignidad, a religious, agricultural community established by German immigrants in 1963, about 340 kilometres south of Santiago. In the real world, Colonia Dignidad, which I shall refer to as The Colony, was a place of serial paedophilia and other sexual crimes, whose leaders worked closely with the DINA and Pinochet. It was also said to have connections with Nazis on the run, men like Adolf Eichmann, Martin Bormann and Josef Mengele – and Walther Rauff. A year after the Coup, in 1974, Pinochet was filmed on a visit to the Colony.

In Bolaño's novel, The Colony was a place of 'pagan orgies, sex slaves and secret executions'. Here, red flags were flown, 'with a white circle in which a black swastika is inscribed'. In the novelist's account, 'the only war criminal to have spent time in the colony (a number of years in fact, entirely given over to horticulture) was Walther Rauss'. According to Bolaño, it was later claimed that Rauss 'had taken part in certain torture sessions during the early years of Pinochet's regime'.

In this fictionalised account, Herr Rauss met his end when he had a heart attack, while watching a football match on television, 'East and West Germany playing during the 1974 World Cup in West Germany'. As with much fiction, Bolaño's account was not entirely without truth: the World Cup was held in West Germany that year, and East and West Germany did play against each other. East Germany won 1-0, a bitter result for Chile, as it dumped the country out of the competition.

As for the rest of Bolaño's novel, it appeared, on first glance, to be the stuff of imagination and mythologies. There was no hard evidence that the real Walther Rauff was interested in football, or that he visited The Colony, or was a torturer, although there were rumours and unsubstantiated tales to that effect. Nor did he die in 1974. That year, and for several more, the real Rauff managed a cannery in Punta Arenas where the flesh of king crabs was packed into small tins and exported to the tables of hungry Europeans.

Let us return to *By Night in Chile*. Other characters included a married couple who Father Urrutia Lacroix came to know. The woman was pretty, a young writer with brown hair and large eyes. Bolaño called her María Canales, and she was married to 'a North American called James Thompson'. They shared a large house, a sanctuary where Canales hosted literary 'gatherings or receptions or soirées or parties'. Occasionally, Father Urrutia Lacroix was present, to enjoy the stories and the company of other writers. 'They all deny it now,' the priest recalled of those who said they weren't there, at gatherings encouraged by Pinochet.

Father Urrutia Lacroix recalled an occasion when a wandering guest found the basement. There he came across a body, tied to a metal bed, 'abandoned but alive', recuperating from an unknown ordeal. With the onset of democracy, after Pinochet's departure, strange tales emerged about the house. One concerned the husband, 'James Thompson', a DINA agent whose house was a place of interrogation and torture, where people were killed. It was said that Thompson travelled to Washington to kill one of Allende's ex-ministers, and organised assassinations in Argentina and Europe. Arrested in the United States, Thompson confessed to his crimes,

implicated a few Chilean generals, entered a witness-protection programme, and was never seen again.

As for María Canales, on the priest's account, she was left with
nothing. She knew what her husband had done, repented, and was
left fearful and barely able to breathe. 'The Jews were planning to
demolish the house,' Bolaño had her say to the priest, so nothing
would be left. 'They're going to knock the house down. They'll rip
out the basement. It's where one of Jimmy's men killed the Spanish
UNESCO official.'

The account was fictional but, like the Colony, not entirely. The
house that fired Bolaño's imagination actually existed. 'A true story,'
Bolaño would say, 'I repeat: this isn't fiction, it's real, it happened
during the Pinochet dictatorship and more or less everybody knows.'
Bolaño came across the story in an article by Pedro Lemebel, pub-
lished in 1994, about a house of literary salons in Santiago on Vía
Naranja, at number 4925. This was the home of the real James
Thompson – Michael Townley, the DINA agent who murdered
Carlos Prats and Orlando Letelier. Townley was married to the real
María Canales – Mariana Callejas, who hosted literary salons at the
house and wrote short stories. One of her stories – 'Conoció usted a
Bobby Ackermann?' ('Did You Know Bobby Ackermann?') – won a
literary prize offered by *El Mercurio*.

In the house of Townley and Callejas, real people were detained,
tortured, killed and disappeared. The 'Spanish UNESCO official'
was Carmelo Soria, the UN diplomat recast in Bolaño's novel as
a 'UNESCO official'. It was here at this house, Carmen Soria told
me, that her father's neck was placed on a step and snapped. Here
in the basement, the DINA established Project Andrea, where the
chemist Eugenio Berríos developed sarin gas to eliminate Pinochet's
opponents. Here, it was rumoured, gas was sprayed on Soria, in the
presence of a Cuban immigrant who would be, just two months
later, involved in the killing of Letelier.

And it was here, in this house, that Mariana Callejas wrote *La
larga noche* (*The Long Night*), a collection of short stories bound
into an ominous black cover on which a large eye peers from behind
the bars of a cell. I bought a copy in an old second-hand shop in
central Santiago, inscribed by the author to her new friends Enrique
and Max.

I read 'Un parque pequeño y alegre' ('A Small and Cheerful

Park'), a story of bombings and torture, acts of the kind in which her American husband excelled.

I read 'Heil, Peter', featuring a German character who comes to South America and lives with memories of his father's friendship with Hitler.

# 19

Reading Bolaño, and encountering the character of María Canales, prompted me to learn more about the real Mariana Callejas, and to read her stories. Fiction introduced fact and brought me to the place where Carmelo Soria had lost his life, on a step.

In Santiago, on a summer's day in December 2021, I visited the neighbourhood of Lo Curro, with my Chilean assistant Monserrat and a friend of hers from Santiago. We passed the palace built by Pinochet and garishly furnished by his wife Lucía. Today it is the Club Militar de Chile, available to rent for weddings and other private functions.

The entrance to the Vía Naranja was protected by a barrier and a sleepy security guard in a cheap uniform who enquired about our business. 'Private visit,' Monserrat and I said in chorus. He raised the barrier and waved us through, allowing us to enter a street of curves, gated homes, manicured gardens and pools, verdant and lush, with sublime views across the city. We reached the place where number 4925 should have been, but it was long gone, as the fictional María Canales predicted. In its place were two new homes, numbers 4241A and 4241B. We lingered in a place of torture and mass killing, a residential paradise with no sign to indicate the horrors that had occurred here.

Across the road, a gardener tended an extensive, lush lawn. We waved, he wandered over. His name was José, he'd worked here for forty years. Yes, he remembered the original house, knew of its notoriety and the horrors that occurred in the basement. Local families and neighbours didn't want to talk about it, nobody wanted a memorial.

Did they read Bolaño?

'They've been here for decades,' said the gardener. 'They must have known.'

And seen?

José nodded and smiled. Omar, his friend, who had tended the garden next to number 4925 for half a century, knew much more.

'He was here in 1976. He saw many things, he heard many things.'

Like?

'When people were brought in, the screams from the basement, the bags that came out, the cars and the vans.'

Bags?

'Body bags.'

José the gardener pointed across the road to where there was once a basement. 'It's under the swimming pool now. When they put up a new house, they just buried everything, in the corner, then built a little hill over the things they buried.'

Omar had spoken of the comings and goings. 'He would come and stand on the corner of the property, look over.'

And he had carried on working, next to a site of mass murder?

José shrugged. 'We need to work.' Omar took what he saw to the grave.

'I saw Townley three times,' said José. He saw Mariana Callejas too, more often. 'They would come with other people, maybe to show the house to sell it. They were separated, on TV they blamed each other for the events.'

As we chatted, a neighbour, an older man, emerged from his house and into his garden, a considerable distance away. He looked towards his gardener, took out a camera and pointed it towards us. 'If anyone asks, say you are looking to buy property,' said José, 'do not say your real business.' He noticed that the security cameras on top of the street lamps had swivelled in our direction.

'We don't want to cause you difficulties, shall we leave?' I said.

'You won't cause trouble. They are the ones who got into trouble, not me. Anyway, I don't care. They can't do anything to me, these people. I wish they'd fire me, then I'd get compensation.'

As we lingered, a handsome, tanned man in a uniform on a motorbike roared up to us. 'What are you doing here?' the policeman asked. You are breaking the law, he continued, you must leave. 'They say you have been going to houses and ringing doorbells.' We had done no such thing, we said, we were just looking for number 4925, but it was gone.

He asked for names and identity cards, which we declined to

provide. 'You cannot perform an identity control on us,' said my Chilean companion. He radioed headquarters, told them we were only walking around. 'Here in Lo Curro, walking around is regarded as suspicious.' He apologised. 'I'm just sent here.'

We told the policeman about number 4925, what happened there. He listened, said he wasn't surprised, or that there was no memorial.

'Are you communists?' he asked suddenly. He said this with a straight face, and expected a straight answer. We laughed.

'Do we look like communists?'

'No,' he conceded, with a friendly smile. It was just that we were here, in a wealthy neighbourhood, and that made us seem like we could be communists. He lived in La Victoria, a leftist village, and was a member of a trade union. 'I won't be voting for José Kast,' he said, a reference to the right-wing presidential candidate, a defender of Pinochet, whose German father had joined the Nazi Party.

We promised not to linger. The policeman offered a wave, got on his motorbike and sped off. We stood on the street, thinking about Townley/Thompson and Callejas/Canales, and the line that divided fact and fiction.

'What about Bolaño's characters?' asked my assistant, Monserrat. 'Were Raef and Rauss based on a real character?'

# SANTIAGO, 1963

## 20

Roberto Bolaño's characters of Raef and Rauss were indeed based on a real person. I first came across Walther Rauff's name in Bruce Chatwin's *In Patagonia*, which I read as a student. It left me with a powerful sense of the region – Bolaño considered that the book brought fame to the 'magical realism' of the area – but the memory of Rauff faded. Only recently, when a friend in Santiago reminded me of the lines, did I return to Chapter 96 and Chatwin's unexpected evocation of a man in Punta Arenas who dreamed and hummed, a passage that opened the imagination:

> He drives to a factory that smells of the sea. All about him are scarlet crabs, crawling, then steaming. He hears the shells crack and the claws breaking, sees the sweet white flesh packed firm in metal cans. He is an efficient man, with some previous experience of the production line. Does he remember that other smell, of burning? And that other sound, of low voices singing? . . . Walter Rauff is credited with the invention and administration of the Mobile Gas Truck.

The passage has a quiet voice and 'glacial' effect, thought Sybille Bedford, a fine observer of legal detail. Another reviewer was struck by the 'sinister nostalgic gaze' of the words, of the connection they drew between travel and violence.

Rauff's name next came up, unexpectedly, as I was researching my book on the Ratline, in the personal archive of Otto Wächter. The former SS leader and Nazi Governor of District Galicia, based in Kraków, was on the run when Rauff wrote to him, in May 1949, three typed pages sent from Damascus. Leave Europe and head to South America on the Ratline, Rauff advised. Accept your situation and 'climb back up the ladder'. Don't waste time harking back to the glory days of Nazism. Avoid the Arab world, head for South America. Best greetings, your Walther Rauff. Wächter died mysteriously in Rome, two months later, but Rauff followed his own advice and ended up in Chile.

'Walther Rauff?' said Laura González-Vera, Carmelo Soria's widow. 'Sure, everybody knows the name, because he designed Nazi-style camps in Chile and advised Pinochet.' The Chilean Army was very German, she wanted me to know, and 'Rauff planned poisonings by the DINA'. This she stated as fact.

It turned out that Rauff featured in literature – beyond Chatwin and Bolaño – and many news stories. By the mid-1980s, he had a mythical status, living in the Las Condes district of Santiago, near Laura González-Vera. He had two sons and several grandchildren, hung out with old Germans, drank whisky, listened to West German radio, celebrated the Führer's birthday, and hummed Nazi tunes.

He wrote letters. He was safe in wonderful Chile, he assured his sister in West Germany. He had friends with easy access to 'the House of Pinochet'. He was protected by 'many high-ranking officers'. Occasionally, he said, there were efforts to extradite him, but they would end up in the garbage.

Pinochet, on the other hand, was circumspect about the relationship. 'I do not know Rauff,' he told a journalist from *Newsweek* magazine, in March 1984. That was a lie, as he well knew.

## 21

I gathered material on Rauff. An academic biography, hundreds of articles, photographs and grainy newsreels. There were archives in Chile, Germany and the United States. At the Bodleian Library in Oxford, Rauff's name appeared in a worn moleskin notebook that belonged to Chatwin. 'Commandant Rauff' from 'P.A.', the traveller wrote, a man associated with 'mobile German vans'.

The archives in Washington DC held dozens of CIA documents. One was a military interrogation of Rauff, from May 1945, offering an account of his life.

I was born on 19 June 1906 in the small town of Köthen, into a Protestant family, he told a British officer. He didn't say he was baptised at the Sankt Hedwigs Kathedrale in Berlin, as he would tell a famed journalist decades later, or that Johann Sebastian Bach composed the first book of the Well-Tempered Clavier (BWV 846 to 869), as well as the French Suites for keyboard (BWV 812 to 817), in Köthen.

His father Otto worked for a bank, his mother Louise looked after him, the home and his older brother and sister, Ernst-August and Ilse. He went to school in Magdeburg, near Berlin, then at eighteen joined the German Navy. As a cadet, his first posting took him to South America on a friendship tour. In late 1925, the SMS *Berlin*, a cruiser, reached the Chilean port of Valparaíso, a city of many hills. Making his way to the Naval Academy, Rauff passed the San Rafael Seminary, where one of the pupils was ten-year-old Augusto Pinochet.

The *Berlin* sailed 3,000 kilometres south to Punta Arenas in Chilean Patagonia, past Dawson Island and Tierra del Fuego and through the Straits of Magellan, named after Ferdinand Magellan, who led the expedition that navigated the strait in 1520 (with Juan Sebastián Elcano who Leina Schiffrin, my Spanish mother-in-law, has now persuaded me is a forebear of her family). Punta Arenas was made prosperous by the connection it offered between the Atlantic and Pacific oceans. Established by European colonisers, the city's powerful German population arranged for Rauff and the crew to visit the city cemetery, on Christmas Day. There they added four shell casings to a monument in honour of Admiral Graf Spee and German sailors who perished when the British Navy sank four cruisers near the Falkland Islands, a decade earlier.

Rauff liked the town, with its bustling Plaza de Armas, the centrepiece a statue of Hernando de Magallanes towering above a Selk'nam warrior, a nod to colonial history. He visited German-owned shops, like the Sara Braun company, and admired the home of the Prussian-born German consul, Rodolfo Stubenrauch. Rauff felt welcome.

Back in Germany, over the next decade he made his way up the naval ranks. Around the time that Hitler became Chancellor in 1933, Rauff married Charlotte Borbe, the daughter of a beer brewer. In 1937 he joined the Nazi Party, member number 5216415, and was given charge of a naval flotilla. That same year he met Edith Richter, twice married, eight years his senior, with a sixteen-year-old son. The affair led to his divorce from Charlotte and military court proceedings that judged him to be an adulterer. He left the Navy at his own request and was discharged with all honours, he would say.

Rauff needed work. An acquaintance at the *Sicherheitsdienst*, or SD, the intelligence branch of the SS and the Gestapo, introduced him to Werner Best, a lawyer and SS intelligence officer close to Heinrich Himmler. 'Rauff is a fresh, purposeful individual, suitable as an SS leader, both ideologically and in his inner attitude', his Nazi file recorded.

He joined the SS a year later, in 1938, as member number 290947, and declared himself to be *gottgläubig*, beholden to Adolf Hitler rather than the Protestant Church. Now married to Edith, the couple lived in Charlottenburg, at Mommsenstrasse 47, and Rauff worked at SD headquarters in Berlin, walking the same corridors as Himmler, Otto Wächter and Adolf Eichmann. He came under the tutelage of Reinhard Heydrich, the SD's leader, a man Rauff first met at a lecture for naval officers in 1928. Heydrich appreciated Rauff's organisational abilities, a man who didn't ask questions and got things done.

In October 1938, he and Edith had a son, Alf, then a second in 1940, Walther junior. Promoted to SS Hauptsturmführer, Rauff now worked in the 'Technical' division of the *Reichssicherheitshauptamt*, Hitler's Reich Security Office, in section *Amt IID*. In June 1941, as Germany cast aside the Molotov/von Ribbentrop Pact with the Soviets, and its army headed eastward, Heydrich engaged Rauff on a most secret project: prompted by Germany's occupation of vast lands, today part of Belarus and Ukraine, Rauff would assist in efforts to disappear the Jewish population. Traumatised by observing a mass execution in Minsk, Himmler had decided that execution by bullets was too stressful for decent SS men and instructed Heydrich to find more efficient means. 'Heydrich was a perfectionist, not a fanatic like Himmler and Hitler,' Rauff would later say of the man who tapped him to become a mass murderer. 'He looked at things coolly, from a technical standpoint.'

On the new project, Rauff's team included Dr August Becker, a chemist who honed his skills in the Nazis' *T4 Aktion* euthanasia programme, using carbon-monoxide gas to kill 'incurable' patients. Rauff designed a prototype gas van that was tested on Soviet prisoners at the Sachsenhausen concentration camp, north of Berlin. Locked into the back, prisoners were killed by internally fed exhaust fumes in less than eight minutes, their bodies then cremated. The process was deemed a success, so Rauff recruited Friedrich Pradel to manage a fleet of vehicles, working with Willy Just, a technician. Rauff had no qualms about the work: it would lessen the emotional burdens of those who killed in the public interest.

'There was a detachable exhaust hose taken from the outside to the floor of the car,' a colleague explained. 'When the engine was started and the connection made, exhaust gases from the engine went through the pipe and into the hose, and from there into the exhaust pipe mounted inside the car, where the gas was distributed.' Rauff was involved in the minutiae, ensuring 'occupants' couldn't tamper with the pipe's entry point into the wagon. Under his direction, the design was constantly improved.

He commissioned five prototypes, three tons of metal that could gas fifty people in a single operation, in just a few minutes. From Berlin, two vans headed north to Riga, in Latvia; one went south, to Simferopol, in Crimea; the two others were used at the Kulmhof camp between Berlin and Warsaw. Over the next year, Rauff oversaw the construction of hundreds of vans. He was involved in their design, manufacture and operation, and the procurement of spare parts from Gaubschat in Berlin-Neukölln (many years later, the company's name was acquired by Wartburgmobil, whose motto is: 'We connect people').

Rauff maintained a calm, positive and professional disposition. This was simply a job to be done, in the struggle against the Soviets and Jews, one to be implemented with care, passion and control. If the delivery of a 'special vehicle' to the Mauthausen camp in Austria was delayed, he'd helpfully arrange for canisters of carbon-monoxide gas to be delivered for use before the van's arrival.

Rauff received regular updates. He was informed when people worked out the fate of those who entered the camouflaged 'death cars', some of which were disguised as ambulances. He was advised on efforts in Kiev to perfect the quantity of fumes delivered, so that

gassing was done 'correctly': some drivers pushed the gas pedal too firmly, thinking that a 'full gas' approach would get the job done more quickly, whereas it caused death by painful 'suffocation' rather than gentle sleep. With Becker the chemist Rauff perfected techniques to allow the vans' occupants to 'slip peacefully away'. A gentle killing meant fewer facial distortions and excretions, and therefore 'less time needed to clean up'.

In June 1942, Rauff received a telegram from Riga. 'Every week, a transport of Jews arrives for special treatment', but three gas vans (two Diamond models, one Saurer) were insufficient to deal with the large numbers. Riga requested an additional van (the larger five-tonne version) and hoses. 'When is the provision of a further van to be expected?' Rauff asked. When would spare exhaust hoses be available? Rauff was a most efficient man.

On 5 June 1942, Willy Just, the technical inspector, sent Rauff details of operations at Chelmno (Kulmhof). The document with his name on it would come to haunt Rauff. Over six months, Just reported, 'ninety-seven thousand have been processed by the three vehicles in service, with no major incidents'. He proposed 'technical changes' for Rauff's approval: a larger 'load space', shorter operations, greater stability (so the 'load' didn't shift around). Internal lights should be left on, after the rear doors were shut, so 'the load' didn't panic and scream and rush around as darkness set in. Cleaning would be assisted by placing a sealed drain in the middle of the floor, one with 'a slanting trap so that fluids could drain off during the operation'. Willy Just requested 'a decision' from Rauff, which presumably followed.

'Whether at that time I had doubts against the use of gas vans I cannot say,' Rauff would later state. 'The main issue for me was that the shootings were a considerable burden for the men who were in charge thereof, and this burden was removed through the use of the gas vans.' The details did not bother him.

An operator at Chelmno offered a first-hand account of the gassing of Jews from the nearby ghetto in the city of Lodz, renamed Litzmannstadt by the Germans:

The people were told that they had to take a bath, that their clothes had to be disinfected and that they could hand in any valuable items beforehand to be registered. Undressed, they were sent to the cellar of the castle, then along a passageway onto the ramp, then into the gas van. In the castle, there were signs marked 'to the baths'. The gas vans were large, about four or five metres long, 2.2 metres wide and two metres high. The interior walls were lined with sheet metal. A wooden grille was set into the floor. [. . .] When the lorries were full of people, the double doors at the back were closed and the exhaust connected to the interior of the van.

The account turned out to be personal, for me. Researching my book *East West Street*, I learned that in July 1939, my mother, as a one-year-old infant, was taken to Vienna's Westbahnhof train station and into the protective care of an evangelical missionary from Norwich, Miss Elsie Tilney, who took her to safety in Paris. They had gone to the station with my mother's eleven-year-old cousin, Herta, who was due to travel with her. At the last minute, however, the older girl could not bear to be separated from her mother Laura, my grandfather's sister. Mother and daughter remained in Vienna. Two years later, in October 1941, they were  transported from Vienna to the Litzmannstadt (Lodz) ghetto. Within months, they were disappeared. From the timings and details in Willy Just's report, I understood that Herta and Laura were likely to have been among the 97,000 people whose lives ended in one of Walther Rauff's dark-grey vans.

As this operation unfolded, Czech partisans targeted Rauff's protector, Reinhard Heydrich, attacked his car and succeeded in assassinating him. It was now June 1942, and the act coincided with Berlin's decision to move away from gas vans and on to extermination on a far greater scale. As Belzec, Sobibor and Treblinka became operational, Rauff needed a new job.

## 22

In December 1942, Rauff was posted to Tunisia, recently occupied by Germany, tasked with ridding the country of Jews. Speaking no French, he hired a Jewish refugee from Austria as his interpreter.

'A small man,' Maximilien Trenner recalled, and reminiscent of Hitler, Rauff was prone to rages, turning 'red with anger' when agitated. He was 'exceedingly dangerous' and 'totally committed to the extermination of the Jews'.

On his first day, Rauff gathered Jewish leaders at his headquarters, 168 avenue de Paris in Tunis. He instructed that 2,000 young Jews be made available for labour within twenty-four hours, failing which he'd take 10,000 instead. When the community provided only a hundred labourers, a furious response followed. 'I have already killed Jews in Poland and Russia and want you to know what you can expect,' Rauff declared. They would be shot, he said, as 'traitors, cowards, Jew dogs, swine'.

Rauff was short, close shaven, ice cold, of bilious complexion, and 'imbued with an air of racial superiority', another observer recorded. When calm, his voice was hoarse and guttural, words spoken brittlely and precisely. Excitement produced 'an avalanche of inarticulate, harsh, rhythmic, brusque sounds'. When angered, he tapped his feet agitatedly and brandished a short stick.

Rauff was driven by anti-Semitism and anti-communism. The Jews started the war, so the brethren in Tunisia must 'take their responsibilities'. He made labourers wear large yellow stars on front and back, 'so that we can see you from a distance, and shoot you if you try to escape'.

Those weeks brought hostage-taking, executions, torture and massive fines levied on the community. Rauff plundered, helping himself to a dozen typewriters. 'To be able to make lists,' he said. 'A true savage,' said a young lawyer who watched Rauff subject his father to a mock execution. 'His only concern was for the job he had been ordered to carry out.'

Rauff's time in Tunis ended abruptly. In May, just a few months after he arrived, the British 7th Armoured Division routed the Wehrmacht and took the city. Rauff fled, leaving behind a traumatised community, with many lives lost, and still today descendants recall his name with a sense of horror. His own recollection would be very different. Measures against Jews? There were none. 'Many worked for us voluntarily without anything ever happening to them.'

Rauff returned to Berlin, where he was honoured for his work in Tunis. General Karl Wolff, Himmler's deputy, awarded him a German Cross, in silver. In early July 1943, Rauff was sent to Corsica, as a plainclothes intelligence officer using false papers signed by the Paris police, to create a cell of French collaborators in the event of an Allied takeover of the island. He remained for two months, but fled when Hitler ordered German troops to evacuate the island, on 12 September.

He went straight to Italy, to serve as Kommandant of *Oberitalien-West*, the head of the SS and Gestapo in Milan, working under General Karl Wolff. Rauff set up his headquarters at the Regina Hotel, near La Scala and in time for a new opera season that featured much by way of Wagner, Mozart and Beethoven. The Regina became a feared place of detention, torture and murder, from which many Italians disappeared.

In early December, Rauff was involved in the first deportation of Italian Jews to Auschwitz, and organising draconian measures against partisans. In the summer of 1944 he personally led operations in the Aosta Valley, near Courgné; in the Susa Valley, near Fenestrelles; and in the province of Cuneo. Examples of the horrors he unleashed were not hard to find. On 21 July, in the village of Robecco sul Naviglio, after partisans killed a German Army marshal, Rauff personally directed the reprisal execution of five men and the deportation of fifty-eight more to Germany, and the destruction of numerous homes. 'If it happens again,' he warned the Prefect of Milan, 'the measures will be harsher and more innocent people will be affected.'

For a year, Rauff oversaw a brutal policy of reprisals against civilians, in manifest violation of international laws. On his authority, fifty civilians were executed in Cumiana; twenty-seven in Turin, after partisans killed a Wehrmacht soldier; and another twenty-six executed on Colle del Lys, their corpses openly mutilated. (Eighty years later, these and other atrocities perpetrated by the German Reich in Italy were the subject of proceedings before the International Court of Justice, with Germany arguing – successfully – that Italy, by the actions of its courts in allowing civil claims, violated its obligations to respect the immunity which Germany enjoyed under international law.) For his work in Italy, General Wolff honoured Rauff with a second German Cross, this time in gold.

In the summer of 1943, the Allies landed in southern Italy and the tide of war turned. Rauff joined General Wolff in negotiating a deal with the Americans, known as Operation Sunrise. In return for peace, he and Wolff hoped to avoid prosecution. In February 1945, Rauff travelled to Switzerland, to negotiate with Allen Dulles, head of the local branch of the Office of Strategic Services, forerunner of the CIA. Karl Wolff appreciated his comrade's efforts. 'You were key in those last two months of war,' he would say.

On 24 April 1945 Rauff met Mussolini, and five days later the Germans in Italy signed a ceasefire with the Allies. The next morning, 30 April, Colonel John Davis of the US Army made his way through angry crowds outside the Hotel Regina, entered the building and arrested Rauff and his staff, including his secretary, Miss Emilie Lukasch (who previously worked for Eichmann, and served in Litzmannstadt). Rauff was escorted out in in a Death Head cap and a full-length, black leather SS coat. 'The Italians cheered us!' Rauff would recall. 'They thought we were Americans.'

In Florence, he was incarcerated with Wolff and interrogated by a British Army officer ('a good Englishman, not a Jew,' Rauff would say). Major Michael Wedekind reported that Rauff was hostile and uncooperative, a typical SS man, with 'contempt and perpetual malice' for the Allies and proud of his criminality. He was cynical and arrogant, 'more cunning and devious than intelligent', posing so serious a threat that he should be executed. If that was not possible, Rauff should be imprisoned for the rest of his life.

## 23

Over the next months, Rauff was moved around Italy, from Rimini to Naples and then Ancona. His second wife Edith and their two children, Alf and Walther junior, were back in Germany. In October 1945, confronted with documents on his role in the use of the gas vans, Rauff signed an affidavit confirming the authenticity of his signature and the documents.

He sought to minimise his role. 'I do not know the number of death vans that operated and cannot give an approximate figure,' he stated. 'Insofar as I am aware, these vans operated only in Russia.' He knew this to be a lie, that Chelmno and Litzmannstadt were in Poland. 'I was never present when the death vans were operating with persons in them being killed,' he declared. His role was purely 'technical'.

The documents were introduced into the proceedings at Nuremberg's Courtroom 600. On 20 December 1945, the twenty-second day of hearings, US prosecutor Colonel Robert Storey spoke Rauff's name into the record, reading out extracts of the gas-van documents and his affidavit. The Nuremberg judgement handed down a year later made no mention of Rauff or the vans. By then he was in a prison camp in Ancona, detained alongside members of Otto Wächter's Waffen SS Galicia Division, and SS officers Karl Hass and Erich Priebke. In the 1990s, the two men's role in the murder of 335 Italian civilians in Rome's Ardeatine caves during the war would cause Priebke to be extradited from Argentina, and the Italian courts to convict both men of crimes against humanity.

Rauff was off the hook, but now keenly aware of the dangers posed by documents concerning gas vans that mentioned him by name. 'I have some responsibilities that could cost me my head,' he wrote to his nephew. He must take care.

He was transferred to Rimini and Naples, from where he escaped, using wire-cutters to cut through a fence. As an Iron Curtain descended across Europe, he made his way to Rome, hunted by the US

Army Counter Intelligence Corps. Its agents included a young Henry Kissinger, working as an instructor on denazification, communism and the Soviet threat. On opposite sides, there was no indication that their paths crossed in Italy, but within three decades the two men would find themselves on the same side, supporting Pinochet and the Coup in Chile.

In Rome, Rauff took refuge in an apartment on the Viale Giulio Cesare, the home of an Italian university professor and his wife and their two sons. 'A simple apartment, a lovely place,' he recalled, 'I looked after the children.' Professor Dupré and his Prussian wife Hedi thought Rauff to be decent and trustworthy. He hung out with German priests at the Collegio Teutonico in Santa Maria dell'Anima, where Bishop Hudal 'helped a lot'.

Hedi Dupré found a room for Rauff at the Vigna Pia monastery, where he worked in the gardens, looking after the cows. In 1948 Edith and the two boys joined him, and Hudal got him an International Red Cross passport. Hunted by the Allies, Soviets and Jews, he flew to Cairo – 'we were given a very warm welcome' – and then Syria.

Arriving in Damascus in November 1948, Rauff was recruited into the Syrian Army, and later worked for the police, reorganising the country's intelligence service. In March 1949, following a military coup, he became a security adviser to the new head of state, Colonel Husni al-Zaim. The CIA, established two years earlier, was keeping tabs on him. 'Subject and his wife are in Syria,' the organisation reported, he was working as 'an adviser to the Syrian Sureté'. A former Nazi comrade, now an American source, reported that Rauff was reorganising Syrian intelligence 'along Gestapo Lines'.

Rauff worked closely with Colonel al-Zaim who, like Hermann Göring, enjoyed pinning many medals onto his uniforms. 'Rauff, how do I look?' al-Zaim would enquire. 'Wonderful!' Rauff re-cruited Germans, including former SS leaders and Wehrmacht officers arriving from Italy. The CIA reported that he was involved in torture, and unpopular with Syrians and Germans. A 'cold egoist', one colleague reported, a man without principles motivated solely by personal gain.

In May 1949, he wrote to Otto Wächter, his SS colleague in Italy, who had taken refuge in the same monastery where Rauff was hidden. This was the letter I found in the Wächter family archive.

Three months later, President al-Zaim was executed and Rauff, charged with terrorism, was expelled from Syria.

The family moved to Beirut ('an oasis, it was wonderful'), where a German padre converted him to Catholicism. They took a Greek steamer back to Italy ('on the Führer's birthday!'), where Edith suggested they head for Marseille. Rauff resisted ('they don't like me in France', because of his time in Tunis), so they returned to Rome and the Dupré family. There, he encountered Shalhevet Freier, a German-born Israeli intelligence officer heading covert operations in Europe. Freier recruited him as an informant on Syrian affairs, apparently knowing nothing of Rauff's past. The pair stayed in contact for two years.

Hunted, Rauff now followed his own advice, as tendered to Otto Wächter, setting his sights on South America. He hoped for Brazil or Argentina, but when Ecuador's embassy in Rome offered visas he seized the moment. Edith's son from her first marriage – Hans Karste Richter – lived there and told Rauff he'd find work in Quito.

## 24

On 5 December 1949, the Rauffs sailed from Genoa on the *Conte Grande*. 'I played skat with a Jewish conductor who worked at the opera in Berlin and had a daughter in Ecuador,' he recalled. The family disembarked at Guayaquil, spent a night at the Majestic Hotel ('Jewish owner, I waltzed in, said my name was Walter Rauff, the Jews were terribly friendly, especially with the children'), then headed to Quito.

'SS Colonel Walter Rauff has arrived in Quito, Ecuador,' the CIA reported. It kept tabs on his correspondence (intercepted by the Italian intelligence service) and noted, without irony, that Rauff's first job was as a car mechanic for the Mercedes Benz dealership in Quito. He learned basic Spanish and moved on to become a salesman for an Ecuadorian company that sold pharmaceutical products for the American company Parke-Davis. He travelled around Ecuador, selling goods to 'astonished Indians'. He later represented Opel, the West German automobile company – whose first sale in Ecuador was to the Papal Nuncio, licence plate CD-1 – and then worked as a sales manager for Gustavo Möller Martínez, a German-Ecuadorian company representing West German corporations. Throughout, he kept a low profile, and used variations of his name, including Raliff.

He and Edith corresponded with the family in West Germany. Life is not without challenges, he wrote, and although his immigration status was sorted there were issues with the local Jewish community. Eventually he felt safe enough to revert to his real name, obtaining a passport from the West German Embassy. His request for a Navy pension was rejected due to his SS service. He wondered whether the Jews were behind the decision, Rauff wrote to his sister, complaining about the renaissance of 'the Jews of Bonn' and his own sense of victimhood. His fondness for the Horst Wessel song 'Die Fahne hoch' and whisky-doused celebrations of the Führer's birthday did not dim.

The sons were not thrilled with life in Ecuador. At sixteen, Alf enrolled at the Chilean Naval Academy in Valparaíso, which his father had visited three decades earlier. A year later, Walther junior joined the Chilean Army's officers' academy. The moves were supported by the Rauffs' new friends, a group of Chilean army officers posted to Ecuador. Amongst them was a forty-one-year-old major, Augusto Pinochet, who with his friend Carlos Prats provided references.

Pinochet had arrived in Ecuador in 1956, with his wife Lucía Hiriart Rodríguez – the daughter of a wealthy Senator and government minister – and three children. This followed time at the Military School in Santiago and postings around Chile, as well as a stint teaching at the War Academy in Santiago. In Quito, where Pinochet taught at Ecuador's War Academy, his extracurricular activities included a rumoured affair with Piedad Noé, a local pianist, and a law degree at the Central University of Quito. The latter was not something he ever referred to, but I found the records from July 1957, in the university archives, which confirmed his academic failure. The records revealed that he left after a year, failed to complete most classes, never got the degree, and was prone to the use of different names: having enrolled as Augusto Pinochet Ugarte, there were various changes and he finally abandoned his course as Pablo Pinochet.

Pinochet and Rauff, and their wives, became socially close, bonded by a virulent anti-communist sentiment, respect of matters German and a mutual interest in Nazidom. Major and Mrs Pinochet were 'in my house several times', Rauff would later say, describing the Chilean military man as a friend and protector from Ecuador days. It was Pinochet, he told a journalist, who encouraged him to move to Chile: 'Mr Rauff, it's very lovely with us in Chile, you should move there.'

The Rauffs visited their sons in Chile and liked what they saw. In 1958, with Pinochet's encouragement and support, they emigrated. Rauff's grandson Walther III confirmed the role played by Pinochet, and Carlos Prats, the friend Pinochet would later order to be eliminated.

In Santiago, Rauff initially had difficulty finding work. Then a sympathetic German introduced him to Goldmann, Janssen y Ciá, a company with an interest in the Sociedad Comercial Sara Braun, which owned the hardware store in Punta Arenas. This was a fine place, Rauff recalled, where Germans were welcome. In November 1958 he and Edith headed to Patagonia and the southern Chilean Magallanes province.

Rauff enjoyed the work at the Sara Braun store on Calle Bories, in the centre of town, selling typewriters and similar items. He made his way up the company ladder, and within a year President Alessandri had granted the family the right to reside permanently in Chile. With responsibility for European imports, Rauff travelled around Chile, meeting West German and other business partners.

Life was settling down when, in 1959, a letter arrived from Wilhelm Beisner, an SS colleague from Berlin, Tunis and Damascus. Beisner wanted to introduce Rauff to the *Bundesnachrichtendienst*, the BND, the West German intelligence service. Rauff passed on a copy of his curriculum vitae, focusing on a naval career but omitting his activities in the Reich Security office and SS years. The BND assessed him to be 'tough, almost directly aggressive in character and appearance, cold-blooded and not overly emotional'. He was, they concluded, 'well suited' to the organisation, with a past reflecting a 'special outlook on life'.

Early in 1960, the West German intelligence services gave Rauff a contract with a salary of several hundred West German marks a month, but no pension. He became BND Agent 7410, codename 'Enrico Gómez', working in Punta Arenas alongside his day job, reporting on communists in Chile, Ecuador and Peru.

The BND offered him travel and other perks. In April 1960, to the couple's joy, they were able to return to West Germany, the first time in fifteen years. Rauff travelled as a businessman, accompanying

David Stitchkin, rector of the University of Concepción, a prominent member of the local Jewish community, assisting in a search for laboratory equipment. The real purpose of Rauff's trip, however, was to spend three days at a BND facility near Munich, to be trained in anti-communist surveillance techniques.

The journey happened to coincide with Adolf Eichmann's abduction in Buenos Aires and extradition to stand trial in Jerusalem. As Rauff and his wife landed, *Der Spiegel* magazine published a story about Eichmann that mentioned Rauff's work in Milan, causing Edith to be anxious. Rauff assured her he was protected by the BND. The visit passed without incident, but on their return to Punta Arenas they learned that Beisner had been seriously injured in an assassination attempt. If he was a target, then so was Rauff.

Around this time, Edith was diagnosed with cancer. The costs of medical treatment were covered by a new job with a West German company, Leinau, and by the BND, which now paid Rauff a generous monthly stipend of 3,000 West German marks. Rauff travelled to Ecuador, Peru, Venezuela and around Chile, recruiting sub-agents, including his son Alf and stepson Hans Knacke. By the spring of 1961, when Edith was gravely ill, the BND postponed a second trip of Rauff's to West Germany. Due to 'the unresolved Eichmann trial situation,' they said.

Edith died in September, and was buried in Santiago's central cemetery. On Rauff's return to Punta Arenas, the BND complained to the widower about the quality of his work. He failed to get to Cuba and missed the rise of Fidel Castro, they complained. They halved his stipend and told him he needed more training.

In February 1962 Rauff returned to West Germany, travelling under his own name but using an address in Quito. In Hanover he stayed at the Central Hotel (today the Kaiserhof) – just a few hundred metres from the offices of the federal prosecutors who were busy preparing a warrant for his arrest, for the gas vans and mass murder. He visited his nephew, Hans-Jochen Emsmann, a young naval officer, and attended a naval reunion with colleagues from the class of 1924. At the BND facilities in Bavaria, he trained in microfilm and encoding, and was warned not to allow the quality of his reports to decline any further.

By March 1962 he was back in Punta Arenas, living in an apartment on Calle Bories, above the Grand Palace cinema. He worked nearby, on the corner of Magallanes and Waldo Seguel, near the Plaza de Armas, coming to terms with a widower's life, one son elsewhere in Chile, the other in West Germany. He was now well integrated into the city's business community, with Chilean and German acquaintances, and membership of the prestigious Club de la Unión. No one knew of his past, or his BND work.

The world of espionage was now less exciting than business, so he found a new West German partner, Herr Reinhard, with capital provided by Habag, a company in Düsseldorf. Rauff started to work as a manager with the *Pesquera Bonacic*, a cannery in Porvenir, across the Strait of Magellan on the island of Tierra del Fuego, a two-hour ferry ride from Punta Arenas. He enjoyed the shuttle back and forth, a pleasant crossing, leaving from Tres Puentes, with its white naval barracks and sky-blue roofs. The view was grand, the seabirds active, the ocean deep and dark. Dawson Island was visible in the distance, and beyond it the snowy, grand peaks of Patagonia.

In Porvenir, a German immigrant named Dietrich Angerstein had founded the *Pesquera Bonacic*, with Karl Kreusel, a businessman who may have been either a real-estate man from Hamburg or a Stasi agent from East Germany. The *Pesquera Bonacic* harvested *centolla*, the meat of giant king crabs, which was packed into small aluminium tins and sold across Chile, South America and beyond to Europe, with a '*Pesquera Pirata*' label.

Dietrich Angerstein has recently written of those pioneering days, in *Cóndor*, a German-Chilean weekly established in Santiago before the war. The article makes no mention of Rauff, but it offers a photograph of the company's flagship fishing boat, which was called the *Walter*. This, I would later be told, was a boat that Rauff sailed.

I contacted Angerstein to obtain permission to reproduce the photograph. He was happy to talk about the *Walter* and the *Pesquera* in Porvenir, which he managed until 1963. Rauff was around, he recalled, a man who was not sociable and had limited relations with the German community, and who he did not hire, on advice from the German Embassy. Angerstein did not want the photograph of the *Walter* to be used in a book about Rauff, he said, and did not really wish to speak about Rauff.

Here, at the end of the world, however, Rauff believed himself to be safe.

He was wrong.

## 25

As 1962 drew to a close, Rauff spent his working day packing the flesh of king crabs into small tin cans. 'The season ran from the first of July until the end of January, and in the off season we sealed other sea life in the cans.' In the evenings he wrote reports for the BND, on local communist activity.

This was his life when, on the evening of Monday, 3 December, as the end of the season approached, he was at home in the Punta Arenas apartment, above the Grand Palace cinema. At 11 p.m. there was a knock on the front door. It was the police. They told him he was under arrest for the crime of murder, indicted by a court in Hanover that wanted to extradite him to West Germany. His crime? Packing human beings into gas vans.

He was escorted out of the building, past posters that announced the week's films, *The Queen of the Pirates* (*La Reina de los piratas*), and, in glorious colour, Rock Hudson and Doris Day in *Lover Come Back* (*Vuelve Amor Mío*). He was taken to the local police station, then to the airport and Santiago. Yes, he told the waiting journalists, he was once a Nazi, in intelligence, now he was 'another war victim'.

The *Prensa Austral*, the local newspaper in Punta Arenas, ran a story that revealed details of his past: 'Co-director of Eichmann's

Office Arrested in Our City'. The article described his work with gas vans that exterminated over 90,000 Jews, but did not mention the name of the 'important' local company for which he worked.

'I am innocent, I have no idea what I am accused of,' said Rauff. I was merely a 'desk colonel'. I 'signed papers'. I 'never ordered or witnessed the killing of any Jews'.

## 26

Rauff's arrest was a precursor for what later befell Augusto Pinochet: two men arrested at 11 p.m., on charges of mass murder, with a request for extradition from one country to another.

As with Pinochet, the events leading to his arrest began much earlier. In Rauff's case, it was in 1957 that his name came up, as state prosecutors in Hanover were investigating some of his colleagues in *Amt IID* in Berlin for their connection to the gas vans that operated at the Semlin camp, near Belgrade, Yugoslavia.

One detail led to another. The prosecutors came across the affidavit that Rauff signed in October 1945, confirming the authenticity of various reports. For reasons that are not clear, the prosecutors did not then proceed to investigate Rauff any further.

A year later, however, in December 1958, a new national body was created to investigate Nazi crimes. The Central Office of State Justice Administrations, known as the *Zentrale Stelle*, or the Z Commission, was based in Ludwigsburg. The prosecutors returned to the gas vans, initially focusing on Dr August Becker, the chemist, who was arrested. In an American archive they found the June 1942 report by Willi Just detailing operations at Chelmno that targeted the 97,000 Jews, addressed to Rauff. Prosecutors now searched for him, initially in Ecuador. In Santiago, the German Embassy in Chile was not keen to collaborate.

The Z Commission's investigations coincided with the Eichmann trial in Jerusalem, where Just's report was introduced into evidence. Eichmann's lawyer questioned his client about the gas vans. I didn't work on that project, Eichmann told the judges, that was Rauff. Yes, he conceded, the project was conceived and prepared in the very same building in Berlin, but Rauff worked in 'a distant corner'.

The document and Eichmann's answers caused the Z Commission prosecutors to focus on Rauff. They determined he was deeply involved in the gas-vans project, with full knowledge of the use to which they were put, including instructions to *Einsatzgruppen* units in eastern Europe. The prosecutors charged Rauff with aiding and abetting murder, and asked the Hanover district court to issue a warrant for his arrest and extradition. Concerned about the statute of limitations, the Z Commission acted fast, and shared information with the West German press.

Rauff was apparently unaware of these developments. He knew that Becker and other colleagues had been indicted for their work on the gas vans, but not that an arrest warrant had been issued in his name, as early as April 1961. Like Pinochet, three and a half decades later, Rauff assumed he had some sort of immunity or protection, in his case as a serving BND agent.

He also believed he was protected by the West German Embassy in Santiago, by the ambassador, who was a fellow traveller. Hans Strack had joined the Nazi Party in 1936 and served as Consul General in Hungary as thousands of Jews were deported to Auschwitz. On receiving the request for Rauff's extradition, Ambassador Strack chose not to pass it on to the Chilean authorities. Instead, he obtained a legal opinion of his own, on the validity of the request under Chilean law.

Strack instructed Miguel Schweitzer Speisky, a Professor at the University of Chile and a noted authority on Chilean extradition law, who happened to be Jewish. As Pinochet's Minister of Justice, a decade or so later, it was he who intervened to allow Laura González-Vera to observe her husband's autopsy, as his son Miguel had been her childhood friend. Small world.

Professor Schweitzer Speisky advised Ambassador Strack that the Z Commission's request would be rejected by Chile's courts. This was for two reasons. First, the crimes for which Rauff was charged – the use of gas vans to kill tens of thousands of Jews – occurred in 1942, twenty-one years earlier, so the proceedings in Chile were time-barred by the country's fifteen-year statute of limitations. Second, the arrest warrant charged Rauff with murder, and that was the wrong crime: the acts alleged were genocide, a crime for which the Chilean courts had no jurisdiction. This was because genocide only became a crime under Chilean law in 1953, when the country

became a party to the 1948 Convention on the Prevention and Punishment of Genocide.

Strack passed Schweitzer Speisky's advice on to West Germany.
The Foreign Ministry in Bonn amended the extradition request to
include a new charge of genocide and sent it back to Santiago. Strack
sought a second legal opinion, this time from Eduardo Novoa, who
gave a green light. On Friday, 30 November 1962, eighteen months
after the extradition request was first issued, the West German Embassy finally forwarded it to the Chilean authorities. The following
Monday evening, Rauff was arrested.

On 6 December 1962, Rauff appeared before Judge Rafael Fontecilla, the President of the Supreme Court in Santiago. Rauff denied
the charges and said he would oppose the extradition request. He
was lawfully settled in Chile, with a right of residence, he said. Yes,
he knew of the gas vans, and their use for mass murder, but he only
ever followed orders, in accordance with the German principle of
*befehlsnotstand*, higher orders. If he had refused to carry out the
orders, he risked being sentenced to death.

## 27

After the initial hearing, Rauff issued a short statement. 'The accusations are false, I am innocent, I had nothing to do with any killing
of Jews.' Chilean newspapers published a photograph of Rauff
seated in the back of a police car, wearing a hat. This was the image
that opened the imagination of Roberto Bolaño and which many
others remembered.

Rauff assured his sons he wouldn't be abducted, like Eichmann,
or assassinated. He was well connected with the upper echelons of
Chilean society, including the military, who understood German
military structures. He would be safe.

'Who is the best lawyer for my father?' Walther junior asked.
'Miguel Schweitzer', he was told. 'They were a bit crazy, so they
went to Schweitzer, an excellent lawyer – but a Jew!' Rauff later told
a friend. 'I'm interested in this case,' Schweitzer told him, 'but I can't
do it because I'd have everyone against me.' He wrote an opinion but
declined to act as Rauff's lawyer in the case. Instead, they retained
the services of Enrique Schepeler, a Chilean lawyer, and Robert

Servatius, Eichmann's lawyer in Jerusalem (an anti-Nazi, *The New York Times* reported, but with no qualms about acting for old Nazis or other 'prisoners of history').

'They treated me quite decently, with kid gloves,' Rauff recalled. They gave him cigarettes and books (including Charles de Gaulle's wartime memoir), his cell door was left unlocked, and he was allowed visitors. They included sympathetic senior Chilean Army officers, the Minister of Justice, German diplomatic staff, and a lady named Armida Zúñiga, known as Nena, who became a regular. 'Rauff is a correct man,' declared Ernst Schäfer, the West German consul in Punta Arenas. Chile's Attorney General intervened in the case to argue against extradition, and there was considerable public support.

The hearings in Santiago lasted several days and were widely reported around the world. A silent *British Movietone* film showed Rauff being escorted out of a police van and into the court building by officers, surrounded by reporters. He was neatly dressed in a light-coloured suit, left hand in a pocket, wearing a tie, a white handkerchief in his breast pocket, a wan smile and confident in his demeanour.

On 21 February, Supreme Court Judge Fontecilla gave his ruling. The evidence established Rauff's direct role in the construction and enhancement of the gas vans, but he could not be extradited on genocide charges, as Professor Schweitzer predicted, because the crime was not part of Chile's Criminal Code in 1941, when the crimes occurred. On the other hand, he could be extradited for the murder of the 97,000 Jews, as the request was not time-barred: the applicable limitation period was governed by West German law, not Chilean law, so the fifteen-year period was not relevant. Fontecilla based this conclusion on 'opinions of various international law writers'.

Rauff wept, told reporters he'd not expected the ruling, and claimed to be 'broken'. 'I obeyed orders that perhaps forced me to kill, but a good soldier carries out his orders, he does not dispute them.' For many in Chile his argument resonated: the country's military was deeply influenced by nineteenth-century German settlers and Prussian military traditions, including the goose-step march, German marching songs and military helmets, and the need to follow orders without question.

From Antofagasta, in the north, the West German consul reported the views of two senior Army officers who had known Rauff in Ecuador. He was, they reported from personal knowledge, a cultivated and discreet man, and the pair expressed serious concerns about the court's ruling. As with Nuremberg, it was wrong to criminalise actions that followed military orders, an approach that would undermine discipline in Chile's Army by encouraging soldiers to disobey orders. The consul did not name the officers, but it was apparent that one of them was Lieutenant Colonel Augusto Pinochet, who of course had known Rauff in Ecuador and served in Antofagasta as commander of Infantry No. 7's Esmeralda regiment.

Rauff appealed the ruling to the full Supreme Court. Hearings were held in March and April, and the time limit for bringing cases emerged as the key issue. Eduardo Novoa, acting for West Germany, argued that for the most serious international crimes there could be no time limit for prosecutions. If Rauff was not extradited, impunity would reign for the gravest crimes.

As the hearings proceeded, Rauff received news that the BND had cut him adrift. The organisation had known for some time that prosecutors were interested in him, but now, fearing the relationship with Rauff would become public, the BND terminated his employment. The decision was backdated six months, to October 1962, before Rauff was arrested, so it could not be said that West German prosecutors requested the extradition of a serving BND agent. Rauff, who later unsuccessfully challenged the termination, instructed his son to destroy incriminating BND documents. In the years that followed, he never spoke publicly of his role as a BND agent.

On 26 April 1963 the judges of the Supreme Court pronounced judgement: by six votes to one they ruled that Rauff's appeal succeeded and he couldn't be extradited, because Chile's fifteen-year statute-of-limitations period excluded jurisdiction over acts committed in 1942. 'The mass extermination of human beings for racial reasons is a crime which is repugnant to the sense of justice of the civilised world,' the judges declared, but it was Chile's limitation period that applied, it was not inconsistent with international law, and it time-barred the case. The majority endorsed Professor Schweitzer Speisky's opinion.

After 123 days in custody, Rauff was released. *¡Viva Chile!* he proclaimed outside the prison. Walther junior organised a party at his house, attended by several high-ranking military officers. If Augusto Pinochet attended, neither man publicised the fact.

Left-wing newspapers reacted harshly to the judgement. 'A paradise for Nazis,' declared *El Siglo*. Right-wing papers, on the other hand, barely reported the ruling. Back in Punta Arenas, Rauff gave a rare television interview to NBC news, the American broadcaster. Seated at a large, old-fashioned typewriter, Rauff offered a monochrome impression – dark shirt, white face, black hair, black-rimmed glasses with thick lenses.

He spoke mechanically, in English, a rasping and distinct voice with a strong German accent. 'My case was decided in Chile. The Chilean government gave me permission to live and to work here, and therefore I am under protection of the Chilean government, like any Chilean citizen, and therefore there is nothing to be afraid of,' he told journalist Tom Streithorst. He feared assassination or kidnapping, but he was innocent, he had merely followed orders.

A week later, NBC interviewed his friend Miss Elsie Fleischer, a New York city nurse who'd recently visited him. 'He is such a human and warm personality,' she told the interviewer, and in Tunisia he 'stopped the order' to put 30,000 Jews to death. Did you ever hear Rauff express regrets? 'He's not a sob sister,' Miss Fleischer replied. What happened in Germany was 'terribly wrong', but so is constantly 'bringing up those things and haunting people'.

After the judgement, the University of Santiago convened a conference on the case. Most speakers, both faculty and students, were critical of the Supreme Court ruling. A notable exception was Professor Schweitzer Speisky, whose advice to the West German ambassador had proved accurate. He saw no need to change Chile's extradition laws, as extradition should be an exceptional occurrence.

The law students in the audience were attentive to the lively exchanges: on extradition and impunity, on genocide and other novel international crimes. Professor Schweitzer Speisky's twenty-two-year-old son, also called Miguel, was in the audience that day. As a student, he would later say, he assisted his father in writing the opinion that contributed to Rauff's freedom.

Miguel Schweitzer the son could not have imagined that many years later he would receive a phone call about another extradition case. It too raised novel issues, and would change his life.

# PART II

## JUSTICE

*It was like an earthquake at all levels, I think things will never go back to the way they were.*
Roberto Bolaño, 1998

# LONDON, NOVEMBER 1998

## 28

'I was called on the Friday, immediately after the arrest of General Pinochet, by a good friend of his.' It was the evening of 16 October 1998 in Santiago, said Miguel Schweitzer, and thirty-five years since, as a law student, he had worked with his father on an opinion that would end Rauff's extradition to West Germany. In the intervening years, the childhood friend of Laura González-Vera – Carmelo Soria's wife – qualified as a lawyer, opened a law firm and became politically engaged.

In the 1970s he advised Agustín Edwards, owner of *El Mercurio*, Allende opponent, Pinochet and Nixon supporter. Miguel Schweitzer supported Pinochet and the Coup, and after the Letelier assassination in September 1976 he worked as Pinochet's lawyer in negotiating the agreement that handed Michael Townley to the Americans and saved Manuel Contreras and Pinochet from further American investigations. In the 1980s, he served as Pinochet's ambassador in London, and then Minister of Foreign Affairs.

Miguel Schweitzer received the phone call because he was a trusted and reliable confidant. Fifty-eight years old, jowly, smiling, well-groomed, a man of charm and intelligence, he was Pinochet's true believer.

'They wanted a legal assessment. I'd been ambassador in London, was well-connected, and had intervened effectively when Amnesty International tried to arrest Pinochet on an earlier trip.' The call didn't come out of the blue. 'Some said there was no risk, as he had immunity, others worried about a new Labour government and Foreign Secretary, Robin Cook.' Pinochet opted to travel, under cover of an official mission to buy military hardware. He was told he had full immunity, 'so there was no risk', Schweitzer recalled. Pinochet had friends in high places, including Margaret Thatcher, and had supported Britain when Argentina invaded the Falklands/Malvinas in April 1982. He thought he was untouchable.

'They wanted a trusted person to take care of the legal issues, so asked me to travel to London immediately. I said it was ridiculous, Pinochet would be free by the time I arrived, it would be over in a day or two.' Schweitzer smiled at the memory. Mrs Pinochet was the one who persuaded him. 'She was alone, didn't speak English, needed somebody to guide her.'

Schweitzer suggested Hernán Felipe Errázuriz should go. Also a lawyer, Errázuriz had been Pinochet's ambassador to the United States and his last Foreign Minister. 'Hernán Felipe was very, very dear to Pinochet, much closer to him than me, the General loved him,' said Schweitzer. 'They were so close that when Hernán Felipe separated from his wife, the only person he told was Pinochet. Imagine! Pinochet loved him like the son he wished he had.'

In the end, Pinochet's friend Carlos Cáceres, who ran the private Pinochet Foundation, persuaded both men to travel. Schweitzer and Errázuriz left Santiago on the Sunday night, 18 October, having had no contact with the Chilean government. 'President Frei was against Pinochet,' said Schweitzer. 'We arrived on Monday morning, with an overnight bag, not even a suitcase. We went to the Connaught Hotel, then to Kingsley Napley, the law firm, to sign a contract with the lawyers who'd defend the General on the extradition procedure.'

Schweitzer opted for them because years earlier they'd helped on an earlier attempt to arrest Pinochet. 'Back then, I turned to Cecil Parkinson, a former minister who was close to Margaret Thatcher, he recommended Kingsley Napley.'

## 29

On Schweitzer's suggestion, the Chilean Embassy in London contacted the firm, and reached Michael Caplan, a partner.

'It was a Saturday morning, I'd been to synagogue, there was a phone message about a new extradition case, a big one, about General Pinochet. The arrest of a former head of state, unprecedented!'

Caplan spoke wistfully. 'I'd vaguely heard of Pinochet, and of Chile, but didn't quite know where it was!' Experienced in extradition law, he knew nothing about immunities. 'I mugged up in the next 48 hours. Does a former head of state have immunity? I knew of the Eichmann trial, universal jurisdiction and Nuremberg, and I'd studied some international law, but not much.' He realised the novelty of the situation, and its significance. 'There wasn't an international law textbook on these issues about immunity for a former head of state, they were open questions.'

He didn't hesitate to take the case. 'As lawyers we do this type of work, it's not for us to judge the popularity or otherwise of a client.' Caplan went to the office on Sunday, then to The London Clinic to meet Pinochet, where demonstrators were already gathered. A Chilean diplomat met him. 'A model of absolute courtesy,' Caplan recalled.

Room 801 was guarded by a police officer and the diplomat interpreted, as Pinochet spoke no English. 'He seemed to understand what I was saying, and wasn't in any way aggressive.' Caplan was handed a copy of the arrest warrant. 'I looked at it quickly, didn't spot any issues.' He read it again at home on the Sunday evening, noting the charge of murder. 'It looked a bit odd, but I can't say I picked up the point.' He didn't know Baltasar Garzón had specified genocide and torture as the crimes warranting extradition.

On Monday morning he met 'Lady Pinochet', and in the afternoon Schweitzer and Errázuriz came to Caplan's office. 'We got on exceptionally well, they spoke perfect English, certainly Miguel did. They listened to what I said, understood this would take time, were extremely patient.' He paused. 'Very different characters, but powerful in their own ways. Miguel was engaging, Felipe quieter but sometimes with a greater clarity of thought. They were committed to the General, understood what was happening, helped a great deal.'

Caplan gave them a copy of the arrest warrant signed by Nicholas Evans. 'He should have rejected the application, not signed it,' Schweitzer said immediately. 'The moment I saw it, with errors and mistakes, I thought everything would be sorted out quickly.' He immediately spotted the connection with the Rauff case, from 1963, on which he had worked with his father, which raised similar issues: is the right crime murder or genocide? 'The mistake in the form was enough to annul the document.'

Beyond the error, Schweitzer told Caplan, Pinochet had full immunity. 'I told Michael to go to court for an order of *habeas corpus*' – an order that Pinochet be released immediately as his detention was manifestly unlawful, in violation of immunity rules. 'Michael said there was no precedent to challenge the arrest warrant, as it was issued and signed by a judge. Hernán Felipe and I insisted, and later we convinced Michael and the other lawyers.'

Schweitzer believed, as Pinochet did, that the arrest was politically motivated, driven by Spanish communists – led by Juan Garcés – frustrated by their failure to ensnare General Franco. The Chilean lawyers were not fans of Spanish judges. 'The communists went to Garzón because they knew the other judge, García-Castellón, would not act. Then Garzón found a link between his Argentine cases and the Pinochet case, through Operation Condor.'

Schweitzer was certain too that other forces were at play. 'This was political. Robin Cook was a militant, in Chile during the Allende period, totally against Pinochet.' He was wrong, but Hernán Felipe Errázuriz embraced the same view. 'I didn't know the details,' he told me, 'but I have no doubt that Robin Cook was involved from the beginning.' Cook died in 2005, so I was only able to check with several of his advisers from the time. All told me that while Cook welcomed the arrest he was not involved in its occurrence.

Schweitzer and Errázuriz hoped to get Pinochet home by the end of the week. 'Everyone worried that there might be an attempt to assassinate him,' said Errázuriz. 'There was at least one well-planned attempt in 1986, which was almost successful, killing five of his protection squad, and wounding eleven others, and his car received several bullets.' The attempt was well organised, 'mostly by members of the communist party, some of whom were at liberty, and the British police were aware that at least one or two of the participants were living in Europe'. When we spoke about this, decades later, Errázuriz maintained the fear was real. 'One of the organisers is still living in Switzerland,' he insisted.

The pair urged Kingsley Napley to hire the best barristers. 'Michael Caplan chose Clive Nicholls, a famous extradition lawyer, who brought in Clare Montgomery and Julian Knowles.' The barristers immediately confirmed a problem with the arrest warrant and the charge of murder. 'Clare, who is so bright and forthright, was the one who insisted': murder was not an international crime over which the English courts had jurisdiction, unless the perpetrator or victim was British. Montgomery would later tell me, en passant, that if she'd been hired on the Saturday afternoon, instead of the Monday, Pinochet could have been home before Schweitzer reached London.

'There was a sense of disbelief about the error, once we realised it, as it was serious and could not be amended,' Caplan said. They worried that Garzón too would spot the error and apply for a second arrest warrant, one which specified an international crime over which the English courts did have jurisdiction. They had to move fast.

Caplan was instructed to file an immediate application with the courts. 'Having read the arrest warrant, I didn't see how we could lose,' said Schweitzer. On Monday afternoon, Caplan asked the Home Office to rescind the warrant, as it disclosed no extraditable crime. 'I wrote in fairly strong terms to the Chief Clerk at Bow Street.' He asked to be informed if Spain issued a second arrest warrant.

Schweitzer and Errázuriz visited Pinochet at The London Clinic, in Room 801. Worried about assassination, they appreciated the security and police presence. 'He was sedated, not really in this world, it wasn't clear if he understood what was happening,' said Schweitzer. 'His wife Lucía was there, rather shocked. We said we'd take charge of all the legal responsibilities, and we did, me and Hernán Felipe.'

On Tuesday, Caplan reiterated the request for the warrant to be withdrawn. No reaction. On Wednesday he wrote a third letter, threatening court proceedings. No reaction. Deadlines came and went. 'We gave them until 4 p.m. on Wednesday, no response. I wrote to say 5.30 p.m. A lady from the Home Office phoned to say they couldn't commit to the deadline. Then silence. It was too late to go to a judge on the Wednesday night, as he'd adjourn the case until the next morning.'

Thursday morning, more silence. Caplan wrote a fourth letter, with a midday deadline. 'We really didn't want to go to court, worried that if we lost we'd be in a worse position.' Schweitzer now instructed Caplan to go to court, so he called the Metropolitan Police to say he was applying for a writ of *habeas corpus*. 'How do you spell that?' the policeman asked.

On Thursday, 22 October, midday came and went. At ten to one, Caplan issued the writ. A hearing was set for that afternoon, as the team worried about a second arrest warrant. 'Should we have gone to court on Monday?' Caplan wondered, years later. 'Maybe if we had the court would have granted our writ of *habeas corpus* and directed the General's release.' Still, Pinochet would not have been able to leave. 'Spain could have appealed and got a court order to keep him in London.'

Years later, Schweitzer looked back on those early days. 'Could we have done anything differently? Should we have gone to court on the Monday? The point always worried us, Hernán Felipe and myself. Was there anything we could have done to avoid what happened next?'

## 30

What happened next was a consequence of the fact that Baltasar Garzón did indeed spot Nicholas Evans's error in selecting 'murder' as the charge.

In Madrid on the evening of the arrest, Garzón received a series of updates on developments in London, phone calls from John Dew. The British diplomat confirmed that a magistrate had signed the arrest warrant. 'I thanked him, surprised, as I thought the judge wouldn't sign, or someone would warn Pinochet and he'd flee. I couldn't believe it, so I started to think about the next steps.'

Garzón was grateful to John Dew. 'His intervention was absolutely critical. If I hadn't had that lunch with him and then a first conversation, without this relationship Pinochet would not have been arrested. It was all about the right people being in the right place at the right moment.'

'I acted on my own, not on instructions from London,' Dew told me. 'Maybe someone in the embassy expressed concern that Garzón would feel rebuffed, he was a pretty important figure, I didn't want to lose the contact.' He paused. 'But if in the end it had a good effect, that is fine, isn't it? Personally, it was a huge issue, about accountability, holding a dictator to account.'

After midnight on the Friday, Dew called again, as Garzón dined with friends, the bullfight in Andalucía being over. 'He told me Pinochet had been arrested in the hospital room. I thought: *¡Enhorabuena! ¡Felicidades!*'

Dew's attitude?

'He was pleased, he wanted it to happen. He could have stopped it, he could have killed this,' said Garzón. 'With the arrest I knew the shit was about to hit the fan. I had to warn Clemente Auger, the President of the Audiencia Nacional, my court.'

Auger had already heard the news and about Garzón's role. 'Wonderful, impressive, incredible,' Auger told him. 'How did you do it?' '"On the basis of Operation Condor," I said, and Auger was entirely supportive,' Garzón told me.

Word spread quickly around Spain's political elite and reached Prime Minister José María Aznar, on his way to Porto for a meeting of heads of state. He was not delighted. In the meantime, as Dew shared details about what had passed in London, Garzón learned that Evans had charged Pinochet with murder, not genocide or torture, or another international crime over which the English courts had jurisdiction.

'As soon as I heard the charge was murder, I knew we had a problem,' Garzón said, as murder in Chile was not an international crime. 'I went straight back to Madrid, to prepare a second request for Pinochet's arrest, one that included international crimes over which the English courts had jurisdiction.'

Garzón spent much of the weekend in his chambers at the Audiencia Nacional in Madrid. 'I called everyone in, the employees, the lawyers, told everyone to start work on a second extradition request. We finished on Sunday evening, it was 118 pages long.' The second warrant included more details of international crimes and victims. 'I added new names to the case, of many Chileans, given to me by Juan Garcés.' Once again, the case of Carmelo Soria featured. Written in Spanish, Garzón's team worked overnight on an English translation to be filed on the Monday morning.

The prosecutor Carlos Castresana recalled Judge García-Castellón's irritation at the news of the arrest, on a case that was his. 'On the Friday I told Garzón I'd think about it over the weekend, by the time I returned the case was gone,' García-Castellón would say.

'He was offended,' Castresana recalled, 'Garzón stole my case.'

García-Castellón eventually agreed that Garzón would run the Argentina and Chilean cases, and the Spanish courts would confirm that Garzón could deal with all aspects of the Chilean file, including Operation Condor, the 'Caravan of Death' case and other crimes.

'In the end I had jurisdiction over the entire matter, so everything was fine,' said Garzón.

By Monday morning the second arrest warrant was ready to go. 'At nine o'clock we sent it to Interpol, with all the necessary information and supporting materials. We included genocide, terrorism and torture, all international crimes, all with universal jurisdiction.' By then, news of Pinochet's arrest had spread around the world. Reactions were strong and mixed.

In Spain, Attorney General Eduardo Fungairiño was furious. He filed a legal challenge to argue that Garzón had no jurisdiction to request Pinochet's extradition. Prime Minister Aznar supported him, while publicly expressing the hope that legal proceedings would operate independently and expeditiously.

In Madrid, Carmelo Soria's widow Laura González-Vera was thrilled. 'I was happy.' She only met Garzón much later. 'I admired him, his persistence.'

In Santiago, her daughter Carmen Soria was more cautious. 'The arrest encouraged me, but I worried what the political parties of the *Concertatión* would do, what Foreign Minister Insulza would do.' Within twenty-four hours of the arrest, she received the first of many death threats. 'I had to leave the country again, three days later, and go back to Spain.'

Erika Hennings was also in Santiago when she heard the news. 'It was a day of immense joy, celebrated on the streets. With another friend, we decided to bring a similar case in France.' A week later, working with the lawyer William Bourdon, a case on universal jurisdiction against Pinochet was filed in the French courts. Similar cases were filed in Belgium and Switzerland, which joined in seeking Pinochet's extradition. Spain, however, was first in the pecking order.

In Chile, the government filed a protest with the British government, but found itself in a bind. Foreign Minister José Miguel Insulza, who had worked with Allende and spent fifteen years in exile after the Coup, was on his way to a television studio when he heard news of the arrest. Insulza was incredulous. 'Are you sure?' he asked the Chilean ambassador in London. 'The first thing I did was call President Frei', who was with Aznar and other leaders in Porto. 'We talked a lot that night.' Frei was 'quiet and composed'. They agreed they must defend the rights of Chile, not Pinochet, and that included the right of a former head of state to travel freely, immune from the risk of arrest.

It was for Chile, not Spanish judges or British courts, to deal with Pinochet's crimes, they agreed. That was the public line, but privately Insulza was delighted by the arrest. 'Of course, on the human side, but I knew the government had a problem and I was responsible for addressing it. I felt the victims would get more justice in Spain, but we were under pressure to do something.'

He called Robin Cook in London. The British Foreign Secretary said it was for the courts, he couldn't do anything. 'Can't you just expel him?' Insulza asked. 'Cook told me he'd love to do that!' Insulza's own Socialist Party was divided: some wanted a trial in Spain, others thought Pinochet should be allowed to return to Chile immediately with a British apology.

Insulza coordinated with General Ricardo Izurieta, who had succeeded Pinochet as Commander-in-Chief of the Army just a few months earlier. 'The government would defend Chile's rights and prerogatives,' Insulza told Izurieta. He repeated the point to the Socialist Party, and it became government policy. We are defending Chile, not Pinochet.

In the meantime, Garzón's second request reached London and made its way to Ronald Bartle, a senior magistrate at Bow Street court in central London. On the morning of Thursday, 22 October, as Michael Caplan prepared to go to court to challenge the first arrest warrant, Bartle signed the second one. It included charges of torture, hostage-taking and conspiracy to commit these acts.

Bartle's signature had immediate consequences. Pinochet's lawyers arrived at the High Court to argue an application for *habeas corpus* on the first arrest warrant, expecting it to be opposed by the Crown Prosecution Service (CPS), on behalf of Spain and Garzón. The CPS team was led by Alun Jones QC, a member of the same barristers' chambers as Clive Nicholls and Clare Montgomery. It was a dramatic moment. 'As we got to court, around two o'clock,' Caplan recalled, 'Alun Jones steamed in and said, "We've got the second warrant."'

Caplan instantly saw that their application for *habeas corpus* was doomed. 'There was nothing we could do, as the second arrest warrant had extraditable crimes, the Spaniards got it right, so the application for *habeas corpus* disappeared.' The case changed direction. 'Our case became an application for judicial review of the decision to issue the second arrest warrant, on the grounds that Pinochet, as a former head of state, had total immunity from the jurisdiction of the English courts.'

The High Court set an urgent hearing for the following Monday morning, 26 October.


# 31


The hearing was unprecedented: never before had the former head of state of one country been arrested by and in another, for committing international crimes.

The arrest of a head of state impugns the country itself, so international law has rules to prevent such actions, giving a serving head of state or government immunity from legal process. This means the courts of one country cannot exercise jurisdiction over the head of state of another country. Where an international crime is in play, there may be exceptions, especially if an international court is involved. The arrest of Augusto Pinochet raised a different issue: was there an exception to the immunity rule for a former head of state if an international crime was in play, and did the exception apply to a case before a national court, as opposed to an international court?

There are two basic reasons for the immunity rule. First, it is a practical necessity: to represent a country around the world, a leader cannot be at risk of arrest by another country. Second, immunity respects the status and dignity of the state: to make a claim against a head of state, or maybe also a former head of state, is an affront to the State itself. This was the point made by José Miguel Insulza, the Foreign Minister, to President Frei.

The origins of the immunity rules are a bit hazy, although the ideas may be found in legal writings that go back to the sixteenth century. This was the context in which the French jurist and philosopher Jean Bodin evoked the wickedness of 'impunitie', and his Italian counterpart in the eighteenth century, Cesare Beccaria, would express the hope that 'no place on earth' would allow the most serious crimes to go unpunished. Immunity and impunity often go hand in hand.

By the nineteenth century, national courts were facing issues about judging the conduct of another state, its leader or diplomats. In 1812, in the Schooner Exchange case, Chief Justice Marshall of the US Supreme Court explained the rationale for the immunity rule: the 'exemption of the person of the sovereign from arrest or detention within a foreign territory' is necessary to safeguard 'his dignity, and the dignity of his nation'. In the decades that followed, national courts ruled that the immunity of a serving head of state was absolute. He or she could not be made to appear before the courts of another country.

The first inkling that immunity wasn't absolute came in 1919: the Treaty of Versailles, signed after the First World War, provided in Article 227 that former Kaiser Wilhelm II of Germany could be arraigned for warmongering, an 'offence against international morality and the sanctity of treaties'. Implicitly, the Treaty limited his immunity insofar as an international crime had been committed. The former Kaiser fled to The Netherlands, which never brought proceedings against him.

Three decades later, the agreement establishing the International Military Tribunal at Nuremberg explicitly dispensed with immunity. The 1945 Nuremberg Charter declared that the responsibility of any individual for their actions was not affected by their position as a senior official, or even as head of state. The Tokyo Tribunal, established in 1946, had the same rule. That was why Karl Dönitz, who succeeded Hitler as German head of state, could be prosecuted at Nuremberg. The same went for Hans Frank, head of the General Government in German-occupied Poland.

Nuremberg opened a door, at least before an international court. In 1948, the drafters of the Genocide Convention took matters a step further, agreeing that any person who committed genocide 'shall be punished, whether they are constitutionally responsible rulers, public officials or private individuals'. This language excluded immunity for any person, before international and national courts. The Convention extinguished the right to claim immunity because the crime was considered to be so heinous.

The idea was taken further in the 1990s, when the Security Council created the first international tribunals since Nuremberg and Tokyo, for crimes committed in the former Yugoslavia and in Rwanda. The Security Council agreed that before these tribunals a head of state – or a former head of state – could not claim immunity for genocide, crimes against humanity or war crimes. In July 1998, states drafting the Statute of the International Criminal Court (ICC) adopted the same approach. Around this time, Slobodan Milošević, the President of Serbia, was indicted for crimes against humanity and genocide before the International Criminal Tribunal for the former Yugoslavia.

Change was therefore in the air. By the time Jean Pateras, the interpreter, informed a pyjama-clad Pinochet that he was under arrest, it was broadly recognised that a former head of state could not claim immunity for an international crime before an international tribunal. The position with regard to immunity before national courts was different. Not long before Pinochet's arrest, Sir Arthur Watts, a former legal adviser at the Foreign Office in London, delivered a series of lectures in The Hague which touched on the issue. 'It can no longer be doubted,' he concluded, that under general international law a head of state 'will personally be liable to be called to account' for international crimes. That conclusion, however, did not address immunity before national courts. When Pinochet was arrested, this was an open issue. That was why the proceedings in London were so novel and remarkable.

## 32

A few days after the arrest, Alun Jones, acting for the CPS, travelled to Madrid to meet Judge Garzón. The main focus was now Pinochet's immunity.

Jean Pateras accompanied Jones. 'I loved working with Alun! He was nice, nervous, excited about the whole thing,' she recalled. Garzón was 'very charming, very flamboyant, he took us to lunch at a nice restaurant, off the Plaza Mayor, in a coat like a matador's cape, absolutely grand, a queen bee, treated like royalty as he entered'. The experience was not perfect. 'Garzón loved the most disgusting food! Offal, scrambled eggs with brains, stuff like that, plenty of wine.'

Did she like him?

'A little bit too arrogant and full of himself.' She stopped, retreated. 'Then all these ghastly things happened to him, didn't they?' Plainly there was affection. As for Garzón, he thought Jean was 'rather impressive'. The conversation focused on Pinochet's claim that he was entitled to immunity, an issue Garzón had not prepared for.

In the meantime, the press started asking questions about immunity, searching out the views of academics. On the Sunday evening before the hearing began at the Divisional Court, I gave an interview to the BBC World Service on legal issues raised by Pinochet's arrest.

'Is he entitled to immunity, as his lawyers claim?' asked Zeinab Badawi, the interviewer.

I don't know, I replied. The situation is novel, practically nonexistent, and the academic writing limited.

Should he be entitled to immunity?

I don't know.

But what should happen, she pressed, what would be the right outcome? Insistent, she sensed a hesitation. Many years have passed, there is apparently no recording, and I cannot recall the precise words I spoke. However, I made clear that it would be odd after Nuremberg, Yugoslavia and Rwanda if a former head of state could claim immunity on charges of international crimes, even before a national court.

My personal view was influenced by the story of my grandfather, who lost most of his family in the Holocaust, which I wrote about in *East West Street*. In July 1998, shortly after he died, and just a few months before Pinochet was arrested, I was peripherally involved in the negotiations in Rome for the Statute creating the International Criminal Court, which excluded all claims to immunity in proceedings before that Court. I contributed to writing the Preamble to the Statute, and wrote the line, with my friend Andrew Clapham, which affirmed 'the duty of every State to exercise its criminal jurisdiction over those responsible for international crimes'. The words, which were inconsistent with immunity, affirmed a duty not previously articulated in international law. Andrew and I expected them to be removed, but they never were.

## 33

Pinochet's case opened before the Divisional Court at the Royal Courts of Justice in London on the morning of Monday, 26 October

1998. The hearing generated much attention, the courtroom filled with observers and press. Outside, protesters and supporters waved placards and opposed each other, noisily and angrily. 'Asesino!' shouted one side. 'Communistas!' shouted the other.

The lawyers gathered, for Pinochet on one side, for Spain and the CPS on the other. Pinochet's lawyers asked the Court to set aside the first arrest warrant, as English courts had no jurisdiction for a crime of murder committed outside Britain, and to quash the second one on the grounds that a former head of state had complete immunity. He should be released immediately and allowed to go home. Spain's lawyers focused on the second arrest warrant and immunity.

'There was a general feeling that the hearing was unusual,' Michael Caplan recalled. 'It was unique and moved so quickly.' Amnesty International and other human-rights organisations pressing for Pinochet's extradition to Spain had no time to intervene, and Chile's government couldn't decide if it wanted to be formally involved. The Home Secretary, Jack Straw, was represented as an observer, as the Extradition Act of 1989 envisaged a role for him if the judges ruled that Pinochet had no immunity. He was advised by Jonathan Sumption, one of the country's leading barristers.

'There was a sense of disbelief,' Caplan recalled. 'How could there be an application for Pinochet's extradition to Spain? He wasn't Spanish, no crime was committed in Spain, and none of the victims were Spanish.' The last point was not correct, I pointed out. There was Carmelo Soria, and other Spaniards. 'I only learned that much later,' Caplan said, 'after we went to court.'

The hearings lasted two days, before a panel of three judges. Tom Bingham, Lord Chief Justice, presided, widely lauded in Britain as 'the greatest judge of our time'.

Miguel Schweitzer was pessimistic. 'I knew we had to win, in law, but wasn't sure we would, because of the media and the political pressure, because Jack Straw and Robin Cook weren't exactly neutral, they seemed to be on the human rights team.' He had no contact with the British government, as liaison with Chile was handled by the embassy, via the Latin America desk at the Foreign Office.

Pinochet did not attend the hearings. 'His mood was, I would say, in a Spanish way, *estoico*,' said Schweitzer. Stoical. 'He never talked much. He would say, "Yes, if it has to be done, it has to be done." "If it has to be accepted, it has to be accepted." He never gave an order, although some in his circle had strident views about what we should do. There was one who wanted to kidnap the General and take him back to Chile!' They continued to worry about assassination.

Schweitzer grinned at the memory. 'Yes, truly. We had to do a lot, Hernán Felipe and me, to avoid our people doing stupid things.' He rattled off a list of stupid things, like the Pinochet supporter who flew people in from Chile, to protest outside the court. 'The one who organised it thought it helped, but I thought it was counterproductive.' He smiled. 'I was against it, because of my background and training. I fight in the courts, not on the streets.'

## 34

On Wednesday, 28 October, the Divisional Court gave its judgement. Pinochet had an absolute right to immunity, a unanimous ruling.

This was a case about extradition, Bingham wrote, an international procedure to prevent a person accused of a crime from evading trial and punishment. Spain, as the requesting state, had asked the United Kingdom, as the requested state, to send Pinochet to Madrid to stand trial on criminal charges.

He set out the background, concisely. Pinochet, a national of Chile, not Spain, served as President, first of the Junta, then of the State, from 11 September 1973. On 11 March 1990, after he stepped down, he was made a Life Senator, with full parliamentary immunity in Chile. Bingham said little about the crimes, beyond what was in the second warrant, on torture, kidnap and disappearance.

As to the first warrant, signed by Nicholas Evans, it was 'plainly bad in law'. The murder of Spaniards in Chile – including Carmelo Soria – was not an extradition crime in England, whose courts had no jurisdiction over a murder – or even many murders – committed overseas by a non-British person. This was no criticism of Evans, Bingham stressed. He acted 'at short notice in a situation of great urgency and with very limited time for reflection'. (Evans was sanguine: 'I got myself into a muddle,' he told me sheepishly but with a large grin, and 'over the weekend learned that I had completely messed up, so was quite happy that someone else took over!')

By contrast, the second arrest warrant, signed by Ronald Bartle, raised international offences that were extradition crimes. The charges set out by Judge Garzón included orders allegedly given by Pinochet 'to eliminate, torture and kidnap persons and to cause others to disappear', to be implemented by the DINA within the framework of Operation Condor. 'It is important to emphasise,' wrote Bingham, that the court expressed 'no view on the truth or falsity of the accusations.'

Bingham summarised the rules of English law. They were largely set out in the State Immunity Act of 1978, which gave a former head of state immunity for 'criminal acts performed in the course of exercising public functions'. Pinochet argued that his acts were carried out as public functions, they were not 'private or personal conduct'. In other words, he was 'exercising sovereign power as head of state of the Republic of Chile', and he was not charged with 'personally torturing or murdering victims or causing their disappearance, but with using the power of the state of which he was head to that end'.

The 1978 Act provided for no exceptions to the general rule on immunity, not even for torture, disappearances or other international crimes, Bingham explained. 'If the former sovereign is immune from process in respect of some crimes, where does one draw the line?' It was not for him to draw a line between a sovereign act and a personal act, even if the act was a crime against humanity or genocide.

Bingham accepted that some rules of international law – he mentioned the 1948 Convention on Genocide – required the punishment of anyone who committed genocide. But the 1948 Convention could not be invoked before the English courts: the United Kingdom was a party to the treaty but had not incorporated it into English law. (This is not unusual: some treaties are incorporated, others are not, and in either case the country is bound by the treaty as a matter of international law – the key point is that an English judge can only apply an international treaty if it has been explicitly incorporated into English law.)

It followed that the rule extinguishing immunity for genocide did not apply in Pinochet's case, and there was no other English law to remove the immunity he had in respect of any other crimes. The Criminal Justice Act of 1988, for example, incorporated aspects of the 1984 Convention against Torture into English law, but neither the 1984 Convention nor the English Act explicitly removed immunity. Unlike the Convention on Genocide, the 1984 Convention against Torture said nothing about immunity.

Bingham said there was no international practice to offer assistance. It was true that the Nuremberg Statute, and the tribunals created in the 1990s for the former Yugoslavia and Rwanda, excluded immunity. But these were international courts, completely different from a national court.

Equally, the practice of other countries offered no assistance. Bingham had not found a single case in which a former head of state charged with an international crime was unable to claim immunity before a national court.

This was the logic of the law. Before a national court Pinochet was immune for any act carried out in the exercise of his functions as head of state, including torture and disappearing people, Bingham concluded. So long as the acts were official, there was immunity. He rejected Spain's argument that torture, disappearance and other international crimes could never be treated as official acts. Unfortunately, added Mr Justice Andrew Collins, in a separate opinion, history showed that state actions sometimes included the extermination or oppression of particular groups, and treated them as official acts.

It followed that Pinochet had immunity before the English courts. The judges had no option but to quash Garzón's second provisional arrest warrant. Bingham recognised there would be 'acute public concern' that a leader who had committed torture or another crime against humanity could escape trial and punishment, but that was the law, and it tied the judges' hands. Their job was to interpret and apply that law, even if the result might be an unhappy one.

As the case was significant and novel, Bingham allowed Spain to appeal the ruling directly to the House of Lords, the highest court in the land, if it wished to do so. He had consulted with Lord Browne-Wilkinson, the presiding judge in the House of Lords, who agreed the case was of singular importance. Any appeal had to be filed within five days, no later than Monday, 2 November, and would be limited to one question: as a former head of state, did Pinochet have immunity before the English courts, for acts committed while he was head of state?

Pinochet would remain under detention. He could not leave the country, or set foot outside his room.

## 35

Schweitzer was 'very happy' with the judgement, but also 'frustrated, as we couldn't take the General home'. It was, he believed, the first time a successful appeal for *habeas corpus* did not give rise to an immediate release.

The General's reaction?

'Stoical, as always,' Schweitzer whispered. 'We reported to him, told him the appeal to the Lords meant there'd be no immediate resolution. He gave us his backing, as always. "If you say that is what has to be done, that is what has to be done."'

Mrs Pinochet?

'She was pleased with the result, confident that we were doing what had to be done. We reported to her, subtly, she never interfered.'

In Chile the reaction was mixed. The General's supporters were delighted, his opponents appalled. In Britain, many understood the ruling was merely a preliminary skirmish. 'First Battle on Extradition', *The Times* reported on its front page. A Chilean minister praised Britain's legal system, adding that the government favoured legal action against Pinochet but only in Chile. The Medical Foundation for the Victims of Torture proclaimed that the ruling 'made England a safe haven for dictators and former dictators'.

Legal observers offered different perspectives. My friend James Cameron, a fellow international lawyer, wrote an op-ed saying it was widely accepted that 'states and their representatives are immune from prosecution by other national states'. No, wrote another academic: certain acts were 'so offensive to mankind as a whole' that states could not evoke immunity 'on behalf of individuals who engaged in the conduct'. Amnesty's lawyer, Geoffrey Bindman, who watched the hearing, was unhappy that the CPS failed 'to focus on the human rights or international law aspects'.

Michael Caplan was satisfied. 'As the judgement was read, I waited for the "but", to alert us that we would lose, yet it never came.' He sensed there was 'a mood swing against immunity, towards the idea that there should be no hiding place, but the law hadn't quite got there, hadn't developed into a hard rule.' 'We're virtually there now,' thought the Pinochet team.

Caplan received a call from the clerk at the Judicial Committee of the House of Lords. The hearings would open on 4 November, a week away, which left little time to prepare, but enough time for human-rights groups to try to intervene. Caplan was anxious about the timing. 'When you rush things, problems arise.' The team also recognised they needed an international lawyer on the team. 'The immunity issue is going to mushroom out.'

A few days later, Jean Pateras, the interpreter, visited Pinochet at The London Clinic with the police, to tell him that he would be moving. She was accompanied by Peter Dean, the medical doctor advising Scotland Yard. 'The police worried he'd die in custody in Britain,' Dean told me, many years later, over lunch with Jean. 'That would have been a disaster.'

Dean had been contacted a couple of days after the arrest. 'Hello doc, we've got a General Pinochet under arrest, we'd like you to come and see him,' he recalled. 'The first time I saw him he was not a happy bunny. "Do you fully understand why you are here," I asked him. He snapped out of a grumpy, angry mood. "I was President for seventeen years, head of the Army for twenty-five, they are treating me like a common criminal, I am not a common criminal."'

'He was like a fox, controlling but charming,' Jean interjected.

'Yes, one who never showed any remorse,' Dean added. 'He told me he was a soldier, that his country was at war.'

'For him it was all about communism!' said Pateras. She stopped herself. 'He wanted you to know that he was in charge, that he was the Commandante, that he knew everything.' He once said to her: 'Jean, I know you are married, where you live, that you have two daughters.' She found this mildly threatening.

'With the Chileans, he was always the boss,' said Dean, 'a proud man who never wanted a wheelchair.'

Pateras told him he was moving to Grovelands Priory in Southgate, north London. As the group left, waiting outside The London Clinic, security was tight. 'The family was stressed but very polite,' said Jean, who was warned by the police to be careful with her words. 'Don't call him a fucking bastard,' they told her, 'as people could lipread and the cameras might pick it up!'

There was a big police escort, the fear of an attack palpable. Pinochet travelled in an ambulance with the family, she followed in a police car. That evening, the *Evening Standard* put the story on its front page, a photograph of the convoy and a woman wearing a long white scarf. 'The general's daughter, Veronica, outside The London Clinic today,' said the caption. 'I looked at the photograph and thought, that looks like me,' said Pateras. 'It is!' A journalist suggested she sue for the embarrassment of being wrongly identified as Pinochet's daughter. She did. 'I got five grand, which was quite nice!'

## 36

I was in Paris when I heard of the Bingham judgement, working on a case between Hungary and Slovakia, on the impact of two Soviet-era barrages on the environment of the Danube River. In that pre-internet age, word arrived by newspaper, in *Libération*. 'First Victory for Pinochet in London', ran the headline. 'General Pinochet has won, the Chilean dictator will escape justice.' The paper reported that most lawyers expected the outcome, that Pinochet would soon be back in Chile.

I stayed in Paris the following day, Friday, 30 October, to attend a ceremony at the Pantin cemetery, to place a headstone on the grave of my grandfather, Leon Buchholz, who had died a year earlier. In the Jewish tradition, this marked the end of the period of mourning. As I left the hotel, an urgent call came from my barristers' chambers in London. 'General Pinochet's lawyers would like to hire you to argue against the appeal in the Lords.'

I'll call back later, I said, after the cemetery. I did not accept or turn down the instructions.

As I have previously noted, my wife Natalia waited at the entrance to the cemetery. She made clear her views, as the child of a mother who was a refugee from the Spanish Civil War, that I should not do it.

At the time, neither of us was aware of the family connection to Carmelo Soria, whose torture and murder started the case.

To act for Pinochet was like acting for Franco, in her view. By the time we left the cemetery I had decided not to take the case. The bar rules had an exception to the 'cab-rank' principle, on 'professional embarrassment': during the interview with Zeinab Badawi with the BBC, a few days earlier, I expressed the view that Pinochet should not have immunity for international crimes. I could decline the instructions, and I did. Twenty-seven years on we are very happily married.

We returned to London, and the next morning, a Saturday, I attended an academic conference. It was on the newly created International Criminal Court, but there was much talk of Pinochet. A lawyer with Human Rights Watch said the organisation was thinking of intervening in the case before the House of Lords. Was I available to be involved? No problem, I said. 'I remember your encouraging enthusiasm,' she reminded me many years later. 'Harmony in the family!'

Human Rights Watch needed a solicitor, so I suggested Richard Stein, an irreverent and fearless lawyer at a small firm in London, and brought in Jonathan Marks as my junior and Ed Fitzgerald as leader. That evening, the Human Rights Watch legal team gathered to draft an application to intervene. The document addressed the organisation's credentials, the errors in the Divisional Court reasoning, and the materials on international rules and the practice of national courts that we wanted to put before the Law Lords.

As we waited to learn if the application was successful, James Cameron accepted the brief from Pinochet on which I had passed. 'I had to,' he would say, 'it was the first one in, so I turned down the Attorney General and Amnesty', who approached him later. Best of friends on opposite sides. 'This is Chile's business and its political history,' James believed. 'There was a sense of pride, a determination to settle political differences at home in their own way, without the unwelcome intervention of a Spanish magistrate who overstepped his jurisdiction.'

Given Spain's total failure to address the crimes of Francisco Franco, or the brutality resulting from its colonisation of the province of Chile, as recorded in the sixteenth-century epic poem *La Araucana*, the argument was a reasonable one. Spain's actions reflected a different form of intervention, and Judge Garzón's actions had engendered tremendous irritation and anger in Pinochet's legal team.

'He was considered vain, a show-off, looking to self-aggrandise, largely interested in his own glory,' James told me. The painful irony of Spain's failure to deal with its own past was very much present. 'In Spain, matters were not resolved, politically or culturally, which was maybe why its political leadership was uncomfortable acting as a conduit for Garzón,' James added. 'I found that quite helpful for performing my role.'

## 37

The day after Bingham and the Divisional Court ruled in favour of Pinochet's immunity, the Audiencia Nacional in Madrid held a hearing of its own. This was the case brought by Chief Prosecutor Eduardo Fungairiño, hoping to close down the cases being investigated by Garzón and García-Castellón, to stop the extradition. Fungairiño asked the Audiencia to rule that Spanish judges and courts could not exercise jurisdiction over crimes committed in Argentina and Chile, even in relation to international crimes.

The two cases were heard together by a panel of eleven judges. The Madrid courtroom was packed and emotions ran high. Pinochet's victims sat alongside Argentine mothers of the disappeared, who held white handkerchiefs and photographs of their loved ones. Juan Garcés addressed the court, but for many the standout advocate was Carlos Slepoy, a legendary Argentine lawyer exiled in Spain.

'Let the genocidaires feel cornered, let humanity be freed from this plague, so the world may breathe a little easier,' he told the judges. 'Why did you become judges? To do justice, no? Now you have the opportunity to do so, as never again.' Please rule unanimously, he urged the judges, to send a clear message.

They did. The next day, all eleven judges ruled that Spanish courts had jurisdiction over international crimes. 'Spain Can Judge Pinochet for Genocide', declared *El País*. Paradoxically, Fungairiño's case, which was brought to help the Chilean military, had the very opposite effect, endorsing Castresana's approach to genocide in

Spanish law. The judges confirmed that the killings and disappear-ances in Chile came within the Spanish definition of genocide, as did torture and all Pinochet's actions to eliminate leftist political groups. With over fifty Spanish nationals identified as victims of Pinochet, including Carmelo Soria, Spain was free to take jurisdic-tion over Pinochet.

Garzón and Castresana were delighted. Garzón detailed the crimes, the locations, the techniques, and the names of thousands of victims. The last was a seventeen-year-old boy, Marcos Quesada Yáñez, detained in June 1989, then tortured and executed. Garzón gave centre stage to Londres 38, including the disappearance of Alfonso Chanfreau and ninety-seven other detainees.

He emphasised Manuel Contreras's testimony, given three years earlier: 'I reported daily' to Pinochet, the DINA director had stated, 'in a state of absolute subordination', and 'strictly obeyed . . . all I was ordered to do'. Pinochet was informed on 'the fulfilment of all orders given', and he alone 'arranged for and ordered the missions to be carried out'. He was responsible for every act of torture at Londres 38, for every disappearance and for every killing.

Carmelo Soria also got attention in Garzón's request. He was a diplomat with privileges and immunities, abducted in an official car that bore a UN registration plate, wrote Garzón, providing graphic details of his mistreatment at the Vía Naranja house, at the hands of a DINA unit 'responsible directly to Augusto Pinochet through Manuel Contreras'. Garzón cited Laura González-Vera's testimony. No one had been held accountable for the killing of Carmelo Soria, wrote Garzón. Only now, years after the case, did I understand the connection with my wife's family.

Garzón sent the documents to London. They were copied, intro-duced into lever-arch files, and entered into the record before the Law Lords. Jean Pateras was given a full set, so she could interpret for the police. Garzón's documents were in the boxes she gave me when we'd met. 'I never forgot what was on those pages,' she said.

# 38

On Monday, 1 November, bolstered by the ruling in Spain, lawyers for the Crown Prosecution Service lodged Spain's appeal to the

House of Lords. 'The Divisional Court was wrong to hold that Senator Pinochet has immunity,' it argued.

No, the Divisional Court and Bingham got it exactly right, replied Pinochet's lawyers. The 1978 State Immunity Act gave the former head of state 'absolute immunity', and it was not trumped by any rule of English or international law.

David Lloyd-Jones acted for the Attorney General as an *amicus curiae*, a neutral friend of the court. He recognised there was 'some support' for displacing immunity in cases of torture, but that position 'did not yet constitute a rule of public international law'.

Human Rights Watch and several non-governmental organisations applied for permission to intervene in the case. Amnesty International played a leading role, part of a group that included Redress, the Medical Foundation for the Victims of Torture, and two British victims, Sheila Cassidy and William Beausire. 'The House of Lords asked our views about Amnesty and the other interveners,' Caplan recalled. 'We considered that was a matter for the House of Lords, not for us.' He paused, he smiled. 'Some people will say the best decision I made in the case was not to object to the intervention of Amnesty.'

A panel of three House of Lords judges quickly ruled on the applications to intervene. They allowed the Amnesty group to intervene in writing, and to address the judges with oral arguments. Human Rights Watch, on the other hand, for reasons not explained, was limited to just intervene in writing.

## 39

The hearings opened on the morning of Wednesday, 4 November. Fearing the Law Lords might issue a quick ruling that allowed Pinochet to return to Chile, Human Rights Watch filed a precautionary application with the European Court of Human Rights. It requested an urgent order that Pinochet not be allowed to leave Britain, even if the Law Lords upheld the ruling of the Divisional Court. The application was brought on behalf of Pinochet's victims, including Alfonso Chanfreau, Erika Hennings and their daughter Natalia. The European Court would reject the application, but it introduced me, at that early stage, to the Chanfreau story.

The hearing was held in Committee Room 4, on an upper floor of the Palace of Westminster, in the shadow of Big Ben. This was not a courtroom in any usual sense. 'Drab', thought Reed Brody of Human Rights Watch, but I felt otherwise about the Gothic stonework and furnishings. Think Harry Potter, or a minor English public-school refectory – a rectangular room, four windows over-looking an inner courtyard, four doors, rows of chairs, a bright-blue carpet, paintings of dead men in gilt frames, and much by way of red: chairs, desks, walls.

Through the Gothic doorways we filed, into a packed room. The five Law Lords would sit at one end, in padded leather chairs, behind a crescent-shaped wooden table topped with burgundy-red leather. Each judge had a small wooden bookshelf on which to place files. The first row had a wooden podium with a small table on either side, then three or four lesser-padded chairs for the senior lawyers, known as Queen's Counsel. From the vantage point of the judges, Pinochet's lawyers sat on the right, led by Clive Nicholls and Clare Montgomery, and Spain's lawyers were on the left, led by Alun Jones.

In the next row sat Michael Caplan and the barrister for the At-torney General. Amnesty, and the other human-rights groups sat in the third row, on lesser-padded chairs. Behind them, in seven unpadded rows, eighty-four chairs in all, the public and the press, including Pinochet supporters and opponents. Among them, ran a rumour, was a representative of Henry Kissinger, along with María Isabel Allende, the former President's daughter, and Orlando Letel-ier's son, Orlando.

I sat in the third row, on a marginally padded chair, between Reed Brody and a middle-aged, well-perfumed man, elegantly at-tired, with a fleshy, friendly face and a decent head of well-tended white hair. In dulcet tones, that first morning, he introduced himself with a handshake and a warm, heavily accented English. 'Miguel Schweitzer, from Santiago'.

We would spend many days as neighbours, but on that first day I knew nothing of his past, save that he was Pinochet's trusted lawyer and, it was whispered, adviser on human rights. 'It is true,' he later told me, 'that in the 1980s I advised that Chile should sign up to some human-rights treaties, on torture and other things.'

In those pre-internet days, there was no way of knowing his other roles, as ambassador and Foreign Minister. Nor did I know of his trips to Washington to negotiate on Michael Townley and Orlando Letelier, or who his father was, or that he worked on the Rauff case (which I'd never even heard of), or that he was connected to the widow of Carmelo Soria (who was also unknown to me). We had no idea about his connections, in Punta Arenas and elsewhere, or his work.

The truth is I liked him, and so did James Cameron, who worked closely with him. 'Miguel was like a decent Chilean wine, stylish and smooth, rather gracious, handsome and well-groomed. He was the kind of man who smells good, speaks beautifully, worldly and knowing, very likeable, gets things done.'

The days ahead were bonding, a kind of legal Stockholm Syndrome. Whatever our differences, and they were significant, all present were connected by their participation in the most significant international criminal case since Nuremberg. Miguel Schweitzer tolerated me, I tolerated him. We came to like each other, and we did not know, on that first day, that we'd still be in touch two decades later.

He was a talker, but only really opened up after it was all done and dusted. 'The case was like a homecoming,' he later said. Educated at a British school in Santiago – The Grange, whose headmaster, George Lowe, climbed Everest with Sir Edmund Hillary – he loved London, as Chile's ambassador, going to Buckingham Palace and the Lord Mayor's banquet. He admired Britain so much that he sent his boys to Cheltenham College, to learn rugby, and was mortified when Pinochet recalled him as ambassador. '"You were becoming Mrs Thatcher's ambassador, not mine!" the General told me.' Yet the case before the Law Lords was 'a pinnacle' for him, he loved every minute. 'Very impacting,' he said.

On the dot of ten thirty, the five Law Lords entered. They were chosen from eleven available judges, all men (five years passed before the first woman, Brenda Hale, would be appointed), all white, all senior. We did not know how they were selected, or why Gordon Slynn presided. A former advocate general of the European Court of Justice in Luxembourg, well-versed in matters of international law, I knew him well, a delightful person with a mischievous twinkle and a mane of well-tended, thick grey hair.

Just a few weeks earlier we'd been together at a seminar on

'democracy and the global economy' at New York University, gossiping as President Bill Clinton and Prime Minister Tony Blair debated what was once called 'The Third Way'. Blair foresaw 'a large change' in global politics, although quite how large it would come to be – September 11th, Iraq, Brexit, Trump, Putin were all in the future – no one in the seminar could foresee.

It also happened to be the day when Kenneth Starr's four-hour examination of Clinton, on his relationship with Monica Lewinsky, was publicly broadcast. In those circumstances, Slynn was mightily impressed by Clinton's sangfroid and intellectual acuity, as was *The Financial Times*. A 'vintage Bill performance', the newspaper reported, 'smooth, eloquent, humorous and oozing confidence'. At a reception that evening, Clinton explained to a small group of us why he decided not to sign the statute of the International Criminal Court.

A few weeks later, Slynn was presiding over a case that would determine Pinochet's future. He sat with Tony Lloyd, Donald Nicholls, Johan Steyn and Leonard Hoffmann, the last two of South African origin, all graduates of Oxford or Cambridge Universities. They wore suits, no gowns or wigs, unlike the barristers. They were assisted by James Vallance White, whose formal title as Fourth Clerk at the Table gave him the role of running the judicial office of the House of Lords. 'To me it was just another case, near Christmas,' Vallance White later told me. 'Everyone knew it was important, but my memory was simply expecting the judgement to go the way of the Divisional Court.' That view was widely held.

David Hope, Scotland's most senior judge before becoming a Law Lord, did not sit on the case. 'I missed the cut by one,' he wrote in a five-volume diary published after retirement. (Vallance White told me that one Law Lord was away and five others were sitting on another case, so those five in effect selected themselves.)

*Lord Hope's Diaries* broke a taboo, that judges do not disclose what has passed behind the scenes. He left out matters that were 'private' or 'best forgotten', but revealed more than might be expected. He wrote of the 'confusion' prompted by the case's sudden arrival, of tensions between the judges, and of reactions at various points. 'God, I wish *you* were sitting,' Slynn told Hope outside Hoffmann's room, shortly before the hearing, without revealing the reason for the exasperation. Slynn apparently tried to persuade Hoffmann not to sit, but Hope believed his colleague was 'determined' to 'play his part in securing the prosecution of General Pinochet'. Hope also revealed that Bingham assumed Hoffmann and Steyn would rule against Pinochet and his own ruling.

Waiting in Committee Room 4, the lawyers and journalists were blissfully unaware of such matters. We observed and waited, as the judges entered, with a sense of anticipation.

## 40

What followed was oral advocacy in the English style, which gave the proceedings an element of theatre. Committee Room 4 was a stage behind closed doors. The proceedings were not broadcast, but journalists were present and able to report.

Papers were shuffled, throats cleared, doors shut and protests drowned out. Slynn offered a few words of introduction. 'I am certain that Gordon looked towards Lennie, expecting he might say something to the parties, but he never did,' Vallance White recalled.

Alun Jones stood to address the judges, for the CPS and Spain, the appellants. 'The High Court of Justice erred in holding that the defendant enjoys immunity from the proceedings against him,' he said, then got his points across, with a muffled passion. Pinochet committed 'savage and barbaric crimes', in Chile and elsewhere. These were not part of his official functions. The 1961 Vienna Convention, and the most relevant English statute, the 1978 Act, offered no immunity to a former head of state for such international crimes.

This conclusion, he continued, was consistent with international agreements on universal jurisdiction, which required countries to prosecute or extradite any international criminal who set foot on their soil. The old rules on immunity were of a bygone age: the United Nations Charter, Nuremberg, and the conventions on genocide, hostage-taking and torture, confirmed that Pinochet's crimes could not be treated as official acts. To recognise his immunity would unleash impunity.

Jones was assisted by Professor Greenwood, an academic lawyer and a fine advocate, of a conservative disposition, once my and James Cameron's teacher. 'He and I agreed we were on opposite

sides of our own views of the law!' Cameron later recalled. Greenwood homed in on Article 39 of the 1961 Vienna Convention on
Diplomatic Relations, on the immunities of former diplomats.
Pinochet only had immunity for 'acts performed in the exercise of
functions as a member of the mission', Greenwood argued. Under
Article 39, a diplomat's immunity normally ended when he left the
country, but persisted for 'acts performed . . . in the exercise of his
functions'.

If a former diplomat had no immunity for unofficial acts, why
should Pinochet? Greenwood argued that this rule was part of a customary rule, that it removed Pinochet's immunity for crimes against
humanity or genocide, as these were not official acts. Amnesty International and Human Rights Watch supported the argument.

Pinochet's lawyers took a different approach. Clive Nicholls laid
the foundations, Clare Montgomery delivered the detail. If one
lawyer stood out in the case, it was her, as the judges listened like
schoolboys appearing before a fearsome headmistress. Immunity
was firmly established in international law, she submitted, and no
treaty or practice changed that fact. Yes, immunity could be lost
before an international court, like Nuremberg, but the House of
Lords was merely a national court. Spain hadn't found even one
treaty that did away with immunity before a national court, and
there was no 'crystallized principle' of customary international law
that trumped immunity under English law. Montgomery's approach
was simple and brutally effective. A female voice touched the courtroom in a way that never happened at Nuremberg.

So the arguments ran, before a packed, thrilled, anxious courtroom. There was back and forth as legal texts were parsed, pulled
and stretched, turned this way and that. This was the magic of words
in a treaty or statute, open to a multitude of interpretations. The
law is never a given. There was point and counterpoint, as obscure
instruments of English law commingled with treaties pulled from
the recesses of history.

The hearing lasted five days before Slynn pulled down the curtain,
with an elegant closing statement. The judges would deliberate, a
judgement would follow. Leaving Committee Room 4 on that fifth
day we had no idea which way the decision would go. Many felt that
way, including David Hope, who noted 'a split of views' among the
judges.

'Sitting there, watching each judge, were you doing like me, trying to calculate, is he for us or against us?' Miguel Schweitzer asked. 'Why did they ask that question? What does it mean?' He was impressed by the hearing: the formalities, the courtesy and preparation, the fairness, the papers, the way lawyers responded to questions with no time to prepare. 'Very impressive,' he repeated. 'In Chile, only very seldom will a judge interrupt you or ask you a question.'

Which way did Schweitzer think it would go? He sensed Slynn's innate conservatism, a scepticism about anything too new. Yet he also noticed Hoffmann's pointed questions, and antipathy towards Pinochet. 'Obviously against us,' he later recalled. It was hard to disagree.

Two weeks passed, life went on. In Santiago, over dinner with friends, the Chilean poet Nicanor Parra spoke of old age and dead friends, cats and car accidents, Shakespeare's fate and Pinochet in London. The Lords would rule against immunity, he predicted. 'Prophetic,' thought Roberto Bolaño, one of the guests.

The Judicial Office announced that judgement would be delivered on the afternoon of 25 November. Each judge would state his decision in a public hearing, in the main chamber of the House of Lords.

## 41

Expectation and anxiety hung in the air, as we entered the Palace of Westminster, passing supporters and opponents of Pinochet. He himself was not present. In the main chamber we stood, wigged and gowned, barristers crowded together in a wooden pen. Jones and Greenwood, Montgomery and Nicholls, and my friend James Cameron, just behind, poker-faced, hands clasped, looking towards the red-leather banquettes occupied by a scattering of elderly peers, just in front of me. Was that Lady Thatcher? Was that Norman Lamont, Pinochet's most active local supporter? The public and press were in the gallery, looking down, under the panelled ceiling. Across the chamber, on a bench near the Woolsack, Hoffmann and Lloyd huddled in amiable conversation.

Michael Caplan was there with Miguel Schweitzer. 'It could go one way or the other, and you knew it would make one hell of a difference,' Schweitzer recalled. 'It was the General's birthday, the plane was ready, the engines running. If we won, he was ready to leave, with luggage, into a car, straight to the airport.'

James Vallance White stood, announced the case, bowed, sat down. Gordon Slynn rose, red folder in hand. 'My Lords, I beg to move, the report of the Appellate Committee be now considered.' The report was the judgement. 'For reasons set out in the speech which I have prepared, I would hold that the respondent as a former head of state is immune from arrest. I would dismiss the appeal.' He returned to the Woolsack.

One-nil for Pinochet.

Lloyd rose. Chile was entitled to claim immunity on behalf of the General under the 1978 State Immunity Act and at common law. 'I would therefore dismiss the appeal.'

Two-nil.

Nicholls rose. 'I would reverse the decision of the Divisional Court, allow this appeal, and hold that the respondent, Senator Pinochet, is not immune from the criminal process of this country.'

Two-one.

'I would allow the appeal,' said Steyn, in a gentle South African lilt. 'On a correct interpretation of the law, General Pinochet has no immunity whatever.'

The equaliser. Pinochet two, Spain two.

That left Hoffmann. I placed my right hand on Reed Brody's left shoulder and whispered: 'We've won.' 'I know,' he said, incredulous. Miguel Schweitzer also knew. 'At two-two, when it came to Judge Hoffmann, I knew that we would have to go back to the General and tell him that we lost.'

Hoffmann stood. The striped shirt and patterned tie were fabulously mismatched, a slight air of naughtiness on his face. He was the centre of attention, around the world, a judgement broadcast live. 'My Lords, I have had the advantage of reading in draft the speeches of my noble and learned friends, Lord Nicholls of Birkenhead and Lord Steyn.' Long pause. 'I agree with them that Senator Pinochet does not have immunity from prosecution, and I too would therefore allow the appeal.'

A distant and unknown voice exclaimed loudly, a single word, unintelligible. Surprise? Joy? Horror? Across the Chamber there rose the gentle sound of a gasp, a collective intake of breath, as the implication sunk in. In such moments the human brain functions in slow motion. A burst of cheering from outside pierced the Palace walls.

Three-two for Spain. Historic, revolutionary even. It was as though in a single moment the global legal order shifted on its axis, away from the sovereign, towards the individual, away from the perpetrator, towards the victim. In an instant, the impunities associated with the crimes of the sovereign were stripped away.

Slynn rose to explain what had passed. A majority confirmed the quashing of the arrest warrant signed by Mr Evans, and restoring the one signed by Mr Bartle. The Divisional Court ruling was cast aside. He sat down.

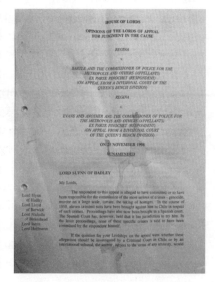

The chamber emptied to the sound of hushed, low voices. Outside, printed copies of the judgement awaited, fifty-six typed pages on pale-green paper. I still have my tea-stained copy. Not one judgement, but five separate opinions, which was unusual. Only by reading each could you find a centre of gravity.

There were points in common. The five Law Lords agreed that if Pinochet had been head of state he could claim immunity. As a former head of state, however, the majority ruled he could not. The reasoning was complex, an interplay between English law and international law. The central point of difference between the judges turned on the interpretation of the 1978 Act and Article 39 of the 1961 Convention, and a single question: were Pinochet's actions in relation to killing, torture and disappearance to be treated as official conduct?

Two judges thought his actions were official, so he had immunity. Three others, the majority, thought they were not official, so he didn't. Each judge wrote in a style of his own, as the law is not a mechanical process. The act of interpretation – of the 1978 Act, the 1961 Convention, the treaties on genocide and torture, and so on – is personal. The law has no single logic, so each judge drew different consequences from the existence and practice of international courts, and from the views of writers and governments. 'In an appeal in which no fewer than 16 barristers were involved over six days, it is not surprising that issues proliferated,' wrote Steyn.

Slynn's judgement was the longest, twenty-five pages of anguished struggle between conscience and the law. Deeply committed to the rights of individuals against the excesses of the state, he concluded that the 'basic rule' of immunity was not displaced. National judges must 'go cautiously', and caution meant that immunity was not 'cut down' by the 1978 Act or the 1961 Convention. To remove Pinochet's immunity required the law to speak in 'clear terms', and it had not done so. Article 39 of the 1961 Convention got close but did not explicitly end immunity. Moreover, Slynn concluded, a president could torture and kill in an official capacity, so that the 'appalling nature' of Pinochet's alleged crimes did not mean they were unofficial acts.

Lloyd agreed. Pinochet acted 'in a sovereign capacity', his orders to torture or disappear people were official acts, implemented by the DINA, protected by immunity under international and English law. No treaty or act did away with immunity. The horrific nature of the crimes, or the fact Pinochet might not have immunity before an international tribunal, changed nothing. And, Lloyd added, defensively, immunity didn't mean impunity. Pinochet could be tried in Chile, or in another country (if Chile waived immunity), or before the ICC (once it was operational). The sentiment seemed optimistic.

The three judges in the majority wrote much shorter opinions. For each, the result was the same but the route was different.

Lord Nicholls concluded that Article 39 of the 1961 Convention limited immunity to official acts, and torture and disappearances could never be official acts. International law outlawed such conduct, even by a head of state, and to give Pinochet immunity would make a 'mockery' of those rules. Since Nuremberg, those who perpetrated international crimes could not 'shelter themselves behind their official position to be freed from punishment'. His words mirrored those written for British prosecutor Hartley Shawcross at Nuremberg, fifty years earlier, by Hersch Lauterpacht, who put 'crimes against humanity' into international law.

Steyn wrote that the loss of immunity was 'the only sensible reconstruction of the legislative intent' of the 1978 Act and 1961 Convention. If Pinochet's acts were official, no line could ever be drawn between what a head of state could and could not officially do, so even Hitler's 'final solution' would be treated as official conduct. Pinochet's lawyers conceded that a head of state who killed his gardener in a fit of rage, or ordered a person to be tortured for personal enjoyment, was not engaged in official conduct. In this way, they recognised a line separating official and unofficial conduct. It followed that since Nuremberg the murders and disappearances perpetrated by DINA in secret, on Pinochet's orders, were not official conduct. Steyn alone addressed the facts set out by Baltasar Garzón, the evidence of a 'systematic campaign of repression', with 4,000 individuals 'killed or simply disappeared' by the DINA. Pinochet was not entitled to an immunity 'of any kind'.

The last judge was Lord Hoffmann. He wrote just thirty-three words, and offered no reasoning of his own. 'I have had the advantage of reading in draft the speech of my noble and learned friend Lord Nicholls of Birkenhead and for the reasons he gives I too would allow this appeal.'

## 42

Pinochet was not at the House of Lords to witness the ruling. He spent his eighty-third birthday watching it on a television screen at Grovelands Priory, with Lucía and the children, a few supporters, police officers and Jean Pateras.

'Everybody was happy, eating cake, preparing to watch the judgement,' Pateras recalled. 'A *tarta chilena*, dulce de leche with pastry, milles feuilles, delicious!' A plane was waiting at nearby Northolt airport. 'We watched on television. I was in one room with the police and the doctors, he was in another with his family, surrounded by Burberry and Harrods bags, suitcases packed and ready.' The prospect of a return to Chile prompted 'masses of shopping'.

Her feelings were mixed. 'I only really got to know what an evil son of a bitch he was . . .' The voice trailed off. He didn't deserve to go home, and secretly she hoped the judgement would go against him, although she didn't expect it to. 'I thought everybody wanted to get rid of him, as he was costing taxpayers huge amounts. What's it got to do with England, people said. I thought he would leave. Everybody did.'

At two-two, as Hoffmann stood to speak, she too realised what was coming. 'Oh my God, what are we going to do?' she wondered. After Hoffmann's decision, a police officer instructed her to prepare Pinochet for the practical consequences. 'Go in and tell him.' She did. 'I said to him, "I'm sorry it went against you, we are taking you to another address where you will be under arrest."'

His reaction?

'He had a tear. Everybody else was crying. They had all been happy, eating birthday cake, then they were crying.'

One tear?

'He broke down and cried in front of me, yes. He just said, "Umm."' Jean was silent. 'So, I said to him, "Can you please get ready because we will be leaving very soon", and then I walked out.'

## 43

Pinochet stayed on at Grovelands Priory for another week, departing on 2 December, to the relief of the staff. He left with heavy security,

an ambulance with police escort, much luggage and a gaggle of protesters in tow. His new home was 28 Lindale Close, in Wentworth,
near Virginia Water, a prosperous neighbourhood south-west of
London, close to the famous golf course.

'A poxy little house, not particularly nice,' Jean thought, with
cream carpets and leather chairs. Two of the four bedrooms were
occupied by Scotland Yard officers, along with a small room next
to the kitchen filled with screens displaying outdoor surveillance
camera footage. Pinochet had room for an exercise bike and many
photographs, of himself, the family and Margaret Thatcher. The
dining room was fitted with 'stuff to control him', Jean recalled,
cameras and listening devices, and a strong police presence.

'The concern about a possible assassination was constant, that
was why there was so much protection, with police living on the
premises, and many security cameras,' said Hernán Felipe Errázuriz. On arrival, Pinochet wanted to inspect the garden. Jean
was instructed to tell him he needed prior authorisation. 'I told him:
"(a) you can't go out alone, (b) you can't go anywhere without a
police officer, and (c) you always have to ask permission."' Later,
when a set of remote-control toy cars were installed in the garden,
he enjoyed racing them around the lawn with the grandchildren,
but he always needed permission first.

Pinochet was not thrilled. It was all 'fury and thunder', Jean Pateras recalled. 'So I said to him, "Sit down here, they will tell you
when you can go out in the garden."' For the most part, he behaved
correctly. Only once, she said, while awaiting the ruling, did he act
inappropriately:

He was in a room with his cronies, can't remember who. Miguel
[Schweitzer] was there. As I left the room, he said something that
made them laugh. In those days I was twenty-five, quite attractive,
good body, all that sort of stuff. I stopped. 'What did you say?
What did you say? Obviously you said something, because you are
all laughing.'

Miguel said, 'No, no, es una tontería, something stupid, don't
worry about it.' That's the only time Pinochet ever said anything
that was even slightly rude to me.

'I did not like Pateras from the beginning,' said Hernán Errázuriz, when I mentioned the episode. 'She was false, she pretended to like the General but I knew she didn't.'

For Miguel Schweitzer, the moment of judgement was 'the most impacting experience' of his entire life. 'Indescribable', and devastating, but he was sanguine. By the time Schweitzer got back to Grovelands Priory, Pinochet had calmed down. 'Again, it was stoicism, in the sense of, "Hmm, now what happens?"'

We will fight on, Miguel Schweitzer told him. We will continue to resist extradition, and do whatever it takes to avoid the consequences of the Law Lords ruling. Schweitzer would dedicate himself to that task.

Into his lap there now fell a new line of attack.

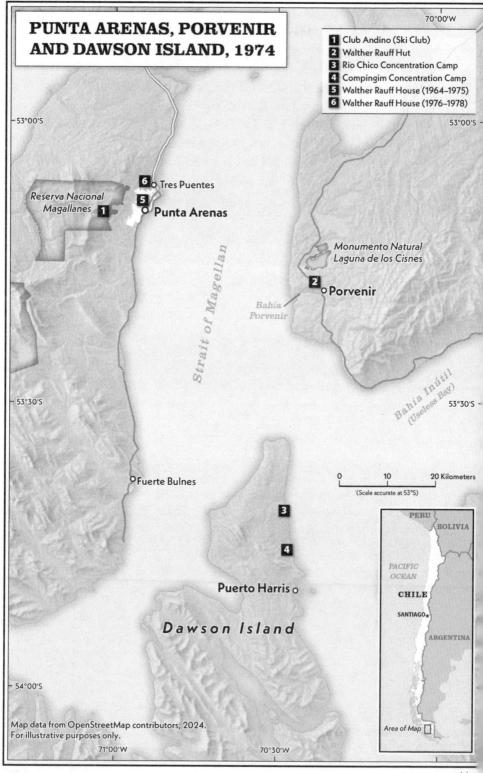

# PUNTA ARENAS, PORVENIR AND DAWSON ISLAND, 1974

1 Club Andino (Ski Club)
2 Walther Rauff Hut
3 Rio Chico Concentration Camp
4 Compingim Concentration Camp
5 Walther Rauff House (1964–1975)
6 Walther Rauff House (1976–1978)

70°00'W

53°00'S

53°00'S

6 Tres Puentes

Reserva Nacional Magallanes

5 1 Punta Arenas

Monumento Natural Laguna de los Cisnes

2 Porvenir

Bahía Porvenir

Strait of Magellan

53°30'S

Bahía Inútil (Useless Bay)

53°30'S

0 10 20 Kilometers
(Scale accurate at 53°S)

Fuerte Bulnes

3

4

PERU
BOLIVIA
PACIFIC OCEAN
CHILE
SANTIAGO
ARGENTINA

Puerto Harris

Dawson Island

Area of Map

54°00'S

Map data from OpenStreetMap contributors, 2024.
For illustrative purposes only.

71°00'W

70°30'W

Map

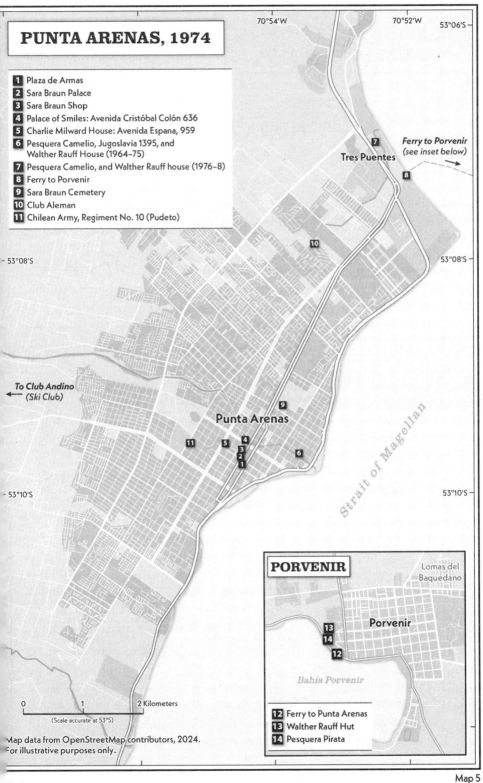

# PUNTA ARENAS, 1974

1. Plaza de Armas
2. Sara Braun Palace
3. Sara Braun Shop
4. Palace of Smiles: Avenida Cristóbal Colón 636
5. Charlie Milward House: Avenida Espana, 959
6. Pesquera Camelio, Jugoslavia 1395, and Walther Rauff House (1964–75)
7. Pesquera Camelio, and Walther Rauff house (1976–8)
8. Ferry to Porvenir
9. Sara Braun Cemetery
10. Club Aleman
11. Chilean Army, Regiment No. 10 (Pudeto)

70°54'W  70°52'W  53°06'S

Tres Puentes

*Ferry to Porvenir*
*(see inset below)*

53°08'S  53°08'S

*To Club Andino*
*(Ski Club)*

Punta Arenas

*Strait of Magellan*

53°10'S  53°10'S

### PORVENIR

Lomas del Baquedano

Porvenir

*Bahía Porvenir*

0   1   2 Kilometers
(Scale accurate at 53°S)

Map data from OpenStreetMap contributors, 2024.
For illustrative purposes only.

12. Ferry to Punta Arenas
13. Walther Rauff Hut
14. Pesquera Pirata

Map 5

# PUNTA ARENAS

## 44

After the Supreme Court of Chile ruled against his extradition to West Germany, Walther Rauff returned to Patagonia. He was free but notorious, his name associated with gas vans and mass murder, now mentioned in the same breath as Eichmann, Mengele and Klaus Barbie. During a visit, the new West German ambassador asked that Rauff be kept away, his membership of the local German Club was terminated, and he needed a job.

My name will fade from the spotlight, Rauff assured his son Alf, and the newspapers will lose interest. In need of money, he purchased a second-hand refrigerated van and, with Alf, travelled around Chile selling fish and king-crab meat. The project was ended by an accident ('full of fish, the refrigerated van was totally smashed and with that the business came to an end').

Rauff returned to Porvenir and the *Pesquera Bonacic*. It was May 1964.

## 45

There are plenty of people in the area who remember Rauff from that time. In Punta Arenas, I met Vladimiro Poll, a retired fisherman of Estonian origin, from Porvenir, who had fished for *centolla* (spider crab) with his father, some of which was sold to Rauff.

'I first saw Rauff in Porvenir, around 1960,' Poll recalled. 'He had his own boat, the *Walter*, which may have come from Germany. It was painted black, different from the other, colourful boats, and I sailed on it with my father and uncle.'

Poll worked with the German owner of the *Pesquera Bonacic*, located on Bahía Inutile, near Porvenir. 'They called it Useless Bay because it was so shallow.' Rauff was reliable. 'He spoke Spanish with a strong accent, paid a decent price for the *centolla*, and treated me kindly.'

Did you know of Rauff's past?

No. Vladimiro Poll was not inquisitive, and such questions made him uncomfortable. This was a left-wing area, he said, many fishermen were sympathetic to Allende, the local senator and Socialist candidate in Chile's 1958 presidential elections. Vladimiro Poll did not wish to talk about politics or Pinochet's Coup.

I took the ferry from Tres Puentes to Porvenir, docking near a memorial park to honour the Selk'nam people, the indigenous community of Tierra del Fuego exterminated by nineteenth-century European settlers. In Rauff's time, Porvenir passed in silence over matters of genocide, whether of the Selk'nam people or that occasioned by Rauff.

Today, the town welcomes visitors with lifesize figures of Selk'nam warriors and industrial artefacts. These included an old furnace, painted bright yellow and black. 'The boiler was used in Rauff's crab cannery!' the guide said with a smile. The town's buildings were equally colourful, a salmon farm in the distance, boats bobbing on the bay, the Anclamar restaurant.

I went to find people who knew Rauff, hoping to obtain first-hand accounts of the man and his character. I was not disappointed: every local I met knew his name, some remembered seeing him, and a few – mostly genial ladies in their seventies or eighties – had had personal encounters with the old Nazi. Their recollections were strikingly consistent.

'I worked for him at the *Pesquera Bonacic*,' said Emma Barrientos, cosily ensconced in the front room of her clapboard home, surrounded by bobbins and spools of brightly coloured threads. 'My job was to dismember the crabs, to remove the flesh from the legs.' Rauff was a 'decent boss', worked long hours, a quiet manager who didn't nag or lose his temper. 'His Spanish was so bad no one understood what he said, except "Buenos Días!"'

'He was welcomed as an outsider,' Emma said. 'He lived alone in a small cabin on the hill behind the fishery, with a German shepherd dog.' The building was still there, a short walk. 'At the factory, everyone knew the stories of his past, the older ones said he was a

Nazi who did terrible things.' No one talked details. 'I was young, didn't believe the stories.'

A photograph of Emma seated at a till hung on the wall, smiling with a fashionable beehive hairdo. 'I worked at the supermarket where he shopped. Always alone, in a green jumper and a long coat. He bought whisky and two packets of Lucky Strike cigarettes.' 'Lucky Strike!' she said, in a deep, rolling growl, with a guttural 'r'. 'Shtrrrrike!' she roared affectionately. 'He was *mi jefe*, my boss.'

We had lunch at the Anclamar, a vast plate of fresh *centolla*, and after that met Adelia Andrade and María Vivat. 'I was sixteen when I started at the *Pesquera* in 1962,' said Adelia. 'We were fifty or sixty people, in a long flat building, a warehouse on one floor. The boss was José Bonacic, a Croat. Rauff arrived in 1964, as the manager.'

'He was quiet, didn't speak much, kept to himself, seemed like a good person,' said María. 'We were told he'd escaped from somewhere, that he once killed many people.' The ladies weren't curious. 'We were young, the stories were long ago and far away. All we cared about was finding a husband and putting the crabmeat in tins.'

Sometimes they would tease him about his past. 'We'd joke about him putting us in the big boiler,' said Adelia. 'He'd look at us silently, listen, smile, say nothing. He didn't get upset.'

'He had an ear that was bitten,' said María.

'Wasn't that his dog?' asked Adelia.

I showed them a photograph of Rauff in Porvenir in 1966. 'Yes, that's him. Sometimes he wore a suit, but usually a jacket and pants, with different colours.'

They reminisced about his cabin on the hill, behind the factory. 'It had a great view, across the ocean, so he could see who was coming, to protect himself.' The two ladies never went inside, but often saw him on the street. 'Always with a dog, never a woman.' Pause. 'There was a brothel in town, back then, maybe he used that?'

After the ladies, I visited Juan Torres Toro, a retired schoolteacher.

He didn't work at the cannery but his father had. 'Everyone knew the rumours and stories of his past,' Juan said. 'I often saw him on the street, with a German shepherd called Bobby, like a police dog but more tender and faithful.' He couldn't remember if Bobby's ear was bitten, or Rauff's.

'My father told us how much his boss liked to drink. Once, Rauff gathered all the cannery workers, to explain the whisky. "I drink to forget and so I can sleep at night," he told them. I haven't forgotten that.'

Juan suggested we walk along the edge of the bay, the coast of Tierra del Fuego, to the factory. It was one storey, walls of corrugated iron painted the colour of a pale-blue sky. Here Emma, Adelia and María had boiled, dismembered, scraped, gathered and pushed flesh tightly into aluminium cans, to be sealed and labelled. This was Rauff's place of work, a refuge close to the penguins and flamingos of Useless Bay.

The cabin was just behind, on a small hill, overlooking the cannery. One floor, wooden walls, a couple of rooms, a tiny kitchen, a huge window with a view across the Straits to Punta Arenas, and simply furnished. 'My only contact with the outside world is the radio and books,' Rauff told a journalist, hoping to obtain 'a more universal vision of human beings and events'. He had friends and enemies, like anyone, but no fears for the future, and hoped to write a memoir. The article's magazine cover showed him crouching, radio and whisky close by, a Lucky Strike in hand. 'A quiet man,' opined the mayor. 'Cultivated and kind, he creates no problems for anyone.'

Eugenio Gligo Viel remembered the cabin. The Porvenir home of the writer, poet and collector is also a private museum. He greeted me in shorts and, on each foot, a giant furry slipper, a big brown dog with a little red tongue. Eugenio Gligo was with Offel Busto, his friend, a delightful man, round and short and with a memory of his own.

'There is a man in Punta Arenas, who had a photograph of himself with Walther Rauff,' said Offel Busto.

'I met Rauff in the 1960s,' said Eugenio Gligo. 'He told us they forced him to be a Nazi.' He knew the cabin and the stories of Rauff's past, his love of typewriters. The last time he saw him in Porvenir was in 1971. 'I did see him one more time,' he added enthusiastically, 'but he was dead, it was in Santiago, in an open casket.'

I expressed surprise.

'There were so many legends and myths, you see, I went to the funeral to see the body, if it was really him, and it was.'

# 46

In Porvenir, in the mid-1960s, Rauff did not get away from the gas vans.

Pablo Neruda wrote about him and the Chilean courts, which failed to extradite a war criminal who lived quietly in Patagonia. 'I cannot deny that this man understands vans,' wrote the poet. 'Nor can I deny that my country's justice system has a well-adjusted conception of reality: it protects those who efficiently organise mass murder and the use of vans.'

A West German judge wrote to Rauff, asking him if he would testify in a West German case about the gas vans. Safe in the knowledge he couldn't be extradited, Rauff consented. He testified on the construction of the vans, but denied knowledge of the use to which they were put. He liked the judge, but the feeling wasn't mutual. Rauff was hard, cold, brash and arrogant, the judge reported.

By the time the case came to trial in West Germany, one defendant was dead, Becker the chemist was too ill to appear, and the evidence against Willi Just was deemed insufficient. Rauff's testimony did help to convict Friedrich Pradel and Harry Wentritt, for aiding and abetting the murder of 3,832 human beings.

The case dragged Rauff's name back into the spotlight, so he declined to testify in the case of Werner Best, Heydrich's deputy and the man who inducted him into the SS. My memory has gone, he said. It was time to avoid publicity, paper trails and photographs, and anything else that might cause difficulties.

He put his energies into the *Pesquera Bonacic*, harvesting crabs, making sure the tins were packed tight, managing the workers. Many were supporters of Salvador Allende. 'My best workers are those who cannot read or write,' Rauff would proclaim. And the best worker was one who was deaf. 'They can't even listen to the radio!'

One day a man named Humberto Camelio came over from Punta Arenas, wanting to buy the cannery. Rauff liked him and his Italian roots, and the family, which had a local supermarket and the Ford dealership in Punta Arenas. The cannery is 'old junk, a pigsty', Rauff told Camelio, but he'd be delighted to work with him. The Camelios bought the *Pesquera Bonacic*, which soon became the *Pesquera Camelio*, with Rauff installed as the manager.

The Camelios knew of his past and, like him, were virulently anti-communist. He was given an office in Punta Arenas at Jugoslavia 1395 (today Croacia Street). His workers, including many communists and socialists, were poorly paid but well treated. Their discipline was 'outstanding'.

He kept the cabin in Porvenir, and the Camelios soon gave him a new home, a prefab next to his office. 'It arrived on a sleigh', just one bedroom, but 'what more did I want, as a single older man?' He lived there for ten years, until the cannery moved to Tres Puentes, near the Navy facility, on the outskirts of Punta Arenas.

His life was solitary. 'There is a social life in Punta Arenas, but I've totally secluded myself.' Rauff kept his head down, away from the wilder aspects of Punta Arenas, a town where 'porno films' were made and local Yugoslavs 'drank like pigs and played wildly'.

Armida (Nena) Zúñiga, who had met him on a prison visit in Santiago, soon joined him. 'I let Nena come in, and we lived together.' He called her his 'carer', not his wife or love, and considered himself to be single. Still, he admired her politics – 'she devours communists' – and the sense of security she brought. 'No one will be able to get me,' he'd say. But Rauff was so fearful that each time he went out, always with his dog, he left her a note with his expected time of return.

## 47

The *Pesquera Camelio* workers recalled Rauff's 'military style' and deep attachment to an old Olympia typewriter, and occasional incidents. The Jewish businessman who threatened to kill him. The Israeli hit-squad rumours. The fights with local workers. 'The man who invented the gas chamber had a gun in his office, and a dog, a large German shepherd,' one fisherman recalled.

The Camelios provided him with a secretary, Margarita Alegría Romero, a diminutive lady of great warmth, humour and energy. She worked as a cashier at the Camelios' *Listo* supermarket, until José Camelio and his sons Humberto and José junior bought the cannery. 'In 1964 I moved to the *Pesquera Camelio*, to produce tins of *centolla* for export to Europe, and did every job imaginable!' She said this with a guttural laugh. 'I weighed the meat, packed the flesh into cans, stuck labels, any job they needed, I did it!' 'Señor Rauff' arrived at the end of 1964, and helped the company prosper (during the Pinochet years it would be honoured as 'Chile's Exporter of the Year').

Each morning, Margarita's boss arrived with a little wave, then disappeared into his office. He was discreet, solitary, meticulous. 'His main concern was that every tin should be filled as tightly as possible with crab meat,' she said. 'He made sure the *centolla* legs were properly packed in, not hanging over the side.' With nimble hands, she deftly showed how he did it, fingers pincered, flipping imaginary legs that hung over the side back into the can, then patting the meat down firmly. 'Macabre,' she said, knowingly. She knew about his prior activities.

'We called him *El Viejo Nazi*.' The Old Nazi, not a term of endearment. 'Everybody knew about the gas vans, and the older workers were wary. "Why is this criminal working here?" they'd ask.'

Margarita worked with him until 1968. 'I stepped in, initially to take messages and phone calls, in Spanish, which he understood.' He took his own calls, work and personal. 'He had a separate telephone in his apartment, with a different number, and was so secretive and controlling that he stopped me taking calls, even from the Camelio family.'

Still, she mused, he treated her well. Margarita showed me a letter of reference he wrote when she left. 'I confirm that Señora Margarita Alegría Romero always worked to our entire satisfaction, performed her duties and was not absent from work except in justified situations.' This was the same signature as on Rauff's letter of May 1949 to Otto Wächter.

He was a man alone. 'No friends or sons visited, although there was a woman who cooked for him, and two Yugoslavs lived nearby, although they despised him, as they knew he hated Communists, including them.'

Was there a temper?

'I never saw it, but I imagine so, from the way he issued orders, so controlling on every detail.' She paused, then said: 'Actually, the truth is, we couldn't stand him.'

Do you remember Rauff? she asked her son Juan Carlos, a cartoonist. 'Yes, and his dog! I was eight, there was a myth around that he was a Nazi Jarpa.' (This was a reference to Sergio Onofre Jarpa, a virulently anti-communist right-winger, later a minister in Pinochet's government.) Juan Carlos continued, 'I learned about Nazis in Chilean comic books, where the bad ones were always Nazis,' he said, with a chuckle. 'Maybe knowing him made me become an illustrator!'

Mother and son remembered 'incidents'. 'People sent by Wiesenthal' – I hadn't mentioned the Nazi hunter – 'found him in the Braun

hardware store, next to the Cinema Palace, and tried to shoot him.'
The story made the newspapers, but Rauff didn't press charges, to
avoid publicity, and then disappeared for a few days. After that the
factory gates were kept shut and more guards hired. 'I saw how fearful he was,' said Margarita.

Given what she knew, would she be surprised if he had supported
Pinochet after the Coup?

'I would not, because of his past and his character.'

Could he have been involved with the DINA?

'I think he would do it. He did it before, and he could do it again.'

On that note, we said our farewells.

A year on, her son sent me an illustration: 'My mother and her
old boss'.

# 48

In November 1970, much to the dismay of Rauff and the Camelios, local man Salvador Allende was elected President of Chile. It was his fourth attempt, on a leftist platform, in support of workers' rights and nationalisation of the country's resources.

'I know Allende,' Rauff told his sister, 'he has visited my cannery several times.' Allende tried to invest. 'We always exchanged friendly greetings – à la Chilena, but I don't like him. He's a filthy rich man with a ferocious hunger for power and political ambition', and he would be 'crushed' by the communists. 'The situation is worse than Cuba,' he added, 'and I'm thinking of emigrating to Argentina.'

Fearing a revival of extradition attempts, Rauff adopted a cautious approach. 'Courtesy and precaution forbid me to write about the overall situation in Chile!!!' he told his nephew, while signalling reassurance. I've been elected to the board of the local lifeboat association, and am developing even closer relations to the Navy. 'The Admiral, the Chief of Staff, and the officer for public relations for the 3rd Naval Zone are aware of my dark past, but invited me to give a lecture on the German Navy to the officers.' His 'good friends' included 'several generals' and the head of Chile's secret police, he told his sister Ilse, and he had excellent contacts with Navy leaders, including Admiral Pablo Weber, who would embrace him publicly.

Two years into his presidency, Allende gave a speech condemning racism and anti-Semitism. Rauff believed this prompted the Nazi hunter Simon Wiesenthal into renewing his efforts to send him to West Germany, as a new UN treaty was agreed to end limitation periods for international crimes.

In August 1972, Wiesenthal wrote to Allende. 'International law takes precedence over national law', it was time to end Rauff's impunity. Rauff heard of the new effort. 'Mr Wiesenthal wrote a letter saying that I had not only killed Jews but also a bunch of socialists, communists and whatever else.'

Allende politely rejected Wiesenthal's request. The Nazis committed 'grave crimes', but he was bound to respect the Supreme Court's judgement. Wiesenthal then turned to West German prosecutors, who obtained legal advice and concluded there was no prospect of getting Rauff back.

Wiesenthal's efforts put Rauff's name back in the spotlight. In

July 1972, a new play on impunity – *La gran prescripción* (*The Great Statute of Limitations*) – opened in Santiago, with the main character (Walther Kock) based on Rauff. The play received poor reviews and the run was short. 'Everything that needs to be said about genocide has been said,' one reviewer complained, and the production was not rescued by the portrayal of Rauff by Roberto Parada, a leading Chilean actor.

As the play opened, there was growing political and economic instability across Chile, and mounting opposition to Allende. Strikes and conflicts, nationalisations, inflation and food shortages engendered talk of a military coup. Businesses in Punta Arenas had largely shut down, Rauff told his nephew, 'My cannery is the only one still working', he'd taken steps to avoid strikes ('my workers don't grumble, they go along with it'), and he prayed for a military intervention. 'I could give the commanding general of the Army's 5th Division some good advice,' he added. 'With a single SS division I would rule the whole country very well, but they won't let me.'

On 23 August 1973, General Carlos Prats resigned as Commander-in-Chief of the Army. Allende appointed Augusto Pinochet to succeed him. Two weeks later, on 9 September, a group of senior military officers met at the home of Admiral Pablo Weber, Rauff's friend, to plan the details of a coup.

In the early hours of 11 September 1973, Augusto Pinochet supported the attack on the Moneda Palace. By the end of the day the Coup was completed, Salvador Allende was dead, and Rauff's old friend from Ecuador was Chile's new leader.

## 49

Augusto Pinochet headed a four-man military Junta. Its stated mission was to 'restore the Chilean way of life, justice, and institutional order', and extinguish the 'principles of Marxism-Leninism' that had infected the country.

As Pinochet took control, hundreds of decrees and laws dissolved Congress and courts, outlawed political parties, halted elections and dismissed mayors. The Junta proclaimed a nationwide state of emergency, constrained unions and universities, ended the right to strike, and created dark new institutions. Rauff welcomed it all.

The DINA became an all-powerful intelligence and police service. Drawn largely from officers of the Tejas Verdes Regiment in San Antonio, west of Santiago on the Pacific coast, it acted on the direct instructions of the Junta, gathering intelligence to 'protect national security'.  Manuel Contreras headed the DINA, a gruff and brutal man who had entered the Army in 1944 and was photographed as a cadet by renowned photographer Miguel Rubio Feliz. Contreras served as Secretary of the Army General Staff under Allende, then director of the School of Engineers at the Tejas Verdes barracks in San Antonio. From 11 September 1973 he reported daily to Pinochet, and was given unlimited powers to detain, torture, execute and disappear. His deputy was Colonel Pedro Espinoza.

The events that followed the Coup are not disputed. Tens of thousands were detained, thousands were tortured and killed, and many were disappeared. In Chile the first book on the disappeared was published in July 1990, three months after Pinochet left office. *Tras la huella de los desaparecidos (In the Footsteps of the Disappeared)* listed the names of 682 men and women, of whom 51 were last seen at Londres 38.

The author was León Gómez. He was held at Londres 38 in 1974, arriving with six colleagues. He was the only survivor among them.

# 50

Until 11 September 1973, the building at Londres 38 was the headquarters of Chile's Socialist Party. It was soon expropriated and made over to the DINA, to be used as a secret interrogation and torture centre. It operated alongside many other sites in Santiago and around the country, used to target leftists: members of MIR (the Revolutionary Left Movement), communists, socialists and other undesirables. Most victims were aged between twenty-one and thirty, a majority were workers, the rest mainly academics, professionals and students. At least 3,216 people were executed or disappeared, and 31,856 were tortured.

The terror was perpetrated around the country. In Punta Arenas and Porvenir the armed forces established places of repression in full public view. Rauff knew exactly what was going on. 'A bit of shooting in the morning and by afternoon they had all the Marxists rounded up,' an elderly lady told Bruce Chatwin during his visit, not long after the Coup.

Rauff's employers, the Camelios, supported the Coup and the repressive acts that followed, and one member of the family, Salvador Camelio, served as Secretary of the Military Tribunal (known as a War Council) in Punta Arenas, under the direction of the Third Naval Zone, with which Rauff was connected. This body conducted secret trials and could apply the death penalty.

The Old Naval Hospital on Avenida Cristóbal Colón, in the centre of Punta Arenas, became a notorious detention centre. Over 1,000 people were detained, interrogated and tortured here, a place that came to be known as the Palacio de las Sonrisas ('Palace of Smiles'). Many who entered would disappear forever.

On José Ignacio Zenteno Street, close to the *Pesquera Camelio*, hundreds of detainees were incarcerated at the barracks of the 10th Motorized Infantry Regiment, the Pudeto Regiment.

The Punta Arenas football stadium served as a place of detention, holding dozens of prisoners. 'We were beaten and exposed to several kinds of torture methods,' one detainee reported. 'From their windows next to the stadium, people saw exactly what was happening.'

Political prisoners arriving at the airport from Santiago were taken to the pontoon dock of ASMAR (*Astilleros y Maestranzas de la Armada*), the state-owned boatyard in Tres Puentes that built and repaired Navy vessels, and with which Rauff worked, to be transported by barge to Dawson Island, across the Straits of Magellan. There, a special camp awaited, constructed with labour and materials from Punta Arenas, to hold Allende's ministers and advisers, including Orlando Letelier, Sergio Bitar, the Minister of Mines, and Miguel Lawner, an architect. The three survived and wrote of their experiences.

In the first weeks after the Coup, over 1,000 people were tortured in Punta Arenas. The scale was so great that everybody knew a local who was taken or disappeared.

One day after the Coup, Silvio Bettancourt, aged twenty-three, appeared before the military authorities in the town. The unmarried petrochemical engineer, active in a leftist organisation, fled from his home. Last seen on the outskirts of Punta Arenas, he disappeared.

On 29 September, José Álvarez, a twenty-eight-year-old worker, left home to visit the shops. The Army shot him dead on the street, for resisting arrest.

On 27 October, Juan Vera Oyarzún, fifty-three years old, a Communist Party official and former municipal officer, was arrested near the Argentine border. He was never seen again.

On 1 November, Carlos Mascareña Diaz, twenty-one years old, student and MIR activist, was arrested and transferred to Puerto Montt, where he was tortured, sexually assaulted and killed.

On 7 November, Juan Carlos Ruiz Mancilla, aged twenty-one, a student of engineering, was arrested at his parents' home and flown to Temuco, to be executed in the Tucapel Regiment barracks.

José Tohá, forty-seven years old, a lawyer and minister in Allende's government, who had also worked closely with Pinochet, was tortured on Dawson Island. In March 1974 he died in a military hospital in Santiago.

The Cementerio Sara Braun has a memorial with the names of many victims. The last is Susanna Estrella Obando, killed on 26 July 1988, aged twenty-three.

# 51

Porvenir did not escape the crimes. The retired schoolteacher Juan Torres Toro told me of one case. The Army arrested three local men, he said, 'I took the last photographs of them alive.' After their bodies were found, outside town, the military took his film and negatives. Juan Torres shook his head and looked towards the window. 'Porvenir? Small town, big hell.'

Rauff's life was transformed by the Coup. 'I am protected like a cultural monument,' he wrote to his nephew. He supported all that Pinochet did. 'He is doing a very good job.' The accusations against the government were unfounded, he said, there were no 'dead bodies lying in the street', and West German accounts of Pinochet's 'bloodthirstiness' and atrocities were 'nonsense'. He knew Pinochet personally, he assured his sister Ilse, he had entertained him at his home in Quito. 'I will not die in a country ruled by communism!' Rauff enthused, and 'that is worth a lot'.

Still, the past impressed upon him the need for discretion. With the Coup, he was careful about what he said and wrote about his contacts. A loose word, or a signature on a document, might cause difficulties. Say nothing. Write nothing.

Occasionally, however, he couldn't stop himself. After the Coup, Pinochet appointed his friend Admiral Weber as Intendiente (Governor) of Magallanes province. A few weeks later, in February 1974, General César Mendoza, winner of an equestrian silver medal at the 1952 Helsinki Olympics, and one of the four members of the Junta, in charge of Chile's *carabinieri*, turned up in Punta Arenas. To Rauff's great delight, Mendoza and Weber agreed to visit the *Pesquera Camelio*.

The *Prensa Austral* reported the occasion. The two men donned rubber boots, and General Mendoza spoke of the workers' 'expertise' in preparing 'highly regarded Magellan king crabs'. The visit passed without a hitch, Rauff reported to Ilse. Mendoza was 'highly capable, not pompous at all, very matter of fact'. As for 'Our Admiral' – his friend Pablo Weber – he greeted Rauff with affection and familiarity. 'How are you, Walther?' They spoke in Spanish, not German, and Rauff took care not to be photographed. 'I always, always stay behind the camera,' he told Ilse.

The reason for General Mendoza's trip was entirely unclear, and Rauff did not elaborate. The visit offered an expression of mutual support, between the Junta, the *Pesquera Camelio*, the family and their manager. Mendoza spent eleven more years on the Junta, and only resigned in 1985 when his police murdered a number of political opponents (one of whom was José Manuel Parada, the son of the actor who played Rauff in the 1972 stage play). As for Admiral Weber, a month after the visit he was transferred to Santiago, to work in Pinochet's office. Following the visit, Rauff had contacts at the very top table.

Of this, however, he said little in the letters he regularly sent to West Germany, to his sister and her son, although he did once offer a proud confession to his nephew: 'I can say with pride that from President Pinochet downward I have had many high-ranking officers, industrialists and other riff-raff come to visit me in the cannery.' The purpose of such visits? 'To pay respect for my achievements in this industry.' He was disquieted, however, when a visiting West German television crew saw right through his efforts to hide his true identity. 'Delighted to meet you, Mr Rauff,' said the reporter.

He reiterated his support for the new regime. 'Keep up' the pro-Pinochet propaganda, he urged his sister, but be discreet. He expressed gratitude that he wouldn't 'bite the bullet' in a Communist regime. He complained about Chile's bad press around the world, and the 'crap' spouted by German newspapers. He complained too about the 'fucking exiles' who attacked Chile while being paid in Russian roubles and Cuban pesos, and the stupidities of 'democratic' governments around the world.

He ranted about 'Heinrich Kissinger', the US Secretary of State, a 'flat-footed Indian' (an anti-Semitic epithet frequently used by senior Nazis). 'I am fed up to the back teeth with him, constantly on radio and television.' On the positive side, at least 'Señor Heinrich' could see there were 'no piles of corpses on the streets' of Santiago.

This he knew, as he too went to Santiago, to the *Pesquera Camelio* office, sometimes spending weeks away from Punta Arenas. He and Nena travelled on Air Force planes, I learned from Nena's nephew Raúl Donoso, a student at the university in Punta Arenas ('Rauff was short, wore a coat with a fur trim, was distant, talked little and walked in a military style,' Donoso recalled, and was very private: he didn't stay with his aunt, who told him that she and Walther 'prefer to live by ourselves'). In Santiago, Rauff stayed with Walther junior, to whom he was closer than Alf. On one occasion he delivered German certificates offering proof of the family's Aryan roots.

He complained about the Camelios. Humberto, the patriarch to whom he owed his work, was 'an awful pain in the ass!', and son José, and grandson José junior, weren't much better. They babbled, knew nothing of the *Pesquera*'s work, gave useless advice and paid miserably. And, he added, they had 'no human side', even if they treated him with kid gloves, as he worked 'eighteen-hour days'.

The letters passed in silence over other matters, about which I learned elsewhere.

Rauff said nothing of disputes with workers at the *Pesquera Camelio*, and cases that went to court, including one in which his testimony, on an allegation of theft by two workers, was treated by the judge as unpersuasive.

He made no mention of his close contacts with the Navy, or ASMAR, the state-owned boatyard in Tres Puentes, from whose pontoon a barge transported prisoners to nearby Dawson Island.

He never wrote of the DINA, even as rumours circulated abroad about his connections to Pinochet's secret police and Manuel Contreras, and he did not share that the BND took steps to find out whether the rumours about him were true.

He did, however, worry that his correspondence might get into the wrong hands, and asked his nephew to keep secret those letters that he did write. 'Not for publication in *Stern* or *Das Bild*,' he instructed. 'This letter is only for the family, not to be released to *Die Welt*.' He didn't say what the concerns were, although the letters' occasional references to Simon Wiesenthal offered a hint. He clipped newspaper stories about the Austrian Nazi hunter, and sent them to the family, signing himself off – in one Christmas card – as a 'state-certified war criminal'.

He sent photographs to his family too, indicating he felt safe enough to travel and be photographed in well-known public places. In March 1976, with Nena and her daughter he celebrated his seventieth birthday in Valparaíso at the Club Bote Salvavidas, a famous restaurant in the port.

# 52

At the *Astilleros y Maestranzas de la Armada*, or ASMAR, at Tres Puentes, on the outskirts of Punta Arenas, there worked a young mechanical engineer named Proserpina Fierro. Recently awarded a doctorate, Fierro was due to take a job in Brazil until Pinochet personally ordered her to stay in Chile. Following his instruction, she opted for Punta Arenas and a job at ASMAR. Soon after she started work there, in 1974, her fellow workers persuaded her to visit the nearby offices of the *Pesquera Camelio*, to obtain scallop shells to decorate an office party:

> I went to the *Pesquera Camelio*, entering through a side door into a large building, one with very few windows. I was directed to a staircase and walked up. At the top, I entered a vast, dark space. At the far end of the room, some distance away, I saw a desk, on which there was a big, old-fashioned typewriter. On each side of the desk was a large dog, a rottweiler, and next to each dog stood an attentive guard. Behind the desk was a man. It was Señor Rauff, and this was our first meeting.

Initially formal and stiff, Rauff soon loosened up, as he came to understand the young woman's friendly intentions. The guards left, the dogs remained. The two spoke, he agreed to give her some shells. A connection was made, and over time they came to know each other. 'He was interested in my work, and seemed to like my attitude,' she would later say. 'I was interested in the factory's processes, he took me to the boats, the small cutters that retrieved the fishing nets.'

She learned of his close relationship with the naval facilities:

> My colleagues at ASMAR would repair the *Camelio* boats, and sometimes I helped. We had naval interests in common, he was knowledgeable, I knew about his background in the German Navy. He helped me too. Sometimes parts would arrive for our naval boats, with technical instructions in German, and I asked for his help. Once, he reached out to me because he was after a special part, which ASMAR could make, to repair the gears of one of his boats.

Many, many years later she would say she knew nothing of his past, his other life. 'I was young and wasn't preoccupied by such things. I saw him as being fully integrated into this local Magallanic society. I didn't need to inquire or ask questions.' His relationship with Humberto Camelio seemed 'cordial', as was the connection with his son [José] Porotin Camelio [Rial], who she knew better. 'There was no hierarchy, it wasn't apparent who was the boss.'

During the Pinochet years they avoided talk of politics. 'The situation in 1975 was difficult,' Proserpina Fierro would say. 'The Camelios were very right wing, sympathetic to Pinochet, so was most of the business community in Punta Arenas.' The military world, of which she was a part, working on Navy ships, was strongly supportive of Pinochet. 'Forty per cent of the population in Punta Arenas was connected to different parts of the military,' she said, and there was a conflict with Argentina, over the Beagle Channel. 'The world I was part of supported Pinochet. The Camelios were of that world. Rauff was part of that world.'

Of his past, Proserpina Fierro would say she knew nothing. Nor was she aware of rumours that began to circulate around the time she came to know Walther Rauff. That he had connections to Pinochet, and that he had an association with the DINA.

## 53

The first story about Rauff appeared in July 1974, in *Le Monde*. As Pinochet replaced Chilean public officials – ministers, ambassadors, mayors – one new appointment stood out. 'A certain Walther Rauff, whom the junta has just placed at the head of the DINA, in other words the intelligence services', the French daily reported.

The article touched on his 'particularly suitable' Nazi past, 'in charge of the mobile gas chambers', and work in Tunisia for which he was 'wanted'. The image presented did not flatter, a man with 'teeth blackened by tobacco, dark blue-green eyes, almost non-existent eyebrows'.

The article prompted a strong response from the Secretary-General of Pinochet's government, Colonel Pedro Erwing. The story was inspired by 'international Marxism' and 'totally false', he said, it was seeking to portray the government as 'fascist'. It also raised eyebrows in Washington, given President Nixon and Henry Kissinger's strong support for Pinochet. Three decades earlier, Kissinger had been working for the US Counter Intelligence Corps, which was hunting Rauff.

The CIA investigated and concluded that Rauff 'has never had slightest association with any Chilean govt, including junta'. 'Total fabrication,' the CIA reported from Santiago, on the allegations, 'plucked out of thin air'. *France Soir* reported the Chilean government's denial. Yet the CIA's report, now available in an archive, contained obvious errors – Rauff wasn't living in Porvenir, and he wasn't a farmer.

The idea that Pinochet could be advised by a former Nazi and SS officer was no less problematic for the West German government, which supported Pinochet's anti-communist stance. A West German diplomat doubted the government would 'incriminate itself' by associating with a man so notorious that he'd recently been the subject of a theatrical play performed in Santiago. Nevertheless, worrying that the story could be true, the BND reached out to Rauff. 'R. himself declares that he has not received any offer to work for DINA.' As with Colonel Erwing's vigorous denial, the words were carefully crafted and open to interpretation. They did not end the rumours.

In Rome, a second Russell Tribunal – a people's tribunal initially organised by the British philosopher Bertrand Russell on the Vietnam War – examined repressive regimes across Latin America. It received information that Rauff worked for the Chilean military. No evidence was cited in support.

In Moscow, the Soviet Union's newspaper of record, *Izvestia*, reported Rauff to have an office at '38 Londres', where detainees were tortured and then taken to Tejas Verdes, near San Antonio.

In Paris, the *Ligue Internationale Contre le Racisme et l'Antisémitisme* reported that Rauff was engaged in 'new tasks' for Pinochet's government. The claim was unsupported by evidence.

The rumours blossomed, not burdened by detail. If a source was cited, it might be an 'unnamed author'. Simon Wiesenthal declared that even without evidence the information should be treated as credible. Rauff must be presumed to be a DINA 'advisor'.

Support for the presumption was not universal. The writer Rose Styron visited Chile in February 1974, with Amnesty International. Noting that Rauff was named in reports of 'Nazi influence' on the DINA's work, including allegations he helped to construct a prison camp on Dawson Island, she concluded the 'rumours' to be unsubstantiated.

In May 1975, the *New York Times* published a front-page story on Rauff and denied that he was a DINA adviser. 'Jewish community, human rights lawyers and clergymen . . . strongly denied such accusations', the paper reported.

Once a story is off the ground, however, there may be no bringing it down. In the months and years that followed, reports multiplied that Pinochet's government benefited from Rauff's services. The details differed, with tweaks and errors. A year after the Coup, the *Harvard Crimson*, a student newspaper, confidently asserted that Rauff was 'chief advisor' to the DINA's head, wrongly identifying Héctor Sepúlveda – rather than Manuel Contreras – as its chief. It offered no evidence to support the bold assertion.

In East Germany, the magazine *Panorama DDR* described Rauff as a 'most important advisor' to the DINA, an organisation that emulated the Gestapo.

In Mexico, at an international meeting, the lawyer who advised West Germany on the request for Rauff's extradition, back in 1963, 'confirmed Rauff's involvement in the DINA'.

The drip, drip, drip of stories worked their magic. By April 1976, as Henry Kissinger prepared to travel to Santiago, the CIA was shifting its position. One report – based on a 'usually well-informed source' – concluded that Rauff was 'working within the Interior Ministry of the Chilean military government'. Wiesenthal asked Kissinger to raise the Rauff issue with Pinochet, which he declined to do.

Following Kissinger's visit to Santiago, and the murder of Orlando Letelier that September, a CIA source suggested that Rauff was still associated with the BND and 'reportedly' advising the DINA. Another source, close to Pinochet's government, advised that Rauff was 'not employed by the Chilean government in any capacity'. However, many Chilean exiles believed him to be a 'principal advisor' to the DINA, and Walther junior to be 'involved in intelligence'.

By the end of 1976, the CIA concluded that Rauff 'may have some close connection with DINA', perhaps as an 'unofficial advisor'. The organisation treated Chilean denials with caution: in its view, Pinochet and his government would have 'no desire to attract world attention for having a Nazi war criminal as an advisor'.

# LONDON, DECEMBER 1998

## 54

A quarter of a century later, on 25 November 1998, the House of Lords rejected Pinochet's claim to immunity, as he celebrated his eighty-third birthday. The ruling received 'almost universal acclaim', David Hope recorded in his diary, bringing letters of congratulation and delight to Hoffmann and Steyn. Calm returned to the Law Lords' corridor, after weeks of disruption, an end to belligerent press calls, and huge quantities of paper passing through the fax machine.

For María Isabel Allende the ruling was 'a truly great satisfaction'. Miguel Lawner, the architect and Dawson Island detainee, watched the judgement being delivered in the company of Eric Hobsbawm, the British historian, who was in Santiago. 'We interrupted his lecture to follow the vote on television, and when the fourth judge spoke, I thought we had won and started to cry.' Lawner and Hobsbawm marked the occasion with a visit to Isla Negra, Pablo Neruda's home, joined by Allende's widow, Hortensia.

Other reactions were not so positive. A 'sadistic and cruel' birthday present, complained Pinochet's son Augusto junior. The ruling undermined his father's rights and those of mankind.

As Tony Blair's government said nothing, Margaret Thatcher expressed horror. In Europe, political leaders generally welcomed the ruling, while the United States offered a muted reaction.

'A landmark,' reported *The Financial Times*. 'A singularly unflinching statement,' wrote a columnist in *The Guardian*, 'bold and principled, taking a stand on behalf of the globalisation of fundamental human rights which will be seen as a milestone'. Many articles singled out Lord Hoffmann, 'the cleverest of the law lords', whose questions cut away at verbiage and 'waffling barristers'.

On the evening of the judgement, my wife Natalia and I invited the Human Rights Watch team to our home for supper. We watched a discussion on *Newsnight*, the BBC news programme, with one participant, Evelyn Matthei, a Pinochet-supporting Senator beaming in live from Chile. Hoffmann's wife Gillian 'has been working for many years in Amnesty International', Matthei complained. 'What does that matter?' retorted the host with a sneer. 'If it is true, then the ruling wasn't impartial,' replied the Senator, as Amnesty participated in the case.

Senator Matthei's words left an impression. We were not aware of a connection between Hoffmann and Amnesty International, but if true the claim raised a reasonable concern. Others noted the moment. 'I wondered if the point would be taken up,' said James Vallance White, the Clerk to the Law Lords. 'I never imagined it would go as far as it did.'

The intervention came to the attention of Miguel Schweitzer. 'Information came to us that Hoffmann had a relationship with Amnesty International, so Hernán Felipe and I decided that we must check if it was true, and if so then do something.'

Schweitzer raised the matter with Michael Caplan, who hadn't watched the programme but felt 'duty-bound to inquire further'. He hesitated, as it was unheard of to challenge a Law Lord or a judgement of the country's highest court. He discussed the matter with the Pinochet team, then wrote to Jack Straw, the Home Secretary. The judgement may have been affected by bias, he suggested, because of Lady Hoffmann's relationship with Amnesty, an intervener in the case. Amnesty confirmed that Lady Hoffmann worked with its secretariat, but downplayed her role, which never touched on anything to do with Pinochet.

On 7 December, Caplan received an anonymous phone call. 'My secretary came into the office and said: "There's a man on the line who says he's got information about Lord Hoffmann and Amnesty."' The caller, who did not give his name, said Hoffmann was a Director of an Amnesty International Charitable Trust. Caplan checked the claim at Companies House. It was accurate.

The next morning, *The Times* ran a story with the same information. Amnesty wrote to Caplan, confirming that Hoffmann was indeed one of the two directors of Amnesty International Charity Limited (AICL), an entity that funded Amnesty International Limited's (AIL) charitable activities (the other director was a barrister who argued Amnesty's case in the House of Lords). Hoffmann was

not, however, employed or remunerated by the charitable arm or
AIL, played no role in the Pinochet matter, Amnesty said, and was
not a member of Amnesty International.

'This was delicate,' thought Schweitzer. 'We analysed the situation and concluded that it was possible that Hoffmann would have
been influenced by his position.' He instructed Caplan to write to
Bindmans, Amnesty's solicitors. 'A pretty aggressive letter came
back,' Caplan recalled wryly. 'How could we even think of chal-
lenging a Law Lord or his wife?' Nevertheless, to protect Pinochet's
rights Caplan advised him he must take 'all necessary steps, however
novel, unpopular or difficult'.

Clive Nicholls, Pinochet's lead barrister, was sceptical about a
challenge. 'You must be out of your mind,' he told Schweitzer. 'The
House of Lords is centuries old and there has never been a legal
challenge to the impartiality of a judge.' Schweitzer did not blink.
In Chile, a judge in such a situation would not be seen as impartial,
why should Britain be different? Hoffmann should have disclosed the
information at the hearing or recused himself, as usually happened.
Schweitzer insisted they return to the Lords and ask the judges to set
aside their own judgement.

James Cameron, the international lawyer on the Pinochet team,
recalled Nicholls's initial anxieties. It was the failure to disclose the
relationship as a director of Amnesty that hardened views. Nicholls
was sceptical, but Clare Montgomery was clear that a problem
existed. 'Once it gets down to first principles – fairness, justice,
due process – I am comfortable making the challenge,' Cameron
said. The main doubt was procedural: how do you challenge a
judgement of the House of Lords, a court from which there was no
appeal?

'Nicholls was very honest,' said Schweitzer. 'He said, "Can you
imagine what's going to happen to me, as a barrister, if I assert that
a Law Lord has not been impartial?"' Eventually Nicholls was persuaded, but with one condition. 'He said to me: "I cannot take the
decision on my own, it must be for the whole team to decide, and it
must be on a direct instruction from the General. If he instructs me
to challenge the judgement, I will challenge the judgement."'

Schweitzer set up a meeting with Pinochet, to obtain that clear
instruction. '"You have to give your formal instruction," I told him
before the meeting.'

'We piled into Clare Montgomery's car, wedged in tight, and went off to Wentworth, through security and into the house,' Cameron recalled. Schweitzer greeted them on arrival, 'the go-between and interpreter'.

'I prepared the General, in advance, with a note, to tell him what we were going to do,' Schweitzer explained. 'I made an initial presentation on behalf of the team. Pinochet talked very little, which was in character. He said, "Yes. No. Do it. Don't do it", that kind of thing. He rarely gave lengthy explanations.' The lawyers were anxious, as was Schweitzer, who knew that the right outcome needed a particular tone. 'You could feel the tension,' said Cameron.

As Clive Nicholls spoke, laying out the issues, for and against raising a challenge, Schweitzer translated. Caplan was strongly in favour of action. 'One of the few occasions when I was more forthright than others.' Schweitzer said: 'Pinochet listened, then said, very formally, "Yes, I fully agree with this, and I assume all responsibility."'

The conversation was brief. 'At a certain point we saw Pinochet drift away, not really interested,' said Cameron. As the meeting ended, the old man in a cream-coloured cardigan uttered a few words in Spanish, which Schweitzer translated. 'If you think it has to be done, then do it. I have given you a mission, which is to return me home. That is your mission. How you carry out your mission is entirely a matter for you.'

Instruction delivered, a group photograph was taken. Pinochet offered a benign smile, surrounded by members of the team, some of whom appeared more comfortable than others. Miguel Schweitzer, on the far left, beamed. 'Can you believe it?' he said, 'it's the only photograph I have of the team with the General!'

'Pinochet said he wanted a photo taken of him and I,' said Caplan, hidden behind the General. 'We had one of us taken separately, I must have it somewhere.'

'That's the only time I met him,' said Cameron, standing tall at the back, a golfer amused to be near his club at Wentworth ('familiar territory, very bourgeois'), and well aware of Pinochet's diminished stature. 'An old man in a cardigan, power seeping away, vaguely bored by the legal discussion, until he spoke the closing words. "I have given you a mission", that was the phrase, well-used.' Words that might equally have been addressed to Manuel Contreras in the 1970s, to deal with Prats, Soria and Letelier.

'We left the house, got back to the cars, and giggled, a nervous laughter,' Cameron remembered. 'I said: "Do you think he might have said that before?" I knew the answer, of course. We had our instructions, now we had to build a case.'

## 55

Prior to any challenge, the House of Lords ruling remained in force. Under the Extradition Act, with the immunity issue resolved, Jack Straw as Home Secretary would decide on the next steps, whether to exercise his discretion to sign an Authority to Proceed. This would allow a magistrate to decide whether the conditions for extradition were met. If Straw didn't sign, the case was over and Pinochet could fly home.

As Pinochet gave his team their mission, Straw opted to issue the Authority to Proceed. This would allow Spain's request to move ahead, before the requests of Belgium, Switzerland and France, one of whose nationals was Alfonso Chanfreau.

Straw explained the reasons for his decision, although he was not required to do so. He felt a need to address the arguments of Pinochet, Spain and Chile, as well as the interveners and various British government departments. To give reasons might avoid future difficulties, political or legal.

The Home Secretary explained the need to give 'particular weight' to Britain's treaty obligations under the European Convention on Extradition. He authorised Pinochet to be extradited for six 'extradition crimes' for which the Lords ruled he had no immunity, relating to murder, torture and hostage-taking, including conspiracy, between 1973 and 1990. The crimes did not include Baltasar Garzón's charges of genocide, or any other crimes which were not extraditable criminal offences in English law.

Straw rejected all of Pinochet's arguments to allow him to go home. The General had no immunity, and the offences charged were not 'political'. The charges were not barred by the passage of time, given their gravity. It would not be unjust or oppressive to extradite Pinochet to Spain. There was no evidence he was unfit to stand trial.

Straw also rejected Chile's request that Pinochet be returned to Santiago to be tried there, as no request for his extradition was made. The mere possibility of a future trial in Chile did not outweigh Britain's obligations to Spain, under the Extradition Convention, and Spain was entitled to judge Pinochet. Claims about the effects on Chile's political stability, or on Britain's national interests, were rejected.

Straw's decision prompted much attention and scrutiny, and mixed feelings. In Madrid, Garzón, Castresana and Garcés were relieved. In Santiago, Carmen Soria was thrilled. In London, Schweitzer and Errázuriz were disappointed but not surprised. 'I tend to believe that Straw acted in an impartial, normal way,' Schweitzer told me.

Pinochet must now appear before a magistrate, to confirm his identity and be told about the next steps. Friday, 11 December was set for a hearing on whether the conditions for extradition were met, and to set the conditions for Pinochet's life in Wentworth, including visits and activities.

The hearing was held at the high-security court at Belmarsh prison, in south-east London, before Graham Parkinson, a magistrate. This was Pinochet's first public appearance. A convoy of police cars drove him from Wentworth. 'An extraordinary moment,' Caplan recalled, as the police worried greatly about an attack. Pinochet, who 'fully understood what was going on and was quite relaxed', travelled in one car, as Caplan, Schweitzer and Errázuriz followed in a police van, wearing protective bullet-proof vests. The security was intense. 'He went in a special car, a helicopter followed, the streets were closed,' said Errázuriz. The risk of an assassination attempt was thought to be real.

Jean Pateras was there too, at Pinochet's request.

'They asked me to interpret his words. They gave me a piece of paper, with a line or two on it, something about "my country".'

His mood?

'Same as always, never anything but arrogant and polite, absolutely polite.' Jean enjoyed the outing, rather unique, she recalled, for a former head of state to appear before the courts of another country charged with international crimes. 'Actually, I felt bloody good, seeing him in court. I think he was probably a bit embarrassed, but he wasn't going to show any emotion, just quiet fury.'

As the group arrived at Belmarsh prison, Pateras sensed a darkening of the mood. 'Very tense and concerning,' she recalled. Worried that Pinochet's words in court might be picked up by the media, Caplan advised him to say as little as possible. 'He wanted to say something, so we spent quite a lot of time with the court interpreter to get that right.'

Schweitzer was with Pinochet at every moment, mainly concerned that he not be made to stand in the dock, and look like a criminal.

'We realised that if he entered the courtroom in a wheelchair, we could avoid that situation.'

Could he have walked in?

'Yes, of course, but that was a bit of a thing we made up, important for two reasons. First, the wheelchair would be below the gallery where the press sat, so there was no way to film him. Second, he would be right beside the judge.'

In this way, there would be no photograph or film of Pinochet in the dock. A court drawing lacked the punch of a real image, of a colossus laid low. 'We prepared him, told him what he must say,' Schweitzer said:

> I wanted to be absolutely sure he said the right thing, so I wrote out a handwritten note for him, in big capital letters, for when the judge asked him if he wanted to say something. It said: 'My name is General Pinochet, and I reject the charges.' That was what I wrote. One line, in Spanish.

Pinochet went over the line carefully. 'I saw him practising his lines for Court,' Jean Pateras recalled. '"If I'm in my wheelchair, I don't have to stand up and acknowledge the Court," he told me.'

The magistrate went through the formalities, established Pinochet's identity and explained the process. When asked if he wished to say something, the former President put Schweitzer's sheet of paper to one side. 'He couldn't care less!' said Schweitzer:

> He just said what he wanted to say. That he was General Pinochet. That he was a Senator. That he didn't recognise any court other than the Chilean courts, and certainly not the Spanish courts. He totally ignored my words!

Later, Schweitzer gave the sheet of paper to one of Errázuriz's daughters, as a birthday present. 'I think she left it behind, so I don't know where it ended up!'

The hearing lasted twenty-seven minutes, then the magistrate wrapped it up. He committed Pinochet to be detained at the house in Wentworth, and announced that a full committal hearing would be held early in the new year. 'Pinochet broadly understood what was going on, and was stoical,' said Caplan.

The group returned to Wentworth, for tea. 'The General wanted me to sit next to him,' Jean Pateras said, as Dr Peter Dean, Scotland Yard's forensic medical examiner, checked him over. 'To make sure he was alright, which he always was.'

'We got back, had tea, little sandwiches with cucumber and eggs, or ham and cheese. It was all very nice. I felt a bit embarrassed to be there,' said Pateras. Pinochet was bothered by one thing, she recalled. 'Did you hear all the noise, people screaming at me? *¡Asesino! ¡Asesino! ¡Asesino!*' he said, as he chewed a slice of cucumber. 'One of his cronies said, "Oh don't worry, it's a motley crew, rent-a-mob, nothing serious." I just kept quiet, it was all a bit embarrassing.'

Schweitzer had a particular memory of that day:

> The General had a walking stick. As we entered the building, I said to him, 'As you know, I haven't charged time for your defence, but I collect walking sticks, I have a fine collection. My fee for this entire case will be your walking stick.' He looked up at me and said, 'Yes, in Chile, once we are back, you will have this walking stick.'

# 56

As he prepared for the hearing at Belmarsh prison, Caplan contacted James Vallance White, the Clerk at the House of Lords. 'I think he came to see me, after the telephone call,' Vallance White recalled. 'The suggestion came from me, that if he really wanted to take up the Hoffmann issue he must put in a petition, but I confess that I didn't think, back then, that it would get off the ground. It had never been done before.'

Vallance White alerted Lord Browne-Wilkinson, the senior Law Lord, who was with Lord Irvine, the Lord Chancellor and head of the Ministry of Justice (Irvine was said to be 'unconcerned' by the news). Gordon Slynn, on the other hand, who recognised a problem with Hoffmann 'from the very start', and felt he should have been firmer, turned 'white as a sheet' when he heard about Caplan's call.

On 10 December, Caplan filed a petition to challenge the judgement, because of Hoffmann's connections with Amnesty International, through his wife and as director of its charitable arm. 'The petition

was received, presented to the House, referred to the Appeal Committee,' said Vallance White. Amnesty went to the High Court
for an order to stop Pinochet from leaving the country, which was
immediately rejected. Premature and novel, ruled the judge. You can
make a challenge if Straw decides to let him leave the country.

A few days later, five Law Lords who weren't part of the first ruling met to discuss how to deal with an unprecedented application.
Nico Browne-Wilkinson was in charge. 'Not before time,' thought
David Hope. 'Nico chaired, the most painful thing, he never recovered from it, very, very painful,' Vallance White recalled, noting
Browne-Wilkinson's distress at having to deal with the fallout from
Hoffmann's failure to disclose his links to Amnesty. 'Lennie [Hoff-
mann] was away in Hong Kong, I had a telephone conversation with
him, he was pretty upset.'

As the application was urgent, the Law Lords decided the hearings
would be held the next morning. Initially, they rejected Amnesty's
application to intervene, as Pinochet's lawyers were 'perfectly capable' of dealing with the issues. Amnesty reacted negatively, causing
Browne-Wilkinson to change tack and allow them in. Fairness, he
decided, as they were involved in the earlier hearing and had a special interest in the judgement under challenge. Human Rights Watch
did not seek to intervene. Amnesty's involvement made me 'angry',
Reed Brody told me.

The hearings ran over two days, again in Committee Room 4.
Browne-Wilkinson presided, sitting with Lord Goff, brought out of
retirement, and Lords Nolan, Hutton and Hope. Once again, an
all-male, all-white, all-Oxbridge panel of judges. 'Many of the faces
in the audience in the committee room were from the affected countries – Spain and Chile, judging by dark hair, brown skins and shape
of face,' Hope wrote in his diary.

The case for Pinochet was led by Clare Montgomery. You can
annul the judgement, she submitted, and must do so to protect the
integrity of the court, as the links between Hoffmann and Amnesty
raised an obvious possibility of bias. Her arguments were 'neat,
polite, precise', Hope thought, 'and very intelligent'. The advocacy
was economical and determined, the facts 'rather shocking'.

Anxiety and apprehension permeated the Committee Room.
Michael Caplan, seated behind Montgomery, noted Goff's question.
'How do you think this would look to someone sitting at the back of

the court?' Silence. 'From that moment, we knew the judges under-stood there was a point to our argument,' Caplan recalled, although 'you never can be sure'. Alun Jones, arguing for Spain, accepted that the earlier judgement could be set aside, but argued, without much passion, that it shouldn't be. By the close of the hearing, on the afternoon of Wednesday, 16 December, Caplan sensed a decision in favour of Pinochet. He was not alone.

The judges deliberated the following morning, and needed little time. The unanimous and unprecedented ruling came in the after-noon, setting aside the judgement in Pinochet No. 1. Written reasons followed a month later, with Browne-Wilkinson writing the main opinion. The case was 'exceptional', the interest unprecedented, and Pinochet's conduct 'highly contentious and emotive'. Those who were sure of his guilt wanted him to stand trial, whereas his supporters saw him as Chile's saviour. Others thought only Chile had the right to address the question of his criminality, not Spain or Britain or anyone else.

Browne-Wilkinson then addressed the facts. Amnesty worked through two separate entities: Amnesty International Limited (AIL), and Amnesty International Charity Limited (AICL), a charitable arm which raised funds for AIL. The charity's two unpaid directors were Hoffmann and the barrister Peter Duffy, who argued for Amnesty in Pinochet No. 1. Pinochet's lawyers did not learn of Hoffmann's role until after the judgement, although there were rumours about his wife's connection with Amnesty.

Browne-Wilkinson set out the applicable principles: a judgement could be set aside if a party was subjected to 'an unfair procedure', including a danger of bias, in light of the principle that 'a man may not be a judge in his own cause'. If Hoffmann had an interest in the case he could not sit, unless he had disclosed that interest and no party objected. In this case he had made no disclosure, so there was no opportunity to object.

The ruling relied on the nineteenth-century case of *Dimes v. Proprietors of Grand Junction Canal*, where the judge failed to disclose that he owned shares in the defendant company, giving him a financial interest in the outcome. Amnesty's interest was not financial, but to obtain a ruling that Pinochet had no immunity. Since Amnesty and the AICL charity were connected and had the same goals, as a director of the latter, Hoffmann could be said to have a direct interest in the outcome. Having failed to disclose this, he was automatically disqualified. There was no actual bias, but a perception of possible bias existed. Having so decided, there was no need to address his wife's work with Amnesty.

The judges did not point a finger of blame, or say that the failure to disclose was entirely innocent. In his separate opinion, David Hope wrote that Pinochet was 'entitled to the judgement of an impartial and independent tribunal', and judges knew not to sit in a case where they had 'the slightest personal interest'. This was especially important where Amnesty had long campaigned against Pinochet. Hope's diary offered more colour and context. 'There was never any doubt in our minds about the result once we had heard the facts,' he wrote, and by lunchtime on the first day Pinochet's lawyers were 'pushing at an open door'. Hope claimed that Slynn advised Hoffmann not to sit, and thought Hoffmann was 'foolish' to discard the advice. He also thought that Hoffmann's position on his wife's work with Amnesty – there was no problem – was reasonable, but his silence on the directorship was not. James Vallance White shared Hope's perspective, and was clear that the earlier judgement must be set aside.

Hope's diary noted that the ruling 'generated no real protest'. Outside the Palace of Westminster, Pinochet's opponents lingered then melted away. The initial judgement on immunity was dead, the case was back at square one. A new hearing would take place, before different Law Lords.

Michael Caplan and the Pinochet team were delighted. 'We're back in this case, but where do we go from here?' The British government was embarrassed. 'In the highest degree unfortunate,' Lord Irvine told a journalist. He'd 'ensure that this does not happen again'.

In Madrid, Castresana thought the decision was reasonable, but Garcés was horrified ('I assumed the Pinochet lawyers knew about Hoffmann'). Garzón was incandescent, knowing he and Jones would have to start all over again, that their historic victory was snatched away. Amnesty's lawyer thought the Law Lords had gone 'overboard', that the application was an 'extremely far-fetched, remote and improbable argument'. In Santiago, Pinochet's opponents were as distressed as his supporters were thrilled. I knew it would be a long game, thought Carmen Soria. The Chilean government now had to decide whether to intervene in the new case.

There were isolated calls for Hoffmann to resign, but no crescendo of voices. 'Lennie has brought our system into disrepute,' Hope thought, but couldn't be forced out. He made a mistake, he must decide what to do. Hoffmann would have known, Hope added, 'that if he did not sit the chances of the case going in favour of Pinochet would be increased', and that outcome was now 'more likely'. Vallance White also thought the new panel would 'go back to the Bingham judgement'.

# 57

Hoffmann did not resign, and the Lord Chancellor supported the decision. A quarter of a century on, I reached out to Hoffmann. There was a modest connection, as my father was his dentist for many years, and he lived nearby. I dropped a note through the letter box, opposite the house where the poet John Keats once lived.

A few weeks later a handwritten reply arrived. 'I am entirely willing to talk to you about Pinochet, but I rather think you must already know more or less all the information I can provide . . .' Spring passed, then summer. In the English autumn, we agreed to walk on Hampstead Heath. 'I can pick up some marmalade at Kenwood,' he suggested, near the house where the legal saga began, with Nicholas Evans's signature of the first arrest warrant. We wandered past swimming ponds and swans, and headed into the woods.

He had not wanted to talk about this. An academic was once in touch, long ago, but he declined. 'I didn't know him.'

Have you read Hope's diaries?

'No. Did he say anything about me?'

'Yes,' I bumbled, scrambling to recall the details. 'Lennie was determined to [sit],' Hope wrote, words I paraphrased.

'I didn't take any steps to make it happen, but I certainly wasn't sorry to sit,' said Hoffmann.

So what happened?

'It was a cock-up.'

A cock-up?

'Yes, a cock-up. I talked about it with Gordon, he wasn't concerned about my past relationship with Amnesty.' Hoffmann told

Slynn he'd advised Amnesty a few years earlier, on the organisation's charitable status:

> Gordon was more worried about Gillian, who worked as a sec-
> retary for Amnesty. He thought I shouldn't sit, but I couldn't see
> why my wife's role should be an issue. Why should I be excluded
> because my wife works for Amnesty International? That seemed
> wrong in principle. Gordon didn't agree. He would have preferred
> I decide not to sit.

The sun peered through the clouds:

> I told him I had another connection with Amnesty, as chairman
> of a separate charitable company, which hived off its educational
> activities and did some fundraising. I think Pinochet's lawyers
> contributed, Kingsley Napley, so I didn't think it was a secret I
> was involved. Gordon said he wasn't worried about that. It was
> separate, charitable. In the end, he didn't object.

Did you mention these points to any of the other judges?
'No.'
Did you think about disclosing the fact to the parties?
'It never occurred to us to do so. That's why it was a cock-up. We should have, in retrospect. If we had, I doubt the parties would have objected.'
Yes, that's what some of Pinochet's lawyers told me, I said.
He didn't mention that another person raised a concern. Only later did I learn that James Vallance White had been dispatched to raise an issue about Lady Hoffmann's work with Amnesty. 'He sent me out with a flea in my ear,' Vallance White recalled. 'When Gordon Slynn went he got the same treatment. Gordon told me he wished he'd been firmer.'
As we walked, Hoffmann and I recalled the moment the judge-ment was disclosed, like a penalty shoot-out, he the scorer of the winning goal.
Why didn't you write an opinion of your own? I asked.
'I thought the Nicholls judgement more or less said what I would have said, although I didn't agree with everything he wrote.' Later, a senior judge shared that Hoffmann, who he saw on the evening

of the judgement, told him it was best not to write a judgement, 'because of Gillian's link'.

We reached Kenwood House, big, white and beautiful in the evening glow. A man at the shop said they were fresh out of marmalade.

What did you think of the ruling to set aside your judgement? I asked.

'I didn't think it was inevitable, or even the right thing, but I didn't object to it. It was a reasonable view.'

'It damaged your friendship with Nico Browne-Wilkinson?'

Silence. I hesitated to push the point.

'It wasn't what the judgement said, but how it said it, and what it didn't say. There were no words to say our approach was reasonable, no usual courtesies, when a judge makes a mistake. They didn't say anything, I thought that was wrong.'

And Nico Browne-Wilkinson became depressed by what had happened?

Silence, again.

Would Hoffmann like to see a draft of my account of our conversation?

'You can show me if you want to, but no need.'

The sun was down, the gates around Kenwood were locked.

'We'll have to climb over the fence,' he said. We did, six feet of metal, with sharp prongs at the top. I joined my hands to offer him a step up and over, then followed. Not bad for a retired judge in his eighties. I tore my trousers.

## 58

A few months later, I came across an interview Hoffmann had given to an oral-history project at the British Library, back in 2011. I hadn't known about it when we met, he didn't mention the project, and it was only made available on the internet after we'd spoken.

The earlier account was consistent with our conversation, with some details added. Hoffmann spoke of the distress caused by the media, the decision not to give interviews, a Chilean refugee who greeted him in a restaurant and asked to shake his hand. He thought the set-aside judgement was 'rather cold, an unfriendly act'.

Hoffmann's relationship with most of the judges was not damaged, however. He felt affection for Slynn, who behaved 'entirely properly' throughout, although that may just have been 'politeness'. Steyn and Lloyd were sympathetic and invited him to lunch.

'I've always been very grateful for that.'

The others?

'I didn't have any close relationship with them, and that just continued.'

The first and only time a judgement of the House of Lords had been set aside, he mused. 'A major thing, a constitutional event.' Still, he had doubts. The principle relied on had only been applied to a case involving a financial interest, not other circumstances. 'I had no financial interest and no connection with Amnesty as such, the campaigning people who were appearing before us, no connection whatever.' The ruling extended the law to deal with his situation, he believed. 'Quite a bit of an extension.'

Looking back, how do you feel?

'It's the kind of banana skin that could happen.'

I met with James Vallance White, but only after the conversation with Hoffmann – tea and fairy cakes at his cosy home in Pimlico, with his wife. He confirmed what I knew, that Hoffmann had told him he couldn't be saddled with his spouse's activities. 'My wife and I have our own lives, I can't be responsible for her,' he told Vallance White.

Vallance White shared a recollection. 'At the beginning of the hearing, I think I noticed Slynn look towards Hoffmann, as though he expected him to say something, but he never did.' If he had made a declaration, no one would have objected, I suggested. 'Of course,' said Vallance White, 'I bet he wishes he had.'

What about Hope's suggestion that Hoffmann was determined to sit on the case?

'I'm not so sure,' said Vallance White.

His wife interjected. 'He was gagging to do it,' she surmised. 'Your wife didn't want you to act for Pinochet, he wanted to sit on the case.'

# PART III

## IMMUNITY

*There is a man in Punta Arenas who . . . hears the shells
crack and the claws breaking, sees the sweet white flesh
packed firm in metal cans.*
Bruce Chatwin, *In Patagonia*, 1977

# NIGHTS IN PATAGONIA

## 59

Walther Rauff made a new life in Punta Arenas, the 'southernmost town in the world' according to Esteban Lucas Bridges, explorer and author of *Uttermost Part of the Earth* (1948). A fine and sympathetic account of the region by an Englishman who grew up there, *Uttermost* was one of Bruce Chatwin's favourite boyhood books and inspired him to write *In Patagonia*. I needed to go, in the footsteps of Bridges, Rauff and Chatwin, in the company of their books.

Like Roberto Bolaño, I came to understand that there is no bright line separating truth and fiction in Chatwin's pages. He visited Punta Arenas shortly after the Coup, so Allende and Pinochet don't dominate. Rauff's appearance in the penultimate chapter – dreaming of pine forests and humming German Lieder – was unexpected. The writer heard rumours of the efficient man who invented the gas vans and ran a king-crab cannery, but from Chatwin's moleskin notebooks it seemed they didn't meet. I imagined the two passing on a street, or standing on the Plaza de Armas, at the unveiling of the bald bronze bust of José Menéndez.

Punta Arenas is 'utterly to my taste', Chatwin wrote, with 'overtones' of Edgbaston, Birmingham, his father's city. The Patagonian town was a nineteenth-century construct, a colonial settlement of log huts, wooden stockades and convicts. A century on, it was a place of vibrant trade and commerce, as the Straits of Magellan offered a direct route between the Atlantic and Pacific, until the Panama Canal opened in 1914. After that the town returned to greater obscurity, inhabited by people of many backgrounds, including Croats, English and the Germans who welcomed Rauff. By the time he first visited, in 1925, most of the indigenous population had already been exterminated.

I visited several times, and met many interesting characters, including ladies who filled tins with the flesh of king crabs, under the close supervision of Rauff. Every Sunday, in the Plaza de Armas, the city honours a group. When I was there it was the turn of the *Bomba Alemana*, the German firefighters, which allowed me to chat with a smiling lady who had rosy cheeks and bright-red lipstick. She wore a tunic full of medals and a *Stahlhelm* that would have warmed Rauff's heart.

The signs of German influence were many. The Lutheran church; an old postcard of the German school, with a portrait of Hitler in the background; a shop's cabinet filled with Nazi memorabilia and embroidered swastikas. At Vieja Patagonia, a café-cum-emporium, the owner offered to find Rauff's old typewriters, or a pair of his shoes. The Museum of Punta Arenas gathered a fine collection of Austrian and German artefacts, as well as José Menéndez's ancient automobile and rusting Shell-Mex oil cans emblazoned with inverted swastikas.

It's a dreamy place, is Punta Arenas, with fading colonial buildings and neatly laid-out streets, grey and low and windy, and so very far away. I stayed at a hotel carved out of a wing of the old Sara Braun Palace, with a wood-panelled bar named after Ernest Shackleton. As he prepared to cross the Antarctic the explorer had lodged with Chatwin's ancestor. It was here that I first met men who were imprisoned on Dawson Island.

'I saw Rauff once, on Hermann Eberhard Street,' said Alejandro Ferrer. The street was named after the German explorer who, in a cave near Puerto Natales, discovered the ancient sloth skin that inspired Chatwin's journey and book.

'No doubt Rauff was a torturer, we all knew about that and his work at the *Pesquera Camelio*,' said Baldovino Gómez, a former school inspector. The Camelios were a reactionary family, Ferrer added, fervent supporters of Pinochet and the Club Andino, the local ski resort they founded. 'The Camelio kids skied in Europe, which no one else in town did.' Shortly before the Coup, the *Prensa Austral* published a story with a photo of José Camelio, sporting a moustache and dark glasses, preparing to fly to Europe with sons Eduardo, José and Jorge, to learn the French style of skiing, more modern than the Austrian technique.

Ferrer was arrested shortly after the Coup, taken to the local Pudeto Regiment barracks, then to Dawson Island. His crime was to be a socialist. 'I was there for Christmas, with Orlando Letelier, who played a guitar and sang old Mexican songs.' Ferrer himself then burst into song, a few lines from *Grítenme Piedras del Campo* by Cuco Sanchez, 'Soy como el pájaro en jaula', I am like the bird in a cage. The two of them, Ferrer and Gómez, chuckled at the memory.

The local university invited me to give a talk about Rauff. The audience was not so young, but Andrea Pivcevic, a former student of mine, showed up, and reminded me of a party I gave on a summer day in London, when I pointed over the garden fence to the room where Nicholas Evans signed Pinochet's first arrest warrant. She now runs a small airline with penguins painted on the aircraft tails. 'The only airline to offer flights to the Antarctic!' she said with pride.

'I was a friend of one of Rauff's sons,' one attendee said.

'How did he die?' another inquired.

'Will you go to Porvenir?' asked a third, a former Dawson Island detainee.

Rauff's shadow was tangible, delicate and persistent.

'Proceed with care and respect,' someone said.

'Why do you come here looking for a German Nazi when you could write about the crimes committed by Chileans?' asked another, pointedly critical. It was a decent question. I explained my interest in continuities and connections between Europe in the 1940s and

Chile in the 1970s, between Rauff's reception in the region and what I had heard about the extermination of the Selk'nam.

That evening, we went to the restaurant of the Hotel Savoy, transported to another age. We ate *centolla*, the southern king crab that dominated Rauff's later life. René the waiter, a man with very fine eyebrows, wore a white wing-collared jacket that bore his name and a black *corbata de cordón*, the bootlace tie that gave the evening a sense of history.

I visited the large cemetery, with its German, English and Croatian gravestones. A red plaque honoured the town's German colony, a black memorial with the four shell casings that Rauff and his colleagues placed on each corner. 'Dedication by the *Cruiser Berlin*, Punta Arenas, 25.12.1925.'

The building where Rauff was arrested is there, on Calle Bories, but the Grand Palace cinema is long gone. This was also where he was attacked by a Jew, Margarita Alegre told me. I wandered along Croacia Street (formerly Jugoslavia) to number 1395, once occupied by the *Pesquera Camelio* and Rauff's prefabricated home, today an empty lot.

At Tres Puentes, near the Navy and ASMAR facilities, where the fish were processed, I peered inside the home Rauff moved to in 1975. 'Much better than the single-person hut' on Jugoslavia, he would say. At Sotito's, his preferred restaurant, I ate *centolla*. At the former Club de la Unión, where he dined, I admired the wood-panelling.

At the Museum of Punta Arenas, the ponytailed director spoke of efforts to gather testimony about Dawson Island. 'No one wants to talk about the place,' he said. 'It's a taboo subject because the torturers still occupy every corner of our town.' Punta Arenas was 'a silent community, a place of total impunity with a dark, hidden history'. There were few visible memorials to mark the crimes of the Pinochet years. The plaque that hung on the wall of the football stadium disappeared during a protest. The Pudeto Barracks had nothing. The Old Naval Hospital (the 'Palace of Smiles') was burned down before it could be transformed into a museum of human rights.

And Rauff?

'He was one of ours, the subject of so many rumours,' the museum director said, 'a man with a terrible past who lived openly and freely in our town.' The sense of impunity goes back generations, he said. To make his point he showed me an old photograph, taken on Dawson Island in 1899. It showed hundreds of members of the Selk'nam and Kaneka indigenous communities being held, under the watchful eyes of Chile's President and Germany's consul in Punta Arenas.

Within a few years, the original inhabitants of these lands were gone.

## 60

On the mythologies, there was no better guide than Chatwin. I walked the streets with a dog-eared and heavily annotated copy of *In Patagonia*, starting at the Palacio Sara Braun, on a corner of the Plaza de Armas. I hoped to see the bronze bust of José Menéndez, 'bald as a bomb', as Chatwin recorded, but it was gone, torn down during a recent protest, painted green and purple, then placed at the foot of the Selk'nam warrior statue with a sign: 'Menéndez Braun, Asesinos'.

Known as the King of Patagonia, José Menéndez was born in Spain and came to Chile via Argentina. He played a key role in the extermination of the Selk'nam, assisted by his foreman Alexander McLennan, known as The Red Pig. McLennan appears in Chatwin's book and is brutally portrayed in a recent film, *Los Colonos* (*The Settlers*).

I crossed the Plaza to the southern corner and the Braun-Menéndez Palace, constructed with stones from France. Here, in a dining room with velvet drapes and white damask, Chatwin admired the amorous geese painted by José Ruiz y Blasco, the father of Pablo Picasso, who was said to have done the feet. An Englishman with a history degree from Oxford told Chatwin that the talk of Indian killings was 'a bit overstretched', that the Indians of Tierra del Fuego were a 'pretty low sort', not like the Incas or Aztecs. 'No civilization or anything,' the Englishman opined.

On the Avenida Colón I stood before the 'Palace of Smiles'. There, I read Sergio Reyes' account of his treatment – beaten, immersed in human excrement, subjected to electricity. After that he was sent to the Pudeto barracks, then Dawson Island. Somehow he survived, and still hopes for a measure of justice. Destroyed by fire, the fading green frontage of the Old Naval Hospital was a monument to impunity and nothingness. Opposite stood pillars of sad concrete bearing the names of the sons and daughters of Punta Arenas who were executed.

Up the hill I went, along Avenida España, to number 959. It was green in Chatwin's day and still is, the iron gate that marked the entrance to the 'solid Anglican gloom' of a double-gabled house with two towers, one square, the other octagonal. Here lived Charles Milward, or 'Cousin Charley', who sent Chatwin's grandmother the slice of sloth skin that opened a small boy's imagination. Milward spent hours in the octagonal tower, armed with a telescope, spying on the warehouses of Tres Puentes and the island across the Strait, where Allende's ministers would later be corralled.

In Punta Arenas, Cousin Charlie Milward was a most generous man. He offered a gift to the British School and the Anglican Church of St James, a plot of land behind his house. Here, on a Sunday morning in February 1975, an American Baptist minister took the Matins service. 'He asked us to pray for Pinochet,' Chatwin wrote, 'but we were uncertain of the spirit in which our prayers were offered.'

Further along the street, down the hill, I stopped at the offices of the *Prensa Austral*, in whose archives Rauff featured. 'The Co-Director of Eichmann's Office Arrested in Our City', a headline reported on 6 December 1962. He worked for an 'important' local business, not named, Rauff said. 'I am innocent and have no idea what I am accused of.' Yes he was a Nazi, he said, yes he served in a secret intelligence unit, but he was 'just another victim of the war'.

From the archives it was apparent that the local newspaper followed every step of the extradition proceedings, from arrest to release. When Rauff returned to Punta Arenas, everyone knew of his work with gas vans. His demeanour was 'even more reserved and silent than usual', the paper reported.

Over time, interest in Rauff diminished. In March 1974, a decade after he returned, the paper reported General Mendoza's visit to the *Pesquera Camelio*. It didn't mention that Pinochet's colleague was welcomed by the cannery's general manager, a former Nazi who disappeared tens of thousands of people.

Mendoza visited not long before Chatwin was in Punta Arenas. This I learned from a letter the writer sent from the Hotel Cabo de Hornos, on the Plaza de Armas, in February 1975. These were active days for the Pinochet regime, the 'Palace of Smiles' operating at full capacity, with rumours about Rauff in the air and the pages of foreign newspapers.

From Chatwin's correspondence I learned that after Punta Arenas he returned to Europe, renting a small house in a village in southern France. This was where he wrote *In Patagonia*. 'Our terrace marked with a pretty indistinct arrow,' he scribbled on a postcard to his father, in December 1975, with an address: 12 Rue Droite, Bonnieux.

I read the postcard in Bonnieux, where I spend a part of each year writing. I left our house, wandered up the hill to the Rue Droite, and sat on the steps of number 12, thinking about the meaning of coincidence. Francis, a local mason, ambled by.

Do you know who owns this house? I asked.

'Madame Maillet,' he said, 'the owner of our local bookshop in Apt, the lovely Librairie Fontaine.'

I called her. She had no inkling that *In Patagonia* was written in her family's house and our village. She was thrilled, and so was I. We had dinner in the room in which Chatwin wrote of Rauff, and later she invited locals to an evening there, to pay homage to a writer who had walked from the village of Bonnieux to Le Baumanière at Les Baux, a restaurant sixty kilometres away ('a solitary and enormous lunch,' he told a friend, '*Paté des anguilles aux pistaches, Noisettes aux Chevreuil* etc', explaining that he'd 'conceived a plan of walking to all the best restaurants in France').

# 61

Far from Bonnieux, in Punta Arenas and other parts of Chile, I hoped to meet descendants of the families involved in this story.

The Camelios were still prominent in the city, but seemed less than keen to be in touch. A friend in Santiago reached out to Silvana Camelio, the daughter of José, Rauff's employer. 'He was like a second grandpa to us,' she recalled. 'He managed the fishery like a Swiss clock. He controlled the personnel, knew all about tides and logistics, that was pretty much all I heard over dinner. In my family you had to be a boy to be more involved.'

She suggested a conversation with her brother, Eduardo, but he was not keen. His daughter, however, a schoolteacher and a poet, was more open. 'My father was a kid when Rauff worked for the fishery,' Mariana Camelio wrote to my friend Rodrigo Rojas, a poet. From the family she recalled a story from the mid-1970s, when Rauff's dog was killed. The Camelios gave him a puppy, a German shepherd that he called Rex. Her father, a young boy at the time, didn't forget Rauff's reaction. 'It was the first time the little boy saw a grown man cry.'

I obtained a copy of Mariana Camelio's recently published book. One poem, 'Laguna Grande', about a 'grandmother I do not know', struck a chord, chiming with Chatwin's language and Rauff's work. She allowed a translation in English to be read during a lecture I gave in Liverpool, in honour of the Irish poet Seamus Heaney:

> one day we found king crab skeletons
> from the main house we saw
> red spots on the peat

We exchanged messages, and participated together at an event at the Bodleian Library in Oxford, on Chatwin's book *In Patagonia* and the archive. Mariana's presence, by video from Patagonia, enriched the conversation, a direct connection with place and the person.

The night before the event she sent a photograph of Rauff, with her grandfather and great-grandfather José, taken in the late 1970s, in Punta Arenas. It could have been his leaving party, and it was the first time I saw Rauff in colour. He stood awkwardly, between father and son, one hand in his pocket, the other holding a Lucky Strike cigarette. He wore a light-coloured Pepita suit, the tie pushed under the jumper, a handkerchief folded into the breast pocket. The glasses were familiar, the posture awkward, the face troubled. He looked uncomfortable in the presence of a camera.

A few months later I met Mariana and her boyfriend in Germany, where they were travelling. She drew a family tree, spoke of Italian origins and family silences. 'I only recently became interested in Rauff,' she said, 'and started to speak with my father, who remembered him from the 1970s.' She offered to show me around Punta Arenas, which a few months later she did.

I saw the school where she taught, and the wooden house she

shared with her boyfriend and cats, a garden flush with plump rasp-
berries. We visited her mother's art gallery, Rauff's house at Tres
Puentes, and the natural-history museum run by friends, with art-
works and the skeletons of whales and penguins.

'Let me take you to Rauff's house at 1395 Jugoslavia.'

'It's gone,' I said.

'It is elsewhere,' she replied. We drove to the Club Andino, a few
minutes away, the local ski resort established by her family. 'They
moved the house here, it's used to store ski boots and other things.'
We walked past the Club house, up the hill, a ski slope, until we
reached a clump of trees, their trunks covered in a fine moss. Here
was the house in which Walther Rauff lived with Nena.

Mariana persuaded her father to join us for a meal that evening.
'He'll say very little,' she warned. He joined us at a small restaurant,
where we ate *ceviche* rather than *centolla*, but the conversation did
not flow so easily. Eduardo Camelio didn't really want to talk about
Rauff, but he opened up a little.

'As a boy, when I was six or seven years old, I was scared of him,'
he said.

Yes, the family knew about his past when they hired him. 'My father knew the details.' Eduardo plainly wished to minimise Rauff's role. 'In Nazi Germany he was a minor character, not like Himmler or Hitler. He told us he only signed documents about the gas vans, to get his young assistant off his back. At the fishery he was just an employee, my father was in control.'

Rauff was strongly anti-communist, like the family. 'He said fascism was better than communism.'

Rauff refused to give interviews, he despised journalists. '"The evils of the twentieth century are journalists and cancer," he'd say.'

'He never spoke of himself,' said Eduardo, 'except when he was drunk, after a whisky or two.'

Eduardo Camelio remembered General Mendoza's visit. 'He didn't come to see Rauff,' he insisted, although how he could know was not clear. 'Pinochet visited too, in 1976, or maybe 1978.'

Eduardo recalled the dog his father gave Rauff. '"This creature gives me back the will to live," Rauff said, then wept. Rex slept with him and Nena.'

Eduardo also remembered Miguel Schweitzer. 'There was a holding company, called Distribudora Graham, or something like that. My father and the Camelio family had an interest, together with Miguel Schweitzer.'

'Everything is connected,' said Mariana.

Do you want to know about the rumours of Rauff's connection with the DINA? I asked Eduardo.

'That's an interesting question,' he said, but not one he wished to address. My question punctured the mood, introduced an element of discomfort. Our dinner was soon over.

# 62

Eduardo Camelio did suggest we meet Marcelo Brossard, who invited the three of us to his neat bungalow on the outskirts of Punta Arenas.

'I started at the *Pesquera Camelio* in August 1973, just before the Coup,' he said. 'I worked as Rauff's secretary. He was strict, meticulous and punctual, and treated me like a lieutenant.' He started at Jugoslavia Street, but a year or so later moved to Tres Puentes. He worked on production, statistics and the fishing boats. 'Rauff had notebooks, wrote everything down.'

Almost immediately, unprompted, Brossard said that Rauff never left Punta Arenas. 'He only travelled once, it was in 1973, two or three days in Santiago.' He said this with certainty. Mariana and I had the impression it was intended to head off any suggestion that Rauff might have spent time elsewhere during the early Pinochet years.

In response, I showed him the photograph of Rauff and Nena at a restaurant in Valparaíso, in March 1976. Brossard looked at it. 'They lived together, but I never did know if she was a wife or a domestic.' The mere fact of the photograph – and its date – surprised him. He had no explanation. 'Rauff stayed out of the picture, in the shadows, he didn't want to be noticed, never allowed photos.'

Brossard had no memory of General Mendoza's visit to the *Pesquera Camelio*, in March 1974. I showed him the photographs published in the *Prensa Austral*. He recognised the ladies. I mentioned what Eduardo Camelio said of Pinochet's visit.

'No,' said Brossard, 'Pinochet didn't visit the factory, he sped past in a motorcade, as we waited outside the factory.' Rauff swivelled his head from left to right, fast. 'He was disappointed that Pinochet didn't stop to greet him.'

Until I told him, Brossard said he wasn't aware Pinochet and Rauff knew each other from Ecuador. 'Occasionally he talked of the past, the German Navy, Rommel in North Africa, Italy, the voyage to South America. He never mentioned Quito or Ecuador. I knew he was a colonel in the Gestapo, and he told us that after the war Nazi officials prepared a travel schedule, and he was offered Punta Arenas.'

Brossard understood my smile. The many lies of Walther Rauff.

'He was very anti-communist, and extremely anti-Semitic. Once, the grandfather arrived at the factory with two or three businessmen who were Jews. When Don Walther saw them coming, he disappeared, went off to his office, to hide.'

Because?

'Fear and anger. He didn't wish to see any Jews.'

Like Eduardo Camelio, Marcelo Brossard did not wish to hear anything about rumours of Rauff's activities after the Coup. He said he knew nothing of Rauff's connection with people at ASMAR, or the Navy, and wasn't curious to know more.

Could Rauff have had a secret life of which you were not aware? 'I don't think so.' He swatted away the question. 'He was just too busy working.'

Brossard did not wish to talk about Pinochet or the DINA. He was happy talking about whisky and Lucky Strike cigarettes, Rauff's 'nice grey Ford Transit', and Miguel Schweitzer, who also visited the *Pesquera Camelio*. 'He was a friend of Humberto and José Camelio.'

# 63

Miguel Schweitzer has a son who is also called Miguel Schweitzer, and he happens to live in Punta Arenas. A few years earlier, in 2016, President Piñera appointed him as the Governor of Magallanes, the same position held in 1974 by Rauff's friend Admiral Weber.

He was happy to meet. Over dinner, he spoke of his father's links to the Camelio family, which went beyond friendship. 'My father did legal work for the *Pesquera Camelio*,' he said. 'The connection was through my mother, my father's first wife, who was the cousin of Ema Camelio, who was Humberto's wife.'

Later, Paula Polanco, the second wife of Miguel Schweitzer whom I knew in London, confirmed the connection. 'Yes, my husband did some legal work for the Camelios in the 1980s. He settled the firm's bankruptcy proceedings, although he didn't really like that work.'

I did once ask Miguel Schweitzer, Pinochet's lawyer in London, about Rauff, before others told me he knew the Camelios and did work for them.

'Of course I know the name of Walther Rauff,' he said.

Just the name?

'I knew him well,' he continued. 'I had various types of relations with Walther Rauff. First, Rauff himself, second, with his son. Because Walther Rauff was intended to be extradited by the West German government, which asked my father – back in 1962 – to be the lawyer for the government of Germany in the extradition of Rauff.'

Miguel Schweitzer, whose father later became Pinochet's Minister of Justice, was a student then. 'I participated in the writing of my father's legal report, for the West German government. We understood that that extradition of Rauff couldn't succeed, because of the statute of limitations. Human rights issues were not what they are today. We gave an opinion, and declined to represent Rauff, who ended up with Enrique Schepeler, a quite famous criminal lawyer.'

'The application by the West German government for the extradition of Walther Rauff was rejected,' he said. 'And by the same token, a semi-relative and political relative of mine, who had a very good fishing business in Punta Arenas, Camelio, had contracted Walther Rauff the son, who worked with him until he died.'

Miguel Schweitzer, who I sat next to in the Pinochet hearings, seemed to be connected to everything and turn up everywhere, a Zelig-like figure. In the 1950s he was a friend of Laura González-Vera. In the 1960s he worked on Walther Rauff's extradition case. In the 1970s he negotiated the Letelier deal with the Americans. In the 1980s he was Pinochet's ambassador in London, then Foreign Minister, and did bankruptcy work for the Camelios, semi-relatives. In the 1990s he was Pinochet's lawyer in London.

'I know quite a lot about the Rauffs,' Schweitzer continued.

Do you think he worked for Pinochet? I told him about the rumours I had heard. 'I can tell you the details. I would have to go back and try and see what we can remember,' he said, then changed direction, sharply. Hernán Felipe Errázuriz, who worked for the Ministry of Foreign Affairs at the time, thought Rauff should be extradited, when the West Germans asked again, in 1984. 'He was looking at it politically, I told him that he was wrong.'

He returned to the subject of Rauff and Pinochet, two men he knew.

'Yes, we can help. You say there is good, important evidence about Rauff's involvement? You won't find it, because there wasn't any. It's not a matter of being withheld or hidden. There wasn't anything.'

It wasn't clear if Schweitzer was saying I wouldn't find any evidence of Rauff's involvement with Pinochet or the DINA, or that Rauff never worked for them and wasn't involved in the crimes.

## 64

'Rauff was not an easy name to grow up with in Chile,' said Walther Rauff III, the grandson of Walther Rauff the Nazi. 'The name causes difficulties, even discrimination, I have lost work because of it, so have chosen a quiet life.'

We first met at the Roggendorf, a German café in a Santiago suburb that made real apple strudel, and stayed in touch. He was generous in response to my requests. Bearded and solid, in his mid-fifties, Walther III was born in Santiago in 1967, a genial and gentle man in a pink sports shirt and beige shorts. There was no immediate resemblance to his grandfather. Like Mariana Camelio, he said that the past was not a subject much talked about in the family.

His father arrived in Chile in the late 1950s. He enrolled in the Army school, but soon left to go into business. 'It gave him a decent life,' said his son. Walter II followed in his father's footsteps, leaving Navy school after a year, then working for various companies, including one established by a man of German origin who was said to have Nazi sympathies.

He was relaxed talking of his grandfather, a man he remembered with affection. 'We knew that Pinochet befriended him in Quito, and suggested that his sons should move to Chile, to attend military school.' Pinochet's friend and victim, Carlos Prats, assisted by sponsoring the sons' applications.

Living in Punta Arenas, Walther III rarely saw his grandfather but recalled those encounters with warmth. 'I got on better with him than my father,' a boisterous and showy man. 'My grandfather was quieter, treated me more as a partner.'

Once he visited his grandfather in Punta Arenas, but never went to the *Pesquera Camelio*, or Porvenir, and had no desire to go now. 'I'd prefer to go to Berlin with you and my daughter,' he said to me, 'to learn about my grandfather's life there.'

The memories were vivid. 'My grandfather was not a tender person, he was sarcastic, with a dark sense of humour, which I liked,' he said. 'When he came to Santiago, he often brought cans of crab meat, because of his job at the Camelio factory.' In the mid-70s, they smoked cigarettes and played cards, for hours.

'My family supported the Coup', to end the political turmoil and shortages. After the Coup, he saw more of his grandfather, as a pattern emerged. 'He came quite often to Santiago, stayed at our house, slept in my bedroom. He was well dressed, always wore a tie. He was bald, shaved each morning, often carried a book, was a heavy smoker and had a nice gold lighter.' Something else stood out: 'My grandfather wore ugly glasses, with thick lenses.'

What did your grandfather do all day?

'Each morning, he would leave, in a suit. He said he was looking for work.'

Looking for work?

'I don't know what that meant, I was a boy.'

After Rauff retired from the *Pesquera Camelio*, in June 1978, he moved to Santiago with Nena Zúñiga, his companion. He got a small house in the Los Pozos district, near his son, and spent time with his grandson. 'Nena was nice, took care of him, treated him like a God.' Walther III didn't recall anything odd about the house. Army people visited, his father's friends, there were parties and card games. 'And no, there weren't swastikas in my grandfather's house!' he said with a chuckle.

'Years ago I went to the Imperial War Museum in London,' he said, 'and saw a document that mentioned my grandfather and the gas vans. I am aware of the allegations, but I loved him as a grandson.' He accepted his grandfather was an active Nazi who committed crimes during that period.

'I like to think he did not want to do what he did, that if he could, he would have been a conscientious objector.' In the family, the Nazi period was a delicate subject, one to be avoided. 'My grandfather was a doer, one who carried out tasks he was instructed to perform. He was not a decision maker.' Occasionally, if a grandson asked questions about that period, the grandfather fobbed them away. A single word. Yes. No. Maybe.

'May I ask a question?' Walther III asked me on another occasion. 'I am not sure if my grandfather really liked Hitler, I think he was quite elitist, what do you think?'

'Your grandfather was a true believer,' I said. 'To the very end of his life, each year he celebrated Hitler's birthday. To the end of his life, he was an anti-Semite.'

The grandson said nothing. When I mentioned the CIA documents, or rumours of a connection with the DINA, Walther III looked at me, without expression. 'When I was a boy, we were a common, boring household, I didn't notice anything strange. I never smelled that anything was going on.'

He recalled that his grandfather liked to write, and when Rauff died, his 'notebooks' went to his son, Walther junior. Walther III thought they ended up with his father's second wife, Beatriz Vázquez, his widow. 'I doubt he wrote about the past,' said the grandson. Relations with Beatriz the stepmother were not good, so Walther III doubted if she still had the books, or would share them.

Still, he was curious. 'I don't care if my grandfather was a demon, I just want to know what he did, if anything, in the Pinochet years.'

The grandson accepted the evidence as to his grandfather's role with the gas vans, but had difficulty with rumours about a role in the DINA years. 'I don't believe my grandfather worked for the DINA or Pinochet.' He said this clearly and repeatedly.

I gave him copies of his grandfather's letters, the ones that mentioned General Mendoza's visit to the *Pesquera Camelio*, the friendship with Admiral Weber, the reflections on 'Heinrich Kissinger', on how under Pinochet he felt safe, like a 'protected monument'.

'I don't know anything about these matters,' said Walther Rauff the grandson. 'I don't want to open that door.'

# SANTIAGO, 1979

## 65

In July 1978, Rauff left Punta Arenas for Santiago, with Nena. He looked on his time with the Camelios with pride. 'I created the most modern factory in Punta Arenas, and for a while in the whole of Chile,' he told a friend, 'everyone expresses respect for the industry I created.'

At seventy-two, decades of Lucky Strike cigarettes and whisky had taken a toll on Rauff's health, and he'd undergone surgery on his stomach. Having failed to arrange his pension, the Camelios would still pay a modest salary, supplemented by a West German naval pension (but 'only for the period from 1924 until the Nazi period,' he complained, barely 'enough to pay for the dog food'). A Chilean pension was not possible without a local birth certificate, a fact that Rauff blamed on the legal adviser of the Punta Arenas registry, who he believed to be Jewish.

He acquired a bungalow in Santiago at 7243 Los Pozos, in the Las Condes district, close to Walther junior and the grandchildren. He invested in a maritime brokerage established by his son – South Pacific Corretaje Marítimo Ltda – opting for a company flag that bore a similarity to the design of its Nazi counterpart, but with a purple background, rather  than red. He worked on translations, occasionally for a fee, and read books on the Nazi era. Werner Brockdorff's *Flucht vor Nürnberg* (*Escape from Nuremberg*), in which he featured, was 'all nonsense, with everything made up'. The grandchildren observed him scribbling into notebooks, and he even managed the first seven pages of a memoir, whose working title was 'From Adolf Hitler to Sara Braun'.

He listened to *Deutsche Welle* radio and immersed himself in West German newspapers sent by his sister Ilse. There was much to irritate him. Rudolf Hess's incarceration at Spandau prison was a disgrace. The government's refusal to give Karl Dönitz, Hitler's successor, a military funeral, was unforgiveable. Criminal cases brought against former Nazis were an appalling idea. The American television series *Holocaust* – 'a very good business for the Jews' – was a disgrace. 'Poor Germans, having to watch such crap,' he said, and hoped the series wouldn't be broadcast in Pinochet's Chile. It was.

His letters offered vitriol and expressions of anti-communist, racist and anti-Semitic hatred, with accounts of birthday celebrations for Hitler and complaints about Kissinger and Jews. Judge Fontecilla's 1963 extradition ruling still rankled, the judge's wife was a Jew! He hoped a friend's daughter would not fall in love with 'a Negro'.

Rauff wanted to visit West Germany, but couldn't because of Simon Wiesenthal. A friendly West German diplomat in Santiago – 'nice man, his father of the same persuasion as me' – warned that the risk of arrest was too great. Rauff remained obsessed with Wiesenthal. 'Coming to terms with the past' is a 'nonsense', he told friends.

Rauff didn't always check out his correspondents. Ernie Z, a German-born journalist in North America, passed Rauff's letters straight to Wiesenthal, confirming he was alive and well and living in Santiago, 'well protected by the dictatorship', and that remorse wasn't his thing. 'I am no fanatic, but regret nothing I have done in my life, and would change nothing.'

The news stories didn't go away. An article in *Le Monde* on the Nazi revival, by a renowned French sociologist who fought in the Resistance and spent time at the Ravensbrück concentration camp, mentioned Rauff's 'placement with the DINA'. Chile's cultural attaché in Paris, Dr Julio Retamal, responded firmly: his country had no connection with the 'appalling ideology' of Nazism, and the claim about Rauff was 'invention' and unproven 'calumny'.

Such articles caused Rauff to worry he might suffer the same fate as Eichmann, or worse.

## 66

On the evening of 25 June 1979, Rauff's son Walther junior received an unexpected phone call. General Karl Wolff was on a tour of South America, in the company of a writer, helping him with his memoirs. The two were in Santiago, Wolff explained. He'd found Walther junior's phone number in the local telephone directory and was hoping to meet his father.

The former SS-Obergruppenführer, Himmler's one-time deputy, had been Rauff's comrade and boss in Italy. At the war's end, Wolff cut a deal with the Americans – Operation Sunrise – assisted by Rauff, and so avoided the Nuremberg trials. Wolff was later convicted by West German courts, spent five years in prison, and then seven more, for aiding and abetting the murder of 300,000 Jews at Treblinka. He was released early, in August 1969, on grounds of ill health.

Rauff was thrilled to meet his old boss, after a thirty-five-year gap. 'I've expected everything in my life, but not this!' he told Wolff as they reminisced about Operation Sunrise and sharing a prison in Florence with Frau Himmler and her daughter. Rauff resisted Wolff's informality. 'Mr General, I insist, or should I say Obergruppenführer, as my military education does not allow me to refer to you as *du*.'

Over four days, the writer taped the conversations and took photographs. It was a while before the materials became available, including transcripts and tapes, which ended up in the archives at Stanford University in California. They reflected the warmth between two old Nazis. 'I'm against the press, not against writers,' Rauff told Wolff's friend, as he shared the first seven pages of his memoir. Perhaps the writer might help him once Wolff was done.

Rauff wore a light-grey Pepita suit and a chequered tie. The writer noted his 'corpulence', the 'tightly combed back' hair, twinkly eyes and 'thick horn-frame' glasses. He recorded the details of Rauff's small home (three rooms, kitchen, bathroom, a small courtyard, all 'well-furnished in traditional Chilean style'). It was as neat and tidy as a German home should be, Wolff thought, and well stocked with whisky bottles from around the world. Rex the German shepherd, the gift of the Camelios, barked madly, as Rauff served glasses of

white wine, personally labelled for Don Walther Rauff by the Viña Linderos winery.

The writer thought Nena seemed to be a 'wonderful companion'. Each year, Walther celebrated the Führer's birthday, she said. 'Good, good, good,' said Wolff. She's 'an enemy of communists and Jews'. 'Good, good, good,' said Wolff. The writer noticed that when a delivery man approached the house, Rex barked wildly. 'He's delivering the gas,' Rauff explained. 'In Chile it comes in cannisters.'

Rauff spoke of his years in the Navy, his warm feelings for Hitler ('he would have done well to learn from Napoleon'), and his love of whisky and smoking. He spoke of his 'Berliner Schnauze', a propensity to speak frankly, and the morning paper. Did you see that Brazil refused to extradite Gustav Wagner, the commandant of the Sobibor extermination camp? said Wolff.

'Wagner was with me in Damascus, a splendid man,' Rauff retorted.

Rauff spoke of the 'gas vans thing'. It was a much 'exaggerated' project, he said, one that began before he joined the SS. He said he was implicated because he signed a document to get the 'annoying' chemist Dr Becker off his back, and now the killings were forever 'on my head!' If only the documents were destroyed, and there was no Wiesenthal. If only Heydrich hadn't put him in charge, 'because I organise things and get them done'. He didn't know how many gas vans were made, he never saw one in action. When three were parked in the Gestapo's yard on Prinz-Albrecht-Straße, he didn't even look inside.

He boasted and bragged and complained. The Jews who lied about his time in Tunis. Dealing with his wife's illness. His connections with the intelligence services in Nazi Germany and the BND in West Germany, and now in Chile. His connections with the German Embassy in Santiago were excellent, he would say, as they were with Chilean Generals and Pinochet.

'In Chile I am a monument,' he told Wolff and the writer. 'General

Pinochet was in my house in Ecuador several times', and 'all the Generals are my friends'. 'I have been in Chile for twenty-one years now, I became good friends with intelligence people.'

Curiously, Rauff offered no details on his work in intelligence, in any of the four periods. Equally striking was the fact that Wolff and the writer never asked Rauff a question about his work with any of the intelligence services. It was as if the subject was out of bounds. The DINA was not mentioned. This despite the fact that the writer knew of Rauff's work with the BND, and he had seen the materials in his files about the rumours of Rauff's work with the DINA.

My instinct was that the silence was not accidental.

On their last day together, Wolff invited Rauff and Nena to lunch at the Munich restaurant in Santiago, with beer and cigarettes. On parting, Wolff offered Rauff a book about Rudolf Hess. 'To my dear loyal friend, retired Colonel Walther Rauff, in heartfelt solidarity in memory of our time together in Italy 1943–1945,' Wolff wrote in the book.

Wolff and the writer left, continuing the tour of South America. They flew to Bolivia, to meet Klaus Barbie. They searched for Martin Bormann and Josef Mengele, without success.

Rauff was energised by the visit. He was not, however, aware of its true purpose.

This I discovered by accident.

# 67

I was searching for information about the gas vans when I came across Rauff's name in a Jerusalem archive, in a manuscript written by Yossi Chen, a former operative of Mossad, the Israeli intelligence agency. Written in Hebrew in 2007, it existed in a single copy, fifty pages of which were devoted to Rauff. They focused not on his wartime activities, but on events that occurred in 1979 and 1980.

I obtained a translation into English. It told me that Wolff's journey to South America had a different purpose: it was a reconnaissance mission called Operation Stainless Steel, in the service of Mossad, intended to gather information on Rauff so as to bring him to trial in Israel, or failing that, to execute him.

Mossad had focused on Rauff in 1949, when it was created, for his role in gas-van operations. The article referenced Willi Just's technical report, on the murder of 97,000 Jews, Rauff's 1945 affidavit, and Eichmann's testimony. There was a photograph, said to depict a 'gas van invented by Rauff camouflaged as an ambulance'.

From the files I also learned that Mossad followed Rauff's 1963 extradition proceedings, and that fearing an Eichmann-style abduction he had requested extra protection. The files described Rauff's recruitment by Mossad's Shalhevet Freier in Rome, and that it was only when Rauff was arrested in December 1962 that Freier realised who he'd recruited. 'Walther Rauff, a war criminal and murderer of the Jews, was a source of intelligence for the officials of the State of Israel prior to its establishment,' a Mossad agent reported. 'Walther Rauff met with Israeli representatives, provided them with information and received money in exchange – that is a fact.'

In 1977, Prime Minister Menachem Begin instructed Mossad to focus on Rauff and other Nazi war criminals. His government decided to catch Rauff and bring him for trial in Israel or, if that wasn't possible, to kill him. A new Mossad department was created – named the 'Message' (רסמ in Hebrew). In March 1978, Rauff was given the code name 'Bone Destroyer', and Mossad instructed Freier, by then a research physicist at the Weizmann Institute in Israel, to travel to Chile to find him. A local Mossad agent in South America found the name of Rauff's son in the Santiago telephone directory.

Mossad believed that Rauff owned the *Pesquera Camelio*, and a Punta Arenas businessman reported him to be living near the fishery, where he liked to walk his German shepherd dog. After *El Mercurio* published a story suggesting that Rauff had moved to Santiago, Freier's trip was postponed, as Rauff's whereabouts were uncertain. In November 1978, Señora Peñaloza, a Chilean lady who taught English at a Jewish school in Santiago, informed the Israeli Embassy there that Rauff was living at 2960 Alonso de Ercilla Street. When the information proved to be incorrect, Freier's trip was again postponed.

In December 1978, Mossad came up with the idea of using a friendly journalist to gain access to Rauff. The intelligence agency identified G, a senior reporter with a weekly German newspaper, as the right person, and he was travelling to South America to research a story. He was considered to be 'excellent and trustworthy', and willing to assist in the hunt for Nazis. I realised G was the 'writer' who had accompanied Wolff on his trip to South America, in reality a journalist of the kind despised by Rauff.

In January 1979, a senior Mossad agent met G in West Germany, and it was agreed he would tour South America with Karl Wolff, who would 'open doors'. Wolff 'did not know about G's secret activities and missions on behalf of the Mossad', or that G had previously worked for Mossad to gather intelligence on Nazis.

In June 1979, G and Wolff embarked on a two-month tour, starting in Santiago. On 26 June, they visited Rauff at his home, Los Pozos 7243. G duly provided Mossad with full details – Rauff was 'about 1.68 metres tall, with blue eyes, dark hair with dark grey bristles on his scalp, wore glasses, and had a plump body'. He was reasonably well off, living with a woman of Chilean descent and a lively German shepherd dog that 'never stopped barking'. G offered details about the house, surrounded by a garden and a hedge, enclosed by a brick wall with a large iron gate. He warned that passers-by could easily be seen from the living room, and the house was well lit at night. Rauff rarely left home and had no car, so he often walked to the Avenida Colón to buy groceries from a store he liked, or to hail a cab.

In November 1979, at a meeting in Hamburg, G gave Mossad two reports, one on Rauff, the other on Klaus Barbie. He provided a description of Rauff's neighbourhood, photographs of the house, and details allowing Mossad to draw up a floor plan with precise measurements. He also gave information about Rex, the highly excitable German shepherd.

Rauff has a 'dishonest' look, G reported. He hoped his information would allow Mossad to 'hurt' the old Nazi.

G 'has no doubt as to our intentions,' Mossad concluded. It would now decide how to act.

## 68

Operation Stainless Steel targeted Klaus Barbie and Walther Rauff at the same time. Mossad decided to act quickly, before either man could be alerted by a story that G might write in *Stern*, his magazine. The operation would be carried out on 17 December. This was delayed, and it was decided to kill Rauff first.

In February 1980, a surveillance mission was undertaken on his house, including escape routes. Over several days, Rauff was observed as doors and windows stayed open in the warm summer evenings, while he watched television. The alley was quiet but the dog barked loudly and aggressively if anyone approached.

The execution date was set for Thursday, 17 March 1980. Nine agents were assigned to the hit, including a shooter, a back-up, security personnel and car renters. Dozens more were involved behind the scenes. The preferred option was to execute Rauff as he left the house or returned to it. The back-up plan was to entice him into the front yard and execute him there, or inside the house. Nena Zúñiga would be killed only 'if she constituted an operational risk'.

The Mossad team flew to Santiago a few days in advance. A document would be left at the scene, stating Rauff's name, his SS number and crimes, Chile's refusal to extradite him, and a black and white Nazi-era photograph. The document was signed by 'Those Who Shall Never Forget', with a blank space for the execution date.

On the evening of the operation, rented vehicles were prepared, communication lines tested, exit routes checked. At nine o'clock, the team set up in a parking lot near Rauff's home. If he failed to take a walk, the team would return each evening until the operation was executed.

With two executioners in the parking lot near the house, Rauff failed to appear. The two returned the next day. Rauff again failed to appear, so the two approached the house. Nena suddenly emerged, alerted by Rex. At the front gate, when she blocked their entry, they enquired in Spanish about a random person. 'The woman replied rudely and raised her voice aggressively: "What do you want!" She started to shout, angry and impatient, in Spanish, "You have nothing to look for here!"'

At that point the dog went ballistic, barking loudly and continuously and running about. The assassins worried about the neighbours, and weren't sure whether Rauff was inside. The dog continued to bark, Nena shouted ever louder. They thought about entering the house to 'eliminate' Rauff, then decided to abort the operation. If they tried to enter, the woman's shouting might attract neighbours or passers-by, and she might even attack them. Having decided not to kill her, and with no other options, they retreated, left, and decided not to return immediately. Rauff was now alerted that something was up. For reasons never explained, the operation against Rauff was abandoned.

Mossad harboured a deep sense of frustration and failure for many years. Rauff's name remained on the list of targets. In March 1983, G returned to Chile, and fed back to Mossad that Rauff was still living at the same address.

I found the document's author, a former Mossad agent called Yossi Chen. 'I didn't really know who Walther Rauff was,' he told me, so the story merited only a modest chapter. He wasn't involved in the operation, but its failure was 'personally painful'.

He wrote the chapter in the 1990s, he said, so his memory was far from complete. Now retired, he had worked with some of those involved, but most were no longer alive. The operation against Rauff was classified Top Secret, so G's name and others were blanked out.

'Who was G?' I asked.

Yossi Chen chuckled.

'I know who G is, but I can't tell you.'

'I think I know who G is,' I said.

'He was a liar,' Chen blurted out. He laughed.

'He is still alive, in his nineties.'

'He is? Well, he was a con man,' said Yossi Chen. 'He was the one involved in the deceit about the memoirs of Hitler.'

That was the confirmation I wanted.

'The Hitler Diaries,' I said. 'G is Gerd Heidemann, right?'

Yossi Chen laughed. 'Yes. A liar and a con man.'

The writer who accompanied Wolff was renowned and notorious, a journalist with *Stern*. Four years after the visit, he sold the rights to his story on the lost diaries of Adolf Hitler for 10 million deutschmarks. When the diaries were exposed as fabrications, causing embarrassment to many – including Oxford's renowned Regius Professor of Modern History, Hugh Trevor-Roper – Heidemann was fired from the magazine. He was charged, tried, convicted, and sentenced to four and a half years in prison.

He declined to meet with me.

Rauff never learned the true purpose of the visit from Wolff and Heidemann.

# 69

After the visit that nearly cost him his life, Rauff carried on as before. Grandchildren, German radio and newspapers, letters, walks, the Horst Wessel song 'Die Fahne hoch', Simon Wiesenthal, whisky, Hitler's birthday.

A year after the failed assassination, an Australian journalist found the name of Rauff's son in the telephone directory. William Bemister filmed Walther junior's house – 'a sleepy street, some kilometres from the city centre' – as two small girls cycled around. One was Rauff's granddaughter, the other said she knew where Rauff lived. They led him to the small house at Los Pozos 7243, with the iron fence, exactly as Heidemann reported. Rex the German shepherd was there in the yard, agitated and barking madly.

An older woman opened the front door. She wore a colourful summer dress, yellow, red and blue, and spoke Spanish in a high-pitched voice. Here was Nena, protective and angry as ever. No, she didn't know anyone called Rauff, and got angry with the girls. 'Inexplicably hostile,' Bemister reported. She shouted to the girls,

'Which one of you brought the gringos here to cause trouble?' 'Walther Rauff sold out for a packet of sweets,' said Bemister. Nena slammed the door shut with such fury that Bemister had no doubt this was where Rauff lived.

For a week, he and the crew hung around. One day, outside the son's house, a short elderly man in a blue shirt with white dots approached. Bald, with thick glasses, he walked nonchalantly, turned towards the camera and stopped at the entrance. Bemister approached.

'You live here in Santiago, don't you?' he asked.

'Yes,' said Walther Rauff. His English was decent, the German accent gruff, like the one heard in the Porvenir supermarket, buying packets of Lucky Strike cigarettes.

'You're staying here today, are you?'

'I must phone up to the jurists,' Rauff responded tetchily.

'Solicitors? Are you still fighting your case?'

'Noooo,' Rauff exclaimed, safe and satisfied. 'It's finished, completely finished! I am not guilty. I want to say only the verity.'

'Only the whole truth?'

'Not more.'

'Will you say that in an interview with me?'

'No,' Rauff responded briskly. 'You are not here only for me, or other things too?'

'You say you are being blamed for these things that happened, why don't you just say it's not true?'

Rauff thought about this, squinting.

'You know, we have now seventy-three years, for Mr Wiesenthal we are dying and they are failing the clients for him.'

'What do you think of Mr Wiesenthal?'

Rauff chuckled nervously. 'No, less than me.'

'It's like the hunter and the hunted?'

Rauff chuckled, and went inside his son's house.

## 70

In 1982, a financial crisis in Chile caused the *Pesquera Camelio* to file for bankruptcy. The Camelios hired Miguel Schweitzer, the son of Pinochet's Justice Minister, to deal with the legal issues. 'He did it for the family,' Schweitzer's second wife, Paula Polanco, told me, 'but didn't enjoy doing it.' The arrangements that followed safeguarded Camelio family assets, and ended Rauff's monthly payments.

A year later, on a visit to the supermarket, Nena Zúñiga suffered a fatal heart attack. Rauff did not attend the funeral rites, her nephew told me, or the funeral.

Around the same time, Klaus Barbie, the 'Butcher of Lyon', was arrested in La Paz and extradited from Bolivia to France. Charged with crimes against humanity, he would be convicted and sentenced to life imprisonment.

The arrest prompted Simon Wiesenthal to write to Pinochet, to request that Rauff be sent to West Germany.

This in turn prompted Beate and Serge Klarsfeld, French Nazi hunters, to focus on Rauff. In January 1984, Beate Klarsfeld flew to Santiago to protest outside his house and Pinochet's office at La Moneda. She was arrested, but her actions prompted Israel to ask that Rauff be extradited to Jerusalem.

A month later, Wiesenthal asked President Reagan to push Pinochet into extraditing Rauff to West Germany. Wiesenthal's push came with a global postcard campaign calling for the extradition.

Reagan encouraged the government of West Germany to call for Rauff to be expelled from Chile. The European Parliament in Strasbourg called for Rauff to be deported to Europe. British Prime Minister Margaret Thatcher asked Pinochet to expel Rauff. It's 'deplorable' that he should be living comfortably in Chile as a free man, she told Parliament. French President François Mitterrand and West German Chancellor Helmut Kohl soon followed suit.

On 1 March 1984, the West German Embassy in Santiago called on Pinochet to expel Rauff to West Germany.

Pinochet was now under serious pressure, with Thatcher's call hurting the most. 'Your father is creating a lot of problems for me with the British government, with this extradition matter,' he said to Walther Rauff junior. Still, he resisted the calls. Rauff had committed no crime in Chile, and the Supreme Court had ruled against extradition. Twelve million postcards will not cause President Pinochet to change his mind, his Foreign Minister declared.

On 5 March, Pinochet gave an interview to *Newsweek* magazine, at La Moneda, under a tapestry emblazoned with a favourite motto (*Por la razón o la fuerza*, 'By Reason or Force'). Noting the old-world charm, Catholicism and anti-Marxist zeal, the journalist asked questions that irritated him.

Corruption in Chile?

'Slurs,' he said tetchily.

Democracy in Argentina, and criminal proceedings against high-ranking military officers?

He was entirely 'calm' on that subject.

Torture and disappearances in Chile?

'If anyone is tortured, he has the right to go to the court to seek justice against wrongdoers,' Pinochet retorted. 'You are free to go to the courts if you wish to verify cases of torture. You will not find any.'

Walther Rauff, the 'notorious criminal'?

The journalist did not know that Rauff had been admitted to The German Clinic in Santiago, with breathing difficulties. 'I will not send him to West Germany,' said Pinochet. 'Principles have to be respected, and the case of Rauff was decided in 1963 by the Supreme Court.'

The journalist persisted.

'I could not care less for Rauff as a person, I don't know him at all,' said Pinochet, which was a lie, but the journalist didn't know that. 'I regret that he committed so many crimes, but that was a long time ago.' The courts have spoken, I can do nothing. 'Of course, if entirely new evidence, totally different from the evidence presented to the Supreme Court in 1963, were presented, the situation would have to be reviewed again.' There was no such evidence.

Couldn't he expel Rauff as an 'undesirable'?

'No, I won't expel him,' said Pinochet. 'He is being used to hurt me and my government, by suggesting we "harbour Nazi war criminals"'. Pinochet understood the distinction between extradition and expulsion: in 1977 he expelled Michael Townley to the United States, rather than extradite him, not wanting to create a precedent that could be used for Contreras or Espinoza, or indeed for him.

'Extradition is quite different from expulsion, which is an internal matter,' he told the journalist. 'Rauff has done nothing in Chile that would make him an undesirable. He has broken no laws. He is old. He lives in Chile, alone, in his private jail: the jail of conscience.'

Rauff was safe, and Pinochet knew his extradition laws.

# 71

After being discharged from The German Clinic, Rauff moved in with his son. He died on 14 May 1984. Natural causes, reported *The New York Times*, whose obituary described Himmler's former 'deputy' as one of the world's 'three most wanted war criminals'. It made no mention of any connection to Pinochet.

'The Rauff file is closed,' declared Simon Wiesenthal in Vienna.

'The Rauff problem is solved,' said Beate Klarsfeld in Paris.

'Rauff Is Dead', ran the front page of the *Prensa Austral* in Punta Arenas, and it offered some local reminiscences.

'Generous, with a good heart, reserved, educated and well read, inseparable from his dog, a German shepherd,' a friend recorded.

'A man who knew much about organisation and discipline,' said an acquaintance.

'A good administrator,' said a fisherman, and 'a suspicious man, who felt persecuted'. He recalled his distinct voice. 'We knew what he did during the war and didn't dare ask questions, but we sometimes aimed jokes at him, which caused him to laugh.'

'A beautiful person,' said a man who sold typewriters with Rauff at the Sara Braun store in the 1950s.

'A man who was afraid and hardly talked,' said his former gardener.

'A typical German,' said a court clerk. 'His black military boots impressed me the most.'

A man who enjoyed his anti-Semitism and 'exploits', with no hint of remorse or regret, said a local who worked for him.

'One of the best administrators at the *Pesquera Camelio*,' said a man in Porvenir. He didn't integrate with the community, and rarely left his home, 'except to go to the lagoon where there were flamingos'.

\*\*\*

Rauff's body was taken to *Der Erlöser*, the German-language Evangelical Lutheran church in Santiago. The funeral service was conducted by Bishop Ricardo Wagner, before a large crowd. His eulogy focused on Rauff's 'love of the sea', and his first visit to Chile, in 1925, but said nothing of his past. 'No one can know with absolute certainty what another person has or has not done,' said Pastor Wagner, prompting a modest protest.

The coffin was taken to Santiago's central cemetery, the procession led by his son Walther junior, with friends, acquaintances and sympathisers. Grandson Walther was not allowed to wear his uniform. 'The Navy school didn't want to be linked to my grandfather.'

The Pastor spoke a few words, the coffin was lowered into the ground, alongside Rauff's second wife Edith. At this point, a large grey-haired man in a black leather, SS-style coat approached the grave. Miguel Serrano, a former Chilean diplomat and prominent local neo-Nazi who adored Hitler, and was the nephew of the poet Vincente Huidobro, invited comrades to raise their right arms in Nazi salute. 'Heil Walther Rauff!', 'Heil Hitler!', they shouted.

'The funeral made me extremely angry,' said Miguel Lawner, Allende's architect and Dawson Island detainee, recently returned from exile. 'How could I accept he be buried in the company of Nazis, led by Miguel Serrano?'

# 72

Four decades later, I met Pastor Wagner at his home in a neat apartment building in central Santiago. Bald and bespectacled, he greeted me with tea. His wife sat next to him, holding his arm in one hand and a Covid mask in the other. 'I didn't know about the man's past when they contacted me,' he said. 'I learned only as I prepared the funeral, when the son told me.'

'How could you do a funeral for such a criminal?' a colleague asked.

'I would have done Allende's funeral,' Pastor Wagner replied. The equivalence said much. 'The dead man doesn't matter, the only important thing is the family.'

The stories of his father's Nazi past weren't true, the son claimed. 'He denied everything, it wasn't my role to ascertain the facts.'

'Had you never heard of Walther Rauff,' I asked the pastor, gently. Be careful, said the wife's eyes. 'Maybe I saw the name in the newspapers, maybe I knew about the extradition case.' He turned to his wife. 'He deserved a burial.'

Did you know the rumours about Rauff's connection to Pinochet, or the rumours he worked for the regime?

Pastor Wagner sidestepped that one. 'I was born in Transylvania in 1939, when the Russians came we escaped and went to Austria. My father fought on the Russian front, the SS wanted him to join but he wouldn't, he volunteered in the Hungarian army. Why don't they judge everybody, like the ones who rape women?' This was a reference to Red Army crimes.

I repeated the question. No, he knew of no rumours. 'We knew he was a Nazi, and I wonder now whether they only asked my husband to officiate, whether others refused,' interjected Mrs Wagner. Sipping tea, the pastor recalled a packed church with many gathered outside, people he didn't know. He remembered the Nazi incident, when Rauff was in the ground. 'A group of men in civilian clothes, doing Nazi salutes and shouting "Heil Hitler".'

'I didn't like it,' said the pastor, and he recalled the 'nasty things' before the burial. 'As we left the church, there was shouting and jeering from groups of Jewish people and the press, left-wingers and communists.' They asked to make a statement, before the funeral, but Pastor Wagner said no, inviting them to be respectful. 'I didn't like it,' he said again.

'It upset him that the crowd bothered the sons, when they were in pain,' said the Pastor's wife.

After the funeral, the papers asked how Pastor Wagner could officiate? It went on for years. 'I wouldn't have changed my mind, even if I knew all the facts.' He heard about people being gassed in vans, but before him was a father's corpse, he had to focus on the son.

Are you sure you buried Walther Rauff?

The Pastor looked puzzled. There's a rumour another body was buried. Hernán Felipe Errázuriz told me that the Israelis asked the Foreign Ministry to view the body, to make sure it was Rauff.

'I didn't know that,' said Pastor Wagner. 'The son must have believed it as he was obviously devastated.'

Did Pastor Wagner see the corpse?

'No. It was, as usual, a closed casket.' He stopped himself. 'Maybe the Israelis came to the church, but I don't remember, or . . .', he paused, '. . . maybe this happened at the cemetery, which is more likely.'

Television footage showed the coffin leave Rauff's house, carried by two men, who lifted it easily into the hearse. Later, when the coffin was removed from the hearse and carried into Pastor Wagner's church, four men struggled.

'What does that mean?' Pastor Wagner asked.

That the body hadn't left the house?

'I wonder if the government killed Rauff,' he said, a reference to Pinochet.

He never saw the Rauffs again, but occasionally thought about the son. 'He was convinced his father was a good man. The problem now is for the grandson, knowing what the grandfather did. That is a problem of many Germans, in these times.' Not just Germans, I thought, but did not say.

The Pastor moved to other horrors. 'In the twentieth century we had two horrible experiments, Nazism and Marxism, with the same goal, a society with no classes, in which opponents were killed or sent into psychiatric units.'

Our eyes met.

'The problem with the Nazis,' he continued, 'was not that they were bad men, but they believed in another understanding of man, one based on the idea of "the other". The ones who signed the orders' – did he mean Rauff? – 'wanted an Aryan society. The beasts were the men in the concentration camps torturing and beating, not the ones who signed the orders. These were good men with good hearts, the others were the devils.'

I didn't know what he meant, and didn't wish to enquire.

Pastor and Mrs Wagner didn't like what happened to Pinochet in London. They hadn't heard of Rauff, and they hadn't heard of Londres 38. Villa Grimaldi rang a vague bell. 'Bad things happened there, but in which totalitarian regime has this not happened?' asked Pastor Wagner.

Was the Pinochet regime totalitarian?

'Yes, but there was a democratic referendum at the end. Pinochet thought he'd win, but he lost, then left. Which other tyrant would have acted like this? Not the Cuban.'

## 73

Walther Rauff's death did not end the rumours about the DINA. The US State Department revisited its files, concluding there was 'no information to substantiate' a connection between Rauff and Pinochet's government. It was possible, however, that he 'served in some unspecified, unofficial capacity'.

'Chileans regularly saw Rauff walking with a briefcase to Londres 38, where his office was located,' a West German newspaper reported a month after his death. The article described Rauff as a *Schreibtischtäter* – a 'desk murderer' – a formulation attributed to Hannah Arendt to describe those who organised mass murder but never personally killed. At Londres 38, Rauff's role was to identify communists, as personally authorised by Pinochet.

'The first interrogations of the prisoners usually took place in Rauff's office', then they were taken to a detention centre near San Antonio. 'Witnesses reported Rauff had political prisoners tortured with gas-emitting liquids that caused severe lung and abdominal pain.' Again, there was nothing by way of witness or documentary evidence.

A few months later, the Chilean magazine *Análisis* ran an article titled 'Dawson, Walther Rauff's Last Concentration Camp'. Rauff was a 'secret adviser' to the DINA, it was claimed, and sent prisoners to Colonia Dignidad, where DINA agents tortured and disappeared them.

It never stopped. A decade later, a writer named Ingo Kletten described Rauff's working relations with the DINA and the Pinochet government, his visits to Colonia Dignidad, and a connection to Manuel Contreras. The DINA connection was said to be 'proven by documents', but only one was mentioned: an affidavit sworn in January 1991 by a man named León Gómez, who described 'the German Nazi Walther Rauff' as one of his torturers at Londres 38.

In 2013, Professor Martin Cüppers published a most detailed biography. He mentioned the 'memorable' Gómez affidavit ('I saw before my eyes one of my torturers, whom I could distinguish [from the others] because of his foreign accent, and I could credibly establish that he was the German Nazi Walther Rauff'). He noted too a claim about a relationship between Contreras and Rauff. On the other hand, Cüppers was struck by the absence of hard evidence, and the failure of any Chilean investigations to mention Rauff. Like the CIA, Cüppers left the door ajar: maybe Rauff's role was informal, responding to requests 'for advice by military officers he knew personally'. In Professor Cüppers' view, that would not amount to work as an 'official advisor'.

Four years on, Carlos Basso, a Chilean journalist, linked Rauff to crimes committed at Colonia Dignidad.

Two years after that, in 2019, Marcus Klein, a German researcher, probed more deeply, and identified a cascading effect: one unsubstantiated assertion was relied upon to support another. If you returned to the ultimate source, it was smoke and mirrors. There was no detail about the Gómez affidavit, and Gómez made no mention of Rauff in his books. 'Rumours can be true or false,' Klein suggested, but he found no evidence that Rauff was 'active in any capacity for the junta and its repressive apparatus'.

Klein speculated about the rumours. They were often harnessed to assertions that Pinochet and Hitler were 'directly linked', so that Pinochet's Chile was 'the epitome of the fascist state of injustice'. Were the allegations about Rauff intended to generate interest in Chile around the world and – this was a most delicate suggestion – 'to appeal specifically to Jewish circles'? Why would the regime associate with someone who would cause them problems? Klein was sceptical about a link between Rauff and Pinochet.

Equally striking, however, was what these writers did not address. Rauff and Pinochet knew each other, from the 1950s. Rauff mentioned the relationship – 'I am like a monument' – that he was protected by the regime. No one picked up General Mendoza's visit to the *Pesquera Camelio* soon after the Coup. No one mentioned the friendship with Admiral Weber. When I went to Chile, if Rauff's name came up, his association with the regime was invariably mentioned. Journalists, diplomats, lawyers, academics, writers – even taxi drivers – made the connection.

I reviewed everything I had gathered or read. So many names and places were mentioned, but three recurred.

Dawson Island, in Patagonia.

Colonia Dignidad, near Concepción.

Londres 38, in Santiago.

I would focus on these, dig a little deeper, find people to talk to.

# LONDON, MARCH 1999

## 74

By the end of 1998, Pinochet had been detained for three months, with no prospect of an early return. Fifteen years had passed since he refused to extradite or expel Walther Rauff.

The start of the third hearing before the House of Lords was set for Monday, 18 January 1999. The case was presided over by Nico Browne-Wilkinson, sitting with six other judges, including David Hope. 'There will be none of the clash of interests and predispositions which marked the previous hearing,' Hope recorded privately and anxiously. 'I cannot recall feeling as deeply uneasy about a case at any time since I went onto the Bench.'

The Chilean government decided to intervene and was authorised to do so by the Law Lords. They accepted that the immunity being claimed in reality belonged to Chile, as a sovereign state. Amnesty and the others who participated with it in the first case were allowed back. So was Human Rights Watch, although we were limited to written arguments. 'A good thing,' Hope noted acidly, as he considered one of us to be 'longwinded' and prone to speak 'in paragraphs'.

Once more, the red-leather seats of Committee Room 4 were packed, and I spent twelve more days seated next to Miguel Schweitzer. 'Pinochet No. 3? With seven judges this time, not just five! Surreal, no?' he exclaimed. Genial and perfumed as ever, with a notable spring in his step, he denied feeling optimistic. 'Everything has been decided once, so there is no way we can win,' he said.

On the other hand, why not?

'It's a new hearing, and we had a little help from the Government of Chile, with its famous lawyer,' he would say, a reference to Lawrence Collins, who was not quite as enthusiastic in his arguments as Schweitzer would have liked. 'Collins argued issues of principle, that a former head of state should not be extradited, but he never once referred to the General.' We all knew why. 'This government of Chile could not appear to be pro-Pinochet.'

On the opening day, silver-haired Baltasar Garzón swept in for the day from Madrid, hoping to add Pinochet to the list of notorious criminals he put behind bars, *The Times* reported. Jean Pateras accompanied him. 'I interpreted everything, bloody exhausting,' she recalled, 'and the *El País* journalist thought we looked like lovers.' They did socialise at her local pub, The Antelope, near Sloane Square, but nothing more.

Back in Madrid, Garzón wanted daily updates. 'I sat in court,' said Jean, 'trying to understand what was going on, and reported back. "Gracias, Jean, call me again tomorrow."'

Day one felt like *Groundhog Day*, the film in which a news reporter awakes each morning to a repeat of what has come before. From the outset, however, it was clear that these seven judges would take a different approach: the facts may have been the same but the legal issues and arguments came out differently. Customary law, the 1961 Convention and the 1978 Statute were barely mentioned. Instead, the judges homed in on torture, and the effect of the 1984 Convention against Torture.

The experience of living through the same case and court but with different judges exploded the notion that the law is applied mechanically to the facts. Change the judges, and everything changes. It's the human factor.

# 75

The Convention against Torture came into force for Britain, Chile and Spain on 10 December 1988. From that day on, they and the other parties were obligated to prevent torture, and punish perpetrators. The Convention defined torture as 'any act by which severe pain or suffering, whether physical or mental, is intentionally inflicted', in order to obtain information, or to punish or to coerce. The Convention applies to acts of public officials and provided that superior orders offer no defence.

Britain, Chile and Spain were required to criminalise torture and complicity, and give their courts universal jurisdiction – allowing them to hold to account any torturer found in their territory, irrespective of nationality or where or against whom the torture was committed. Unlike the Convention on Genocide, however, on which Garzón placed great reliance, the Torture Convention was silent about immunity. Our role in the case, for Human Rights Watch, with the assistance of students at Yale Law School, was to research the treaty's four-year negotiating history. Did the drafters say anything about immunity? They did not. The negotiators said nothing about the immunity of a serving or former head of state.

In English law, as I have mentioned, an international treaty only becomes part of domestic law if it has been formally incorporated. For the Torture Convention, this was done by section 134 of the Criminal Justice Act 1988, which came into force on 29 September 1988. This meant the judges could interpret and apply the Convention. By December of that year, it was in force for Britain, Chile and Spain.

Garzón alleged that Pinochet planned torture before he took office, and authorised it from the date of the Coup, 11 September 1973, and throughout his time in office. In English law, an agreement by two or more people to commit torture in the future – Pinochet's plan – is treated as a conspiracy. The conspiracy charge didn't really feature in the first case before the House of Lords, Alun Jones told me, because his team had no time to develop it. 'We were only able to formulate charges for conspiracy to commit torture in the new case. We did it to cover criminal conduct that continued over a long period of time,' he explained. The argument was deployed because the CPS lawyers worried that the Law Lords might limit their jurisdiction to a later date, for example when the Torture Convention came into force, in October 1988.

'It was a tactical decision,' said Jones, 'to represent the fullness of the case put by Garzón, that Pinochet agreed with others to commit torture before the Coup, and to continue to do so for many years after.' The conspiracy charge would allow the judges to take account of acts of torture from 1973 to 1990. 'I like to think that was my real contribution to the case,' Jones said.

# 76

Once again, as the appellant, Spain went first. It focused on two key issues: first, did the crimes charged satisfy the double-criminality rule, namely were they crimes over which both English and Spanish courts could exercise jurisdiction?; and second, could Pinochet claim immunity for those crimes?

In the days that followed, the arguments narrowed in on the crime of torture and the requirements of the 1984 Convention. 'The torturer is the universal enemy of civic society and human rights,' argued Alun Jones, so immunity for a former head of state was flatly inconsistent with the Convention. He was supported by Professor Greenwood, who argued that beyond the Convention, customary international law also did not allow Pinochet to claim immunity. Browne-Wilkinson, the presiding judge, was puzzled. When did a rule become a part of customary international law? As a law student he'd never really understood the answer to that question. 'The case is going to turn more and more on that point,' he added, which seemed ominous for Spain – the majority in the first ruling concluded that Pinochet had no right to immunity under customary law. The question caused Miguel Schweitzer to cross his arms, turn to me and smile. I never quite forgot that moment, and he mentioned it often, even years later.

'Customary international law develops through the practice of states,' said Greenwood, trying to be helpful. 'The practice must be coupled with the belief that it is required as a matter of legal obligation, not mere convenience. This is known as *opinio juris*, for those interested in Latin jargon.

Browne-Wilkinson had a puzzled look. 'So if we say it is part of international law, it is, and if we say it is not, it is not?'

This seemed significant. Browne-Wilkinson was expressing scepticism as to the approach taken by Hoffmann and the earlier majority. It's just too vague, he seemed to be indicating. He wanted something clearer, a written rule, one in a treaty that states had drafted and signed and explicitly agreed.

'Your Lordship recognises what is, if I may say so, the very considerable responsibility which faces your Lordships' House in this case,' said Greenwood. As far as Spain was concerned, the Torture Convention did no more than codify an existing customary prohibition on torture, adding a few bells and whistles. Customary law didn't allow Pinochet to claim immunity, nor did the Convention.

There was the smell of rubber hitting the road. 'OK, let's look carefully at the Torture Convention,' said Clare Montgomery, 'and see what it actually does.' The Convention only became binding on Britain, Chile and Spain late in 1988, she explained, so logically it could surely only apply to torture that occurred after then, when it was in force for all three countries. It could not apply to torture before October 1988, she surmised, and it couldn't apply to torture in Chile in the 1970s, long before the Convention was even drafted.

Lord Millett intervened. Didn't the Nuremberg tribunal reject the argument that the crimes set out in the Nuremberg Statute couldn't apply to crimes that pre-dated the drafting of the Statute, in August 1945? Didn't the Nuremberg judges rule that 'crimes against humanity' applied to acts that occurred even before August 1945, when the concept was first introduced into international law?

Perhaps, said Montgomery, briskly, but Nuremberg was an international tribunal, and you, the House of Lords, are only a domestic court. Before this domestic court, she continued, there could be no retroactivity: if immunity was not removed by the Torture Convention, it persisted. General Pinochet's immunity persisted. It was absolute, watertight, total.

Millett did not let go. 'Did you not say yesterday that the immunity extends right down the line, even to the local police chief?'

'Yes,' replied Montgomery.

So a local police chief can be tried by an international tribunal, before which immunity is lost, but not before a national court, where immunity persists?

'Yes,' Montgomery retorted. 'Or he could be tried by his home state.' The immunity belonged to Chile, she explained, in respect of all its public officials, however high or low they might be. Montgomery's glory is that if you sound like you really believe your argument, there is a fair chance the judges will buy it.

Millett seemed perplexed, so did Browne-Wilkinson. 'If the former police chief can only be tried by an international court or his home court, why does the Torture Convention require other states to prosecute him?'

This was a key question: how could absolute immunity be consistent with the Torture Convention's obligation that a party must prosecute or extradite any torturer, irrespective of who they were or where they tortured?

The law is premised on a form of logic, the disentangling of threads that pull in opposite directions. Montgomery's proposition of absolute immunity before national courts might go too far for me, Browne-Wilkinson suggested. In half an hour he might feel differently, but right then, he said, it seemed that since the 1984 Convention required its parties to prosecute any person who committed torture, it appeared to offer an 'arguable exception' to immunity.

This was advocacy, in the English tradition, cut and thrust, teasing out the issues. The advocate proposed, the judge probed, back and forth, the pull and push of argument, an intellectual tug of war across words, a clash of logics. On it went, for several days. Argument, response, counter-argument, propositions kneaded and pulled and prodded, until finally some sort of shape emerges, finding expression in a written text that is called a 'Judgement'.

# 77

Each day after the hearing, at four o'clock, the seven judges gathered for tea, to 'stay in touch with their thinking,' Hope recorded. Decades later, he walked me around the Palace of Westminster, and the Law Lords corridor where they worked. The room where they deliberated was small and ordinary given the matters of vital interest being addressed. The judges 'worked very well together,' Hope thought, under Browne-Wilkinson's gentle but firm direction.

'Nico never sought to dominate', and he was 'several fences' ahead of the others, 'even if he sometimes showed signs of unease about his own inclinations'.

A few days into the hearing, Browne-Wilkinson asked other pertinent questions. Could a general right to immunity be removed by a treaty? And if so, did the treaty have to do it explicitly, or was a necessary implication sufficient? Browne-Wilkinson knew from our written submissions, on behalf of Human Rights Watch, that the drafters of the Convention never addressed these questions.

Necessary implication was not enough, said Montgomery, you needed more. A treaty must be explicit to end an immunity, like the Genocide Convention did. 'To my mind, this is the central point,' said Browne-Wilkinson, his mind apparently still open.

Professor Brownlie of Oxford intervened on behalf of Amnesty, like a bespectacled, gruff owl. If Miss Montgomery was right, Pinochet could hide behind 'a wall of impunity'. Why would the drafters of the Torture Convention give a dictator like Pinochet the benefit of immunity after he left office?

Lord Millett intervened once more. A necessary implication was surely enough. The logic of the law meant that immunity was ousted by a treaty requiring a torturer to be prosecuted or extradited to a place to be prosecuted. The faces of the other judges offered no hint of their views on this key point.

Each time an advocate of the Chilean government spoke, it felt as though they were walking a tightrope, not wanting to sound positive about Pinochet. 'Torture is prohibited by international law,' said Lawrence Collins, and Chile accepted that was the position in the 1970s.

'As far back as 1973?' asked Lord Hope.

'Yes indeed,' Collins replied. But the fact that Chile accepted that torture was prohibited by the time of the Coup did not mean it was 'an international crime at that time'. Moreover, immunity was lost only if 'expressly waived' by a treaty, exactly as Miss Montgomery argued. Since the Torture Convention offered no explicit waiver, Pinochet's immunity – and Chile's right to assert it – remained in full effect. It was 'untouched'.

After twelve days of tight argument, the hearings concluded on Thursday, 4 February. 'Far more comprehensive' than the first hearing, Hope thought. Finely balanced and unpredictable, the Human

Rights Watch team thought. The judges demeanour and the questions suggested a different outcome.

The period between the close of the hearing and the handing down of the judgement was not without its moments.

Lord Irvine, the Lord Chancellor, ended speculation on Hoffmann's future. 'A judge of the highest integrity,' he proclaimed, guilty merely of an error of judgement. He would remain in post.

The Vatican urged the British government to allow Pinochet to return to Chile, in the interests of national reconciliation.

Roberto Dávila Díaz, President of Chile's Supreme Court, spoke on the opening of the country's legal year. He was in favour of immunity, he declared, and the immediate return of the General.

After seven weeks, the law lords announced that the judgement would be delivered on Wednesday, 24 March. Two days before, *The Times* announced that the coming judgement would 'boost' Pinochet's 'case for freedom': the newspaper predicted the judges would rule Pinochet had immunity for acts committed before 1988, but would not be immune for any crimes committed after that date, for which he could be extradited to Spain. However, the newspaper explained, the extradition would be 'fatally holed' as most of the acts alleged by Garzón occurred in 1973 and 1974. 'A very disagreeable day,' said James Vallance White of the apparent leak. Amnesty and others complained. An inquiry was held, inconclusively.

# 78

On the afternoon of 24 March, we gathered once more in the Chamber of the House of Lords. Pinochet was in his fifth month of detention, James Cameron and I had not communicated for several weeks. No contact until the case was over, we agreed, in the aftermath of the Hoffmann matter.

At two o'clock, Browne-Wilkinson stood. 'For the reasons given,' he said, 'I would hold that Senator Pinochet does not have immunity as a former head of state for extradition crimes.' He paused. 'I would thus in part allow these appeals.'

'In part'. What did that mean? He left us dangling.

Lord Goff spoke next. Pinochet had complete immunity.

Then Lord Hope. Pinochet lost his immunity, but only from the day that the Torture Convention came into force for Britain, Chile and Spain, on 10 December 1988. *The Times* report was accurate, there'd been a leak. Were any crimes committed after that date, between December 1988 and March 1990, when Pinochet left office? Very few.

Lord Hutton said that Pinochet lost his immunity on 29 September 1988, when section 134 of the Criminal Justice Act came into force. Four judges had spoken, each with a different conclusion.

Lord Saville agreed with Browne-Wilkinson.

Lord Millett, the sixth to speak, said Pinochet had no immunity whatsoever. He could be extradited to Spain to face every charge raised by Garzón.

Finally, Lord Phillips. He would allow the appeal in respect of conduct by Pinochet that constituted extradition crimes. What that conduct was, he did not say.

As they spoke, a multitude of lawyers standing in the Chamber of the Lords, and millions of people around the world watching the judgement live on the BBC and CNN, tried to work out what was decided. Seven judges, six opinions, and the upshot seemed to be that Pinochet had no immunity for torture committed after December 1988. He could be extradited for those acts, but not the earlier ones. Bingham and the Divisional Court, and the five Law Lords who decided the first case, were not followed.

Browne-Wilkinson stood again. He explained that the double-criminality principle meant that Pinochet could only be extradited for conduct that was criminal under both Spanish and English law. As torture and conspiracy to torture outside the United Kingdom only became a crime in English law on 29 September 1988 – when section 134 of the Criminal Justice Act 1988 came into force, implementing the Torture Convention – Pinochet could only be extradited for torture after that date.

'The result,' he continued, was 'to eliminate the majority of the charges levelled against Senator Pinochet.' In fact, all that remained was one charge of torture after 29 September 1988, and two charges of conspiracy to torture that began before that date and continued after it. Pinochet could also be extradited for charges of conspiracy to commit murder in Spain, but ordinary murder in Spain was not an international crime, so for that he had immunity.

Browne-Wilkinson turned to the next question: did Pinochet

have immunity for the single charge of torture and two charges of conspiracy, committed after September 1988? He did not: the immunity was removed by the operation of the 1984 Convention. As these were 'very limited charges', the Home Secretary would have to decide whether to permit the extradition proceedings to continue at all.

Browne-Wilkinson was sending a clear signal to Jack Straw: think carefully before issuing a new Authority to Proceed, given the 'drastically reduced' charges.

We digested Browne-Wilkinson's words, and the conclusions of the seven judges. Six voted against immunity on the limited charges, with Goff the solitary holdout for total immunity. The 6-1 result precisely mirrored the judgement of Chile's Supreme Court in Rauff's case, back in 1963.

It is impossible to do justice to the varied approaches of the judges. A golden thread ran through their reasoning: the Torture Convention required torturers to be prosecuted or extradited, and that obligation was inconsistent with immunity. By necessary implication of the aim of the Torture Convention, Pinochet lost his immunity from December 1988, when the Convention came into force for the three countries.

'The summing up was listened to in silence,' Hope noted in his diary. When Browne-Wilkinson sat, people left the Chamber and there was a 'scrambling in the galleries', to spread the news.

I felt deflated, Miguel Schweitzer looked elated. Yet for both of us the feelings were tempered, as neither side won or lost decisively. 'Both sides greeted the judgement with acclaim,' Hope wrote. The Law Lords passed the buck to Jack Straw, who would now have to decide what to do.

# 79

Outside the Chamber, we picked up copies of the written judgements. Some 122 green pages, a spectrum of diverse views, bookended by the opposing views of Millett and Goff. For the former, international law was a 'living and expanding branch of the law', with Nuremberg catalysing an end to immunity. For the latter, immunity could be lost by explicit agreement of countries, and there was none.

Between these two views was the middle ground, led by Browne-Wilkinson. He could not ignore the 'appalling acts of barbarism' committed in Chile and elsewhere, the large-scale 'torture, murder and the unexplained disappearance of individuals'. Garzón set the horrors out in 300 pages, crystallised by Spain's team into thirty-two charges of torture and murder and other crimes, committed between January 1972, when Pinochet plotted to take office, and January 1990, when he stepped down. The double whammy of the 'double-criminality rule' and the 1984 Convention whittled these charges down to just three extraditable charges.

Hope recognised the 'profound' effect of the reduction to three extraditable charges. It removed the crimes perpetrated by Pinochet's regime against 4,000 victims between 1973 and 1977. Of the original 130 offences identified by Garzón, only three were committed after December 1988: a single act of torture – Marcos Quesada Yáñez – and two charges of conspiracy to commit torture.

Did the drafters of the 1984 Convention intend to deprive Pinochet of immunity for a single act of torture, Hope asked. They did not, he wrote in his diary. The drafters were concerned only with torture on a scale that was an international crime because it was 'widespread or systematic'. More than a single act of torture was needed, which was why conspiracy to torture was so significant: Pinochet's involvement in the conspiracy started in 1973, before the Coup, and continued on a scale so great that it crossed the line into 'an international crime'.

Hope was persuaded on the conspiracy argument by the details of Garzón's 312-page extradition request: Pinochet's participation in an agreement to develop a 'campaign of torture' that pre-dated the Coup and ran for eighteen years, until he left office. The agreement and the campaign were intended to create fear and bring people into line, a conspiracy that embraced every single act of torture committed after the Coup. I read it to include the torture of Gómez and Chanfreau at Londres 38, and Carmelo Soria on the Vía Naranja. Every judge except Goff agreed with the conspiracy argument, that it was an extradition crime for which Pinochet had no immunity.

Still, Hope and the other judges recognised their ruling significantly cut back on the charges for which Pinochet could be extradited without immunity, so Jack Straw would have to decide afresh whether to issue an Authority to Proceed. If he so decided, a magistrate would then have to pay 'very careful attention' to the evidence on the remaining charges, to decide whether a long-standing conspiracy coupled with a single act of torture could allow the extradition.

Hope seemed unsure whether the extradition should go ahead. He was bothered by the 'huge expense' of holding Pinochet 'on so few charges', and the 'diplomatic fall-out'. The benefits of extradition may not outweigh the disadvantages, he wrote. The 'weight will surely now lie with those who say we should send him back to Chile,' he concluded privately, as years of costly litigation would be ridiculous. In his diary, but not in his judgement, he wrote that Browne-Wilkinson and Goff shared this conclusion. The 'odds were now firmly in favour' of a decision by Straw to send Pinochet home.

James Vallance White also thought the ruling would end the case.

Did you think that the drastic reduction in the number of charges was intended to end the case?

'Yes, that was exactly the impression I got. They were hoping that Pinochet would be got rid of, so they were delighted that David Hope came up with a middle way that would allow Pinochet to return.'

A way that looked after the institution?

'Exactly, they were happy to agree with this halfway house, very relieved to have found a way of putting an end to the case that was intellectually and politically satisfactory.'

\*\*\*

The ruling came down on the day Britain and the United States launched military strikes on Serbia, in relation to events in Kosovo, on 24 March 1999. 'It is to curb Milosevic's ability to wage war on an innocent civilian population,' declared Tony Blair, 'for a world that must know that barbarity cannot be allowed to defeat justice.'

The bombing of Belgrade took the Pinochet ruling off the front pages, but it was still widely reported. The general conclusion was that Pinochet had not won completely and still faced a serious possibility of extradition. 'Sovereignty's Worst Day in Memory', ran an editorial in *The New York Times*. A welcome ruling, reported *The Guardian*, adding that although Pinochet would avoid prosecution in Spain for 'the bulk of his crimes', this was 'tempered by the advances the case has made in human rights law'. The *Daily*

*Telegraph*, on the other hand, considered the ruling to be appalling, as did Amnesty's lawyer. 'Completely wrong,' thought Geoffrey Bindman, who preferred the earlier ruling 'because it accepted that crimes such as torture had been crimes for all time, or at least back to Nuremberg, and that they were crimes of universal application.'

Miguel Schweitzer was convinced the Law Lords wanted to end the case. 'Extradition for a single act of torture? That would be absolutely ridiculous, as the violations of human rights in Chile were over by 1988.' He was 'absolutely sure' that Chile's intervention made a crucial difference.

Michael Caplan was less optimistic, and not so clear what the judges really wanted. He appreciated the care of the ruling, and Browne-Wilkinson's nudge, to invite Straw to rethink. 'Very good of him to say it, but I never thought for a moment the Lords could end it altogether. I thought he was saying, "This is where we are, do you really think it's sensible to go on with the case on that basis?"' Caplan shared Schweitzer's view that Chile's intervention made a difference.

Was there coordination between the teams?

'I'm not sure,' Caplan said, a little evasively. 'We were happy to discuss things, if and when they wanted.'

James Cameron and I had not spoken for over three months, but as the case was now over we could resume regular contact. On the evening of the judgement, we flew to Washington to attend an international law conference, where the new ruling was discussed. Was this an advance for human rights, or a setback? Views were divided. In a packed room, we were joined by a friend from Barcelona, Adriana Fabra, who offered a Spanish legal perspective, complete with emotion and even some tears. It was a case that separated friends.

## 80

Jack Straw would now have to decide whether to issue another Authority to Proceed, or to end a case that was limited to one charge of torture and two charges of conspiracy.

Pinochet's team went from the House of Lords to the High Court, to get an order to stop Straw from taking an immediate decision. 'I managed to tee up the High Court to sit that afternoon, served the papers on the CPS there and then,' said Caplan. The judge rejected the application, causing Caplan to worry that Straw might sign an immediate 'Authority to Proceed'.

All options now needed to be explored, and perhaps something else was afoot. Caplan alluded to this years later, when we revisited those days. 'There was a possible undercurrent,' he said a little mysteriously. 'It was no more than that, the possibility of some suggestion of a medical situation.'

As Straw weighed up his options, the CPS and Garzón searched for more torture cases that occurred in the relevant, truncated time period. 'We need precise particulars of all instances of torture arising after 29 September 1988, as a matter of urgency,' the CPS told Garzón. The cases must be authentic, with details of victims and torture methods, and proof that the torture was the result of a 'systematic, widespread and continuing policy of repression'. More cases would bolster the conspiracy charges.

Garzón was assisted by Juan Garcés, who quickly found forty-four more cases of torture that occurred after 1988 and were associated with the Pinochet regime. The details arrived in London within two days of the judgement, on 26 March, as Thatcher visited Pinochet in Wentworth, to express solidarity. Garzón wanted to show that Pinochet's 'systematic plan' of tor-ture started in 1973 and continued until he left office in 1990, part of a single and continuous policy over two decades.

The lawyers in Madrid found another way to strengthen the case for extradition. Juan Garcés and Carlos Castresana provided Garzón with a list of 1,198 names, people who were disappeared and whose fate was unknown on 8 December 1988. The exercise was premised on a judgement of the Inter-American Court of Human Rights, that disappearances were a continuing act of psychological torture for the families, until the fate of the person was established.

In other words, the failure to provide information on the fate of Alfonso Chanfreau, who disappeared in July 1974, perpetrated a continuing torture of his wife Erika Hennings and their daughter. The Inter-American Court approach was confirmed by cases under the 1984 Torture Convention and other international agreements, and rulings by the European Court of Human Rights.

Within weeks, a single case of torture and two cases of conspiracy had been supplemented by forty-four more acts of torture and 1,198 cases of disappearance. Everything was sent to Jack Straw: 'a trolley was wheeled into my office, with twelve lever arch files'. Pinochet and Chile made representations to end the case, while Garzón, Spain, human rights organisations and victims urged him to extradite Pinochet to Spain. The Foreign Office and British intelligence services added their own thoughts, not made public.

'I was like a Trappist monk, not allowed to say a word to a soul, except the officials concerned,' Straw recalled. 'I knew what my instinct was, but felt I must work through this lot.' Years later, James Cameron and I sat in Jack Straw's garden near Oxford, on a blustery, sunny, spring morning.

Straw spoke of his younger days as a politically active student in Leeds, travelling to Chile in 1966, a trip supported by the Fund for International Student Cooperation, which he later learned was a front for MI6, the British secret intelligence service. He met Salvador Allende – 'I may have shaken his hand, can't remember' – and welcomed his election to the presidency four years later. 'Elected fair and square,' Straw believed.

In 1973, Straw was a young barrister, litigating cases for the transport police ('money for old rope'). He followed events in Chile but didn't get involved in protests ('too much else going on in my life'). Occasionally he met Chilean refugees and formed a clear view on Pinochet. 'An extremely unpleasant fascist, killing people in very large numbers, supported by the Americans. I hated him. Happily, I never said it publicly!'

Straw's past caused Pinochet's supporters to detect a conspiracy, one that joined him to Robin Cook. 'Like hell it was!' Straw said. He only learned accidentally that Pinochet was in London, and of Garzón's interventions, a few hours before the arrest, in a *Guardian* article he read on a flight to Marseille. He was upset that the Foreign

Office and Metropolitan Police got wind of something a day earlier, but had not informed him. Still, he thought, Cook was 'on the right side' of the Pinochet story, unlike 10 Downing Street. Blair and his team were 'extremely unhelpful'.

Straw recognised immediately that as Home Secretary the Extradition Act required him to play a quasi-judicial role in any extradition proceedings, so he kept his distance from others.

How did you feel about the arrest?

'Proud and delighted, but I kept that to myself.'

The Divisional Court's ruling?

'Disappointed.'

The first judgement of the House of Lords?

'Momentous, incredibly pleased.'

The Hoffmann issue?

Straw thought about this. 'Furious, absolutely incandescent.'

Just as the Hoffmann issue broke, Straw was required to decide on the Authority to Proceed. 'I had to deal with it with an utterly straight bat, not talk to anybody.' He didn't discuss the matter with Robin Cook ('he knew my instinct, I knew his'), or Tony Blair ('torn, as committed as anybody against murderers and brutal dictators, but matey with Aznar'). The Spanish Prime Minister was on the right, not unsympathetic to Pinochet, and worried the arrest might set a precedent that would stop dictators choosing the path of democracy.

There was no formal coordination between different parts of the British government, Straw explained, but the Home Secretary picked up nuggets of information. He heard of the 'extraordinary correspondence' from Margaret Thatcher to Blair – 'instruct your Home Secretary to release Pinochet,' she pleaded – and Blair's negative reaction. 'It's Straw's decision, not mine.' Blair occasionally tried to engage him after a Cabinet meeting. 'He'd call me in and say, "Can I talk to you about where you have got to?"' Straw declined. Jonathan Powell, Blair's Chief of Staff at 10 Downing Street, sometimes buttonholed the Home Secretary. 'Where has it got to?'

Straw declined to say anything, he told us. He had to decide whether to sign a second Authority to Proceed, and that required complete independence.

## 81

It was now April 1999, four months after Straw signed the first Authority to Proceed, in December 1988. 'There were thirty-three counts for the first Authority to Proceed,' Straw said, 'and now it was reduced to just three.'

Straw was assisted by Jonathan Sumption, a leading barrister. The Divisional Court confirmed he could quash the first Authority to Proceed and decide on a second one. He received the large trolley, laden with lever-arch files. 'I waded through all of them' and there was much of interest. Britain's ambassador in Chile was getting 'twitchy' about the whole affair, and MI6 wanted Straw to 'get rid of Pinochet'. Margaret Thatcher was outraged by the entire episode.

Over several days Straw read and reflected. He wanted to consider the matter 'entirely afresh', noting Browne-Wilkinson's nudge that he take note of the 'very considerable reduction' in charges.

'I reviewed all the representations, from opponents and supporters, with an entirely open mind.' The number of surviving charges of torture and conspiracy was small, but they offered evidence of crimes that were 'serious', and justice required them to be addressed. Straw thought the conspiracy charges were important, allowing him to take account of torture as far back as 1973. The cases of disappearance, like that of Alfonso Chanfreau, also came into play.

Years later, sitting in a blustery garden, Straw was sanguine. 'I was aware that I had to have good arguments for what I was deciding. There was no point in me saying, "The man's a bastard, he ought to be extradited."'

And the small number of charges?

'My strong instinct was that three counts was sufficient. Pinochet was a really, really bad man. I made the point to Tony [Blair] a couple of times: it was no good us having signed these international instruments, preening ourselves, then doing nothing when presented with a case.'

'Did you ever waver?' James Cameron asked.

'No. I had the authority to decide to proceed, I'd gone this far, I was going to make the decision.' He looked at us, blinked, paused, then said: 'I was still furious about Lennie Hoffmann.'

On the evening of 14 April 1999 any doubts were set aside: Straw signed the second Authority to Proceed. Britain's ambassador in Chile, MI6 and Margaret Thatcher would be disappointed, as would Augusto Pinochet. The papers would go to a magistrate, who would decide on the next stage of the proceedings, as the Extradition Act required, on whether to commit Pinochet to be extradited to Spain. Pinochet's stay in London would be extended.

# PART IV

---

# ESCAPE

*Everybody knows that the dice are loaded*
Leonard Cohen, 'Everybody Knows', 1988

# NIGHTS IN THE MUSEUM

## 82

On an autumn morning in London in 2022, an email arrived from my assistant Monserrat in Santiago. 'I have found a book that might be of interest,' she wrote, 'by Galo Ghigliotto, a Chilean writer, and one of the protagonists is Rauff.' She had not yet read the book but was intrigued by the title, *El Museo de la Bruma*. The Museum of the Mist.

The book arrived a few days later, in Spanish with a handsome red-and-black cover. It told the story of a museum established in Punta Arenas, a collection of objects distributed across three main rooms, including photographs and documents.

Leafing through, I read a reference to a photograph of Augusto Pinochet inaugurating José Menéndez Street, probably in Punta Arenas, in 1975, with Rauff amidst the onlookers, standing between two women with flags. On another page, a familiar description of the article in *Newsweek* from March 1984, Pinochet talking about Rauff, saying he didn't know him.

I read on.

A first room in the museum was dedicated to Julio Popper, a nineteenth-century Romanian adventurer who searched for gold in Tierra del Fuego and murdered many members of the Selk'nam community, the indigenous group gathered by the Silesians at Dawson Island. Popper was a genocidaire.

A second room was devoted to Alain-Paul Mallard, traveller and collector, and Bruce Chatwin, explorer, writer and mythographer.

The third room honoured Walther Rauff and the former SS officer's years in Punta Arenas and Porvenir. The museum held objects from his life and times.

A visit to the museum was not possible, as a few years earlier a fire had destroyed the building and all the objects. 'The power of the winds of Tierra del Fuego allowed the flames to work impeccably.' The author spent years searching for replacement objects, in libraries, bookstores, museums, homes and antique shops, until he realised the task was impossible. Instead, he'd make do with words, to preserve the spirit of that which was lost.

The museum paid homage to Patagonia, a special region, distant and splintered in its isolation. Its 'sinister geography' allowed it to become a place of 'extreme impunity', imbued with 'a genocidal impulse'.

I read on.

The collection included many familiar documents about Rauff.

A copy of the infamous letter, tendered as evidence at Nuremberg, from Dr Becker the chemist to SS Obersturmbannführer Rauff, sent from Kiev in May 1942, on the gas vans. The museum offered a Spanish translation.

A CIA memorandum, from March 1950, on Rauff's links to the Israeli secret service.

A statement by Francisco Coloane – a renowned Chilean novelist – from Porvenir, whose neighbour occupied an unpainted, corrugated-iron house. 'Here lives Walther Rauff, the genius who connected the gas exhausts to the inside of the prisoner transport vehicles.'

A statement by Héctor Rivera Antipán, student at the Escuela Las Mercedes in Punta Arenas, who recalled a visit by Rauff, to honour him for his support, introducing him as a saint. Only later did Antipán learn that the man from Porvenir had killed 97,000 human beings.

A statement by Juan Carlos Colihuinca, a petty thief who shared a prison cell with Rauff during the 1963 extradition proceedings, in Santiago. Rauff received preferential treatment, a curtain and a desk, and a lady was allowed to visit. Rauff told Colihuinca that he designed certain devices, but never personally used them.

A statement by G.R., a member of the Phoenix Brigade, on an attempt to assassinate Rauff in Punta Arenas in 1964, which caused the German to move to Porvenir.

A newspaper article by Pablo Neruda from July 1965, titled 'Freedom Fighters'. The poet attacked the legal system for allowing Rauff, a war criminal, to live freely in Chile. 'There is no denying that this man understands vans. Nor can I deny that my country's judiciary, its Supreme Court, has a well-adjusted conception of reality: it protects people who efficiently organise collective murder and transport in vans.'

A letter from Salvador Allende to Simon Wiesenthal, in August 1972. It was for the court to decide on the extradition of Rauff, not the President. Nevertheless, Allende condemned the terrible crimes of the Nazis.

A CIA memorandum from 8 July 1977, translated into Spanish, on the assassination of Orlando Letelier in September 1976 and Rauff's alleged service as a senior advisor to the DINA.

A letter from Klaus Barbie to Rauff, dated 12 October 1983 and sent from Lyon, on receiving news of Rauff's death. In error, as Rauff was still alive (dying in May 1984).

A statement by Blanca Madones, a neighbour in Porvenir. 'We were so afraid of Mr. Walther Rauff,' she stated. 'He looked at us as if we were dogs or horses passing by, as though we did not exist.' Only later did she learn that Rauff really was a Nazi, but no one in Porvenir wanted to talk about that.

A statement from 2014 by Eugenio Giglio, a poet from Porvenir, recalling that many in the community thought Rauff was 'a good old man', who did not 'feel' himself to be a Nazi.

The museum also had objects.

Pride of place went to a Minerva manual printing press, a Heidelberg T model manufactured in 1940. This was said to be the machine that printed the passport with which Rauff travelled to Ecuador.

A gold tooth Rauff obtained in Milan from a bag of objects originating in an extermination camp. He kept it as a lucky charm.

A can of paint used by Beate Klarsfeld to spray the words 'SS Rauff' on the front door of his house on Las Condes Street, Santiago, in February 1984.

A painting by Rauff, titled *Sunsets*, a view over the Bay of Porvenir from his cabin.

A fragment of a recipe for the preparation of sarin gas, said to have been given to Rauff by Eugenio Berríos, the biochemist who worked in the basement of Townley's house on the Vía Naranja, where Carmelo Soria was killed.

The museum also had photographs.

Josef Mengele, posing in Santiago in 1957 with a man who might be Rauff, next to a statue of Pedro de Valdivia, Spanish coloniser and founder of Santiago.

Walther Rauff during a visit to Colonia Dignidad in 1974, photographed in a white karate kimono. He was in the *zenkutsu dachi* position, his right arm extended towards the abdomen of a pupil who was identified as Franz Bäar.

And so on.

# 83

'What a trove of fabulous materials,' I wrote to Monserrat. However, I harboured a doubt, prompted by the kimono. 'Is this for real?'

Delighted that the materials were of interest, she replied. 'The objects are real, but they were destroyed in the fire,' she explained, 'hence, the book uses the museum records to rebuild it. Documents, of course, exist independently of the book.'

I returned to the book. It was almost too good to be true, like the stories of Bruce Chatwin which turned out to be partially invented, or the *Hitler Diaries*, or the writings of Roberto Bolaño, who teased us with his interweaving of fact and fiction, of Mariana Callejas and Michael Townley and the priest retained by 'Herr Raef' to give Pinochet lessons in Marxist theory.

I read more closely. With time, and closer attention, I wondered if this was a finely researched work of poetic imagination.

How we laughed, Monserrat and I, as we came to the realisation this was indeed a work of well-researched fiction. We laughed even more a few months later, on meeting Juan Torres Toro, the retired schoolteacher in Porvenir, who photographed three of Pinochet's victims just before they were executed.

Yes, he said, he knew some of the characters in *The Museum of the Mist*.

Francisco Coloane?

'Oh yes, he existed, but, if he spent more than fifteen days in Porvenir I would be surprised!'

The schoolgirl Blanca Mardones?

'Oh yes, she existed, but if it happened as she said, she would have been a child.'

The poet Eugenio Giglio?

'Oh yes, he lives here, and he is a poet, but not a very good one.' Torres stopped himself, told us Eugenio's real surname was Gligo, then said: 'The black sheep of an impressive family, a priest, then a schoolteacher, who lost his posts due to various allegations of impropriety.' Of course, I realised, I knew this man, I'd met him! The man who wore the brown dog slippers.

Rauff and *The Museum of the Mist*. Why did these pages touch me? Because they seemed credible, emblematic of something more, of Pinochet and the DINA's mythical relationship with Walther Rauff, the old Nazi. They told a bigger story, how a rumour starts, takes off, and then it crosses a line and is treated as a fact, a truth. The book of the museum that never was only made me want to find out more about Walther Rauff.

Let us start with Dawson Island, where Orlando Letelier and other ministers were held. Here, on the Straits of Magellan, it was said, Pinochet built a concentration camp, with Rauff's assistance.

Chatwin called Dawson Island the 'black hump', visible in the distance, across the Straits of Magellan. He wrote of a visit, in 1975, hitching a ride with a local Yugoslav who flew goods in from Punta Arenas.

'I wanted to see the concentration camp where ministers of the Allende regime were held.' He didn't see much, the pages of *In Patagonia* told the reader, as the soldiers at the airstrip confined him to the small plane.

# DAWSON ISLAND

## 84

Within days of the Coup, Augusto Pinochet ordered three dozen men to be detained. They were arrested, flown to Punta Arenas, taken to the ASMAR pontoon, near the *Pesquera Camelio*, and placed on a barge. It sailed for several hours to a desolate island in the Straits of Magellan.

The group included Orlando Letelier and Sergio Bitar, Allende's Minister of Mining, who arrived with a copy of Dostoyevsky's *Crime and Punishment*, in French. Five decades on, the island was notorious and generally off limits. Like Chatwin, my request to visit was refused. 'Military exercises'.

'We arrived at Dawson Island, but didn't know that until later,' Bitar recalled. The camp known as *Compingim*, near the Puerto Harris Army base, was ready in advance of the Coup. It would hold hundreds of detainees, forced to work as manual labourers. To relieve the boredom, Allende's colleagues studied German and arranged seminars. Sergio Vuskovic, mayor of Valparaíso, offered a discourse on language. Jorge Tapia, Minister of Justice, gave lectures on constitutional law. Orlando Letelier addressed matters of international finance. José Tohá, Minister of Defence, explored modern Spanish usage.

After a few weeks, they learned of a new camp being constructed nearby. 'I had a sense of total desperation when I first saw it,' said Bitar. 'It had the feel of a concentration camp.' Tucked into a hollow near the sea, it was surrounded by watchtowers and two perimeters of barbed-wire fences, angled at the top, 'like Auschwitz'. Local detainees from Punta Arenas described beatings and torture, with electricity, or in a sealed transport container, or being submerged in the Strait's icy waters.

Three months on, Sergio Bitar and colleagues moved to the new barracks – Rio Chico, eight buildings, each with forty bunks, one atop the other. 'Dark and dismal', with soldiers who carried machine guns and binoculars. Every detainee got a number: Bitar was *Isla-10*, or I-10. Occasionally there were visits, by the Red Cross, or journalists from NBC or the BBC, allowed to film but not to speak to detainees.

## 85

Bitar remained on Dawson Island until May 1974, when he returned to the mainland and exile in the United States. Eleven years on, he returned to Chile, serving in the governments of Ricardo Lagos and Michelle Bachelet when democracy returned. In 1987 he published a memoir on life on Dawson Island. One passage described a meeting with electrical workers. 'We weren't supposed to speak to them, but we got close enough to have a few words,' Bitar wrote. 'They told us that a German helped design the camp. Rumour spread that Walther Rauff was consulting on the project.'

Bitar's memoir became a film, *Dawson Isla 10*, directed by Miguel Littin, who later was the subject of Gabriel García Márquez's book, *Clandestine in Chile* (García Márquez would later say he was willing to stop writing literature until Pinochet fell). In the film, a stern officer explains the Junta's need for Dawson. 'The new camp is not improvised,' he assures a colleague. 'Its designs are by Walther Rauff, who is personally supervising the camp. You know who he is, don't you?'

Other films mentioned Rauff's alleged role. *Pinochet's Plan Z*, a documentary about bogus Marxist efforts to foment civil war in Chile, featured Rodolfo Mansilla, a sculptor detained at Dawson. He called it 'a miniature model of Auschwitz', one that was 'designed by the military, before the coup, by Walther Rauff', a Nazi who lived nearby in Punta Arenas.

Websites described Rauff as a 'criminal and accomplice' in the construction of Dawson. The *Pesquera Camelio* manager was said to be the camp's 'designer'. A poet evoked his role and relationship with Pinochet:

> The general who assumed power
> commissioned him with his new plan

a forced labour camp
in a remote archipelago.

Dawson detainees spoke of Rauff. Luis Vega, a lawyer, said the barracks were constructed by the old German, who advised on interrogations and other 'special matters', and was protected by the military. According to Vega, the director of the Army's Military Intelligence Service, Augusto Lutz, travelled to Punta Arenas and Dawson in January 1974. 'He visited Walther Rauff', who supposedly assisted in drawing up plans for Dawson. (Lutz was not available for comment as he, like so many, died in mysterious circumstances a year after the visit, having confronted Pinochet on the DINA's excesses.)

Gonzalo González, a philosopher, spent time in Dawson's infirmary with Letelier. Four decades later, on a visit to the island, he compared his lot to that of his father-in-law, detained by the Nazis in occupied Denmark. 'My case was similar on Dawson,' he recalled, 'where the *capo* was the former Nazi SS colonel, Walther Rauff.'

Tales abounded, yet I found no document that mentioned Rauff, or anyone who had actually seen him. It was the stuff of rumour and hearsay. 'When the legend becomes fact, print the legend,' says a character in the film *The Man Who Shot Liberty Valance*.

The allegations gnawed away. During visits to Santiago and Punta Arenas, Rauff would often be mentioned in relation to Dawson. I asked Sergio Bitar about the rumours. At his neat bungalow in Santiago, I encountered a bespectacled and smiling man in a short-sleeved white shirt and shiny black shoes. 'I don't remember writing that!' he chuckled, when I mentioned the line about Rauff.

But he remembered something else. Years later, when he was Minister of Education in the Lagos government, he visited sites of detention and torture around Chile, part of a project to create a network of sites of memory. 'It is important that people do not forget.' Londres 38, Villa Grimaldi, Tejas Verdes, Cuatro Álamos, the house on Vía Naranja, all had other lives as offices, as homes or jails, or as places of tourism or sport. Dawson stood out, the only camp that was purpose-built.

Bitar's ministry selected the sites to be listed. 'In 2003, I listed Londres 38, and also the Villa Grimaldi and the National Stadium.'

He wanted to preserve the National Stadium's original old red seats. 'They must never be replaced.'

As minister, he returned to Dawson with other detainees. 'It was a place where they tried to take our souls,' he said, 'the only camp in Chile with the design of a Nazi concentration camp, I have never seen anything else like that.' The sense of horror was palpable. 'I almost do not remember how the rumour about Rauff began.' The thought prompted a memory, a file of documents on Dawson which he saw when he was Minister of Public Works, in the Bachelet government. He instructed that the documents be deposited in the archives of the Museo de la Memoria.

Bitar circled back to Rauff. 'I bet eighty per cent that he was involved with Pinochet.' As a minister, Bitar knew how things worked in Chile, especially if decisions needed big expenditures. 'You always needed to have sign off from on high, and that would have applied to Dawson.'

'Go to the archives and find those documents,' he suggested. 'And speak to Miguel Lawner, the architect, detained there with us. He will tell you about the camp, how it was, what we saw.'

# 86

Miguel Lawner was in his ninety-fourth year when I met him in Santiago. Tall, elegant, white-haired, moustached, twinkle-eyed, his memory was clear, his sense of humour lively. He did not mince words. 'The camp reminded me of Auschwitz, so I decided to draw it. I wanted people to know Chile built a concentration camp of its own, one that followed the German model.'

As Allende's director of social housing, Lawner was arrested on the day of the Coup and sent to Dawson. 'I expected to be detained', like in 1947, when communists and leftists were detained in a camp at Pisagua, north of Santiago. 'Guess who the commandant of that camp was?' he asked cheerily. 'A young Army captain, Augusto Pinochet!' He referred me to a passage in Pinochet's autobiography. 'I was much concerned that such pernicious and contaminating ideas should continue to be taught in Chile,' Pinochet wrote. The Pisagua camp was like 'a true Marxist-Leninist University which trained people to be agitators', so he turned away a visiting congressional commission, one of whose members was Salvador Allende.

Lawner recalled the daily routines at Dawson, the humiliation of forced labour, contact with local detainees. 'First, they were tortured, then made to build Rio Chico, the new camp,' he said. 'The place was inhuman, with barbed wire, iron sheets, tiny windows.' It was shocking. 'We will die here,' one detainee said to him.

Somehow, he retained a sense of optimism. 'I had never before been somewhere where the power of nature was so strong, fierce rains followed by a wonderful sun, then the most incredible clouds.' The wildlife left a deep impression. 'There was never any silence,' he recalled. 'There is a bird on Dawson, the *bandurria*, with a song that is beautiful and strong. That bird helped me survive.'

So did his love of drawing. Each morning, as detainees were marched around the camp, singing the national anthem, Lawner worked on an inner project. 'As I sang and marched, I measured the distance in precise steps. Uno. Dos. Tres. Cuatro. Cinco. Seis. In my head I drew a precise map.' After a few weeks, allowed paper and pencils, he sketched. He drew inmates and guards, barracks and towers, a detailed plan of the entire site. 'Each barrack was identical, six by thirty metres, with a name: Alpha, Beta, Gama, Delta, and so on.'

Returning to the site, three decades later, he thought nothing remained. 'Then, suddenly, as I looked at the grass, I saw the faintest of lines, a tiny difference, and I could follow the faded outline of each barrack. I found the first one, Alpha, near the road and the sea, then Beta, then Gama. Each of us stood where we once lived, little groups standing in perfect silence.'

Like Bitar, Lawner didn't forget the first impression of the new camp. 'We were putting large wooden poles into the dark and treeless earth, every fifty metres. As we moved along, it came into view. A proper concentration camp, modelled on a Nazi design.'

As workers buzzed around, a lunch break offered a chance to talk with local detainees. 'They told us that a man who did not speak proper Spanish, a foreign man, was involved. He would come and give instructions on what to do.'

Did the man have a name?

'Our comrades from the region said they knew that Walther

Rauff lived nearby, not in Punta Arenas but in Porvenir, in a far and isolated house,' Lawner recalled. 'They guessed that the man who brought the instructions to Dawson must be Walther Rauff.'

Did they guess or know?

'They guessed.'

Lawner knew of Rauff, everybody did, as he was notorious, the Nazi that the Supreme Court of Chile refused to extradite. Lawner knew that Allende had rejected Wiesenthal's request to deport Rauff. 'I knew all about him,' he said. 'I'm Jewish, my mother was from Ukraine, she survived the Nazi occupation. So did my aunt, who remained there for the rest of her life'. An uncle was gassed in a Nazi camp, with his wife and two children.

In a gas van or a camp?

He didn't know but understood the question. 'We were angry when Allende refused to extradite Rauff.'

Lawner spoke carefully. He doubted Rauff had a role in building the Dawson camp. Another detainee, Carlos González, mayor of Punta Arenas before the Coup and again after Pinochet stepped down, talked of Rauff. 'He said he lived an isolated life, in a house near Porvenir, with a woman, that he was drunk most of the day. He wasn't sure Rauff could have been involved in the construction of the camp.' Lawner smiled, with a touch of sadness. 'And so, according to Carlos González, who can be trusted, I have doubts that Rauff could have played this role.'

And you have doubts about your doubts?

'What do I remember? What is memory?' Miguel Lawner's eyes darted and pierced. 'According to the workers who built the concentration camp, who talked with our comrades, a foreign person came and give instructions while they were there. Wouldn't it be strange if there was another foreigner, not Walther Rauff, who went to Dawson and gave those instructions?'

Did the workers see the foreigner?

'I am not sure that they did. No. They talked with construction workers who told them this story, about a foreigner who arrived with instructions.'

He picked up his phone and called a friend. It was Baldovino Gómez, who I would meet in Punta Arenas, in the Shackleton Bar. The two laughed as they spoke. 'Baldovino has no more information on this matter,' he said. 'He too remembers that workers at Dawson said something about instructions from a foreign person, but he has no more information.'

Miguel Lawner changed tack.

'The thing is, it wasn't only the rumours, it was the design of the camp.' He plucked a large volume from the shelf, a book of drawings he made after being released, while exiled in Denmark. With a gentle finger, he guided me around the plan of the barracks, to the places of abuse, to the watchtowers, along the barbed wire.

'The double wire fence was the distinguishing feature. It made me think Rauff might be involved. I'm an architect, I'd never seen this before in Chile, or after.' His finger moved along the ink fence until it reached the entrance. 'I cannot reject the possibility that Rauff was involved. I have been living with this idea all my life. It may be because of the concentration camp blueprint that I never doubted his role.'

'Do you believe in justice?' he suddenly asked. Sort of, I said, explaining that I'd come to understand that justice was uneven in its delivery, and I'd learned to temper expectations.

'I testified at the United Nations in Geneva,' he said. 'I brought the sheet of paper with the drawing I made in Denmark. It was 1975, a large room, many seats, dark. The judges were there, with Red Cross people. I was the only witness to give testimony. I told them: "We were held in a real concentration camp"'. The chairman of the Committee on Human Rights expressed surprise:

> It was a proper concentration camp, I told him, I have the drawings . . . He came to me, took the sheet of paper, looked at it.
> Later he said: 'This is the first time since the Second World War that we have come across a specially built camp that is modelled on the design of a Nazi concentration camp.'

Did it matter whether Rauff was involved? Yes, said Lawner. For Chile, the camp was novel and 'unbelievable'. Rauff's role would show a connection between Pinochet and the Nazis, both motivated by a resistance to communism.

Do you believe in justice? I asked.

He didn't reply.

Was justice done in your case?

'Never.'

Were you paid compensation?

'No. Many received compensation, not me.'

Did the state ever apologise to you?

'No. There has never been any recognition of the wrong done to me.'

So, total impunity?

'Yes. But . . .' Miguel Lawner hesitated. 'Not quite total. Dawson has been recognised as a site of national memory, a protected monument, and that means something.' Nevertheless, the site was generally out of bounds, and few visits were allowed.

And, he recalled, during the horrors of captivity there were also moments of great humanity. Once on a forced march, the prisoners encountered an abandoned, wooden church, built by the Salesians at the end of the nineteenth century. Lawner was allowed to restore it, working with a friendly Army sergeant. On another day, in a spiky calafate shrub, the two men came across an abandoned statue of Monsignor José Fagnano, the founder of the Silesian mission of San Rafael on Dawson. It was cleaned up and returned to the church for its re-dedication, on the Day of the Immaculate Conception, in December 1974.

'Much later, on the same spot, I came across two glass jars,' Lawner said. 'They were made by the sergeant's wife. Can you imagine? Home-made marmalade in a calafate bush, a wonderful act of humanity!'

## 87

The story of the statue and the church was a reminder that Lawner and the others were not the first to be held on Dawson Island in abject conditions, nor the first to experience total impunity. At the end of the nineteenth century, Monsignor Fagnano, he of the lost statue, established a mission on Dawson Island to 'save' aboriginal souls from the extermination being perpetrated by European colonisers. The targets were Kawésqar and Selk'nam (also known as the Ona), indigenous peoples who lived in the area when Europeans arrived, with a culture and ideas of their own. The Spaniards, Germans and British started by lopping away trees, to create sheep farms. Later, they lopped away the indigenous peoples, to create a living space for

Europeans. 'This is a case that can be characterised as a genocide', a Chilean national commission recently reported.

The director of a museum in Punta Arenas showed me a photograph of the Selk'nam and Kaneka people gathered on the grounds of the Colegio de Minas on Dawson Island. Men in suits and fancy hats stood and observed them. Rodolfo Stubenrauch, the German consul of Punta Arenas, was there, with Federico Errázuriz Echaurren, the President of Chile and a forebear of Hernán Felipe Errázuriz, one of Pinochet's lawyers in London.

Esteban Lucas Bridges, the Anglo-Argentine author and explorer, visited Dawson around the time of the photograph. He met Selk'nam women who wove blankets and men who cut timber. 'Splendid specimens,' he recorded. He learned the language, Yahgan, and compiled a dictionary, which can be consulted in the British Library.

He befriended Hektliohlh, a man who spoke with 'terrible sadness' of the effects of incarceration. 'Shouwe t-maten yaw,' he told Bridges – 'the longing will kill me', and it soon did. 'Liberty is dear to white men,' noted Bridges. 'To untamed wanderers of the wild it is an absolute necessity.'

The Selk'nam were hunted by colonisers, encouraged by a bounty, a pound sterling for a pair of ears. Alexander McLennan, the foreman of José Menéndez, was one of the most brutal. His bust was mounted on a pedestal on the Plaza de Armas in Punta Arenas, in the presence of Bruce Chatwin, and was toppled shortly before my first visit.

McLennan, who was known as the 'Red Pig', served in Khartoum with the British Army and revelled in the killings. They were humanitarian, as captivity was cruel. 'The sooner they were exterminated the better,' he believed, and very soon they nearly were. The story is told in a fine film, *Los Colonos*.

For his service, José Menéndez offered McLennan – 'my fine collaborator' – a gold pocket watch and a tie pin. The pin enclosed a sliver of polished green glass, fashioned from the arrowhead launched by a Selk'nam warrior that pierced the flesh of the Red Pig. The British Museum in London has a similar green-glass arrowhead, also made by a Selk'nam.

We may have forgotten what happened, but Hektliohlh's descendants have not. We are not dead and here I am, declared Arpón de Fuego, a Selk'nam leader, before Chile's recent constitutional convention. His voice was tinged with a special emotion.

It was only in August 2023 that Chile finally recognised the Selk'nam as an indigenous community. Chile has also recognised the killing of the Selk'nam as an act of genocide, but the governments of Germany, Spain and the United Kingdom have not. Nor have the corporations or shareholders who benefited greatly from the genocide they contributed to.

## 88

The later crimes of the Pinochet era are recognised by the Museo de la Memoria in central Santiago. Here, I found the documents that Sergio Bitar spoke of, in a file named 'Dawson Island Archive'. The country's head of public works wrote on the cover: 'Please receive these papers, a part of the history of our Chile, documents about a project which, with sadness and impotence, some of our colleagues were obliged to carry out.'

The file held seventy-nine pages of documents, handwritten, typed or drawn. There were letters and scribblings, proposals and sketches, receipts and lists, a testament to the mundanities associated with the creation of the concentration camp. The documents confirmed that planning must have begun before the Coup, along with the conspiracy to torture: by early October 1973, the local Punta Arenas firm of Juan Pedro Martínez & Co. was being billed for construction works *already completed*, and Pinochet's regime was seeking quotes for the camp on Dawson Island. A week later, building materials had been supplied and invoices rendered, for materials sourced in Punta Arenas, from local companies known to Walther Rauff.

Over the next month, the basics needed to build and operate a concentration camp were sourced. General Motors provided one electricity generator, and Mercedes Benz in Argentina supplied two more. Endesa, Chile's state-owned utility, provided electrical works, and Coditec installed a deep-well drinking water pump. 'Of German manufacture', the company confirmed.

In December, accounts were settled for wood, pipes, kitchens and equipment, and a furnace. The project was managed by the office of public works in Punta Arenas, under the direction of Nicolás Izquierdo Vergara. 'May his name live in infamy,' said a former Dawson detainee when I asked if he knew the name.

The Ministry of Public Works and Transport in Santiago approved payments for these 'urgent' works. The Corporación de Magallanes paid the Dirección de Arquitectura in Punta Arenas, supported by the National Secretariat for Detainees in Santiago. The documents detailed expenditures to local companies of 146 million escudos, about US $250,000 at prevailing exchange rates. By December 1973, Camp Chico was ready to receive inmates.

The dossier contained various documents of interest.

There was a passenger manifest, with names of those who arrived at Dawson on a special flight on 7 November 1973, including Izquierdo Vergara. Three weeks later, the Fiscal Inspector carried out an audit. The names of construction workers were laid out, the payments approved by Señor Izquierdo Vergara. Did these men speak of Rauff, or recall a German who offered instructions?

The documents made no mention of his name, or of any other foreign person. If Rauff was involved, these documents did not prove it, and any connection was tenuous, left to be inferred from some sketches. One drawing showed a small wooden hut connected to a fence of wood and wire. Another showed a wooden bunk bed, one sleeping area above the first. The sketches reminded me of things I once saw at Auschwitz, many years before.

It is true that the images shocked, as they did Lawner and Bitar. But shock and fear are not proof. Around Dawson Island there were many rumours about Rauff, but there was no evidence.

He lived nearby, and was involved in a similar enterprise, long ago and far away, but that was not sufficient. I would have to look elsewhere for signs of Walther Rauff's involvement in the crimes of Augusto Pinochet.

# LONDON, APRIL 1999

## 89

On the evening of 14 April 1999, Jack Straw signed the second Authority to Proceed. 'Inevitable,' thought David Hope, as the timing coincided with Blair's decision to go to 'war with Milosevic for crimes against humanity and genocide'. Any other decision would lead to 'criticism of double standards'. Britain could hardly preen itself on its actions abroad, then fail to apply the same principles at home, Straw told Blair. Years of Pinochet litigation lay ahead, many thought.

Baltasar Garzón sent a fresh extradition request to London, limited to torture and conspiracy by the Pinochet regime after December 1988. It arrived at Bow Street, where a magistrate issued a new arrest warrant. 'Between December 9th, 1988 and March 11th, 1990,' he wrote, Pinochet 'agreed with others to commit the offence of torture within the jurisdiction of Spain.'

On the morning of 16 April, Inspector Hewett drove to Wentworth with Jean Pateras, to arrest Pinochet under the new warrant. They were met by Caplan, Schweitzer and Errázuriz, and a Chilean military attaché, who thanked the police for their efforts in protecting Pinochet. The Chileans worried about assassination.

Pinochet greeted the visitors in the sitting room, in a comfortable armchair. 'Smartly dressed in a blue jacket, collar and tie', he clutched his walking stick 'vertically', as it rested on the floor, Hewett noted. 'He looked up at me as I entered and nodded but did not say anything,' Hewett said. Jean Pateras 'squatted down on his right-hand side', Hewett stood facing Pinochet, with Michael Caplan to his left, on a sofa.

'Good morning, Senator,' said Hewett. He proffered an identity card, which Pinochet peered at but did not touch. 'I have here an additional warrant for your arrest,' Hewett explained, and 'a further allegation of torture.' He read out the charges, told Pinochet he was under arrest, read his rights and bail conditions, and warned that anything he said could be used in evidence. Pinochet could not leave the house, except to attend court or for medical or dental treatment. He could exercise in the garden, but only with prior permission. He must attend Bow Street Magistrates Court at a date to be set, and if he failed to show would be 'liable to a fine or imprisonment or both'.

Hewett gave the General a copy of the warrant. Do you understand, do you have any questions?

'Yes,' said Pinochet. He spoke lucidly, without notes:

In the first place, I do not agree with this. Because . . . all these charges, I completely negate them, because I have absolutely had nothing to do with any of these charges. I am being humiliated. I am a General with sixty-four years' service. I am a gentleman who knows about honour. I completely deny all this.

He said he would behave and comply with the order: 'Don't worry.' 'Thank you.'

The encounter lasted twelve minutes. Hewett lingered in the driveway, comparing notes with Caplan and Jean Pateras. Accuracy was important, as Pinochet's words would be used in court. On the way back to Heathrow Police Station, Hewett stopped at the Golf Club, to refresh himself and write up the statement.

## 90

Pinochet's lawyers went straight to the High Court to challenge the second Authority to Proceed signed by Straw. A short hearing was held on 27 May before Justice Ognall, the son of a writer of crime novels. The judge listened politely, then refused permission to proceed with the case. The challenge was 'premature' and would 'needlessly disrupt' the extradition proceedings. Pinochet could make his case in due course, in 'a fully informed manner'.

A date was set for the initial extradition hearing, as required under the Extradition Act, in June, at Bow Street Magistrates Court. This was a formality, when the magistrate would review Garzón's request and satisfy himself that the crimes alleged were extraditable under English law. At Pinochet's request, the hearing date was postponed until the end of September.

Summer took its course. Under the watchful eye of the police, Pinochet received permission to walk in the garden of 28 Lindale Close, and to play toy electric cars with his grandchildren. He watched *Star Wars* films and read books about Napoleon.

He received visitors, drank tea. He gave an audience to journalist Christina Lamb, who noted his voice ('high-pitched whisper') and 'flat and meaty' fingers ('like those of a butcher'), the Catholic icons and Jean-Claude Van Damme videos. She listened to his complaints about a farcical legal process (one ruling and appeal after another, 'like being on a wheel').

Michael Caplan travelled to Chile. 'I met the General's supporters, the speaker of Parliament, the Foreign Minister, representatives of the English and Spanish communities, and the Jewish community.'

The Jewish community?

'Many were supportive of Pinochet,' said Caplan, 'and of course Miguel [Schweitzer] was Jewish.'

Garzón used the time to uncover more acts of torture, assisted by Garcés and, behind the scenes, Castresana. Over the summer, he sent four more batches of torture cases to London. With the topped-up charges, Pinochet now faced thirty-five additional counts of torture.

Miguel Schweitzer fumed about these new cases. 'Imagine, the extradition request being adjusted, ex *post facto*! Back home that would never be allowed.' But that was exactly what happened thirty-five years earlier, I reminded him, in Rauff's case before the Supreme Court of Chile. When Schweitzer's father advised that the case against Rauff was genocide not murder, the West German prosecutors amended their request for extradition, just as Garzón had done.

'And the German request failed,' Schweitzer said, with a little smirk. Indeed it did, but for a different reason: Chile had a fifteen-year statute of limitations, even for international crimes, whereas Spain and Britain had no such rule. You could be extradited there in 1999 for a conspiracy to commit torture that began in 1973.

In July 1999, Pete Sampras beat Andre Agassi in the final of the men's tennis at Wimbledon. Also in that year, and after a long gap,

George Lucas released the fourth Star Wars film, *Episode I – The Phantom Menace*. It is not known whether Pinochet watched it.

In August, Slobodan Milošević and four others were indicted at the International Criminal Tribunal for the former Yugoslavia. The charges included crimes against humanity perpetrated in Kosovo.

In Chile, the campaign got underway for the first round of the presidential election, to be held in December.

In September, as Margaret Thatcher visited Pinochet in Wentworth, a new Chilean ambassador was posted to London, and Ronald Bartle, the magistrate who signed the second arrest warrant, was chosen to sit on the next stage of the extradition procedure.

# 91

Autumn in London brought the first anniversary of Pinochet's arrest. At Bow Street Magistrates' Court, the hearing opened on the morning of 27 September. 'The police picked us up in a coach,' Caplan said, with an unhappy memory. 'It was fraught outside court, one of my team was assaulted.' The courtroom and public gallery were packed, an overflow room offered a live video stream. Pinochet was excused from attending, on medical grounds.

Ronald Bartle took his seat in Court No. 1, the clerk read out the charges. A 'steady monotone', *The New York Times* reported, a graphic account of beatings and burns, detainees bound and suspended, cages, starvation, sodomy. Pinochet authorised rape, the use of dogs, hallucinogenic drugs, electricity, and anything else that might cause a detainee to talk and give names. Miguel Schweitzer listened attentively. 'Some of the most serious allegations of crime ever to come before English criminal courts,' Alun Jones told Mr Bartle, who sat with a poker face.

Detective Inspector Hewett read out the statement Pinochet gave him a few months earlier. 'I don't agree with this,' he said. I deny all the charges – I am a gentleman humiliated after sixty-four years of honourable public service.

Outside the courtroom, Pinochet's supporters outnumbered the opponents, including Juan Garcés, the Spanish lawyer. 'The most important thing,' he told a journalist, was that this was the first time in history that a former head of state was subject to an

extradition hearing for such crimes. 'A form of justice,' said Reed
Brody of Human Rights Watch, the mere fact of proceedings and
charges, and the reading out of the names of those tortured, killed
and disappeared.

Pinochet's lawyers rebutted all the charges, a matter for Chile
alone. Facile, countered Alun Jones, since the Spanish courts and
the Law Lords confirmed Spain's jurisdiction over the crimes, and
the absence of immunity. 'The continuing offence of conspiracy'
covered the fate of all the disappeared, he explained, the torture of
families by 'severe mental pain, suffering and demoralisation'. Julian
Knowles, one of Pinochet's junior barristers, rebutted the argument
for Pinochet with force. 'He clashed quite badly with Alun Jones on
that issue,' Caplan recalled. Matters were getting fraught.

The hearings ran for four days. A week later, Ronald Bartle
summoned the parties to receive his judgement. Pinochet was excused, after two minor strokes and with other ailments, including
diabetes, kidney problems and incontinence. The police were relieved by his absence, as less security would be needed.

Bartle's judgement was pithy. He based his decision exclusively on
the law, he said, not any personal or political inclination. Modern
international law reflected a 'growing trend' to outlaw crimes that
were abhorrent to civilised society. This presaged 'the day when, for
the purposes of extradition, there will be one law for one world'.

Pinochet was entitled to know what he was said to have done, and
the conduct alleged must be shown to be a crime both in Britain and
Spain. Bartle was not concerned with proof of the facts, or Pinochet's defence, these were 'matters for trial' in Spain. He considered
all the information put before him, including the new cases of torture submitted by Judge Garzón, and the details of the disappeared.
The ghost of Alfonso Chanfreau and a thousand others haunted the
courtroom.

Was the 'double-criminality rule' satisfied?

It was. Torture and conspiracy were extraditable offences in
Britain and Spain. The Torture Convention allowed universal jurisdiction, it was part of English law and, as the Audiencia Nacional
confirmed, it was part of Spanish law.

Did Bartle have to satisfy himself, as Pinochet argued, and Hope
predicted, that the torture alleged was 'widespread and systematic'?

He did not. 'One act of torture' was enough for extradition, he ruled, and 'even without the guidance of the highest court in the land, I would have come to the same conclusion'.

Could Pinochet claim immunity?

No, not in relation to acts of torture after 8 December 1988. As for the conspiracy, that was a 'continuing offence', which allowed Bartle to take account of any act that was part of the conspiracy even if it occurred long before December 1988.

The disappeared?

Most significantly, Bartle ruled that 'the effect on the families of those who disappeared can amount to mental torture'. Whether Pinochet intended this, in relation to the 1,198 disappeared, was a question of fact for the trial court in Spain, not one which he must decide.

As the conditions were met to allow Pinochet's extradition, Bartle committed Pinochet to the next stage. All that remained was for the Home Secretary to decide whether or not to extradite him.

'A fundamental step forward,' declared Amnesty International. The ruling allowed extradition for all thirty-five cases of torture, and the 1,198 cases of the disappeared. This sent a powerful signal to prosecutors and courts across the world.

'Historic,' said the UN High Commissioner for Human Rights. 'Those who commit, order or tolerate torture can no longer be sure of a peaceful retirement.'

On the streets, Pinochet's supporters burned British and Spanish flags and raged about communists. Opponents opened bottles of champagne.

Still hoping to avoid a trial in Madrid, the Spanish government proposed a different 'solution'. Foreign Minister Abel Matutes suggested that the matter be referred to the International Court of Justice in The Hague, or to arbitration, to determine whether Spain truly had jurisdiction to try Pinochet. The idea did not take off.

Pinochet was 'frustrated, disappointed and stoical,' said Michael Caplan, 'but aware there was always another hearing'. Outside court, his statement was read out: the Spanish authorities produced no evidence against him, he would now reflect on the next steps. 'As the former President of the Republic of Chile, and Senator, I declare that I am not guilty of the crimes of which I am accused.'

The net was tightening. Under the Extradition Act, the case

was reaching a final stage. Jack Straw, as Home Secretary, would now decide whether to allow the extradition to proceed. Unless, of course, Pinochet could find another way to delay matters.

# LEÓN

## 92

With no hard evidence that Walther Rauff was involved in Dawson Island, I turned my attention to Colonia Dignidad. This was where the DINA tortured and disappeared prisoners, a place Rauff was said to have visited.

Colonia Dignidad was a German colony to the south of Santiago. It was founded in the early 1960s by Paul Schäfer, a former Wehrmacht medical orderly during the war who later ran a children's home in West Germany. Faced with allegations that he sexually abused young boys, Schäfer fled to north Africa. New allegations caused him to go to Chile, where he arrived in 1961, not long before West Germany sought the extradition of Walther Rauff.

As Rauff faced justice, Schäfer purchased an extensive tract of land near Parral, a town about 300 kilometres south of Santiago, Pablo Neruda's birthplace. He established an agricultural and religious colony, inspired by the ideas of William Branham and Oral Roberts, two virulent anti-communist preachers he came to know. *Arbeit ist Gottesdienst*, 'Work is divine service', was the motto that Schäfer chose for the Colony.

The Colony had its own school, hospital, chapel and bakery, and a German-themed hotel with a restaurant selling sausages and other Teutonic fare. By the early 1970s, the community counted several hundred residents, German immigrants and local children who were adopted and Germanised. Opposed to Salvador Allende, the Colony maintained close links with extreme right-wing groups, including Patria y Libertad, and senior figures in the Chilean military. In September 1973, Schäfer welcomed the Coup and Pinochet, and forged a close working relationship with the Junta and the DINA. Pinochet visited the Colony in August 1974, and Manuel Contreras, a frequent visitor, hunted there with Schäfer. The rumours of paedophilia and other sexual abuses, already rife, would be supplemented by rumours of torture and other crimes.

In 1976 the United Nations reported that Pinochet's opponents were being sent to the Colony to be tortured, killed or disappeared. A year later, Amnesty International published first-hand accounts from two escapees, Erick Zott and Luis Peebles. Peebles, a psychiatrist, told of being held in an underground cellar and tortured with electricity by an older man, who he later recognised as Schäfer.

After Pinochet left office in 1990, more details emerged on the close relationship between the Colony and the Pinochet regime, with graphic accounts of systematic child abuse. The Colony's name was changed to Villa Baviera, and in 1997, faced with allegations of sex crimes, Schäfer fled. The police confirmed systematic sexual abuses, DINA crimes and links to the disappeared, some last seen at Londres 38. There were reports of a mass grave, and of bodies being exhumed and cremated. The DINA turned to the Colony, it was said, because the Germans were reliable on torture.

After a journalist found Schäfer hiding near Buenos Aires, he was extradited to Chile, tried and convicted in 2004 of sexually abusing dozens of boys. Sentenced to twenty years in prison, his death in 2010 meant that the crimes he committed with the DINA could not be further investigated.

The Colony's sordid history garnered much attention. There were films and podcasts and a Netflix series (*A Sinister Sect: Colonia Dignidad*). Books and articles alleged Rauff's presence at the Colony, but as with Dawson Island the rumours were not supported by hard evidence.

Two books by Carlos Basso, a journalist and lecturer at the University of Concepción, stood out. The tone and content of *Chile Top Secret*, published in 2017, and *La Secta Perfecta* (*The Perfect Sect*), published five years later, were credible, the research diligent, the findings understated. Basso saw the Colony as 'a concentration camp and place of torture where people from Santiago and Concepción were taken to be disappeared', and believed Rauff had some connection.

# 93

I reached out to Carlos Basso. He was fascinated by Rauff's mer-
cenary spirit, intelligence and pragmatism, and his Nazi and SS
intelligence background. Such characteristics would have been useful
to Pinochet, he explained. 'I am pretty certain he was connected to
the DINA and the Colony', but this was instinct, not proven, based
on years working at the prosecutor's office in Concepción. 'If you are
interested in Rauff,' said Basso, 'you must go to Colonia Dignidad,
undoubtedly the most exotic place in Chile!'

He passed on several documents, two of which stood out. One
concerned the earlier cited Franz Bäar, a long-time resident of the
Colony, the other a training course for DINA agents held at the
Colony in November 1974. In 2005, the police raided the Colony
and found thousands of pages of documents and personnel files.
None mentioned Rauff, but we now know he avoided photographs
and paper trails.

Materials for the training included a twenty-four-page typewritten
document, lectures on intelligence gathering apparently organised
by a man named Lindes. Basso believed the document could have
been prepared by Gerd Seewald, Schäfer's right-hand man and head
of intelligence. Convicted of paedophilia, Seewald died in 2014.

Basso was introduced to Bäar, who was taken from his parents as
a young Chilean boy. Adopted by Seewald, Bäar was given a German
name and a life at the Colony. Schäfer singled him out for special
treatment, as a troublemaker: he was incarcerated at the Colony's
hospital for thirty-one years, subjected to a 'treatment' of drugs and
electricity.

By the time Basso met Bäar and his wife Ingrid Szurgelies, in 2015,
they had left the Colony. 'I met a gentle man, sixty-five years old, a
German mentality, little understanding of Spanish, and the qual-
ities of a child.' Bäar testified to the Chilean courts about Schäfer's
sexual crimes and was treated as credible and reliable. He told Basso
about the lectures delivered to DINA agents.

'I know about the course, it was run by Walther Rauff,' Bäar told
Basso. 'He was a nice friend with two children who spent time at
the Colony.' Unprompted, Bäar mentioned the name repeatedly, and
was correct about the two boys. 'Each time, he told me the same
story, and I have no reason to believe he was lying,' Basso said. 'He

mentioned Rauff in a natural and spontaneous way, without suggesting it was a big deal.'

I spoke with Bäar, via Zoom. He repeated what he had told Basso.

Did you see Rauff deliver the talks? I asked Bäar.

'No, but I saw him at the Colony. I recognised him because I had seen a special film.' He offered no details.

Did Rauff appear in the film? I asked.

Bäar's expressive, kind face, dominated by a single, prominent tooth, offered a generous smile. 'Yes'. He nodded vigorously. 'I needed time to discover who this person was,' he explained, unaware of Rauff's past, of the gas vans. When I suggested we look at some photographs, he agreed, but with a caveat: 'It is very hard to get back memories from those times.'

On screen I shared a photograph of Rauff, taken in the mid-1960s. I did not mention his name. Bäar stared at it for a minute. 'I am looking at the eyes and the nose.' Eventually, he said, 'No, I don't recognise this man.'

I put up a second photograph. The same man, a decade later, in 1976, this time with glasses. 'Is it the same person?' Franz Bäar asked, gingerly.

Yes.

'No, I don't recognise this man,' he said.

I put up a third photograph, a different man. Bäar did not hesitate. 'Yes, this is the man they called Lindes, this is Walther Rauff.'

Except that it wasn't, I said, as gently as I could. The photograph was of Cornelius Krieg, whose file the police found in the Colony archives. Born in Mainz, Germany, Krieg served as an engineer with the Wehrmacht and later moved to Concepción, in Chile. The Colony file said he worked as an instructor on hand-to-hand combat with the Chilean Navy, and held a position with ASMAR, the state-owned naval construction and repair company.

Bäar grinned. 'Ah, OK.'

I reported back to Basso. Krieg had no background in intelligence, Basso said, so he could not have given the talks or designed the course. On the other hand, as an SS intelligence officer, Rauff could have been a lecturer in 1974. There were three clues in the documents, thought Basso. 'First, the speaker mentions an affiliation with the Navy. Second, the talk is on intelligence gathering. Third, Rauff had a background in intelligence techniques, including torture.' He said he'd send me the document.

The twenty-four pages arrived the next day. They were in German, with images of instruments of torture, but made no mention of names, speakers or attendees. The document addressed matters of surveillance, apprehension, interrogation, and physical and psychological techniques. They offered guidance on ballistics, bombs and missiles, and the use of decoys to abduct people, stated to be based on Gestapo methods. The targets were MIR members and communists. These people could be turned, the document warned, but 'a turned agent is never a real agent'.

To my untrained eye, the document felt amateur, and it offered no confirmation of Rauff's involvement. Still, it was curious that the lectures were delivered in German, referred to Nazis, the SS and Gestapo, and Quito, where Rauff once lived. It was not entirely fanciful to raise the possibility that Rauff might be connected.

I sent the document to Dr Kerstin Hoge, an academic at Oxford University, a specialist in German linguistics and phonetics.

'Absolutely fascinating,' she said. She knew of the Colony, a place of 'revolting individuals, events and ideologies', but thought it would not be easy to find a 'linguistic fingerprint'. She'd try.

# 94

A thoughtful assessment arrived a few days later. The document was in five sections, she explained, a mix of transcript and notes, almost certainly involving more than one lecturer. It contained many linguistic errors, indicating that the speakers did not have 'full native competence' in German. Other clues confirmed Rauff could not be the sole author, or perhaps not connected to the document at all.

Dr Hoge was pretty sure that a Spanish speaker or writer was involved. The term *Kinderschule*, for example, was not a German word, but a literal translation of *escuela infantil*, the Spanish for kindergarten, or nursery. The formats used for dates – day, month, then year – followed the South American style, not the German approach.

The use of pronouns indicated that the speakers were men, most likely with a military background. They seemed to be drawn from the lower ranks of the Wehrmacht, not Rauff's more senior level. *Strammer Kerl*, for example, meant 'tough guy', offered a sense of informal masculinity and suggested a lesser educational status or authority.

The use of the composite *Busschofför*, bus driver, used only in the Alemannic dialect area (German-speaking Switzerland, Baden-Württemberg and Swabia in Germany, or Austrian Vorarlberg) indicated that one of the speakers was from there. These were the only places where that word was used. As far as I knew, Rauff had no connection with any of these places.

One lecturer fought on the Eastern Front in the Second World War, against Ukrainian Red Army units. Rauff had no such background. Another was familiar with the story of Peter Simon, a teacher at the German school in Concepción who fled Chile in October 1973. Rauff had no known connection with that city. One speaker 'likely to have been in the Navy' – as Rauff was – received a karate kick from a female naval officer. Rauff was not associated with karate, as far as I knew. Another speaker referenced a meeting with Salvador Allende in Quito, but Rauff had known Pinochet there, not Allende.

In sum, thought Dr Hoge, the 'lectures' were probably delivered by different speakers; some were fluent in German, others had Spanish-speaking origins. She doubted Rauff was among them.

I reported this back to Carlos Basso. He was sanguine. 'Next time you are in Chile, come and visit me in Concepción,' he suggested. 'Go to Colonia Dignidad, then come and see me. I have more things to suggest, in person.'

# 95

I followed the suggestion. To prepare for the visit to the Colony I read books and watched the Netflix series, a German-Chilean production, in which Pinochet made a fleeting appearance, in the August 1974 visit. Children sang, Pinochet wiped a tear, and hung out with Schäfer. There was no sign of Rauff.

I went with Monserrat, from Concepción, then two hours by car, across impoverished lands, flat and soulless. On the outskirts of the estate, we reached a tombstone-like rock, protected by barbed wire, on which the new name was inscribed: Villa Baviera.

A large, colourful map at the Colony's entrance announced the Tourist Complex, Villa Baviera. It depicted the facilities, including a hotel, gardens and swimming pool, bakehouse and engineering works, a cheese factory, the hospital. There was no word of torture or disappearances, or sex crimes, or Erick Zott and Luis Peebles, or the DINA. It was presented as a place of recreation, not pain.

We were accompanied by an Austrian ice-cream maker, who reached out after reading *The Ratline* and learning of my interest in Rauff ('some of my older friends in Chile knew Rauff and know his son reasonably well, and might be of help if needed'). To write a book is to attract unusual characters. The residents of the Colony wandered around in German-style clothing, children who'd reached pension age, descendants of those complicit in the horrors of the past. They still ran the show, replete with German flags and old Mercedes, and a delicatessen selling locally produced Westphalian ham and sausages. The beating heart of the Colony was the Frei House, replete with photographs of famous visitors, including Pinochet in military regalia. Here was Paul Schäfer's bedroom, its windows peppered with hundreds of bullet holes.

Words cannot capture the awfulness of Villa Baviera.

We wandered around the gardens and buildings, had a German dinner in the same restaurant where DINA agents once gathered, a forlorn space populated by a few tourists. We met Harald and Horst, lifelong residents, and sat at the kitchen table eating freshly baked Kugelhupf, a cake my Austrian grandmother used to make for me.

The two spoke of Schäfer, of encounters with Miguel Contreras ('quieter and more educated than others, who were brutal,' said Harald), of DINA agents. Contreras once accidentally shot dead a nine-year-old boy, Hartmut Münch, while hunting chickens with Schäfer. The incident was hushed up but the grave was there to be visited.

There was no love for Schäfer among these ageing men. 'He told us he was against National Socialism, then constructed a similar system of his own,' said Horst. If you ignored the rules, it was off to the hospital, for drugs and electricity. 'We were Germans, taught to follow orders and be very afraid of the Russians and communism,' said Harald.

They spoke of the abuse. 'Schäfer told us the sex was for our education,' said Harald. 'It was for our own well-being, to show he was in charge, not the parents.'

They spoke of 1990, of their sadness when Pinochet stepped down. 'He was good for us compared to Allende, whose victory was seen as the end of the world at the Colony,' said Harald.

They spoke of Schäfer's abrupt departure in 1997. Having grown up with dire warnings about the dangers of leaving the compound, they were shocked when the police cut the fences and broke in. 'We want to save you,' said the police. 'We don't want to be saved,' replied the residents.

They spoke of Pinochet's crimes. 'It was difficult to believe such things had happened,' said Harald, on first hearing the allegations. 'I couldn't believe it, even though some of it happened right here, in the Colony.'

Pinochet's arrest in London in 1998 came as a terrible shock. 'We thought he was our saviour,' said Horst. 'Now I see what he did was a crime.'

They spoke of needing help, how Germany offered money to the residents for its failure to intervene over many years. A one-off payment was offered, $11,000 for a lifetime of horror. Not enough to start a new life, or bring years of impunity to a decent end, thought Harald. The Colony was transferred to a new charity, but the children of the perpetrators stayed in control. 'We want land of our own, they won't let us have it.'

They spoke of therapy. 'Dr Niels Biederman, a psychiatrist, came to see us, paid by the German Embassy,' said Harald. 'I saw him three times, but understood this was not the solution.'

I showed them a photograph of Rauff, which prompted no hint of recognition. Over two days I showed photographs to several residents, but none of them recognised him, or said they recognised him, or expressed any curiosity. This was a 'head down' sort of place, where no one knew the name.

I slept in a hotel room near the restaurant, part of the dormitory where children had been abused. Deeply anxious, I barricaded the door with chairs.

## 96

On the second day I met Jürgen. For a modest fee he showed us around a familiar face from the Netflix series. 'The show is accurate,' he said. He was born in 1964, and had lived at the Colony for most of his life. He took us to the site of a future museum, with a sign: 'A people without memory is incapable of growth.' We peered at photographs of the original members. Only after Schäfer left did Jürgen comprehend the scale of the wrongdoing. He pointed to his parents, Walther and Mathilde. True believers, he said, they were *Russlanddeutsche*, Germans from Russia, traumatised by the Second World War, virulently and forever anti-communist.

'My first sexual encounter with Paul Schäfer was when I was five,' said Jürgen. 'It happened in his bathroom, very nicely decorated.' He offered a horribly graphic account, how Schäfer first noticed him, a boy, a runner, athletic. 'I did what I was told. I took off my clothes. He talked of God and the Bible and said that if I spoke to anyone I would go to hell.' He stopped himself. 'When Schäfer left the Colony, in 1997, he said goodbye, and told us if we were good enough, he would return. We believed him.'

'We also believed that Pinochet was our saviour', that his years in power were 'golden'. The Coup was so special that 'people could listen to the radio, which normally wasn't allowed'. The military visited, so did Contreras ('I sang happy birthday to him!'). Schäfer travelled to Santiago, important people visited. 'I was ten years old when Pinochet visited! He went to the restaurant, he went to the torture place. He was against communism, and so very much loved here. We called him *Opa*, Grandpa Pinochet. Schäfer was *Tío*, Uncle Paul.'

Jürgen remembered some who hung around the Colony. 'There was a man called Lindes, a Nazi. He was often with Schäfer; they hunted together. Another colonist was in the SS, so was a visitor.' I showed him a photograph of Rauff. 'No, not him', but he added a caveat. 'Just as I cannot say that Mengele wasn't here, maybe this man was here too.'

He took us to the potato store, used as a place of torture, passing a trapdoor in the ground. 'This was the cellar, where old cars were hidden, and people were tortured and killed. In the Pinochet years, a hundred soldiers stayed at the Colony, ate in the restaurant, left their weapons outside.'

The potato store was a large barn, with a tiny plaque on the wall. It said: *Sitio de Memoria Ex Colonia Dignidad "Bodega de Papas" Testimonio de violaciones a los Derechos Humanos* ('Ex Colonia Dignidad Memory Site, "Potato Store" Testimony to Human Rights Violations'). 'This was where the torture happened, a space Schäfer gave to the DINA,' Jürgen explained. 'Manuel Contreras was here, in this room.' He paused. 'After Pinochet, the police came and took everything away.'

Villa Baviera was grotesque. It was a relief to leave.

With no evidence of a connection with Rauff, the only path that seemed to be left was the León Gómez affidavit.


## 97


Later, writing up my notes and listening to the tape, I noticed that Jürgen had the same surname as Franz Bäar's wife, Szurgelies. It was also a name in a Chilean news story – at twenty-four, Jürgen fled the Colony, only to be caught and returned – and a case in an international law report.

'Taken by force', a local newspaper reported, until Jürgen was 'locked behind the barbed wire of Colonia Dignidad and nothing ever heard of him again'.

During his brief taste of freedom, Jürgen met an Evangelical priest, who was later contacted by a West German diplomat. Why did young Jürgen flee, the diplomat enquired. The priest said nothing, but on learning of his enquiries, Jürgen's parents, who were dual nationals of Chile and West Germany, went straight to the local court in Chillán. By making enquiries, they claimed, the diplomat violated their rights to privacy and family life under the Chilean constitution.

Not at all, said the West German Embassy, their diplomat was immune from legal process, under Article 39 of the Vienna Convention on Diplomatic Relations, he was just doing his job. No, said the

Szurgelies parents, he interfered and went beyond the usual functions of a diplomat. These were the same arguments raised in the Pinochet case before the House of Lords.

The court ruled that the diplomat acted within the functions of a diplomat and was entitled to immunity. The Supreme Court then reversed the ruling. Distinguishing between official acts and private acts 'has long been a controversial issue for foreign courts', the judges noted, and the immunity rules couldn't trump the parents' human rights under the Constitution, which was 'supreme law' and prevailed over all international rules. The Supreme Court sent the case back to the Court of Appeal in Chillán, which decided the case was moot, so there was no need to rule.

The case was reported in the International Law Reports, immortalising Jürgen Szurgelies and the proposition that immunity was not absolute. Francisco Orrego Vicuña, who was Pinochet's ambassador to London in the 1980s and later advised him after his arrest, welcomed the ruling. 'No State can stand above the requirements of protection of such fundamental rights,' he wrote in a 1991 law-review article, seven years before Pinochet was arrested. The claim to immunity couldn't be 'a bar against the protection of human rights', which must always 'prevail in case of conflict with immunities'.

Seven years later, while in London to add support to Pinochet's claim to immunity, Orrego Vicuña took the opposite position, and even castigated those who argued for the position he'd articulated in 1991. 'What have you done, what have you done?' he asked Christopher Greenwood, one of the lawyers arguing against Pinochet's immunity. How can you argue against immunity, Orrego Vicuña asked me, over dinner at his club, the Athenaeum, before berating me for my work with Human Rights Watch. Back then, I did not know of the article on the Szurgelies case he'd written seven years earlier.

# 98

As Chile's Supreme Court was pondering the relationship between human rights and immunity in the Szurgelies case, León Gómez was writing about Pinochet's crimes and signing an affidavit in which he claimed to have been interrogated by Walther Rauff.

I first encountered the affidavit in Martin Cüppers' biography of Rauff. The mention referenced an article by one Ingo Kletten, which in turn relied on a book by one Friedrich Paul Heller.

The various accounts suggested that the Gómez affidavit was available in the archives of the Institute for Social Research in Hamburg, and the Fritz Bauer Institute in Frankfurt am Main (the latter named after the renowned post-war prosecutor of Nazis). Neither institution had a copy. Nor did Professor Cüppers.

So I searched for León Gómez. His name appeared in several newspaper articles, in relation to the book he wrote on the disappeared. I came across the original proposal for that book, in which he stated that the disappearances from Londres 38 were 'first carried out with the advice of the Nazi criminal Walther Rauff'. Published shortly after Pinochet left office, his book *Tras la huella de los desaparecidos* (*In the Footsteps of the Disappeared*) listed the names of hundreds of disappeared men and women, including Alfonso Chanfreau.

Curiously, unlike the proposal, the book itself made no mention of Rauff.

Gómez's earlier book – *Que el pueblo juzgue, historia del golpe de Estado* (*Let the People Judge, History of the Coup d'État*) – was published in 1988. This listed the names of many perpetrators – Pinochet, Contreras and Espinoza were all there – but not Rauff.

Where was León Gómez? A researcher was unable to locate him, but thought he might be connected to the Londres 38 organisation. I contacted Erika Hennings, the organisation's founder. 'I knew León Gómez,' she wrote, and said she was vaguely aware of an affidavit, but had not seen it and could not vouch for it. She passed on an email address. My researcher wrote to Gómez, and he replied with a telephone number. She called him many times, but Gómez never answered. Months passed. 'He doesn't answer the phone, doesn't reply to the emails,' said the researcher.

A year passed. In October 2019, I travelled to Santiago to deliver a lecture in a series that honoured Roberto Bolaño. I visited the Museum of Memory and Human Rights, where the display included several items connected to my research: a mother's letter to Pinochet's Minister of Justice, Miguel Schweitzer Speisky, seeking help in finding her disappeared son, and a certificate from the Spanish

Consulate in Santiago, certifying the death of Carmelo Soria, due to a cervico-thoracic trauma.

On the morning of the lecture I took an early walk. I left the Plaza San Francisco hotel, turned right and found myself on a cobblestoned street, one with old lamp posts. This happened to be Londres, the street on which many refrigerated vans once trundled. I went to number 38, a low, grey, stone building, with a large wooden front door. It was open, so in I went, walking across the black and white floor tiles. Back then, I didn't know *Izvestia* referred to this place as Rauff's 'office', or that ninety-eight men and women disappeared from here. I wandered the rooms in silence, imagined the mood in 1974.

I gave the lecture, and by the time I was back in London there was still no sign of León Gómez. Nor could I find any trace of Ingo Ketten, whose article first mentioned Gómez's affidavit. An acquaintance in Nuremberg informed me that Ingo Kletten did not exist, he was invented by a man named Dieter Maier. Maier did exist, a former Amnesty International worker who devoted himself to the crimes of Augusto Pinochet. Kletten was one of many pseudonyms Maier used, I was told, as he feared for his life. Another made-up name was Friedrich Paul Heller.

Heller? The Kletten article that first mentioned the Gómez affidavit referenced a book by Heller. The penny dropped: every reference to the Gómez affidavit led back to Dieter Maier, who cited himself. The lesson was clear: proceed with caution when it comes to evidence, as nothing is only ever what it seems. In fact, I'd learned this from my practice in international cases. 'Widespread reports of a fact may prove on closer examination to derive from a single source,' the judges in The Hague once declared. Numerous reports of a 'fact' should be treated as having 'no greater value as evidence than the original source'.

In search of the original source, I looked for Dieter Maier and found him in Germany. Genial and open, he didn't have a copy of the Gómez affidavit, as he'd given it to the Fritz Bauer Institut in Frankfurt. They don't have it, I said. Try the Museo de la Memoria y los Derechos Humanos in Santiago, he said. They don't have it either. I doubted the existence of an affidavit.

Yet Maier insisted that Gómez wrote it. 'Upon my personal request,' he said, so never part of an official file. When the two met in the 1980s, Gómez told him that he recognised Rauff as 'a member of the team that tortured him'. The account was credible, so the words were put to paper and Gómez signed it. 'The affidavit was one or two pages, no more. The key sentence was that when his blindfold was loosened, he recognised Rauff to be present during his torture session.'

'The rights in the affidavit are mine and nobody else's,' Maier told me. 'Gómez wanted me to use it as additional confirmation.' As I pressed, a glimmer of doubt emerged. 'Could a blindfolded person identify a torturer while being tortured'?

Maier told me that in December 1990 Gómez testified about the disappearance of Alfonso Chanfreau, and his testimony was treated by the courts as credible. I found the testimony. Gómez offered a detailed account of his own arrest, in July 1974, his detention at Londres 38, and seeing Chanfreau there. 'I always knew that Alfonso Chanfreau was the most tortured, as he was supposed to be one of the most important leaders of the MIR,' Gómez told the judge. 'He arrived in terrible shape from the torture and had lost many kilos, he was very thin and looked ill, that was the last time I saw him.' The testimony made no mention of Rauff.

In the same case file I found a statement by Erika Hennings, Alfonso Chanfreau's wife. Yes, she confirmed, a number of detainees mentioned that one torturer spoke with a clear German accent. 'It seemed to be a reference to Walther Rauff,' she reportedly observed.

As I digested this material, León Gómez suddenly appeared.

## 99

Gómez contacted my assistant Monserrat in May 2021, two years after we had started looking for him. 'Such a nice man, and he sounds so young!' she reported. He lived in Santiago and was happy to meet.

In due course I returned to Santiago and visited him at his home, modest and tidy, in Renca, a suburb in the north of Santiago. He lived with his second wife, surrounded by volumes on history and politics, and portraits of Salvador Allende. The radio played classical music, he smoked continuously, we spoke for hours, I returned several times.

He was short and very thin. He wore a bright-red plaid shirt, in contrast to his air of deep weariness. His hair was dark, his beard long and grey. He wore silver-rimmed glasses, perched at the tip of his nose. His eyes were piercing and sad but were also strong and fighting.

He was born in Chiloé, an island in the south, into a political family. Allende, or *El Tito*, as he called him, was close to his grandfather, a Socialist Party leader. León saw Allende often, before and after he became President. 'I've known this guy since he was very small,' Allende once said of young León, who knew some secrets, like the President's long-standing affair with his secretary, Mira Contreras, known as La Payita. 'Her daughter visited me in this house,' said León. 'To offer thanks, as I worked at a hospital and helped find the body of her brother, after he disappeared.'

At the time of the Coup, León Gómez was a history student at the Technical University in Santiago. 'I have always loved history, and I always tell the truth,' he whispered. In July 1974, when he was twenty-one, he was detained. 'I was arrested because I was in the resistance, a member of the Socialist Youth', tasked with identifying DINA agents. 'I was turned in by a young woman called Luz Arce.' She was a friend, a socialist, highly intelligent with a photographic memory, who later became a DINA informant. On his account, they went to a restaurant where he was arrested by two DINA agents. (Arce would claim that León turned her in, a claim he denied to me, with vigour but no irritation.)

Gómez was taken to a police station, then to the Tres Álamos detention centre, where he was interrogated and tortured. 'With an electric cattle prod,' he said quietly and firmly, with certitude. 'I was held in Room 25.'

His interrogator was Osvaldo 'Guatón' (Fat) Romo. 'I knew him from Socialist Youth, and he knew me, so he interrogated me, that was how it was.' Romo, who was notorious and boasted of using electricity to torture and the ocean to disappear people, was extradited to Chile in 1992, eventually tried and convicted for numerous crimes, including the torture and disappearance of Alfonso Chanfreau. By then, the Supreme Court had ruled that the Amnesty Law did not cover grave human rights violations, so the courts could exercise jurisdiction. Sentenced to ninety-two years in prison, Romo died in 2007.

Gómez was transferred to Londres 38. 'I recognised the building, as I knew the floor tiles at the entrance, black and white, like a chessboard.' He was held there for about seven days, interrogated and tortured.

Who interrogated you?

'Osvaldo Romo and others.'

Anyone else?

He paused. 'Walther Rauff.'

I had not mentioned the name. Yes, he said, he once wrote an affidavit, many years before.

Did you ever mention Rauff to anybody?

'Perhaps I mentioned Rauff to some friends, but it was only in the 1980s that I really thought about him, when someone said he was a consultant with the DINA.'

Why did you not mention Rauff in your books?

'Because he wasn't Chilean.' León Gómez chuckled throatily. 'If you are not Chilean, you cannot be subject to trial.' His wife Juana, who sat with us, thought his memory was reliable, although he rarely spoke of that period, and never of Rauff. 'Because no one asked,' she said.

When did you see Rauff at Londres 38?

'He was there every day. He assessed the intelligence gathered.' Later, Gómez offered more detail. 'Rauff reviewed the statements and interpreted the answers to the questions. He was a good observer. He knew how to push you.' Gómez spoke without hesitation or doubt.

How did you recognise Rauff?

'I saw his photograph in a newspaper, many years earlier. I was interested in Jewish issues, my family thought we might have Jewish ancestry. It's why I am named León, like my godfather. I was interested in genocide, the Nazis. I saw pictures of Rauff in the newspapers, so I recognised him in Londres 38.'

Did you know about the attempt to extradite Rauff?

'Yes. I knew he was a Nazi officer, that he lived in the south. Some of my party comrades knew him from Punta Arenas, where he worked for fishing companies.' These details were unprompted and spontaneous. I had mentioned none of these matters.

Did Rauff have a connection with Manuel Contreras?

León Gómez chuckled and took a long drag on the cigarette. 'Everybody knew that.'

How?

'*Compañeros*. In the Socialist Party, we all knew each other, we shared information.'

Do you know anything about Rauff's sons?

'Nothing.'

Did Rauff touch you?

'No.' Again, the answer was firm and instant. 'He was more like a psychologist, one who watched me closely. It seemed his role was to judge whether I was telling the truth or lying.'

Was he close enough for you to see his face?

'Yes, he would approach, and would say: "Turn up the electricity, because they are just repeating prepared answers."'

Did you look into his eyes?

'I was blindfolded, but I could see over the top.'

What did you see?

'Evil, hate.'

What language did he speak?

'Spanish with a German accent, although he'd been in Chile for years. He sounded like a German speaking Spanish.'

What did he wear?

'A dark grey suit and tie, I think. Not a uniform. He was dandy, elegant.'

Did he wear glasses?

'I'm not sure, I can't remember.'

Do you remember anything else about his face?

'I remember how very pale he was. I recognised the face because I had seen pictures of when he was arrested in 1962, sitting in the back of a police car.'

Anything else?

'He looked very clean, healthy.'

Did he wear scent?

'He smelled nice, he was well-shaven, impeccable.'

Anything else?

'He would come in and out of the room as if he owned the place.'

Did your comrades recognise Rauff?

'We wouldn't talk much about that. We talked more about which other comrades were there, as they referred to us by number, not name. I was number 81.'

Number 81 described what was done to him. 'They used electricity, beat me in the abdomen, inserted things in my rectum. I knew I was going to be tortured. They wanted names.'

Did you give them any names?

'Only those who were dead or disappeared.'

This happened in the presence of Rauff?

'Yes. He wasn't in every session, but when present he'd listen and give instructions. I sensed he was knowledgeable in interrogations and was comfortable being there.'

I showed him a photograph of Rauff, taken in 1976. Do you recognise him?

'No. He looks like Rauff. They all look the same.'

How then could you be so certain it was Walther Rauff?

'His voice, and because of his accent.'

## 100

After a week Gómez was taken to Cuatro Álamos in the south of Santiago.

'We were transferred in a small white refrigerated van. It was cold inside.' The vans were parked outside Londres 38, to transport prisoners. 'I went to different places, always in a refrigerated van. There was no name on the van, no company sign. People said the vans belonged to a fishery, the *Pesquera Arauco*.' This was the first time I'd heard of this fishery.

He ended up in the regular police cells at Tres Álamos, then allowed to leave. The seven comrades with whom he was held were gone. 'I am the only survivor, they disappeared, forever.' He doesn't know why he survived.

Reporting each day to a police station, and kept under surveillance, he joined a church institution and wrote secret notes. He collected names of the disappeared and then, after Pinochet left office, published them in a book. Later, when the investigations began, he was a witness.

'I testified many times, over many years.' I read the transcript of his 1990 testimony. He was arrested, taken to a 'white Chevrolet van, model C-10, with a grey awning', and saw Fat Romo next to it, with two other men. He testified about Alfonso Chanfreau at Londres 38 – 'he always arrived dead from torture, and that was the last time I saw him' – and later how he was taken to Puerto Montt. 'By then I knew that *Puerto Montt* was the code the DINA used to mean that a person would be executed, then buried on land.'

I asked about Kletten, Maier and the affidavit. 'I remember,' said León Gómez, 'but I don't have a copy.' Nor could he remember when he wrote it. 'There were so many trials.' He paused. 'I got away lightly.' His eyes watered, then he wept, gently, without a sound, as the radio played a Chopin prelude. Perhaps Mario Carroza, a Supreme Court judge and a cousin of his first wife, might know where the affidavit was.

Did you ever go back to Londres 38?

'Yes.' He mentioned the identity parade. 'We can go there together,' he said.

The conversation meandered. We talked about his books, and

Colonia Dignidad. He took a long drag on another cigarette, rubbed his eyes, talked of the disappeared.

'Colonia Dignidad? The sea?' he said.

'I was working for a mining company in the north when that happened. I was delighted when Pinochet was arrested in London. We celebrated and drank Pilsen beer! There was much happiness.'

# LONDON, OCTOBER 1999

## 101

In July 1974, a refrigerated van moved León Gómez around Santiago, and others to places where they would disappear. Twenty-five years later, Ronald Bartle, a magistrate in London, ruled that every such act of disappearance could be treated as an act of torture, a crime against humanity for which Augusto Pinochet had no immunity and could be extradited to Spain.

For Pinochet, the prospect of extradition was very real. 'We decided to launch a new *habeas corpus* application,' said Michael Caplan, to leave no stone unturned. The High Court decided that written arguments would be filed in January 2000. The hearing would be in March.

Pinochet's new case attacked Bartle's judgement, but it also had another purpose: to buy time, as Pinochet couldn't be extradited if legal proceedings were pending. The case meant Straw could rule against Pinochet's extradition, but not in favour.

The need for time was motivated by another factor. As the new case was filed, the Chilean Embassy wrote to Straw to inform him that Pinochet's health had deteriorated, and provided a medical report in support. They were asking for Pinochet to be allowed to return to Santiago, as a matter of urgency.

'The idea of a health issue came through the Chilean Embassy,' Straw recalled, decades later, in his blustery garden. 'To this day, I don't know whether the idea of producing medical evidence, in that way, might have been reinforced by people within the UK government.' His carefully chosen words caused me to go back to the contemporaneous news reports.

The first public hint about a medical issue came in July 1999, three months before the Bartle hearing. Dr Helmuth Schweizer, an Army doctor at Santiago's Military, claimed that Pinochet's health was parlous and he was 'at risk of death'. In September, Pinochet underwent a medical examination at St Peter's Hospital, in Runnymede, near where Magna Carta was sealed in June 1215.

Pinochet's health issues emerged as primaries were underway in Chile, to choose candidates for the presidential election, the second round of which would be held in January 2000. 'The government wanted the Pinochet matter to be resolved before the second round, to help its election prospects,' Miguel Schweitzer explained. 'That was very influential.' The health issue might offer a way forward, he suggested, but denied being involved.

In September 1999, President Frei appointed a new ambassador to London. Pedro Cabrera, former Under-Secretary of the Navy, procured a medical report from two experts in diabetes and respiratory medicine at King's College London. Dr Schweizer, who raised the issue publicly in July, travelled to London with three Chilean doctors, experts in cardiology and psychiatry – one of whom was said to have attended to Pinochet after the 1986 assassination attempt.

At the same time, the Army's Chief of Staff, General Ricardo Izurieta, became actively engaged on the issue. 'I met with Izurieta the whole time,' said Hernán Errázuriz. 'He came to London, met the General, and General Urbina was the link with him.' Izurieta sent other military colleagues to visit Pinochet, to persuade him that his health issues offered a 'humanitarian' way to return. A proud man, Pinochet worried that clemency based on health, which might imply guilt for the crimes, was not acceptable.

The new medical reports raised significant concerns. Ambassador Cabrera shared the details with Foreign Minister Juan Gabriel Valdés and Alberto van Klaveren, a career diplomat. In September, at a meeting in New Zealand, Valdés raised the health issue with Robin Cook, and apparently mentioned the useful role being played by Jonathan Sumption, the barrister advising Straw. Sumption confirmed to me that he advised on the Extradition Act, and that its silence on matters of health did not preclude Straw from ending the extradition on the grounds that Pinochet was not fit to stand trial in Spain.

At the end of September, Pinochet underwent a further medical examination, which indicated that he may have suffered a minor stroke. Following exchanges with Tony Blair, the papers reported that President Frei sent a trusted emissary to London, Cristián Toloza, his speechwriter and a director at the Ministry of Communication and Culture. He was reported to have met with Jonathan Powell, Blair's Chief of Staff, to provide a medical update and a personal message from Frei: 'Let Pinochet return, so the Chilean courts can try him.' Powell 'showed a lot of interest in the medical report', Toloza reportedly told Frei. The newspaper report signalled that Chile's government was actively engaged in getting Pinochet home.

Around this time, Foreign Minister Valdés met with Robin Cook and Abel Matutes, the Spanish Foreign Minister, in New York. Pinochet's health issues are 'the only possible way out,' Valdés told them. French Foreign Minister Hubert Vedrine was said to concur.

In Madrid, Straw met with Jaime Mayor Oreja, his Spanish counterpart. 'I got on very well with him, a very nice man,' Straw recalled. 'He was always asking, "What about Pinochet?" Can't talk about it, I'd say, it's for the courts.' On this occasion, however, Straw offered a suggestion. 'I said, well, produce a sicky to say he can't stand trial. Happens all the time, I don't accept them.' A 'sicky' is a sick note.

The ministerial exchanges encouraged the arguments about ill health. On 25 September, *The Sunday Times* reported that Pinochet had suffered a minor stroke, the health issue that allowed him to miss the hearing before Ronald Bartle. Two weeks later he also missed the handing down of the judgement.

As the foundations were being laid for the ill-health arguments, other developments were underway in Chile. Eighteen months earlier, prosecutor Juan Guzmán had opened an investigation into Pinochet's role in the 'Caravan of Death' case. In September, he finalised a list of seventy-five questions, and now sent them to Pinochet. In early October, a Chilean official in London served the questions on Pinochet. He refused to respond – detained in London, too frail.

This was the context in which Ambassador Cabrera wrote to Straw on 14 October. He sent reports from a leading neurologist at St Mary's Hospital, with other documents provided by Chilean experts. The reports concluded that Pinochet's health had deteriorated:

he was not fit enough to stand trial in Spain and should be allowed to return to Chile.

## 102

Twenty-five years later, Straw had a vivid recollection of Cabrera's letter and its effect. 'They came up with this panel of guys,' he said. 'My instinct in relation to this was: is this bloke fit to travel to Spain? It's up to the Spanish to decide if he's fit to stand trial, because we're not trying him.' Straw hesitated as he spoke. 'I didn't want to make a decision about whether he's fit to stand trial', but was advised that the extradition rules gave the Home Secretary a 'very wide discretion'.

According to newspaper reports, Frei's emissary, Cristián Toloza, returned to London, to urge Jonathan Powell to act on Ambassador Cabrera's letter. What did Chile's Socialist Party want, Powell reportedly enquired. Views were divided, Toloza told him. Some wanted Pinochet to be sent to Spain, others that he be returned to Chile, to be prosecuted.

What was [María] Isabel Allende's position? asked Powell, referring to the former President's daughter.

'Isabel has supported the process in Spain, but I think she now accepts things have changed a lot and that he could be tried in Chile,' Toloza replied.

'Interesting,' said Powell.

'I think Blair wants to find a way out,' Toloza reported back to Frei and Valdés, but believed that any solution must be 'at the appropriate procedural time' and in accordance with English law. Under the Extradition Act, any decision to end the extradition would have to be taken by Jack Straw.

Straw reflected on Cabrera's letter. He consulted lawyers and Professor Liam Donaldson, the country's Chief Medical Officer. 'A good guy, and a friend of my wife,' said Straw. He knew Frei had written directly to Blair, who now wanted to sort the matter out quickly. By now, Straw was aware of the discretion given to him by the Extradition Act, including on medical issues.

Straw decided that if he was going to act on the basis of Pinochet's ill health, he needed an independent and reliable medical report. On 4 November the Home Office sought Pinochet's consent to subject him to an independent examination. The report would be kept 'entirely confidential', he was assured.

***

This was when the health issue first reached Michael Caplan, he said. Miguel Schweitzer had told me that it was Pinochet's medical experts who prompted the Home Office to act, but Caplan thought otherwise. 'I'm pretty sure it was the Home Office who approached us,' he explained. 'I don't think I ever sent a medical report to the Home Office.' It was possible, he added, that 'a report came via the Chilean authorities', but this he did not know.

For Pinochet, the health issue was humiliating. It undermined his sense of well-being and desire to project an impression of continuing power and authority. Nevertheless, since the health issue offered the possibility of an early return, he confirmed his willingness to undergo an independent medical examination.

Pinochet's consent came with conditions. First, the appeal in the pending *habeas corpus* case would not be withdrawn. 'We had a deadline, to get our arguments in for January, it would have been disastrous if we didn't proceed,' said Caplan. Second, the medical report would only be disclosed to Pinochet and the Home Office, not to Spain, the CPS or any of their lawyers. Initially resistant, Straw agreed, but also insisted that the report be given to the Director of Public Prosecutions and the Solicitor General. This was necessary to meet Britain's obligation under the 1984 Torture Convention (which required the authorities to decide whether to prosecute Pinochet in England if he wasn't extradited to Spain).

The Home Office appointed an independent medical team led by Sir John Grimley Evans, an Oxford professor said to be the 'most respected individual in British geriatric medicine'. He was assisted by Dr Michael Denham, former president of the British Geriatrics Society; Professor Andrew Lees, of the National Hospital for Neurology and Neurosurgery; and Dr Maria Wyke, a neuropsychologist, of Mexican origin. 'Four medics with extensive forensic experience,' Straw was assured. 'I was told these were real bastards, really good at cutting through all the people who could stand trial.'

As arrangements were underway, and rumour grew about Pinochet's health, Miguel Schweitzer suffered a heart attack. He recuperated in London, then returned to Chile. 'From 26 December until mid-January, when I returned to London, I wasn't on the scene to address the negotiations on the medical issues.' By now, Chileans had voted in the first round of presidential elections. The centre-left candidate, Ricardo Lagos, supported by the Frei government, came out narrowly ahead of his right-wing opponent, but short of the 50 per cent needed to win on the first round. The second-round vote was scheduled for 16 January. Frei and Lagos wanted a statement from Straw before the date, that Pinochet's next stop was Santiago, not Madrid.

On 3 January, Frei made a public statement. 'We are working to find a solution to bring Pinochet back to Chile,' he said, and revealed the coming medical assessment. 'Some want to make all sorts of difficulties, so he does not undergo medical examinations,' he added, aware that the continued detention of Pinochet would help the right-wing candidate. That day, on his way back to London, Hernán Errázuriz was questioned by a journalist at Santiago airport. Was the medical examination being delayed to help the right win the election?

'How could you think that!' Errázuriz replied (¡Cómo se le ocurre!).

On the morning of Wednesday, 5 January, Peter Dean, the doctor assisting the Metropolitan Police, confirmed that Pinochet was fit to travel to Northwick Park Hospital for the independent medical assessment. Again, security was tight, but Dean, who accompanied Pinochet, was surprised the car didn't have darkened windows. 'Anyone could look in and see him in the back!'

Pinochet was checked in, then had a light lunch. In the afternoon, he had a CT scan, blood samples were taken, and his cardiac pacemaker was checked. The Home Office-appointed doctors then carried out a more detailed physical examination, after which Pinochet was subjected to a neuropsychological assessment by Dr Wyke.

Pinochet's doctors were present throughout, but Peter Dean was excluded, and none of the British lawyers attended. Dean was not the only one to be kept out of the loop. John Dew had left the British Embassy in Madrid and was now head of the Latin America Division at the Foreign Office. 'I knew nothing about the health issue, I was told the Home Secretary was dealing with it. It was addressed orally, there was no paper, nothing. That was unusual for the Foreign Office.'

'I wasn't at Northwick Park,' said Michael Caplan. 'The Home Office made all the arrangements.'

Did he think there was a genuine health issue?

'That's not a question I can answer, I had to rely on the medical reports requested by the Home Office.'

Hernán Errázuriz did attend. 'They think I'm mad!' Pinochet said to him at one point. 'They are wrong.'

Jean Pateras, who did not attend, was sceptical. Over the course of the year or more she interpreted Pinochet, she observed no real deterioration in his health. A Chilean doctor at Northwick Park saw Pinochet's brain scans, she recalled. 'A perfectly normal scan of an eighty-something-year-old man, nothing wrong with it,' the doctor reportedly concluded.

Pinochet was assessed in just a few hours, and the four Home Office assessors took less than a day to review the results and write up a report: Pinochet was not fit to stand trial in Spain, and his condition could not be feigned. Straw invited Professor Donaldson to review the document. A thorough and authoritative assessment, Donaldson reported back, there was no reason to doubt the team's judgement. Jonathan Sumption told me he had no reason to doubt the medical assessment or the conclusions. 'The medical assessment was independent, thorough and genuine,' he said, with obvious belief.

'Did you meet the four medics?' I asked Straw.

'I just read their reports, they said he's not fit. Faced with that situation, as it was presented to me, what the bloody hell could I do? I couldn't say, I would rather have not seen this. I should have said . . .'

His voice trailed off, into a void.

## 103

On 9 January, Straw made a public statement: the medical reports were 'unequivocal and unanimous' in concluding that Pinochet's health had deteriorated, so he was 'not at present capable of meaningful participation in a trial'. No change was expected in his condition. The 'decisive criteria' were his limited memory and inability to process verbal information, so he would not be able to follow proceedings, understand questions, express himself or instruct lawyers. In accordance with the agreement between the Home Office and Pinochet, Spain was not provided with a copy of the report. Nor were Belgium, France and Switzerland, who had also sought his extradition.

Two days later, in good time before the second round of the Chilean presidential election, the Home Office informed the Spanish government that Straw was 'minded to conclude' that Pinochet should not be extradited to Madrid. He invited representations from Spain and Amnesty International. Privately, Straw wanted to disclose the medical reports to Spain and the three other countries – 'under conditions of strict confidence' – but Pinochet refused consent. Amnesty asked for a copy of the reports, but Straw refused the request.

On 12 January, Straw made a formal statement in Parliament, and the Chilean newspapers reported that Pinochet would soon be returning to Santiago. The government of Belgium, which also sought Pinochet's extradition, now formally requested that it be provided with a copy of the medical report. We want to question the authors, they said, and we want an independent medical panel to examine Pinochet.

As concerns about the medical reports grew, Ambassador Cabrera told the BBC that Pinochet could lose his parliamentary immunity when he returned to Chile.

Pinochet opposed the idea of publication of the report. 'It's a medical report,' said Caplan, 'we don't agree to disclosure.' He recalled that Jonathan Sumption urged Pinochet's lawyers to allow the report to be made public. No. 'A lady from the Home Office phoned me at lunchtime,' Caplan said, 'as I bit into a sandwich. It was five o'clock by the time I finished it, when the discussion with the Home Office was over!' The answer from Pinochet was still no. 'You don't disclose medical reports unless you have to, and we didn't have to.'

On 16 January, in the knowledge that Pinochet's return was secured, Chileans voted in the second round of the presidential election. Ricardo Lagos, the candidate of the Socialist Party, won by a tiny margin. He became Chile's first socialist President since Allende. The following day, despite pressure from Judge Garzón, the Spanish government informed Straw that it would not challenge any decision to allow Pinochet to return.

The government of Belgium, however, decided otherwise. It was time to launch a legal challenge of its own, to protect the integrity of the Torture Convention. It reached out to lawyers in London.

# CONCEPCIÓN

## 104

After meeting León Gómez and visiting Colonia Dignidad, I headed off to meet Carlos Basso in Concepción, about 500 kilometres south of Santiago. The city on Chile's coast had significant connections to the Pinochet era and its crimes: a medical student at the city's University, Miguel Enríquez, was a founder of MIR (the Revolutionary Left Movement), which made him an early target of the DINA.

It was here too, shortly after the Coup, that Roberto Bolaño was arrested and held for eight days, on suspicion of terrorism. 'I got out of that hole thanks to a pair of detectives who were at high school with me,' he wrote. Friends in Mexico, to where he headed, would express doubts about aspects of his account.

Bolaño 'created his own myth', was a girlfriend's assessment. He 'liked to play tricks and create mysteries,' said Jorge Herralde, his editor in Barcelona. A literary editor thought it to be without importance whether Bolaño's narratives were 'true or invented', and that 'the only thing that mattered was its literary value'.

The same could be said of Bruce Chatwin's writings on Patagonia, where the line that divides what was experienced or imagined is not always clear.

This is one of the differences between literature and law, between the pages of a book and a courtroom, or a reader and a judge.

## 105

Carlos Basso greeted me at the entrance to the University, an attractive mid-century campus dominated by a looming, elegant bell tower. He is a man of generous proportions and disposition, balding, bespectacled and engaging.

On the way to his office, we passed a colourful mural that depicted the dead and disappeared. In the shadow of a banner that proclaimed ideals of 'Justice and Truth', monotone faces of young men and a woman posed questions.

*¿Me olvidaste?* asked José Carrasco, of MIR. Have you forgotten me?

*¿Donde están?* asked Ricardo Salinas, of the Socialist Party, who disappeared near San Antonio. Where are they?

Carlos Basso told me he could say more in person, but I didn't know what he wanted to share. I had made the journey on a hunch, picking up on Basso's instinct that Rauff played a role at Colonia Dignidad, even if there was no hard proof. We drank coffee and talked more about Franz Bäar, our Zoom conversation, and Bäar's wife Ingrid. 'The guy was Walther Rauff,' Ingrid had told Basso, with absolute assurance and certainty, despite the photograph.

Was she sure?

'Yes, of course,' Bäar had intervened. 'We all knew Walther inside the colony. He came with two German shepherd dogs, always, then one day he stopped coming but the German shepherds remained.'

I was looking for evidence of connections between Rauff and Pinochet, I explained. As I dug deeper into Pinochet's crimes, and the disappearances that became more important in the London proceedings, I had an instinct that Rauff was involved, but I also had growing doubts, in the absence of evidence. There were no documents – they were destroyed by Miguel Contreras in 1977, when the DINA was closed down – and beyond León Gómez there was no other direct witness testimony.

Basso listened attentively as I shared the fruits of a long journey. He told me of a book about an arms dealer named Gerhard Mertins, a former SS man connected to Schäfer, the Colony and Pinochet. Rauff's address was in the files of one of Mertins' associates, said Basso. Bit of a stretch, I suggested. He mentioned María Soledad – 'a very good investigator' – who'd written of Rauff in connection with arms deals for Pinochet.

I want someone who saw Rauff with Contreras, I told him. The conversation traversed Chile, from the Colony, to Dawson Island, then to León Gómez and the interrogations at Londres 38. Basso didn't know about the affidavit, but my mention of it prompted a thought.

'On the pavement outside Londres 38 are stones engraved with names of those executed there, or who disappeared,' he said. 'One of the names is Álvaro Modesto Vallejos Villagrán. He was a medical student, active with MIR. His nom de plume was Loro Matías.'

I hadn't heard the name, so Basso told me the story. Loro Matías was taken from Londres 38 to the Colony by a DINA agent, a young conscript. 'I know him, he has described the journey to the Colony, and explained how the prisoner was handed over to Schäfer.'

I listened.

'Why don't you speak to the former conscript?' Basso suggested. 'We can call him, right now, his name is Samuel Fuenzalida.' It wasn't familiar. He took his mobile phone and dialled.

'Don't mention Rauff's name,' I said.

Basso and Fuenzalida spoke on a video call for a few minutes, in Spanish. I understood the direction of the conversation. Maybe you could show Fuenzalida the photographs I showed Franz Bäar, I whispered. Basso passed on the suggestion. Yes, said Fuenzalida.

I got the photographs up on my phone, and put the screen in front of Basso's phone, with the first photograph.

Fuenzalida looked at the first photograph. 'I don't know this man.'

He looked at the second photograph. 'No.'

He looked at the third photograph. Immediately, with no hesitation, Samuel Fuenzalida's face reacted, softening into a smile of recognition.

'Yes, this one I know. I saw him, at the main headquarters of the DINA, on Marcoleta Street, just a few blocks from Londres 38.' He looked closely at the black and white image.

'I saw him more than once,' he added.

The third photograph was the only one of Walther Rauff, one taken in 1976. Up to this point, no mention was made of his name.

'I saw him in 1974, in January, February and March.'

Basso held his hand over the phone. 'Maybe you can see Fuenzalida when you are in Santiago tomorrow?' he whispered.

'I don't want him to know the name of that person,' I said, 'I just want him to look at the face.'

'Somebody told me this guy was with a fishing company,' Samuel Fuenzalida then said. Unspoken, I assumed he was referring to the *Pesquera Camelio*, in Punta Arenas, but he wasn't. 'We knew the DINA ran a fake fishing company, it was called *Arauco*, the DINA used it for their work, in San Antonio. The fishery had little vans, refrigerated vans, which the DINA used to transport detainees from one place to another.'

This was not the first time I heard mention of the *Pesquera Arauco*, I thought, but couldn't remember why it rang a bell. Only later, reviewing the notes of my conversation with León Gómez, did I notice that he spoke of being transported in a refrigerated van, of seeing several parked on the cobblestones outside Londres 38. He also mentioned the name of the company that owned them.

The phone conversation with Fuenzalida came to a close. No name was mentioned.

We agreed to meet the next morning, in Santiago.

# 106

I met Samuel Fuenzalida in the courtyard of my hotel, on the Avenida Italia. He stood erect and strong, and proud, in a deep-blue shirt, wearing a cap on his head. His face was weathered and worn, with warm eyes. This man had a firm personality, but he was gentle. He had a story to tell.

He was born into a leftist family, and in April 1973, at eighteen, had been conscripted into the Army. After the Coup he was assigned to the DINA, to San Antonio and the Tejas Verdes camp at the School of Military Engineers. Manuel Contreras personally welcomed his unit.

In January 1974, he was transferred to Santiago and the DINA's *Brigada de Inteligencia Metropolitana*, the 'BIM', based at the Villa Grimaldi. He was then posted to Londres 38, where he spent several months, involved directly in the system of torture and some of the ninety-eight disappearances. The most active months were July and August 1974, when a prisoner disappeared every sixteen hours. One was Alfonso Chanfreau.

In 1975, Samuel fled. He went to Argentina, then West Germany, where he was given political asylum. 'I thought I was in danger when they started to kill conscripts.' In 1977 he contacted Amnesty International, which published his account. He gave evidence to the United Nations on the tortures and disappearances. He remained in exile for three decades, and after his return to Chile testified in the trials of several high-ranking DINA agents. The courts relied on his testimony as credible and accurate. On the basis of his evidence, numerous DINA agents were convicted.

Fuenzalida's return to Chile was not easy. For his work with the DINA, as a conscript, he was tried, convicted and sentenced to 541 days imprisonment, for a killing that occurred in 1975. When we first met, he was still prohibited from travelling abroad. 'I was convicted for crimes I did not commit,' he insisted. 'Forty witnesses declared my innocence, still I was convicted.' In 2023, he was convicted and sentenced to a further 541 days, for his role in the kidnapping and disappearance of a photographer, in August 1974. In both cases the sentences were suspended.

He worked at Londres 38 between January and April 1974, before being transferred back to Villa Grimaldi. At both places his commander was Marcelo Moren Brito, the operational head of the DINA, later convicted of crimes against humanity by courts in Chile and France. Fifty years after the Coup, Samuel Fuenzalida was still testifying before Chilean courts. The week we met, he was scheduled to testify against Cesar Manríquez Bravo, commandant at Londres 38, already serving a life sentence.

Fuenzalida and I spoke for several hours. On my first mention of Colonia Dignidad, he said: 'I have been there.' The tone was neutral, the content chilling. 'When I worked at Villa Grimaldi, I was instructed to accompany a senior officer, Fernando Gómez Segovia, to the south, to the place of the Germans. That was what they called Colonia Dignidad. They needed me to accompany a package.'

A package?

'A person. A detainee. He was known as Loro Matías, I knew him, his real name was Álvaro Vallejos Villagrán. He was a medical student, head of the political section of the MIR, the son of a senior non-commissioned army officer, his father worked in the Ministry of Defence after the Coup.'

Fuenzalida didn't know why he was selected for the journey. It was 1974, late July. 'I collected the "package" at Cuatro Álamos', where León Gómez was also being held. 'I knew Loro Matías from Londres 38, where he was a prisoner. When they said he did not need to bring any belongings, I understood he was going to die. He was in handcuffs, tortured and totally broken. Too much had been done to him to allow him to be released.'

At Villa Grimaldi, Fuenzalida saw the detainee files. 'The file of Loro Matías was stamped with the words "Puerto Montt", which meant he would be eliminated "on land".' (The other stamp was 'Moneda', which meant elimination at sea.)

Fuenzalida spoke of the drive to the Colony. 'Fernando Gómez Segovia and I travelled south in a C-10 truck. On the way, we stopped to pick up a permit. We needed that because of the curfew.' At Parral, near the Colony, another truck joined them, with several DINA agents on board.

'We arrived at Colonia Dignidad at about one thirty in the morning. We were met by armed men. I thought we were in an Army facility, because everyone wore a uniform, and held Army-issue machine guns. Later I came to know the identity of two of the men who met us: Gerhard Mücke and Paul Schäfer.' (Mücke, who later testified that at least thirty Pinochet opponents were murdered at Colonia Dignidad, and was convicted for his involvement, died in 2022.)

Fuenzalida continued: 'Schäfer, known as "The Professor", had only one eye, was dressed in olive green, military style. He greeted Captain Gómez Segovia in German. I didn't know German or English. For me, they were all gringos, but it was obvious they knew each other.' He then added:

> Captain Gómez Segovia got out of the truck. He left me alone with the prisoner for a few minutes. Loro Matías asked me to pray for him, for he knew he was going to be killed. They came back and took him out of the truck. They put him in the back of a light blue Mercedes, then drove him to the big house. We followed in our truck. The conversation was in German, so I couldn't understand. I picked up a few things in Spanish, for instance that Pinochet was coming to visit in the next month. This was July 1974, the General did visit in August.
>
> At the big house, we separated. I went to eat, German food. I was upset. I knew the prisoner, I had sympathy for him. Later, the Professor returned, with a black dog – a German shepherd. He stood at the head of the table. Without saying a word, he used his hand to make a slashing movement across his neck. He said: 'Fertig!' Finished. I understood.

Years later, Fuenzalida testified about these facts in court. Paul Schäfer 'was probably the one who murdered Álvaro Vallejos Villagrán,' he told a Chilean judge. Pedro Espinoza, Miguel Krassnoff and Gerhard Mücke, among others, would be convicted for the killing of Loro Matías and each sentenced to ten years in prison.

## 107

As I digested Fuenzalida's account, we returned to the photographs of the previous day. I now had printed copies. He studied them carefully. 'The only man I recognise is the one in the third photograph,' he said. I showed him a different photograph of the same man, taken a decade later. Again, he responded firmly and without hesitation.

'Yes. I know this man. He was with the *Pesquera Arauco*. In the times of DINA, there was a fishing company. I can try to find the name of this man.'

I shared what León Gómez told me, about being taken to the Cuatro Álamos detention centre, in a refrigerated van. A *Pesquera Arauco* van?

Fuenzalida smiled. Yes, prisoners were taken to and from Londres 38 in refrigerated vans of the *Pesquera Arauco*. 'This man Gómez was lucky,' he said. 'Normally the ride in the van was from Londres 38 to the coast, to the town of San Antonio, where the *Pesquera Arauco* was mainly based.'

Fuenzalida knew of León Gómez, because he had met Luz Arce, who Gómez told me had turned him in. Fuenzalida had a different account. 'She told me that Gómez turned her in, not the other way round.' This surprised me, as Arce was a confirmed DINA informer, whereas there was no such suggestion about Gómez. When I put the claim to Gómez, he refuted it forcefully.

Fuenzalida doubted that the man in the photograph was involved in the torture of Gómez. 'The only foreigner was an Italian doctor, who collaborated at Londres 38. I don't think this man was at Londres 38.'

We returned to the photograph, of a man Fuenzalida recognised but did not know was Rauff.

Did you see him in San Antonio or Santiago?

'In Santiago. I don't know his name, but he was part of the DINA, he was in charge of the *Pesquera*.'

In charge?

Fuenzalida nodded.

Where exactly did you see him?

'I saw him at the first headquarters of the DINA, on Marcoleta Street, near here, not far from Londres 38. That was before the headquarters were moved to Villa Grimaldi. I saw him there, many times. I am in touch with other conscripts, they will know him too. We are like a family, we all know each other, we've stayed in contact.'

Did you hear the man in the photograph speak?

'No, but I saw him in Marcoleta.'

How many times?

'Three times, at least. Once, I came to Marcoleta from the Villa Grimaldi with my Commander to drop off some documents. It was in 1974, after I was transferred from Londres 38. This man was in the hall, in the main room, where there was a table, and many people walked around, moving in and out. I didn't see him go into the office. Normally you notice these people because they look different. I knew this man was important because of his manner.' He spoke of how he walked, with a sense of control and arrogance, a powerful and protected man. I recalled Rauff's letter to his nephew in West Germany, around that time. 'I am, so to speak, protected like a cultural monument.'

Samuel Fuenzalida continued. 'I thought the man looked like Henry Kissinger, because of the glasses, *poto de botella*, glasses with thick lenses, like the bottom of a bottle.'

How did he dress?

'He wore civilian clothes, a suit and tie, as they all did. He was elegant, well dressed, neat.'

We looked at another photograph, the same man, Rauff, in 1976, seated at a restaurant with Nena Zúñiga, his lady friend, leaning toward him, by the sea, small boats in the water behind them. The setting was neat, a clean white tablecloth, wine glasses, a bottle of white wine, two large potatoes on the man's plate, a cigarette in his left hand, a white handkerchief in the breast pocket. Fuenzalida examined the photograph. He wondered if the photo was taken in San Antonio.

Did you ever see the man in San Antonio?

'No. I am just speculating about where this could be. I can try to find out.' (I later ascertained it was taken in Valparaíso, in March 1976, a seventieth birthday celebration at the Club Bote Salvavidas.) Fuenzalida continued, without prompts:

Other DINA conscripts told me they would go in a van with prisoners from Londres 38 to San Antonio, that the van would stop, at the second bridge, before the centre. The conscripts got out, the driver carried on with the prisoners. The conscripts didn't know where the van was going. Talking to these people, much later, I learned that by 1974 it was considered that taking the prisoners to Colonia Dignidad was expensive, so instead they took them to San Antonio, where they would be turned into fishmeal.

Fishmeal?

'Yes, fishmeal, feed for farm animals, for chickens.'

I didn't know what Fuenzalida was saying. I didn't process it, take it in, or ask more. We just moved on.

Could the man in this photograph have been at Londres 38?

'Yes, I think so, it is possible.'

Did some interrogators there wear civilian clothes?

'Yes, everyone was in civilian clothes.'

I took a sip of coffee, and asked directly: 'Do you know the name of this man?'

'No,' said Fuenzalida. He looked me straight in the eye. It was clear he had no idea who the man was, or what his name was.

Eventually he asked: 'Do you know who he is?'

I nodded.

'You know his name?' Fuenzalida was surprised, and eager.

'Do you want to know his name?' I asked.

'Yes. Of course I would like to know the name,' he said.

I paused, looked at him, he looked at me. 'The man is called Walther Rauff. Do you know this name?'

There was silence, then Fuenzalida smiled, a big smile. 'Of course, of course I know this name. Everyone knows this name. I just didn't know that it was him, not until now, not until this moment.'

We digested the moment. Could Rauff be connected to some of the activities he had been telling me about?

'Yes,' he said.

I told him about Rauff's other life, his role in the gas vans, his friendship with Pinochet in the 1950s, his role as manager of the *Pesquera Camelio* in Punta Arenas. I told him about connections, how I sat next to Miguel Schweitzer during the Pinochet hearings in London, how his father Miguel Schweitzer Speisky had advised on Rauff's extradition to West Germany and later served as Pinochet's Minister of Justice, how Schweitzer worked for the *Pesquera Camelio* and knew Rauff personally.

'Crazy world,' Fuenzalida said, as he processed the information, the points of detail and connection.

Do you have a photograph of the *Pesquera* trucks or boats?

'No, but I might be able to find one.'

Would other colleagues from the DINA recognise the man he now knew to be Walther Rauff?

'Yes, they would.' He stopped. 'But I don't think they will want to talk to you because they are fearful of the repercussions.'

Would there be any documents from *Pesquera Arauco* or the DINA that mentioned Rauff's name?

'No,' he confirmed. Miguel Contreras destroyed the documents in 1977, when the DINA was closed down, after Orlando Letelier was killed, when the Americans got involved.


# 108

A year later, I saw Samuel Fuenzalida again, in the courtyard of the same hotel. He had information and anecdotes to share, from others who had worked with the DINA. They recognised the man in the photograph, by the sea, with the lady with big hair.

I saw him in the detention camp at Chacabuco, the old saltpetre mine in the Atacama desert, a former colleague wrote. 'He turned up with dogs, trained dogs.'

I saw him, wrote another, in response to the photograph. He was known as 'El Chacal', the Jackal.

I recognise him, wrote a third, who once met a relative of Rauff's, a younger man who turned up at Manuel Contreras's home in Santiago, laden with seafood. 'Shrimp, prawns and king crab, frozen, or tinned. The crabs were whole, just the best parts, the legs and the tails.'

Fuenzalida showed me a WhatsApp message. It was sent by Jorgelino Vergara, who worked with Manuel Contreras from 1974. 'Representatives of the entire southern cone' came to Santiago 'to plan "Operation Condor"', wrote Vergara. 'I attended to them, I was there, and I picked up many things about what was going on.' Rauff was present. 'I can assure you that *El Chacal* was already operating with the high command of the DINA.'

So, Fuenzalida had no doubt that Rauff worked with the DINA?

'Yes, but Rauff's relationship was with high-level members of the DINA, not with inmates like Gómez,' he insisted.

Do you still believe, as you said a year earlier, that Rauff worked with the *Pesquera Arauco*?

'Yes! Yes! I believe what my old colleagues said to me, that they saw him.' Fuenzalida stopped. 'And of course, I saw him at the DINA headquarters, I saw him myself.'

The DINA office on Marcoleta Street was nearby.

'Let's go,' said Fuenzalida.

Off we went, in a small black and yellow taxi.

## 109

Sitting in the back of the cab, a ten-minute ride, Fuenzalida kept talking.

'I have no doubt Rauff was a consultant with the DINA, that he worked for the *Pesquera Arauco*.'

I wondered about proof. I wanted evidence, not speculation, rumour or myth.

'You will have the evidence,' he said. 'Maybe Vergara will even agree to meet you. He told me he saw the man in the photograph and Manuel Contreras together, on several occasions.'

The taxi driver interrupted. 'May I say something?'

'Of course,' we answered in harmony.

'It is not a rumour,' said the taxi driver. 'It is a fact. Rauff worked for the DINA.'

How did he know?

'Everybody knows.'

Of course, but how did he know, really?

'Everybody knows. I am seventy years old. I lived through that period. We all knew Rauff's name. We all knew the stories. We all knew what he had done with the Nazis. We all knew he worked for the DINA.'

The taxi pulled up and let us out on Avenida Portugal, on the corner with Marcoleta. Fuenzalida got his bearings, walked us along Marcoleta, which turned into Jaime Eyzaguirre, past the San Borja Park. We came to a white modernist building, three stories on Baron Pierre de Coubertin Street, nondescript and unmarked, next to a kindergarten.

'This is it,' said Fuenzalida, 'the DINA main offices, in 1974.'

How did he feel being back?

'It's been a few years.' He said this quietly. 'This was the first entrance . . .' He pointed to walls covered in graffiti.

Inside?

'Just offices.'

Where did he see Rauff?

'On the other side, in another building, we must walk around.'

As we walked, he phoned Vergara, told him we were on Marcoleta.

'I remember talking about Rauff with Gerd Heidemann,' he said after the call was over. Fuenzalida met the *Stern* magazine journalist while living in West Germany. 'Heidemann told me Rauff had a role here in the DINA, that he was an instructor.'

How did Heidemann know?

'He said he met him in Santiago at the end of the 1970s, they talked about it.' Heidemann travelled with Karl Wolff, Rauff's old boss, looking for old Nazis, said Fuenzalida. Yet, I knew, there was no word of this in the transcript that Heidemann typed up, no mention of the DINA, no questions about the DINA. If it came up it was in a moment not recorded, or if it was recorded, Heidemann left it out of the transcript.

We walked along Pierre de Coubertin, onto Avenida Vicuña Mackenna, and came to a locked gate, preventing entry onto José Carrasco Tapia street, named after the journalist murdered in 1986 following the failed assassination attempt on Pinochet. A passing resident let us in. We walked to the end of the street and another set of locked iron gates. We peered through, towards a three-storey building.

'This is the exact building where I saw Walther Rauff, on the first floor, several times,' said Fuenzalida.

Today the building is the University of Chile's Centre for Advanced Education Research. There is no plaque to indicate this was the DINA's nerve centre, where decisions were taken to detain, torture, kill and disappear.

Fuenzalida went off to make a phone call.

'Jorgelino Vergara says he agrees to meet you,' he said.

# LONDON, JANUARY 2000

## 110

A few days after Jack Straw announced his intention to allow Pinochet to return to Santiago, I was contacted by colleagues in Brussels. Straw won't let the Belgian government see the medical reports, and they want to bring legal proceedings.

Foreign Minister Louis Michel – 'He was always very much against Pinochet,' said Miguel Schweitzer – identified two legal routes: a case against Britain at the International Court of Justice in The Hague, to stop Pinochet leaving, or a case in the English courts to gain access to the reports.

On 14 January 2000, the investigating judge who sought Pinochet's extradition issued to Belgium started proceedings in Brussels for the medical reports. How 'paradoxical', said Judge Vandermeersch, that Straw thought Pinochet was too unwell to stand trial in Europe, and is sending him back to Chile, hoping there'll be proceedings against him there. 'How can his health situation be different in Chile?' the judge asked.

The Belgian Foreign Minister instructed me and a group of Belgian colleagues to draft an application to the International Court of Justice. On 25 January, I sent a draft to the Court's President, Stephen Schwebel, and spoke informally with him about a case that might shortly be initiated: by refusing to extradite Pinochet to Spain, Britain would violate the 1984 Torture Convention and the 1957 European Extradition Convention.

A few days later, we were informed that Tony Blair had asked a question to the Belgian Prime Minister: are you aware of a case in which one member of the European Union has sued another before the ICJ? The Belgians forwarded the question to us. We were not aware of a precedent. (The first such case was only filed in 2001, by Liechtenstein against Germany, in relation for wartime confiscation of properties owned by Liechtenstein nationals; in 2008, Germany sued Italy at the ICJ to protect its right to immunity in relation to cases brought against it before the Italian courts, in relation to Second World War crimes.) Blair's question, and our negative answer, killed the case before the International Court.

Instead, Belgium opted to go to court in London, to seek a ruling that by refusing to give Belgium a copy of the medical reports on which he had relied, Straw violated English law. Amnesty International and five other organisations filed a parallel case. I acted as a junior barrister in the case, led by Nigel Pleming and Rabinder Singh. On the last day of January the judge ruled that the case was 'not arguable': Straw's decision to refuse disclosure was not unlawful, unfair or irrational and, putting the boot in, Amnesty and the other organisations had no standing to sue.

Belgium appealed to three Court of Appeal judges, who expedited the case. Over two days of hearings, in early February, Belgium's arguments were opposed by Jonathan Sumption for the Home Office. On 15 February, the Court of Appeal unanimously upheld the appeal, ruling that Belgium was entitled to see the reports on which Straw relied.

'Sixteen months have passed since Pinochet's arrest,' wrote Lord Justice Simon Brown, the latest in a long line of English judges who addressed Pinochet's legal situation. 'What should happen to him now? Should he be extradited to Spain to stand trial for the grave crimes of which he is accused? Or should he be allowed to return home to Chile?' Views were divided and it was 'high time the decision was taken'. Belgium sought Pinochet's extradition, as an interested party, and wanted to see the report.

The case turned on fairness, Simon Brown said, and laid out the applicable considerations. The context was 'exceptional' and 'uniquely controversial', a case with serious allegations of international crime. Torturers were the 'common enemies of all mankind', every country had 'an equal interest in their apprehension and prosecution'. If Pinochet wasn't extradited, he'd be 'untriable anywhere in the world'. In favour of disclosure, Belgium must be able to comment on the report, so justice was seen to be done. The arguments against disclosure were modest delay and a certain loss of Pinochet's right to confidentiality. On balance, Simon Brown concluded, fairness and transparency outweighed Pinochet's interests, so Belgium should see the report. The two other judges agreed, so the Court of Appeal ordered immediate disclosure to Belgium, Spain, France and Switzerland. They were also given seven days to send their observations on the report to Jack Straw.

'I had a copy of the report in the safe,' said Caplan, 'someone from the Home Office came round to collect it.' Copies were made available to Belgium, and expecting to see a copy the next day, we prepared to work with Belgian medical experts. Later that evening, Pinochet's medical reports were disclosed by two Spanish newspapers and available on the web.

# 111

To this day it is not known how the medical reports reached the press. Who had an interest in making them public? Publication would generate sympathy for an old man, but the reports also raised serious questions about the adequacy of the conclusion that Pinochet wasn't fit enough to stand trial.

All and sundry could now express their views, and they did. The first report, prepared by Professor Grimley Evans and two colleagues, addressed Pinochet's physical and other medical conditions. Although easily tired, he was cooperative and alert and had a 'good rapport' with the doctors. He scored well on a Mini Mental Status Examination, 'smiled appropriately', and maintained a sense of humour. He was a little deaf, his voice had deteriorated, and he reported a decline in memory, with difficulty remembering people, events, and scents. He told Grimley Evans that once he failed to recognise his own wife, an incident Jean Pateras recalled with scepticism.

He had been mildly depressed, but perked up with medication. In the early months of detention he read and used a computer, but now mostly watched television and wrote fewer letters, with a handwriting less legible. He was homesick, bored and frustrated.

Grimley Evans found evidence of a recent 'transient cerebral dysfunction', and two minor strokes. Pinochet displayed signs of 'Parkinsonian features' and had a 'tendency to fall backwards'. He showed 'slowness in comprehension' and 'difficulty in understanding complex instructions'. A brain scan revealed 'recently progressive cerebrovascular brain damage'. This, combined with 'clinical evidence of widespread damage to the brain', was 'compatible with bilateral damage to temporal lobe structures'.

The doctors found no major problems, but the 'brain damage' they did identify meant that Pinochet would not be able to follow the trial sufficiently to instruct counsel, understand questions or reply to them. Grimley Evans found no indication that Pinochet was deliberately exaggerating his impairments. As significant improvements were 'unlikely', the team concluded that Pinochet 'would not at present be mentally capable of meaningful participation in a trial'.

The second report was by Dr Maria Wyke, who conducted a neuropsychological assessment, and visual and cognitive tests. She found Pinochet to be pleasant and cooperative, and able to answer questions on his and Chile's history. His verbal comprehension and speech were good. He had no difficulty understanding questions or following test instructions. To my reading, this suggested he was perfectly able to stand trial.

However, she continued, having been a person of 'superior intelligence', Pinochet now functioned in a 'low/average range', with 'a moderate/severe deterioration of intellectual function beyond that due to his age'. He had a 'severe deficit' in short-term memory and delayed recall, and was unable to retain information over time. With no evidence of fakery, she concluded, 'he would not be able to cope with the legal complexities of a trial'.

On face value, the conclusions were not compelling, as other reactions confirmed. Many in the medical community thought the reports did not come close to indicating Pinochet was unfit to stand trial. The Spanish government offered no reaction, but Judge Garzón commissioned a report by eight Spanish doctors, which concluded he was 'sufficiently normal' and could stand trial. Belgian experts came to the same conclusion.

Jean Pateras raised an eyebrow when I mentioned the subject of the medical reports. She and Peter Dean, the doctor advising the Metropolitan Police, saw Pinochet regularly over the course of a year. 'For the most part, he was absolutely fine and arrogant, and enjoyed reading. When I asked the police what he did all day, they said he watched *Star Wars* films and loved reading books about Napoleon.' She sensed a ruse. For months he was 'absolutely normal', she recalled:

'Hola, ¿qué tal? ¿Cómo estás? ¿Cómo está vuestro marido? How
are you? How's your husband?' he would say. Then, one day,
when I was there with Peter Dean, I sat next to him and he said:
'You know, Jean, this morning I was talking to my wife, I didn't
know who she was!' I thought, Oh really? He carried on in that
direction. 'I was talking to someone, I forget who people are, I
just don't know what's happening.' I said, 'Oh yeah, pull the other
one!'

Jean drew her own conclusions:

I realised he was going to play the lunatic, the Alzheimer's thing,
or whatever. At the beginning, I remember him being told, or
somebody telling me that they had told him, 'For Christ's sakes,
pretend you are mad, old and mad.' 'I'm not going to do that,' he
said. In the end, he obviously realised that was the only way to get
home.

I shared the reports with a colleague, Professor Howard Robb, Professor of Old Age Psychiatry at University College London. He was
highly critical of the reports. They offered no convincing diagnosis
for the mild cognitive impairment, the mention of cerebrovascular
disease was 'vague', and there was an over-reliance on the physical
examination. The most striking failure, he said, was the total absence of a psychiatric evaluation. This reflected Professor Grimley
Evans' 'antipathy' towards psychiatry, said Robb.

He was also struck by the weakness of the conclusion that Pinochet wasn't faking symptoms. There was no effort to speak to people
who observed Pinochet's behaviour, like the police, or the lawyers
who took instructions, or Jean Pateras and Peter Dean. Professor
Robb was aware that those who spent time with Pinochet saw him
going through his papers, reading, annotating documents, then
signing them. 'He wasn't doing it in crayon!' The reports disclosed
no 'real attempt' to assess Pinochet's capacity to understand or give
instructions. Dr Wyke's neuropsychological results put him squarely
in an 'average zone'. On her approach, 'half the population' could
have avoided extradition to Spain.

# 112

Years later, Jean Pateras introduced me to Peter Dean, and we had lunch together at a pub in Hampstead. He was friendly and open, a man of obvious decency and reliability. 'I travelled with Pinochet to Northwick Park for the medical assessment,' he recalled. 'He was a bit older, a bit frailer, but basically fine.'

Dean first examined Pinochet a day or two after his arrest, then regularly over the next months, including the morning of the visit to Northwick Park. Everything was normal, including his blood pressure. 'On the eve of battle, the old soldier remains calm!' Pinochet once said to him about his fine blood pressure.

Dean noticed no significant change in Pinochet's condition across fifteen months. At Northwick Park he was surprised to be excluded from the assessments. Home Office appointees only, he was told. A few days later, he heard rumours that doctors might conclude Pinochet wasn't fit to stand trial. This bothered him. 'I felt that something wasn't right, that he may have pulled the wool over their eyes,' he said. 'I believe in rights and wrongs, I had a real issue here, felt a strong need to act, so I reached out.'

He contacted the Metropolitan Police forensic medical group. 'I have an issue here,' Dean told them. It went up to an assistant commissioner of police. 'A message came back: "Sit on your hands."'

Dean turned next to the Medical Protection Society, a body that offered advice on legal and ethical issues for medical practitioners. 'I thought they might be helpful, but they just said it was all very difficult.'

His next port of call was the British Medical Association, the trade union for medical doctors in Britain. The ethics department declined to provide immediate advice. 'We need to think about it, they said.'

'By then I was deeply troubled,' said Dean.

Having drawn a blank, he decided to go to the highest level, the General Medical Council, the body that governed ethical conduct for medical practitioners across Britain. The Council suggested he write to Jack Straw. 'Send a letter to us, we'll pass it on to him.'

So Peter Dean, as a medical practitioner with decades of forensic experience who had attended to Pinochet for fifteen months, wrote to Straw. There was no medical basis to conclude that Pinochet could not be extradited to Madrid, he wrote. 'I had no doubt he could stand trial.'

He sent the letter to the GMC. He didn't hear back from Straw, who told me he had no recollection of the letter or Dean. Soon after he wrote, however, Dean told me that he received a telephone call from Liam Donaldson, the Chief Medical Officer. 'He must have got my number from the police and was on an information-gathering exercise,' said Dean. He told Donaldson what he thought, that Pinochet was basically fine. 'The next morning I received a telephone call from a police officer at Scotland Yard. He told me I was no longer on the Pinochet case.'

Did Straw see your letter?

'It was apparent to me, from the fact that I received the call from the Chief Medical Officer, that Straw must have known about the letter.'

## 113

Baltasar Garzón, the Belgian judge and several others sent representations on the medical reports to the Home Office. These arrived on 22 February, the Grimley Evans medical team reviewed them, and stuck to their conclusions. Sir Liam Donaldson told Straw he was impressed with the rebuttal of criticisms. A 'sound and logical' approach, he reported, 'supported by clinical evidence'. Straw reported Donaldson's views as to the 'skill, integrity and independence' of Grimley Evans' conclusions. Nothing was said about Peter Dean's intervention.

Straw considered the representations, and on Friday, 2 March made a statement to Parliament. The Pinochet case was 'unprecedented', requiring him and the courts to navigate 'uncharted waters'. He accepted the reports of Grimley Evans and Wyke and rejected the representations of others. Pinochet was not fit to stand trial, and further proceedings against him would violate his rights under Article 6 of the European Convention on Human Rights, the right to a fair trial.

On legal advice, he rejected the idea that it was for Spain to decide on Pinochet's fitness for trial. In any event, the Spanish authorities confirmed that their standards were similar to the ones he applied.

With no expected improvement in Pinochet's condition, there was 'no judicial purpose' in continuing the extradition proceedings.

Straw said that he received more than 70,000 letters and emails from the public, from across the world. The vast majority urged him to extradite Pinochet. He was attached to universal jurisdiction for international crimes, he assured, and 'very conscious of the sense of injury' that Pinochet's victims and their relatives would feel. 'Ultimately,' he concluded, 'a trial of the charges against Senator Pinochet, however desirable, was simply no longer possible.' Amnesty's lawyer thought differently. 'Incomprehensible legal advice and certainly wrong. Pinochet should have been sent to Spain.'

Straw wished to put a positive spin on the situation. Pinochet had been detained for seventeen months. This sent a signal that 'those who commit human rights abuses in one country cannot assume that they are safe elsewhere'.

Nevertheless, he accepted, Pinochet would 'probably not be tried anywhere'.

# PART V

---

# IMPUNITY

'There is no denying that this man understands vans.'
Pablo Neruda, 2 July 1965

# THE DEAL

## 114

When Jack Straw announced that Pinochet would return to Chile, rumours were circulating about a deal between Britain, Chile and Spain. There were suggestions of diplomatic and telephone conversations between Prime Minister Blair and President Frei.

'Our legislation contemplates a humanitarian exception,' one newspaper reported Blair to have told Frei, offering a way out of the Pinochet problem. 'Strictly confidential,' Blair insisted, as any publicity would 'complicate' matters and be 'difficult to manage'. Frei's son would later report that his father wanted Pinochet home by the time the President left office in March 2000.

Nearly a quarter of a century on, in 2024, the speculation about a deal was widespread, but as with the rumours about Rauff's involvement with the DINA and Contreras there was no hard evidence.

Pinochet 'conned' Straw into believing he had Alzheimer's, Lord Hoffmann told an interviewer. He was not alone in that view.

Jean Pateras thought something must have happened. So did James Cameron, although he had no hard information. 'As one of Pinochet's lawyers, that's how we interpreted it,' he told me.

Michael Caplan was equivocal. 'I've heard rumours, in the background, that the health issue came up between the authorities.' Yet, he wished to emphasise, 'if there were any discussions, I was never involved and never knew of them'.

Miguel Schweitzer, Pinochet's principal Chilean lawyer, was evasive, offering a quizzical look and a raised eyebrow. 'We know there were conversations, probably many, but no, Hernán Felipe Errázuriz and myself, as the representatives of Pinochet, never had anything to do with them.' Pushed, however, he acknowledged facilitating contact with a Chilean medical doctor. 'The one that knows more precisely is Hernán Felipe, speak to him,' he suggested. Errázuriz, at his most diplomatically charming, made clear he had no wish to address the subject.

'There was no deal involving me, far from it,' Jack Straw told me firmly, insisting he would have been kept at arm's length. 'They kept me out of it because I was suspect, wanting to get Pinochet on a plane to Spain.' Yet James Cameron and I sensed a disconnect between what Straw said and the impression he gave. He looked at us, blinked, then said: 'I think Number 10 was involved.' Pause. 'Jonathan Powell.' The name came out of the blue, it hadn't been mentioned. 'Tony was finding this embarrassing . . .'

So, if there was a deal, who was behind it?

'Obviously the Chilean government,' said Straw. Pause. 'People inside the British government? Jonathan Powell. We need to get shot of this, there are other equities involved.' The British intelligence services wanted Pinochet away. 'They kept playing on how important Chile had been in the Falklands.'

Was there a deal?

'Yes,' said Straw. No hesitation, but then a minor correction. 'It's difficult to say.'

On the Spanish side, everyone involved assumed a deal. 'Of course,' said Juan Garcés, there was no other way to explain what happened. Baltasar Garzón concurred. 'It was confirmed to me by Abel Matutes, Spain's Foreign Minister,' he said. 'Matutes said the diplomatic situation was tense, the UK and Chile were in agreement.' Aznar's government did not object.

Carlos Castresana, the Spanish prosecutor who started the legal process, agreed, and told me of a conversation with a Chilean general, on a flight after a seminar in Switzerland. 'I said to the General that I knew of a political agreement between Spain, Chile and Britain to allow Pinochet to return,' said Castresana. He hoped to provoke a confirmation, and it did. He added, 'The General said, "Not true. It was only between Chile and Britain. And I know all about it, I was there."'

# 115

Carlos Castresana introduced me to Javier Urbina, the Chilean general who worked closely with General Ricardo Izurieta,

Commander-in-Chief of the Chilean Army, throughout the period Pinochet was in London. General Urbina and I spoke by phone, then met in Santiago. When I suggested there might have been a *quid pro quo* – no extradition for reasons of health, return, loss of immunity, proceedings in Chile – he said simply: 'Yes, that's right.' Still, he thought the medical issues were 'not entirely made up', a point made by Jonathan Sumption, who advised Straw on English law. 'The medical reports were clear.'

General Urbina summarised the Army's perspective. Pinochet had ignored advice not to travel to London. When the former President was arrested, General Izurieta came under 'intense pressure' to secure his release, and worked closely with Frei, with whom he had a decent relationship but who worried how the Army would react. A main forum for discussion was Chile's National Security Council, on which Izurieta served. It was there, in June 1999, according to Urbina, that the health issue was floated as a possible way out, when Frei assured Izurieta he would 'sort this out, with an agreement with the British'. Around this time, a Chilean newspaper first reported an issue with Pinochet's health.

'June was when the health issue became the catalyst for a way out,' Urbina recalled. Izurieta travelled to Europe, hand-in-glove with Frei's agreement. In London, assisted by General Juan Carlos Salgado, he met Pinochet and his advisers, and someone said to be at the heart of the British government. *El Mercurio*, the pro-Pinochet newspaper, reported the visit, signalling the military's efforts to secure a return, working with Frei's government.

According to Urbina, Izurieta had a good relationship with Chilean judges, as crimes from the Pinochet era started to reach the courts, where they hit the wall that was the Amnesty Law. 'And I had a strong relationship with Miguel Schweitzer, at the time,' said Urbina, contradicting what Schweitzer told me. 'Hernán and Miguel knew exactly what was going on.' On Urbina's account, Pinochet was kept fully informed, with General Salgado acting as the intermediary (he had served as Chile's military attaché in London and was close to Errázuriz). Salgado also met Pinochet's lawyers in Spain.

The armed forces of Chile were 'flexible' on the terms of any arrangement, Urbina explained. 'They did not object to the loss of Pinochet's immunity if he returned to Chile, and General Izurieta talked with many people, including the President of the Supreme Court, to make sure there would be no problems.'

'No problems.' Did that mean 'no immunity'?

Without answering the question, Urbina said: 'So did Frei.'

So did Frei what? Speak to the President of the Supreme Court?

Urbina nodded. The Court's President at the time was Roberto Dávila Díaz, who had, at the start of the legal year, made an impassioned plea for Pinochet's return.

José Miguel Insulza, who moved from Foreign Minister to Secretary-General of Frei's government in June 1999, confirmed the timeline. 'June was when President Frei began a new approach, dealing directly with the British Prime Minister's office.'

Insulza didn't deal with the British himself but he saw President Frei every day, so he 'knew what was going on' behind the scenes. The lead was taken by Foreign Minister Juan Gabriel Valdés, working closely with Izurieta, and by the Minister of the Interior, Raúl Troncoso. The point person was Cristián Toloza.

'Toloza was trusted, he was the guy who went to London, to Tony Blair's office, to speak with Jonathan Powell,' Insulza told me. In Santiago, meetings about Pinochet were on a tight hold. They were conducted in a small office close to the President's office at the Moneda Palace. With 'direct access' from an underground car park, the meetings were very secret.

Did the British come up with the health argument?

'Yes, but it was accepted immediately by the Chilean side,' Insulza said. 'I don't think any British psychiatrist or doctor had examined him.' The process was conducted in two stages: a doctor was retained by Pinochet, then there was a report from independent doctors. 'That was agreed fairly early on.'

And Spain?

'I don't think they were involved in any way.'

The liaison between the British and Chilean governments was at the highest levels, starting with a conversation between the two leaders. 'Mr Blair called President Frei,' said Insulza. Blair's memoir made no mention of this, or Pinochet or Chile.

High-level contacts began in the middle of 1999. 'Toloza made the deal, travelling to London for the first time around July. By September or October, things were moving, but I wasn't much involved,' Insulza recalled. He thought a deal would help elect a centre-left candidate to succeed Frei (who, by the constitution, couldn't stand again), so there was 'political value to Pinochet's return'.

To face charges in Chile?

Insulza nodded.

Was there a *quid pro quo*?

'Well, I do hope so,' said Insulza, with a smile. 'The assumption was that somehow Pinochet would be tried when he got to Chile.' As I pushed, Insulza barely resisted, although he chose his words with care. He and Frei discussed Pinochet's fate, and the President's office had informal contact with Juan Guzmán, the prosecutor investigating Pinochet's role in the 'Caravan of Death' case. 'We never had an official relationship,' Insulza said of Guzmán. 'My impression was that the President, knowing he was very formal, spoke more with somebody in the Supreme Court than with Judge Guzmán.'

Somebody in the Supreme Court? The President? I understood Insulza to be confirming a conversation between the President and the judiciary, on the ending of Pinochet's immunity. 'Maybe Juan Gabriel [Guzmán] or somebody spoke to other judges,' he said, 'on what would happen if Pinochet came back to Chile.'

Would the composition of the Supreme Court be changed, to end immunity for Pinochet?

'I don't know,' said Insulza. 'I assume, given the way the Chilean Supreme Court is appointed, it is not easy to change three or four judges at once. The assumption was there would be some kind of change.'

A change at the Court to accommodate Pinochet's return by ending his Senatorial immunity?

'I think what happened was that the judges more favourable to judging Pinochet, not necessarily the majority of the Court, were given the opportunity to write the rulings.'

When Insulza learned of Jack Straw's decision to allow Pinochet to return to Chile, was anything said about a deal?

'I don't recall that, but . . .' He thought about my question, then added: 'I thought there was some agreement. It was presented as a decision of the British government, but I knew about Toloza's visits to London.'

# 116

Cristián Toloza was not easy to locate. During Pinochet's detention, his name barely featured in media reports, and he never gave interviews. A mutual acquaintance made the introduction, and we met in Santiago. With glasses and grey hair, neatly attired, an engaging smile, he was happy to talk about what happened. 'It is time,' he said. He was now working at the Ministry of Foreign Affairs, and made no attempt to hide his disdain for Pinochet.

Back in 1999, Toloza was President Frei's speechwriter and economic adviser, a member of the core team that dealt with Pinochet's arrest and plans to get him home. 'We prepared as part of an informal group, run by the Minister of the Interior, Raúl Troncoso, with the Foreign Minister and Insulza, the government's Secretary-General.' It was 'a real crisis', like the one in 1995, when the Supreme Court sent Manuel Contreras and his deputy at DINA, Pedro Espinoza, to jail for the murder of Orlando Letelier back in 1976. Frei worried that Pinochet's arrest could lead to violence and deaths, and maybe even an Army takeover. 'Izurieta was clear about the situation, a gentleman, a happy realist, balanced,' Toloza recalled. And yes, Javier Urbina was much involved.

Toloza took the lead because he was trusted and knew Britain. He was trained in clinical psychology, and lived in Exeter in the 1990s, studying for a PhD in psychology (his thesis was on the variability of political attitudes, in general and in Chile). 'I had a feel for the granular pulse of the British,' he said. In Britain he learned about 'thinking for yourself', and this helped him to understand London's approach, so he could explore ideas on the way forward and feed them into Santiago's thinking.

'My training gave me an understanding of the unconscious, the need to take account of all aspects of a situation, including instinct.' Toloza developed a three-step strategy to win over the British government. 'We acted completely independently from Pinochet's lawyers, and I never met Schweitzer or Errázuriz, or Blair, Cook or Straw. I dealt only with Jonathan Powell, Blair's Chief of Staff.' Jack Straw confirmed he never met Toloza, and said he'd never heard his name.

The first step followed the arrest, as Blair's government took political advantage of Pinochet's presence. 'At the beginning we knew they'd be like *un cerdito en el barro*, a little pig in the wood, enjoying the situation,' said Toloza, 'but when they encountered difficulties that would change.' Pinochet's presence allowed the British to promote ideas about judicial independence and the rule of law, and Robin Cook's 'ethical foreign policy'.

'We knew to wait for the moment when Pinochet became a problem, and that happened with the Hoffmann episode, a real embarrassment,' Toloza continued. The 'wait and see' stage ended in April 1999 with the third House of Lords judgement and Jack Straw's second Authority to Proceed. That was when Blair raised the health option with Frei.

The next step was the 'application of pressure' stage. 'I travelled to London to warn the British side of the coming dangers,' said Toloza. The first meeting with Jonathan Powell was exploratory, to build trust, and it went well. Initially, when I myself met him, years later, Powell had only a vague memory of the Pinochet saga. 'I have a feeling the arrest was shocking, and I remember a young guy coming to see me,' said Powell. This was Toloza. Later, with the help of his diaries (Powell was writing a book about Iraq, he explained, so it was no trouble to check that period), he recalled the first meeting with 'a young guy'. It was on 2 June. 'I'm not embarrassed about the outcome,' said Powell, 'just don't recall how we got there!'

'The diary says my Chilean opposite number came to see me to ask us to release Pinochet,' Powell said. 'I set out what we could and couldn't do legally, presumably on the basis of a brief, so I must have been expecting the meeting.'

Two days later, 'I see him again,' Powell recorded. The details of an arrangement were gently teased out: the British were open to a resolution but constrained by English law and the political need to ensure that if Pinochet returned to Chile he'd face justice there. 'Toloza said they wanted to set up a legal process in Chile, and I set out what we needed from them,' said Powell: an end to Pinochet's immunity, followed by criminal proceedings in Chile.

For Toloza, the second meeting offered 'a libretto', something to take things forward. Troncoso had instructed the team 'to do anything it could to persuade the British to release Pinochet', as he wanted a clear commitment before the second round of the Chilean presidential elections. 'In this stage, I went to 10 Downing Street with a clear strategy, to create fear in the mind of Jonathan Powell,'

Toloza said. 'I arrived with a piece of political fiction.'

'We are concerned that Pinochet could die in Britain,' he told Powell. 'He's old, a military man, proud but defeated, an exile for his country.' If he dies in Britain, Toloza warned, 'you will turn him into a martyr and a saint. Is that what you want?' The possibility of assassination still hovered, and Pinochet's death would cause a 'hysterical' Chilean Army reaction. 'One thing is sure: if he dies in London, there will be deaths, Valdés the Foreign Minister and Lagos the candidate for President will be killed.' He explained that the assassination attempt on Pinochet in September 1986 was followed by violence and killings. If Pinochet died in London, a delicate political situation might implode. 'You risk undermining a fragile democracy – is that what you want?'

Powell listened attentively, said little, took notes. His recollection of the meeting did not extend to the details. President Frei followed up with a letter to Tony Blair, reiterating the points, creating a paper trail so it couldn't be said his government failed to do everything it could. 'If Tony spoke to Frei, there would have to be a memo in the No. 10 file,' Powell noted. Yet Blair made no reference to Pinochet or Chile in his memoir, I pointed out, not a word.

This was the background which forced the turn to Pinochet's health. 'I think the British started the medical issues,' Toloza recalled. 'They had legal advice that the extradition procedure could be ended because of a health issue.' Such advice would have come from Jonathan Sumption, I suggested, who was advising Straw. 'I know who Sumption is,' Powell said, 'but don't remember talking to him at that time and have no memory of ever having met him.'

A linkage was discussed: a health issue would end the extradition, allow Pinochet to return to Chile, and once back he'd lose his immunity and be investigated and prosecuted. So that was the arrangement?

'Of course,' Toloza had replied.

The third step began in September 1999, when Toloza met Powell once more at 10 Downing Street. 'It was on 20 September,' Powell confirmed. 'He comes back, pushing their approach harder.' Both sides hoped this final stage would lead to a deal, but one serious obstacle remained: the British needed confirmation that the Chilean courts would end Pinochet's immunity. For that, Toloza brought a piece of paper to London, one that remains secret and unavailable to this day. 'This is very, very secret,' Raúl Troncoso, the Minister of the Interior, told Toloza.

'I went to London with a copy of an internal Chilean Army document,' said Toloza, 'the personal authorisation by Pinochet of the "Caravan of Death" operation, in the days immediately after the Coup, a document that bore his personal signature.'

The document was provided by the Army, it seemed. 'With this document, we have direct proof of the involvement of Pinochet,' Toloza told Powell, and 'a legal basis to put him on trial in Chile.' Toloza confirmed that the Chilean government and military wouldn't oppose the courts, and the move was signed off by President Frei and General Izurieta. Powell vaguely recalled being given a document. 'It must be in the public records office,' he said. If it was, I was not able to find it.

'The document was a photocopy of the original,' Toloza said. 'I gave it to Powell for further British examination. I didn't keep a personal copy, as it was given to me by Raúl Troncoso, expressly to be given to my British counterpart. Our message was that this document was part of a legal process already underway in Chile, it was a secret document, part of an ongoing judicial trial in a specific case.' This was the 'Caravan of Death' case being investigated by prosecutor Juan Guzmán.

By 'secret document', Toloza explained, it was 'probably only available in the "secret copybooks" that allowed the judges, in Pinochet's era, to "manage" special files that weren't available to lawyers or others involved in a case'. From direct experience, he was aware that documents existed that were not publicly available, but he didn't know what happened to them after the dictatorship ended.

The decision on immunity would be for the Chilean courts, Toloza assured Powell, and several cases were already pending against Pinochet. 'The government has communicated to the judicial authorities that they have a green light to proceed in any case against Pinochet,' he added, so 'the British government could liberate Pinochet and be certain that he would be processed in Chile.' This was 'the turning point' in the exchanges: the loss of immunity wasn't based 'on vague promises, but on empiric facts to support the request'.

I asked about the document.

'As it was secret,' said Toloza, 'I just read it once in private, and then had a look again when I gave it to Powell.'

Did he recall what it said?

'From my reading, it was clear that the document offered strong evidence that Pinochet was directly involved in the "Caravan of Death" case, and a sufficient basis for him to be put on trial in Chile.' The document gave 'force and persuasion' to the argument that Pinochet would lose his immunity.

'I remember clearly,' Toloza continued, 'that in its first page there was a written comment by Pinochet in the margins saying something like "aprobado" (approved) and then his personal signature. In Chile, it is a custom called "una mosca" (a fly), where you put your initials on a government document. I showed it to Powell, who was impressed.'

'I don't remember the details, but I have no reason to doubt that's what happened,' Powell told me. 'It's highly credible. Seems likely we wanted to get it sorted out and they wanted to sort it out, and probable they came up with a deal.'

The two men met for a fourth and final time on 18 October, as the deal was being implemented: Straw had received a letter from Chile's ambassador in London, Pablo Cabrera, and advice from Sumption confirming that the Extradition Act allowed Pinochet to return if he was unfit to stand trial. Straw consulted Professor Liam Donaldson – 'a friend of my wife' – and instructed his staff to obtain Pinochet's consent for an independent medical examination.

I asked about something else I had heard, that a document was prepared in the course of the cooperation between the Chilean Government and the Army, to instruct Pinochet on how to act to maximise his chances of returning to Chile.

Toloza confirmed what I picked up.

'A report was prepared for General Izurieta on how Pinochet should fake depression,' he said. 'It was about ten pages long, and suggested how Pinochet should 'perform': he should evoke thoughts about suicide, problems of memory, and say things that were irrational or absurd.

We looked at each other, silently. He smiled wryly.

Did the report reach Pinochet?

'I assume so! Izurieta went to London and saw him there.'

# LONDON, MARCH 2000

## 117

Following his decision that a trial of the charges against Augusto Pinochet was no longer possible, Jack Straw took steps to exclude the possibility of any legal challenge before the English courts. All that remained was a possible case before an international court.

On the morning of Straw's announcement, on 2 March, the Foreign Minister of Belgium gave a press conference. 'After consultation with our legal advisers and our lawyers in London,' Louis Michel declared, 'I confirm that Belgium will not bring the case to the International Court of Justice in The Hague.' This was the consequence of Tony Blair's intervention.

Like Straw, Michel tried to put a positive spin on the announcement. He had been in touch with the Chilean government, he said, which had asked him to provide any evidence available to Belgium of crimes committed by Pinochet. Their own courts were independent, the Chilean government assured him, and all Chileans were equal before the law, including Pinochet. Noting that the President of Chile's Supreme Court had declared, a few days earlier, that 'conditions were met for Chile to judge Senator Pinochet', Michel seemed to suggest that proceedings against Pinochet in Chile might follow. No one really picked up on the hint.

Pinochet was not yet accountable for his atrocious crimes, said Michel, but the previously 'unthinkable' principle that 'a dictator is no longer out of the reach of justice' was now recognised.

The Spanish government remained silent, delighted to be rid of the whole wretched affair.

## 118

Following Straw and Michel's announcements, the day of Pinochet's return to Chile arrived. It was 2 March 2000, and 503 days had passed since the interpreter Jean Pateras informed Pinochet he was under arrest.

Early that morning, Pateras joined Michael Caplan at the house in Wentworth, to accompany Pinochet to an unnamed place of departure.

'It was pissing down with rain and he was in his wheelchair,' she recalled. 'The General was very excited and all smiley.'

Was he *compos mentis*? I asked Jean when we met.

'Absolutely *compos mentis*, yes.' There wasn't much to do, or interpret. '"In you go," I said, "into this car."'

The convoy of six police vehicles and two motorbikes left at around ten o'clock. No one in Pinochet's entourage was told the destination.

'We were concerned right until the last minute of General Pinochet's stay about an assassination attempt,' said Errázuriz. 'Now, there was extra protection, the streets were closed, a helicopter followed, and the plane that was to take us back to Chile was moved around different airports. We and the crew didn't know until the last hour which airport we were going to.'

As they sped off, Jean Pateras's phone rang:

> I was in a police van, it was Garzón, furious. 'Where are you?' he said. 'I don't know, in the car, he's leaving the country.' 'What the fuck is happening? Jean, put me on to the . . .' I cut him off. 'I'm just the interpreter, can't do anything, we're taking him to the airport.' 'I can't believe it! I want that fucking man in my court!' He was ballistic.

Inspector Hewett instructed Jean Pateras to terminate the call and switch off the phone:

> Later, when I got home, there was a barrage of messages from Garzón. I told him, 'I couldn't answer, they told me to turn my phone off.' 'That's disgraceful!' he said. All that time, while we were driving up, he was calling and calling, but the phone was off.

The car snaked its way around London, then headed north. The original plan was to head to Northolt, an airport west of the city, six miles north of Heathrow, but at the last minute the convoy changed direction and headed north-east, to a military airfield near Lincoln, a hundred and fifty miles away.

'It was all hush hush,' said Pateras, the route was kept totally secret. As the convoy made its way up the A1, the dominant mood was anxiety.

'At one point, as we were driving, somebody said "Sniper! Sniper on a bridge!"' she recalled. 'We all ducked. "It's OK, just a cameraman!"'

Without incident, the convoy arrived at RAF Waddington, a military airfield, just before one o'clock. Pateras spotted the blue Boeing 707, a Chilean Air Force plane:

> We got out. He was in the wheelchair, pretending he couldn't walk. I was told not to say anything. We couldn't see any cameras but were told they were all around. They worried the media would read our lips. He was wheeled to the plane in his wheelchair. He said goodbye. I said 'Goodbye! Good luck!'

'Come to the kitchen,' she said to me, 'I'll show you a photograph.'

It was framed, on the wall, in colour. Pinochet smiling, pink-faced and angelic, a cosy blanket draped over his legs, walking stick to hand. 'See the old bastard? He was really happy to be going home, smiling, about to get on the aeroplane. I had my hair all nicely done.' Pateras stood behind him, a scarf clutched to her head, close to Hernán Felipe Errázuriz, tall, in glasses, attentive and anxious. 'Wheelchair bound, still arrogant,' Pateras recalled.

His final words?

'Adios, y muchas gracias. Goodbye and thank you.' Up he went, on an elevated platform, then wheeled into the plane. Michael Caplan, his solicitor, followed, a bit later.

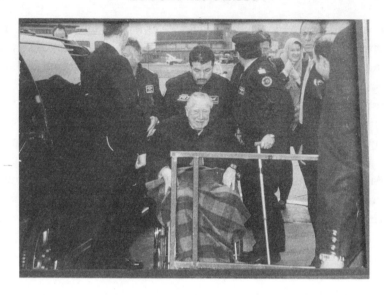

Pateras recalled that morning with some gravity but chuckled at the mention of Caplan's name, Caplan later told me. 'I was quite tense,' he said, worrying about a last-minute court application to stop the plane taking off. 'A judge had been made available at the High Court to hear any legal challenge, I felt it right to be with the General. I had the legal papers in my briefcase, to deal with any such proceedings.' Pinochet was stoical, showing little emotion on the drive or when they arrived.

'Margaret Thatcher gave me a gift for him,' Caplan said, 'but only on the plane, she said, as it left.' Caplan didn't decline. 'You don't say no to a former Prime Minister!' The gift was bulky and, worried he'd forget it, he tied it to the outside of his briefcase. 'I went inside the plane to give it to him, he was very courteous.'

Caplan didn't notice the doors close. 'I handed him the gift, unaware the plane was moving, and said: "This is from Margaret Thatcher." It was a plate, something to do with the last time we beat the Spaniards.'

'The last thing he did was thank me,' Caplan recalled, 'a model of absolute courtesy throughout. Mrs Pinochet was with him, and now they were quite emotional.' When the police noticed Caplan was on board, the aircraft stopped, the doors opened, and he disembarked.

Miguel Schweitzer, who was also on the plane, watched the episode and laughed at the memory:

We were waiting and waiting, engines in motion, but it didn't
leave. Mrs Thatcher had sent a gift, but Michael was delayed. We
spent twenty minutes waiting, nervously, worried there could be
a legal appeal. Fortunately, that didn't happen, Michael arrived,
formally gave the gift to President Pinochet, who didn't open it.
Later, he showed it to us. It was something important, not just
anything, but I don't remember what.

A plate, I told him, that commemorated the defeat of the Spanish
Armada sent to invade England in 1588. 'A token of personal esteem
for the great injustice of his detention,' Thatcher said, an act 'which
should never have taken place'. 'Perfect,' Schweitzer thought, the
Spaniards deserved it.

At ten minutes past one the plane left British soil, with Pinochet
and Lucía in a separate cabin. 'They built up a sort of room for him,
with a bed and a couple of chairs,' said Schweitzer. 'Most of the
journey he slept and rested, we never really had a conversation. I
think he was still shocked, hadn't realised he was going back.'

The flight was longer than usual, as Brazil and Argentina refused
permission to pass through their airspace, requiring the plane to
refuel on Ascension Island. 'When the pilot finally said we were
entering Chilean territory, there was an explosion of joy,' Schweitzer
recalled. 'Somebody brought up a bottle of champagne, which we
opened.'

How was the arrival?

'Atrocious,' Schweitzer snapped back sharply:

Hernán Felipe and me, we spoke two or three times with the
General, saying he must leave the plane in a wheelchair, but he
wanted to leave by the stairs. We told him, 'No, you can't do that.'
He said, 'Why not?' 'Imagine President, General Pinochet, that
you fall down, everybody there is waiting for you, and you fall
down, on television? You got on the plane in a wheelchair, please
leave the plane the same way,' we said to him. It was hard, but he
understood in the end. He said, 'OK'.

It didn't quite work out that way.

The plane arrived in Santiago on Tuesday, 3 March, shortly before
eleven in the morning, local time. Pinochet prepared to disembark

in the wheelchair, as agreed. A military band played 'Erika', a 1938 German marching song favoured by the Wehrmacht and the SS during the Nazi era, then 'Lili Marlene', Pinochet's favourite tune. Walking stick lodged between his legs, he was wheeled onto an elevator and slowly lowered to the ground. The wheelchair was pushed onto the tarmac, where it stopped. In a dark suit and purple tie, Pinochet was helped up, took a few steps forward, hugged General Izurieta, then walked to the terminal, waving and smiling. The band played, supporters cheered, Pinochet beamed.

'The old dictator, said to be incapable of walking or answering questions and mentally enfeebled, seemed in fine form on his return, *bon pied bon oeil*, walking stick in hand, welcoming the supporters who waited impatiently,' a French newscaster reported.

'We forgot to tell him that once the wheelchair was down the ramp and on the ground, he should not get up and walk,' Schweitzer said. He wasn't surprised Pinochet could walk so briskly. 'I'd seen him walking everywhere in Virginia Water, in the house, in the gardens', and the medical reports were, as Schweitzer put it, 'somewhat contested'.

Two decades later, the lawyer spoke more openly. 'One person who examined him, I understand, was clear that he was fit as a fiddle!' said Schweitzer, not mentally debilitated. 'He seemed like an old man, not out of his senses, but I was sure he couldn't face a trial. His memory, his reasoning. For me, it was a true fact that he could not face a trial, but it didn't mean he was foolish or out of his mind. To the contrary, he was never out of his mind. He was normal.'

A true fact?

Schweitzer smiled.

For others too, that moment, broadcast across the globe, left a strong impression.

'I was so angry,' said Jack Straw.

'Disgraceful,' said James Vallance White.

'It really pissed me off,' said Jean Pateras. '"Fuck everybody out there, look what I've done, I'm back!"'

'Disgusting,' said Garzón.

'Appalling,' said José Miguel Insulza.

'Horrifying,' said Carmen Soria.

'I felt consternation and rage, and a deep sense of impunity,' said Erika Hennings.

'His illness seemed like a joke, or maybe a political arrangement,' said María Isabel Allende.

'Augusto Pinochet proclaiming he'd won the game,' wrote Juan Guzmán, the prosecutor.

## 119

For two years, Juan Guzmán had been investigating Pinochet's role in the murder and disappearance of Chileans. The case began when Gladys Marín, Secretary-General of the Communist Party of Chile, filed a complaint, in January 1998, accusing Pinochet of genocide and other international crimes in relation to her disappeared husband, Jorge Muñoz Poutays. Investigations were underway for other perpetrators, but this was the first case against Pinochet. 'Dim,' reported *The New York Times* about the lawsuit's prospects at the time.

Judge Guzmán's investigation brought him notoriety and many problems, but slowly it progressed, and a month before Pinochet travelled to London in August 1998 the Chilean Supreme Court had ruled that the Amnesty Law didn't necessarily exclude all cases, especially if they raised serious human rights violations. Pinochet's arrest in London gave the investigation greater traction, Guzmán would say. By the time Pinochet returned to Santiago the taboo was broken, he was no longer untouchable.

Within hours of his return, lawyers in the 'Caravan of Death' case asked the Court of Appeal in Santiago to open proceedings against him. Three days later, on 6 March, Guzmán asked the judges of that court to rule that Pinochet had no immunity in relation to certain acts of 'permanent sequestration': the abduction, detention and disappearance of nineteen people.

Three months later, the Court of Appeal ruled by a narrow majority – thirteen judges in favour, nine against – that Pinochet had no immunity in the 'Caravan of Death' case. The ruling, which was dramatic in its reception and immediate consequences, was based on 'well-founded suspicions' that he was personally involved in the disappearances. The 'political arrangement' suspected by María Isabel Allende – between the Chilean government and judiciary, between Cristián Toloza and Jonathan Powell – bore fruit.

Pinochet lodged an appeal. On 8 August 2000, the Supreme Court confirmed he no longer had immunity under Chilean law. The vote was fourteen to six, a clear majority. The Court went further than the lower court, removing Pinochet's immunity in fifty-seven cases of murder, where bodies had been located and identified. The ruling was premised on Pinochet's role in covering up the crimes of others. It was a 'big, big moment', Insulza recalled. 'Pinochet's inviolability was shattered.'

The judgement made no mention of any arrangement or the document that Toloza gave to Powell, the one that authorised the 'Caravan of Death' operation, personally signed by Pinochet. General Arellano Stark, who led the operation, told the judges he'd seen the order signed by Pinochet, but neither he nor the Army had a copy of it.

The judges were sceptical. 'It is surprising and difficult to understand that General Arellano does not even keep a copy of a document so important to him,' they recorded, one that allowed him to undertake the mission entrusted to him. 'It is also unclear why the Army, as he claims, does not retain a copy of the same document.'

The document signed by Pinochet exists – somewhere. Cristián Toloza has seen it, so has Jonathan Powell. The Chilean people and judges have not.

The Supreme Court ruling paved the way to move from the investigation of Pinochet to his prosecution. It had broader effects, as though a door had opened. The case against the murderers of the three men in Porvenir, photographed shortly before their deaths by the schoolteacher Juan Torres Toro, reached the Supreme Court. There, Judge Nibaldo Segura argued for the approach the court took in March 1963, in Rauff's extradition case, namely to apply a limitation period. He did not persuade the majority on the Court, who ruled that where a crime against humanity occurred there was no longer a time limit. Rauff was dead, so was his precedent.

With Pinochet's immunity gone, Guzmán reached out to Garzón to compare notes, until the Supreme Court ordered the Chilean to avoid contact with his Spanish counterpart. 'We got around it, at least once through an intermediary,' said Garzón. 'Guzmán came to Spain, and he and I communicated through Hernán Hormazábal, a Chilean refugee who taught criminal law in Girona.'

By the end of the year, Guzmán had two cases running against

Pinochet: the 'Caravan of Death' case, and the 'Conferencia Street' case, which involved a clandestine operation by the DINA's Lautaro Brigade to dismantle the leadership of Chile's Communist Party. Guzmán worried that the Supreme Court, so complicit during Pinochet's rule, would close down both cases.

To move from investigation to indictment, Guzmán was required to interview Pinochet about the alleged crimes. He proceeded on the basis that the seventy-five written questions he had transmitted to London a year earlier – which Pinochet refused to answer – could be treated as the required interview. On Friday, 1 December 2000, Guzmán indicted Pinochet for fifty-eight homicides and eighteen disappearances, in the 'Caravan of Death' case. This was a first.

Pinochet appealed. The Court of Appeal suspended the indictment, as Guzmán hadn't properly interviewed Pinochet. The judges gave Guzmán twenty days to interview the General properly, and assess his fitness to stand trial. The interview was set for 2 January 2001, but Pinochet failed to attend – newspapers showed him relaxing in plush surroundings at home, which caused an outcry.

Miguel Schweitzer and Pinochet's other lawyers advised a change of direction, and a few days later the medical exam was carried out. It concluded that Pinochet was suffering from 'mild to moderate dementia', but not such as to preclude the interview, which took place on 24 January.

'For nearly thirty years, many people in Chile waited for this moment,' Guzmán recorded. Pinochet appeared before him like anyone else under investigation. 'I entered the hall, where two of the General's lawyers, Miguel Schweitzer and Colonel Gustavo Collao, were waiting.' The sofas and armchairs were arranged in a semi-circle, as they were when Inspector Hewett visited Pinochet in Wentworth.

'Miguel Schweitzer was particularly obsequious towards the General,' Guzmán recalled, 'Mister President this, Mister President that . . .' The atmosphere was relaxed and familial, until Guzmán ordered Schweitzer and Collao to leave the room.

'The interview was brief, thirty minutes at most. I asked a dozen questions. I noted that Augusto Pinochet had a good memory and, despite his age, gave the impression of being alert with intellectual capacities intact.' As Guzmán reached the agreed time limit,

Schweitzer returned and whispered a few words: 'Listen, Juan, the General must be very tired, best to leave it here, no?'

Guzmán wrote up his notes in an adjoining room. The door was left open, which allowed him to observe 'a curious scene'. 'I saw the General get out of his chair and go to the other end of the room. He was a little stooped, but he walked quickly and with ease.' Out of sight, or so he believed, Pinochet seemed rather sprightly. 'How badly advised, I thought, how unwise. After all the warnings and claims about his frail health, I observed the duplicity.'

Coffee, biscuits and small talk followed, and Pinochet politely declined an offer to review Guzmán's notes. 'Mister Judge, I have confidence in you, I will sign the deposition without reading it.' A game of cat and mouse, Guzmán thought, one that began with the theatrical moment at the airport.

Guzmán concluded, on the basis of the evidence, that Pinochet committed crimes and was fit enough to stand trial. On 29 January, he issued a fresh indictment and ordered Pinochet to be held under house arrest at his home in Los Boldos. Five months later, despite the clear views to the contrary of some Chilean medical experts, the Court of Appeal suspended the proceedings: Pinochet's health was too fragile. It took a year for the Supreme Court to confirm the suspension.

It was now 2002, and Guzmán was sure he'd reached the end of the road. Pinochet was off the hook. Disappointed, like others before him, Guzmán found comfort in the idea that total immunity for the General was ended, in principle, if not in practice. No immunity, no impunity.

Pinochet too believed the criminal proceedings against him were over, so he resigned as a Senator. 'I have a clean conscience,' he wrote in his resignation letter.


## 120


Life is never quite what it seems, and Pinochet and his advisers were insufficiently attentive to the consequences that his arrest in London had in other places. Washington DC was one such place.

As Pinochet lingered in London, the US Senate Judiciary Committee was investigating money laundering in the US financial-services sector. In 2003, a sub-committee examined the Riggs Bank, where Manuel Contreras happened to have opened accounts in relation to the assassination of Orlando Letelier.

A year on, the sub-committee found that Pinochet had also opened accounts at the bank. In fact, there were multiple accounts in many different names – Augusto P. Ugarte, José Pinochet, José Ugarte, Daniel López, and so on – a reprise of his approach to law school in Ecuador, decades earlier. The sub-committee identified deposits of over US $26 million in cash in his name, in 125 different US accounts, done in a manner to avoid scrutiny.

The sub-committee also determined that senior staff at Riggs Bank had helped Pinochet avoid sanctions and restrictions, including one court order by which Garzón froze his assets. The intermediary between Pinochet and Riggs Bank was none other than General Izurieta, who had served in Washington before he succeeded Pinochet as Army Chief of Staff. While working to bring Pinochet home from London, Izurieta met Joseph Allbritton, the Riggs Bank Chairman, in Santiago.

'Where do I begin to thank you?' Allbritton wrote to Izurieta. 'You graced our suite with the sweet smell of beautiful flowers and Chilean wine. You gave us your time on the very eve of the General's return.'

The evidence on which the US Senate relied caused an outcry when it became public. Investigations were opened in Chile, on allegations that Pinochet filed false tax returns and engaged in fraud, embezzlement and bribery.

Believing himself to be beyond the reach of the law, Pinochet chose this moment to give an interview to Canal 22, a Spanish-language television network in Miami. It was November 2003, and the interviewer was María Elvira Salazar, a virulently anti-communist Cuban American (she is now a Republican congresswoman for Florida). She appreciated Pinochet, she would say, because he had prevented Chile from becoming another Cuba.

The interview was extensive and friendly. A relaxed and genial Pinochet offered the impression of being in rude good health, and brushed away any suggestion to the contrary. He suffered no more than an occasional headache, he told Salazar, and this was easily controlled with medication. He spoke proudly of his health and his political record. He was not a dictator, he continued, and any 'excesses' were committed by people outside his control, for which he bore no responsibility.

'I did not murder anyone, and I gave no orders to murder anybody.' He had no resentments or grudges. 'I am an angel.'

Judge Guzmán watched the interview with a sense of surprise, horror and pleasure, as he realised it would allow him to reopen the Pinochet file. As the US Judiciary Committee reported on Pinochet and the Riggs Bank, he started a new investigation on the General's role in Operation Condor.

In August 2004, the Chilean Supreme Court ruled that Pinochet had no immunity in the case of Operation Condor – the crimes invoked by Carlos Castresana and Baltasar Garzón in the proceedings that led to Pinochet's arrest in London. María Elvira Salazar confessed she felt so bad that her interview had brought such trouble and grief to Pinochet. He was 'now entangled in new legal problems, because of me'. This was around the time that the systematic use of torture by the Pinochet regime was confirmed by a Chilean National Commission on Political Imprisonment and Torture, the Valech Report.

What remained to be determined was Pinochet's fitness to stand trial. Five years after Jack Straw had decided that Pinochet could not be tried in Spain, Judge Guzmán stood in the grand hall of the Supreme Court in Santiago and announced the Court's ruling in his latest application: Pinochet is 'mentally fit to stand trial in Chile' and 'will now be prosecuted for nine abductions and one homicide'. Guzmán placed Pinochet under house arrest.

The interview by María Elvira Salazar and the Court's ruling combined to create a domino effect. In June 2005, the Santiago Court of Appeal ruled that Pinochet had no immunity for financial crimes in Chile arising from the Riggs Bank investigations. A month later, the courts ruled he had no immunity for his role in Project Colombo, involving two killings during the Coup. More indictments followed: for killings, tortures and disappearances at the Villa Grimaldi; for the murder of Eugenio Berríos, the chemist who worked on sarin gas at the Vía Naranja; and for Pinochet's role in the murder of two of President Allende's bodyguards.

Erika Hennings sensed a change, and now called for Londres 38 to be declared a national historical monument. 'We lit candles outside the building, and Michelle Bachelet's government established a process.' Hennings' efforts worked: Pinochet's lease of the building to the Instituto O'Higginiano was terminated and a new organisation, called Londres 38, was given a long-term concession over it.

Pinochet too sensed a tide had turned, and he was in real trouble. On his ninety-first birthday, 25 November 2006, his wife Lucía read out a statement on his behalf, one intended to be more conciliatory:

> Near the end of my days, I want to say that I harbour no rancour for anyone, that I love my fatherland above all else, and that I take responsibility for everything that was done.

At the same time, he expressed support to all those 'comrades in arms' who were 'imprisoned, suffering persecution and revenge' in the face of accountability for the crimes that were committed. It was 'not fair' to target those who acted in the face of the crisis the country faced under Allende.

Two weeks later, on 10 December, he suffered a heart attack. Serially indicted, stripped of all immunities, declared fit to stand trial, and under house arrest, he was taken to hospital, where he died.

'The man who lived his whole life and never paid for even one of his crimes had done it again,' said the writer Ariel Dorfman. 'Once more – one final time – everybody in Chile thought that Pinochet had escaped judgment.'

The Chilean government refused to give him a state funeral. Pinochet's body was placed on public display, in a military uniform, in an open casket at the Santiago Military Academy, surrounded by a military guard of honour. Thousands of supporters queued for hours to pay their respects, as opponents celebrated his demise.

Francisco Cuadrado Prats, the grandson of Carlos Prats – the Army General Chief of Staff assassinated under Pinochet – was among those who attended. He 'walked up to Pinochet's coffin and deliberately, calmly spat on the dictator's face as he lay there in full regalia,' wrote Ariel Dorfman. Queasy and uncomfortable, who could blame the grandson, Dorfman asked. 'His was the tiniest of revolts, barely two or three seconds long, but it spoke for his murdered grandparents and for all the mutilated and missing bodies of his land.'

A few days later, Pinochet's funeral was attended by tens of thousands of supporters. His grandson, Captain Augusto Pinochet

Molina, delivered an impassioned defence of his grandfather, denouncing those who persecuted him. The words caused him to be expelled from the Army. Pinochet was cremated and the ashes deposited at a grave in Valparaíso.

The Pinochet Foundation released a final message. 'I have a special memory of my communications from my captivity in London,' wrote Pinochet. He said he wished that the Coup had not been necessary, but it, and all the actions that followed, were justified. 'It was necessary to implement certain measures, like temporary imprisonment, authorised exile, executions by firing squad after military trials.' Deaths and disappearances were inevitable, he added, it is 'very possible that we will never achieve a complete understanding of how or why they occurred'.

Like Walther Rauff, he offered no hint of regret or repentance, in respect of the consequences of his acts on others.

However, he wrote, at the end of his life he never imagined that he would not be free to wander the streets of Santiago. For himself there was a modicum of self-pity.

'My fate is a type of exile and solitude.'

# EL MOCITO

## 121

One month after Pinochet died, an investigating judge opened a criminal investigation into Jorgelino Vergara. He was a suspect in the 1976 killing of Víctor Díaz López, a Communist leader. Vergara, who was described as a *mocito*, or a junior waiter, was one of many civilians who served in the DINA's Lautaro Brigade.

'A waiter's assistant killed the leader of the Communist Party?' asked the judge. In fact, he didn't, but Vergara's testimony would have dramatic consequences. The forty-four-year-old revealed a previously unknown place of killing, the Simón Bolívar barracks serving as a detention centre in the east of Santiago. He contributed to the convictions of dozens of former DINA agents. He also identified the location of the 'final destination' of four disappeared individuals.

Vergara's accounts were picked up by filmmakers and writers. Samuel Fuenzalida, who told me he had seen Walther Rauff at the DINA headquarters, knew Vergara and suggested I should meet him. 'He might have information about Rauff and the Pinochet case in London,' he said. He recommended a book – *La danza de los cuervos* by Javier Rebolledo – and a documentary film, *El Mocito*.

'I am a good man,' Vergara says in the opening sequence of the documentary, as he skins a rabbit caught in the woods near a building that is described as his home, but which, I was later told, wasn't where he lived. 'I was involuntarily involved in kidnappings and murders, I just looked on.' He bore no responsibility, he said. 'I did not kill, but it is true that others murdered many people without mercy.' Vergara would only talk about what he witnessed before he reached the age of eighteen, in 1978, the moment at which he could be criminally responsible and prosecuted.

Vergara's story was unusual. He was fourteen when he arrived in Santiago, penniless and without a pair of shoes. He got a job there at the home of the DINA chief Manuel Contreras, working as 'a junior waiter'. For the next four years Vergara saw everything and everyone, watching and listening from the sidelines as people came and went, hearing of plans to kill and disappear, and sometimes witnessing the acts.

After the DINA was wound up in 1977, he served in the Lautaro Brigade, based at the Simón Bolívar barracks in the capital. This was a unit that protected Contreras and Pinochet by killing opponents. Vergara observed torture and killings, and assisted in disappearances. He learned of the use of sarin gas and cyanide, met Michael Townley, and knew all about the killing of Carmelo Soria. Working as a guard, Vergara fed and looked after prisoners while they were alive, then assisted in the disposal of their bodies when they were dead. 'The Simón Bolívar barracks was an extermination centre,' he said bluntly. 'To leave, you had to die.'

The documentary film described the journey in his words. Vergara was shown visiting Londres 38, and the family of Daniel Palma, a businessman who disappeared. With the grandson he reviewed headshots of DINA agents with whom he worked. 'I saw your grandfather at Simón Bolívar. He was tortured, then I stopped seeing him.' On a sheet of paper, with no word spoken, he wrote out the names of those who killed Daniel Palma.

'Thank you,' said the grandson.

Vergara's testimony convicted dozens of DINA agents, including the head of the Lautaro Brigade. It catalysed a request for the successful extradition of Adriana Rivas, hiding in Australia. 'Even though I participated in assassinations, kidnappings, and all of that,' Vergara said, 'I didn't participate.'

## 122

Jorgelino Vergara agreed to meet me, to talk about what and who he saw between 1973 and 1977. In November 2022, I joined my assistant Monserrat, Samuel Fuenzalida and a friend of the former DINA man on the ride to Teno, a small town about two hours from Santiago.

Vergara, known as *El Mocito*, greeted us on the main street of Teno, a small and worn agricultural hub. The moustache from the documentary was gone, the face topped by a paramilitary-style beret. Vergara was open and engaged, chatting amiably with Fuenzalida. They obviously knew each other well. As we ate at a local restaurant, chicken and courgettes, nothing fancy, Vergara kept a constant eye on the entrance and the front door.

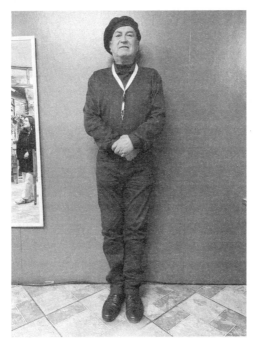

I showed him some photographs.

The first was of Cornelius Krieg, known as Lindes, the man from Colonia Dignidad. The image generated a flicker of recognition, nothing more. 'I remember someone who looked like this, who once arrived at the home of Contreras.'

The second photo was from the 1970s, a man with glasses like those worn by Rauff and Kissinger. 'No,' he said, instantly. 'I have never seen this man.' Eric Morecambe, I said, an English television comedian from the 1970s, from my childhood.

The third photograph caused the lines on Vergara's face to relax, and his eyes to ignite. 'Yes, this one I know. The German. He was in San Antonio, if I remember correctly.'

Not in Santiago?

'No, he didn't come to Contreras's house there. Others did, some who looked like him, they were younger, maybe members of his family, maybe a brother or a son? They came with Christoph Willeke and Chico Müller from Punta Arenas. They brought packages of seafood, from the *Pesquera*.'

These were senior DINA agents. Willeke, of German origin who frequented Colonia Dignidad, had been convicted of crimes against humanity for his role in Operation Condor, and was incarcerated at Punta Peuco prison in Tiltil. Elissalde 'Chico' Müller was a partner in a firm colloquially known as DINA Services, a front company that financed DINA agents and activities.

Do you know the name of the German?

'No. I saw him in San Antonio. I think he was in charge of the *Pesquera Arauco*, already from 1973, when Contreras was still working at Tejas Verdes.' He added: 'They called him *El Chacal*, or maybe that was his son.'

The *Pesquera Arauco* was a fishery in San Antonio. 'I don't remember the name, but I knew he was German and that a German was in charge of the *Pesquera*.'

The man was called Rauff, I said. Back then people didn't know this was his name. Did you see this man in San Antonio?

'No, not in San Antonio. I saw him nearby, in Santo Domingo, where there was a holiday resort for DINA agents.' This was near San Antonio, vacation cabins on a beach, built by Allende's government as holiday homes for workers and their families. In 1973, the DINA took over the cabins and used them to hold, torture and disappear detainees. Demolished in 2013, the Detention Centre at Rocas de Santo Domingo is today a site of national memory.

Manuel Contreras had a house there. 'I saw this man in Mamo's beach house in Santo Domingo. Twice.'

A beach house?

'Yes. At Rocas de Santo Domingo. It was 1974, the first year I went there with the Contreras family. It was the summer. I ran on the beach, barefoot. Mamo's daughter, an athlete, was impressed by how fast I was.'

Why was Rauff there?

'He came as a visitor. I don't know why, or what they talked about, because this man didn't speak good Spanish and Mamo spoke good German.'

Contreras spoke German? Vergara nodded.

Do you remember the German's voice?

'He had a strong accent, so I struggled to understand what he said.'

Three ladies in Punta Arenas who worked for him at the fish cannery said the same thing, I informed him. Vergara laughed. 'Danke schön, danke schön, gute nacht!'

He told me that Contreras and Rauff ate together, served by Mamo's daughter. 'I saw him twice at the house, in 1974, during the holiday period.'

How did he know the German worked for the *Pesquera Arauco*?

'Because he – or others on his behalf – brought seafoods from the *Pesquera* to the summer house, and to the house in Santiago.'

What seafoods?

'Camarones, centolla, salmon.' The reference to king crab was not prompted by anything I said.

Canned or frozen?

'Frozen. To Santo Domingo, always frozen. To Santiago, both canned and frozen.'

Have you heard of the *Pesquera Camelio*?

'No.'

Do you know what Rauff did at the Arauco?

'This is what I heard: that the people who were killed were thrown into the machines. They were not disposed of. They were added to the fishmeal, feed for chickens. It was put in bags and taken to chicken farms.' He stopped, to allow me to digest the horrific implications of what he was saying.

'Can you imagine, when we were eating eggs, we were eating humans?' That was what Jorgelino Vergara, known as *El Mocito*, said to us over lunch. I was lost for words.

Eventually, I asked: 'Did you ever visit the *Pesquera*?'

'No.'

Did they also dispose of people at sea?

'Yes, the ones who came from Santiago. By helicopter though, not by boat, as far as I know.'

Did Rauff have a house in San Antonio?

'I don't know.'

Jorgelino Vergara spoke calmly, with clarity and certainty. If he didn't know the answer to a question, he said so. 'I am not a *pamplinas* [bullshitter].'

Did Contreras and the man in the third photograph know each other well?

'It was a friendship. Yes, they knew each other well, I could tell. When he was there, he was well served, they were attentive to him, in the summer house. He was important, like family. It was like a family visit.'

Rauff spent time with the daughters?

'Yes.'

Would they remember him?

'Yes, of course.'

Are they still alive?

'Two of them, Mayte and Alejandra. The third one, Mariela, died. There was a boy, too, Manuel. Mayte and Alejandra served him food.'

Did you ever see a *Pesquera* refrigerated van?

'No.'

Did you hear about the vans being used to transport detainees to and from Londres 38?

'No.' He stopped to think. 'The only thing I recall were the vans used at Colonia Dignidad, to transport organs. They would sell them, to Germany, Switzerland, Sweden.'

The same countries and networks used for illegal adoptions?

'Yes. The organs were bought and sold.'

Would Adriana Rivas, Contreras's secretary, know about the man in the third photo?

'Possibly, yes, because La Chani, as she was known, was the direct secretary of Mamo in the Cuartel.' He said she was in Australia, awaiting extradition to Chile, in part because of his testimony.

It was clear why Jorgelino Vergara's testimony convicted so many DINA agents. He spoke from first-hand experience. He spoke with understatement. He spoke with clarity and accuracy.

## 123

Vergara went off for a smoke. Do you think he is credible? I asked the others.

'Credible, unattached, speaks freely, cooperative, good memory,' said Samuel Fuenzalida's friend, the driver.

'Same,' said my assistant Monserrat. 'Very clear, seems honest, interesting what he says.'

'And shocking,' I added. Was he confused about the identity of *El Chacal*, as Rauff or one of his sons?

'I think *El Chacal* is Walther Rauff,' said Fuenzalida.

Why didn't he say that?

'Because they don't want him to share the information he has,' Fuenzalida added.

They?

'Some filmmakers he is working with.'

Filmmakers?

'Yes. They told him not to say that Rauff was in the house in Santiago, but he told me he was.'

When Vergara returned from his smoke, I showed him another photograph of Rauff, taken in Porvenir, in the small cabin above the *Pesquera*: 1964, no glasses, cigarette in left hand, in front of the big radio.

'Yes, that is him,' said Vergara. 'He came to a meeting on Project Condor, this is more what he looked like back then.'

Did he come to Contreras's house in Santiago?

'Yes. I think when they met for Operation Condor. In 1974. Or maybe 1975. Between July and November.'

Rauff came to the first Condor meeting?

'Yes.'

Is this *El Chacal*?

'This man is *El Chacal*. There were others with German names, and one was a member of DINA, and he was called *Chacalito . . .*'

Did people mention the name Rauff?

'No, they would just say *El Chacal*.'

Was that the father or the son?

'¡Correcto! The father was El Chacal. The younger one, the son, was called Chacalito.'

Did you ever see father and son together with Contreras?

'No.'

Who else was at that Operation Condor meeting?

He gave us some names, people from Uruguay, Brazil, Ecuador, Peru, Bolivia, Chile, Argentina, Paraguay.

Fuenzalida showed me a message Vergara had sent him a few months earlier. 'I can assure you that El Chacal was already operating with high-level people at DINA,' Vergara wrote. They gathered at Contreras's house, then they went to Casa Piedra, a DINA facility, about 45 kilometres south-east of Santiago. 'Rauff was there.'

Vergara recalled another meeting, attended by Rauff, he said, when a decision was taken to kill a prisoner and deposit her body in the garden of the Italian Embassy in Santiago. 'They killed Lumi Videla to send a message,' Vergara told Fuenzalida, because she was given asylum in Italy.

I checked the story. Lumi Videla was killed on 3 November 1974, at the Villa Grimaldi. Four days later, her body was deposited in the garden of the Italian Embassy. El Mercurio published a cartoon – titled 'International Circus' – a human missile blasted over a wall into a garden. 'The fantastic human projectile fired over the walls of an Embassy!' wrote cartoonist Renzo Pecchenino, who was known as Lukas.

The Pinochet regime blamed her death on asylum seekers.

Who decided to kill her?

'The Condor group,' Fuenzalida replied. (Later, León Gómez would tell me that Lumi Videla was a friend of his and that those prosecuted for her killing included Major Mario Jara, who ran the Pesquera Arauco after the Coup.)

And Rauff was present?

'That's what I remember,' Vergara said. 'Who in the group took the decision, I didn't know. What I know is that the man in the photograph was present at the meeting where the decision was taken.' He pointed to the photo of Rauff, in black and white, on the table.

Jorgelino Vergara had many other stories.

He spoke of Carmelo Soria. 'They took him to the house in La

Curro, the one Mamo Contreras set up for Townley and Berríos, the chemist. The writer Mariana Callejas lived there too, with Townley. They used it as a torture centre, and an extermination centre.' This he said without prompts, accurately.

Did you visit the house on the Vía Naranja?

'No. They killed Soria when they were trying out sarin gas.'

How do you know?

'They talked about it at the Cuartel Lautaro, because they used the same gas to kill other people, Peruvians.'

And Townley?

He came to the Cuartel Lautaro, said Vergara, to test the sarin gas. 'I met him many times, at least ten times.'

Mariana Callejas?

'No. I didn't meet her.'

He remembered when the DINA was dismantled, in 1977. 'Mamo was angry about the rumours he could be extradited to the US, although Pinochet told him he would never let that happen. They created the CNI, which was the same thing as the DINA, but Mamo lost all power. He went to his estate in the south.'

Vergara worked for the CNI until 1985, then left. Ten years later, Contreras was arrested and convicted of the murder of Orlando Letelier. 'I couldn't care less,' Vergara said. Three years after that, Pinochet was arrested in London. 'A good thing, at least the truth might come out.' He had no positive feelings for either man.

'I started to work at Mamo's in 1974,' he said. 'I thought it was the glory moment of my life, but I always had the feeling that something was wrong. At the Simón Bolívar barracks I witnessed executions and other things. I felt bad, and often could not sleep. Everything that happened in that period was a terror, a horror show . . .'

His voice trailed off, then he asked about Rauff.

'A collaborator of Hitler, no?' He remembered something about gas vans. 'They were like sardines in a tin.' Like *centolla* in a can.

'Killed by exhaust fumes?'

He wanted the details. 'I knew about Hitler, but I didn't know about this man or his history. When did he die?'

1984.

'Yes, I remember the farewell, with honours. Miguel Serrano was there.'

We paid for lunch, ambled onto the street and the summer air, searched without success for a coffee. 'No espresso in Teno,' Vergara roared. We stood on the street, said our farewells.

'Funny thing,' he said, as we prepared to part, in a wry tone, matter of fact. 'I called my friend, who runs the chicken farm, to see if he wanted to talk to you. Said he didn't have the courage, didn't need new problems.' Vergara adjusted his beret. 'He once told me he'd found something strange in the fishmeal. A fingernail, a complete fingernail! I told him he should report it, but he never did. Said he didn't want trouble.'

Vergara looked up and down the street, turned to Samuel Fuenzalida, then to me. 'Can you imagine? Chileans thought they were eating eggs!'

He remembered something else about Rauff the German. 'I saw him with Contreras somewhere else near San Antonio,' he said. 'It was at a hotel, La Bahía I think, by the sea.' He said: 'Yes, we can go together.'

# *LA PESQUERA ARAUCO*

## 124

Samuel Fuenzalida and *El Vergara*, also known as *El Mocito*, had connected Rauff to the *Pesquera Arauco*. To that company I would now turn.

Pinochet was a keen supporter of privatisation but not, it turned out, for all companies, and not for the *Pesquera Arauco*. On the day of the Coup, his people acquired the San Antonio fishing company, in part because it had a large fleet of refrigerated vans.

The fishery was established in 1940. In September 1973 it had a fleet of six boats, used to harvest hake. The fish was frozen for export, or used to produce up to thirty tonnes of fishmeal each day. Shortly before the Coup, and many years after he met the cadet Manuel Contreras, photographer Miguel Rubio Feliz visited the *Pesquera Arauco*.

Until Pinochet and Contreras took over the *Pesquera Arauco*, the boats were run by Anatolio Zárate. He was detained on the morning of the Coup and held for several months. One of his torturers, he alleged, was Cristián Labbé, who accompanied Miguel Schweitzer to Washington to negotiate the Letelier deal with the Americans. Labbé, who was later elected Mayor of Providencia, would then be convicted of crimes against humanity, in part based on testimony by Samuel Fuenzalida. Everything is connected.

Contreras became president of the *Pesquera Arauco*'s board of directors, with Espinoza as his deputy. Contreras appointed Hubert Fuchs Asenjo as the company's financial controller, a man who would play a key role in the DINA's financial affairs and, after 1990, be known as the 'first fugitive' in the investigations of the Letelier killing. From the day of the Coup, and for the next eighteen months, the *Pesquera*'s facilities in San Antonio were run by Contreras. Its daily operations were directed by Major Mario Jara, who also worked at the nearby Tejas Verdes barracks.

Contreras, and later the DINA, now controlled a fleet of 310 refrigerated vans, mainly Chevrolet C-10 and C-30 vans, as well as a few Chevrolet Apache vans. After the Coup, the *Pesquera Arauco* vans would be seen near places of detention, including Londres 38. It took decades for the details to emerge, how the vans were used to transport prisoners and corpses across Chile, to and from San Antonio and elsewhere. Corpses one way, fish, shellfish and fishmeal the other.

Around the time of Pinochet's arrest in London in 1998, former detainees testified about being transported in a refrigerated van. León Gómez was among them, as he told me in our first conversation, a detail I was not immediately alert to. In this way, Gómez and Rauff might be connected.

Former DINA agents confirmed that Contreras used the vans. Major Jara, his colleague, testified that the vans 'were used to transport detainees', that he and Contreras drove them around incognito, to 'carry out inspections'. There was testimony too that bodies were stored and disposed of at the *Pesquera*'s facility, and that the *Pesquera* financed DINA activities, including a brigade of female prostitutes.

The evidence was mostly in the form of witness statements presented in court, but a few documents somehow escaped destruction.

Shortly after the Coup, for example, the Minister of the Interior authorised the *Pesquera*'s financial controller, Fuchs Asenjo, to hire armed vigilantes to protect the Chevrolet vans. Pinochet personally approved the request. Former police officers were recruited, men who had worked under the direction of General Mendoza. This was around the time Mendoza visited the *Pesquera Camelio* in Punta Arenas, and met Rauff.

Over time, evidence emerged of the disposal of bodies at sea, in and around San Antonio. In 2016, Pedro Espinoza, Contreras's deputy at the DINA and the *Pesquera*, was convicted of the murder of Marta Ugarte. The forty-two-year-old teacher and dressmaker was arrested in June 1976, held at the Villa Grimaldi, drugged and strangled, then her body was dropped into the Pacific Ocean from a Puma helicopter. The sack in which Ugarte's body was enclosed, tied to a length of railway iron, was poorly secured, so she later washed up on a beach near Valparaíso, ninety kilometres north of San Antonio.

There were accounts too of bodies being held at the *Pesquera*'s cold-storage facilities, or being loaded onto the *El Kiwi*, a German-built tug operating out of San Antonio, to be disappeared at sea. After Pinochet's arrest in London, *El Kiwi*'s skipper and pilot gave an account of a dozen 'wrapped bodies' being loaded onto the boat at midnight, on a San Antonio pier, with the full knowledge of the head of the San Antonio Port, appointed by Contreras. The three crew members were locked into the anchor room as the bodies were dropped into the ocean. The account caused a judge to investigate, but no charges were ever brought.

## 125

As the stories multiplied, calls grew for a criminal investigation into the *Pesquera Arauco*. In 2012 the Chilean police opened proceedings into the *Pesquera Arauco* and another DINA-run company in San Antonio, the *Pesquera Chile*. (The *Arauco* had been sold to the *Chile* in February 1975, then merged into the *Pesquera Nuevo Aurora*. It in turn was then sold on after the murder of Orlando Letelier in 1976 and the dissolution of the DINA the following year.) In 2014, a judge at the Santiago Court of Appeals connected the *Pesquera Arauco* to Operation Colombo, the DINA operation to cover up 119 disappearances, including that of Alfonso Chanfreau. The investigation received hearsay evidence that the *Pesquera Arauco*'s fishmeal plant may have been used to disappear opponents. The judge gathered photographs of the *Pesquera Arauco* and *Pesquera Chile* in San Antonio, along with witness testimony.

Anatolio Zárate, the former director of the fleet, was one who testified. Years earlier he told the United Nations about the disposal of bodies at sea. He now told police about a fellow detainee at Tejas Verdes, a man who ran Arauco operations after the Coup, who 'confided to me that one of the cold-storage units, in the southern part of the facility, was used to store corpses'. Zárate drew a sketch map of the site, to show where bodies were stored. He named ten people said to be involved. The police didn't question them, and no further action was taken.

## 126

In 2015, a different judge began a new investigation of the *Pesquera Arauco*. He concluded that the company was 'captured' by the DINA, and the fishmeal plant 'might have been used for the disposal of detained people'. Without 'biological evidence', however – that is to say, human remains – he was unable to take his investigation further.

The decision was appealed to the Santiago Court of Appeal. In due course, Judge Mario Carroza opened two investigations: Case 201, on the *Pesquera Arauco*, and Case 202, on the disappeared, who could be connected to the *Pesquera Arauco*. Among those he interviewed was Samuel Fuenzalida, who testified on Major Jara's role, and explained the basis of his belief that 'many detainees were turned into fishmeal'. It was hearsay. 'I once heard an officer say, "Turn the detainees into fishmeal", at the factory in San Antonio.'

Several former workers, mostly net repairers living in Tejas Verdes, gave statements to the investigating judge. They described how hake was offloaded from the boats into a pool, placed on a belt which led to the large oven, then baked into fishmeal. The workers offered similar accounts of the day of the Coup, when the military took over and prevented workers from entering the fishmeal production area. The situation persisted for eighteen months.

'A military man took over as boss,' declared Enrique Duarte, aged eighty-one. He heard stories about 'people being dumped at sea, in San Antonio and other parts of Chile, but not in connection with the fishery'. He didn't hear that the military wanted to be 'alone around the oven', or that the vans 'were suspected of bringing bodies to the oven'.

José Siguefreido, aged eighty-six, told the investigating judge that three days after the Coup the boats and plant were back in operation. 'We made loads of fishmeal', with the military 'in charge of security, with dogs'. The fishmeal oven ran at all times, to keep it hot, under the direct control of Major Jara. Siguefreido doubted it was used to dispose of human bodies, didn't recall suspicious movements of trucks, but he did recall 'a German engineer, who he thought was there before September 11th'.

'I have no knowledge of the military ever emptying the fishmeal factory and taking over the operation of the oven,' declared Arturo Poblete, aged seventy-four, to the judge. 'I never saw any detainees, or acts of torture, or human bodies inside the plant,' said Luis Valdebonito, also in his eighties. Nevertheless, it was a fact that workers 'weren't allowed to come close to the vans', and he 'never knew what was inside them'. The oven was 'very large', so 'large animals, like dolphins, sea lions and sharks' could be introduced. 'It is possible that human bodies could also be introduced,' he said, but he never saw the *Pesquera* 'being used to exterminate bodies'.

The testimonies were neutral. They offered no evidence that the *Pesquera Arauco*'s facilities were used to disappear people, or that they were not. What was striking, however, was the consistency of the statements, many sentences and conclusions virtually identical, as though they were written by the same person. I never heard or saw anything, nothing was ever said, I have no record, and so on. Over the years, having read many witness statements, a sixth sense emerges, allowing you to detect the hidden hand of the drafter, one who may have an interest in closing down a line of investigation.

The fishnet repairers offered consistent testimony on the DINA's presence, but no explanation as to why the DINA would occupy a commercial fishery, or why they'd want to control a fleet of refrigerated vans or a fishmeal oven, or why the DINA might remain there until the middle of 1975, which was when the rate of disappearances decreased. No worker explained why the plant was run by Major Mario Jara, a DINA agent, or why they weren't allowed to enter the fishmeal plant or go close to the refrigerated vans.

The statements raised obvious questions, but these were never investigated. 'The line of inquiry was based on hearsay testimony provided by Fuenzalida,' the police concluded, mere 'rumour' offered 'without support'. With 'no concrete evidence', the investigation was terminated.

The authorities failed to act, so Erika Hennings and the Londres 38 organisation stepped in: in October 2017 they initiated a criminal action against the Pinochet-era directors of the *Pesquera Arauco*. They alleged that the fishery financed DINA crimes and was involved in the disappearance of Alfonso Chanfreau and ninety-seven other men and women from Londres 38. Hennings asked the court to investigate kidnappings and illegal burials, and to locate the 'final destination' of the disappeared. One of the judges who investigated the case was Paola Plaza.

## 127

Judge Plaza agreed to meet me at her bustling office in downtown Santiago in November 2022. She was brisk, bright and purposeful, in blue-rimmed glasses, and open with her thinking. She was also incredibly busy, with more than two hundred live cases involving Pinochet-era deaths or disappearances. As we met, she was about to report that the exhumed body of Pablo Neruda, who died just twelve days after the Coup, contained traces of *Clostridium botulinum*, a deadly man-made toxin.

'Everything changed after Pinochet was arrested in London,' she said. The dam broke, allowing new investigations on the disappeared. Her work turned on whether there was any proof of a death: if there was a witness, or evidence of a body, or DNA, the case was treated as murder (*homicidio*); in the absence of such evidence, the case was treated as a kidnapping (*secuestro*). This was how it was for Alfonso Chanfreau, seen at Londres 38 on 13 August 1974 by León Gómez. With no body or other evidence, his disappearance was treated as an act of continuing torture of the family, or as an illegal burial or exhumation. The latter crime was, however, only an infraction, which in Chile is a lesser crime.

The absence of any documentary evidence was an unintended consequence of the US investigation into the killing of Orlando Letelier. It led to the dissolution of the DINA and the destruction of documents, making the investigations far more difficult. Cases went to court, but there was still no overall plan to find the disappeared.

As criminal investigations were underway, Judge Plaza was limited in what she could say. She explained that her office investigated crimes that originated in Santiago – the *Pesquera Arauco* had an office at a food market in Santiago – or at Colonia Dignidad. The Colony was, she believed, probably the 'final destination' for many of the disappeared from Londres 38, transported in *Pesquera Arauco* vans. Crimes committed in San Antonio or at Rocas de Santo Domingo fell within the jurisdiction of judges and courts in Valparaíso.

Fifty years after the Coup, not a single person had been indicted for the use of the Arauco vans or facilities. Mario Jara was prosecuted, but he died before he could be tried. 'Progress has been limited,' Judge Plaza accepted, but it was more than nothing. The use of the refrigerated vans was 'a proven fact', on the basis of witness testimony. The allegations about the *Pesquera*'s role in disposing of bodies at sea, or in the fishmeal plant, on the other hand, were not yet proven. These were allegations with no direct witness testimony. 'A *Pesquera* accountant recently testified that he did not see its installations being used to disappear bodies,' she told me. The formulation, however, tracked the words of the fishnet repairers.

Nevertheless, Judge Plaza had no doubt that the *Pesquera Arauco* was associated with crimes during the Pinochet era, and disappearances. She was focusing on links between the *Pesquera Arauco* and Colonia Dignidad, and 'actions taken to hide or disappear bodies'. She had evidence that Paul Schäfer ordered bodies that were buried at Colonia Dignidad to be exhumed and then destroyed. She had found places of burial, but no human remains. Gerhard Mücke, Schäfer's right-hand man, testified about the murder and burial of 'about thirty' detainees at the Colony, but the bodies were exhumed, removed and destroyed, as part of *Operación Retiro de Televisores* (Operation Recall of Televisions).

On Mücke's account, Pinochet personally ordered the operation, after the DINA was dismantled, to cover up the crimes. Mücke testified that because he and others were Germans, they had been ordered to disappear the bodies; Germans after all were people who 'knew how to execute with perfection a given task'. Convicted of crimes against humanity, for kidnapping and torture, he died in 2022.

Judge Plaza had evidence that some detainees were disappeared at sea, and of the *Pesquera Arauco*'s involvement in other crimes. It may well be, she said, that their involvement was connected to the use of sarin being developed at the Vía Naranja, and the activities of the *boinas negras*, or black berets, the elite group who protected Pinochet and engaged in 'special operations'. The *boinas negras* may have been involved in the murders of Letelier and Soria, she said.

Have you encountered the name of Walther Rauff in your investigations?

'No,' she said, although she knew the name.

Samuel Fuenzalida had recognised the man in a photograph I showed him, as did *El Mocito*, but neither knew his name until I mentioned it, I told her.

She had interviewed Fuenzalida, she said, but before he saw the photograph. He didn't mention the man now known to be Rauff. She had not, however, interviewed Vergara. 'Rauff could well end up being connected to the *Pesquera Arauco*,' she added. 'From now on, he will certainly be on my radar, and San Antonio should be on yours.'

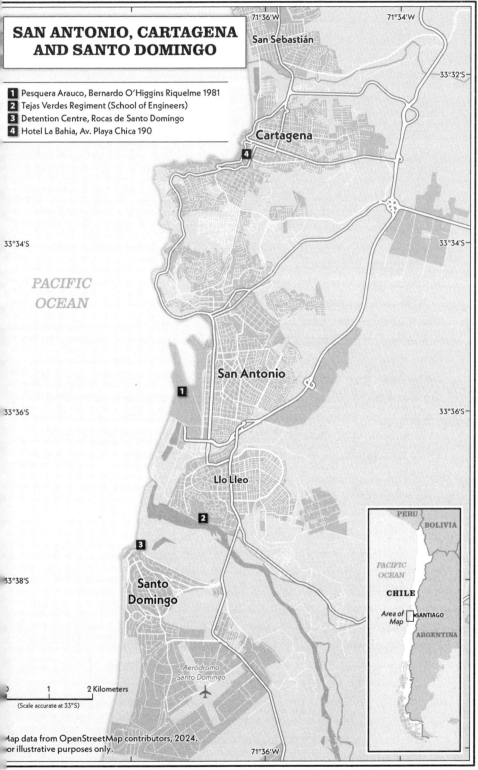

# SAN ANTONIO, CARTAGENA AND SANTO DOMINGO

1 Pesquera Arauco, Bernardo O'Higgins Riquelme 1981
2 Tejas Verdes Regiment (School of Engineers)
3 Detention Centre, Rocas de Santo Domingo
4 Hotel La Bahia, Av. Playa Chica 190

71°36'W

71°34'W

San Sebastián

33°32'S

Cartagena

**4**

33°34'S

33°34'S

PACIFIC
OCEAN

San Antonio

**1**

33°36'S

33°36'S

Llo Lleo

**2**

**3**

33°38'S

Santo
Domingo

Aeródromo
Santo Domingo

PERU

BOLIVIA

PACIFIC
OCEAN

CHILE

Area of
Map □ SANTIAGO

ARGENTINA

0       1        2 Kilometers

(Scale accurate at 33°S)

Map data from OpenStreetMap contributors, 2024.
For illustrative purposes only.

71°36'W

Map 6

# SAN ANTONIO

## 128

San Antonio is a city of hills and coastal dunes on the Pacific coast, about an hour west of Santiago. The Maipu River flows through the city that is home to the Tejas Verdes regiment and the School of Engineers, Manuel Contreras's base, and the *Pesquera Arauco*. Nearby are the fine old seaside resort of Cartagena, to the north, and the Rocas de Santo Domingo, to the south.

I have learned through my work on international disputes that there is much to be gained by visiting a place, that words alone are not able to give a complete sense of geography and the impregnations of history. I wanted to go to San Antonio where, according to Samuel Fuenzalida and Jorgelino Vergara, Walther Rauff developed a second career with vans. They said they'd like to come with me, on a Chilean summer's day, in March, but first I would meet Anatolio Zárate.

He was eighty-six years old when we met and he lives with his wife in a sunny apartment on the upper floor of a building in a Santiago suburb. Natural light bathed the dining table on which he'd laid out old newspapers, with interviews he had given describing the torture to which he was subjected. An unbroken man of intelligence and warmth, he spoke excellent English.

His parents were medical doctors but he opted for life as an engineer, joining the *Pesquera Arauco* in 1970, the year Allende became President. 'I was head of the fleet', responsible for six large boats, of which two came from Cuba, and three from the Soviet Union. The fleet caught two or three hundred tonnes of *merluza*, or hake, every day. Most was frozen for sale across Chile and some was exported to Spain, possibly to be made into fishfingers.

The hake that remained was processed into fish oil or fishmeal, up to thirty tonnes a day, on site. 'The *boca de la planta* – the mouth of the oven – was about a metre and a half by two metres, it could easily take a shark or a sea-lion, or a human body,' Zárate said. He pointed to a tapestry on the wall, a view of medieval Florence. 'About that size'. He testified on rumours about the use of the oven. 'I saw nothing, as I was arrested early on the morning of the Coup, at about half past seven, accused of being part of Plan Z.' He was an Allende supporter.

He was held for a month at the School of Engineers in Tejas Verdes. 'It was a concentration camp. They broke my spine, so I went to hospital, then to the San Antonio prison, then to Calbuco island, in the south, near Puerto Montt.' He was released in December 1974. For the harm he suffered, he receives a modest monthly pension, 220,000 pesos (about US \$250). 'I was very happy when Pinochet was arrested in London,' he said, 'the courts in Chile have been slow, I know, as I have testified many times.'

He knew of the refrigerated vans. 'Chevrolets,' he said. C-10s and C-30s, he thought. I showed him a Chilean C-30 advertisement from 1973. 'That's what the front looked like, but the back was different, a refrigerated square box, big enough to hold a few men.' There were a couple of hundred Chevrolets, maybe more, including a couple of dozen Apaches. He thought they arrived at the time of the Coup. 'I never saw them, as I'd been arrested.' The Army occupied the *Pesquera* plant, and Contreras, Espinoza and later the DINA ran the company. The intervention must have been planned in advance, I suggested,

for the Army to have taken over the plant so quickly, and for vans to have been ordered. 'Maybe,' he said, 'but I never heard of an order for the vans.'

He knew too that the vans were used to transport detainees.

And bodies?

'Ah,' he exclaimed. From the table he took a copy of *La Nación* from 2004, an article about *El Kiwi*, a boat that took bodies from San Antonio and disappeared them at sea. I knew the article, which contained Captain Vincente's first-hand account.

'I was Captain Vincente!' said Zárate, suddenly. He was given a full account by 'Pituco' Reyes, the captain of *El Kiwi*, as the two men sailed another boat from Germany to Chile. They encountered a ferocious storm in the English Channel, near Dover Point, one that caused Reyes to fear for his life. 'I have to tell you something, and he told me the story.' In later recounting what he heard, Zárate used a pseudonym, Captain Vincente – his wife feared the consequences of his involvement.

'No one wants to talk of these things, not even today,' he said.

Was the story accurate?

'One hundred per cent.'

Not a myth?

'No.'

On the subject of myth, I showed him a photograph of Walther Rauff.

'Yes,' he said, 'He lived in Punta Arenas, I know about him, the rumours and myths.' Then he said something else: 'When I was de-tained and tortured, people spoke with foreign accents.'

German accents?

'Yes, German accents. I couldn't see anyone, but I heard the accents.'

Might you recognise the voice?

'Perhaps.'

I have a recording of Rauff, I said. Yes, he'd listen to it. On the laptop I pulled up a clip from *The Hunter and the Hunted* documen-tary, in which the journalist confronted Rauff near his son's home in Santiago. Zárate watched and listened intently.

'Suddenly, the unexpected happened,' said the journalist. 'Ap-proaching from the north end of Los Pozos was the man himself, SS Obersturmbannführer Walther Rauff, the alleged murderer of a quarter of a million human beings.' Birds tweeted as Rauff ap-proached, balding and bespectacled, a cigarette in his left hand, the heavy glasses, in a dark-blue shirt with white dots.

'Where is this?' Zárate asked me. Los Pozos Street, in Los Condes. There at the gate Rauff came face to face with an unwelcome visitor carrying a hidden radio microphone. 'You live in Santiago, don't you?' the journalist asked.

'Yes,' Rauff replied. One word, spoken slowly, in a voice that was deep and gravelly, with a slight tremolo, the sound left by cigarettes, and an unmistakable German accent.

As he heard the word, Zárate's face seemed to freeze, literally. He brought his hands together onto the table and clenched them tightly.

He was immobile and silent for several minutes. I have never seen someone react in this way.

'I must phone up to the jurist,' said Rauff in the documentary. 'My case is finished, I am not guilty, I want to say only the verity.' The truth.

'Yes, yes,' Zárate said to me. 'I remember that voice.' He was deeply shaken, terribly disturbed even. 'Yes, yes . . . oof. Yes.'

We watched and listened again.

'It was in San Antonio, in Tejas Verdes, a concentration camp in the School of Engineers, underground, where I was detained.'

The man with that voice was in the room, he said, asking questions. 'Where are the guns, where are the guns? It was the only thing they wanted to know.' Zárate was wearing a hood, so he never saw his interrogators, but he knew a German accent, for there were many Germans around Valparaíso and San Antonio.

'Oof,' he said. No, he didn't know whether the one with the German accent used physical violence against him. 'There were a few people there, I remember only the voice.'

How certain are you that was the voice?

'Yes, I'm certain. Eighty per cent. I don't know how to say this, but it's a deep sensation.'

As it was for me. Here was a second person, after León Gómez, who said he recognised Rauff and was interrogated by him.

Only later did I make the connection between this moment and the play *Death and the Maiden*, written by Ariel Dorfman, in which a detainee recognises her torturer by his voice alone.

# 129

The next morning, Monserrat and I drove to San Antonio with Samuel Fuenzalida and Jorgelino Vergara, two men who knew a lot about the disappearance of people.

As we approached the city, Fuenzalida suggested we leave the highway and take the old road, the one from the 1970s. 'I know this road,' he said. 'Me too,' said *El Vergara*, 'we used it to go to the Contreras house by the sea, with the dog and the children.' As we drove, we talked about this and that, my trip to Patagonia, the *Pesquera Camelio*, Quito, Londres 38, and Guatón Romo's perfume.

'I wore *Flaño*,' said Fuenzalida.

'So did I!' said Vergara.

We pulled up at *Los Hornitos de Doña Carmen*, a bakery. 'The vans with the detainees stopped here for food,' said Fuenzalida, a place of ancient brick ovens. A few kilometres on, we pulled over, near a sign for the School of Engineers. This was by the old Lo Gallardo bridge, destroyed in the 1985 earthquake that laid waste to the port of San Antonio. 'The vans stopped right here, to allow the prisoners to be transferred to the Tejas Verdes team,' said Fuenzalida.

We drove on, a couple more kilometres, to the seaside town of LLolleo – the name originates from *Llollehue*, the Mapuche word for 'fishing place'. At the Plaza Estrella, in the centre, Fuenzalida and Vergara went for a coffee while Monserrat and I met with a retired fisherman, waiting on a park bench.

Jorge Silva was a short man with strong hands. He wore a jumper with blue and red patterns. I'd heard his words on a German radio programme, a few months earlier. He'd been shown a black and white photograph of an older man, bald with glasses.

'When I see the picture of the old Nazi, I remember,' he said. 'He was in the fish factory with Contreras and Jara and the other murderers.'

Where in the San Antonio fishery? the journalist in the radio programme had asked.

'In the hall, where the net repairers worked,' Silva replied. 'He was there, by the trucks with prisoners in the back. He's the one in the photo, he had a German accent.' The journalist told him the man's name: Walther Rauff.

Today, the old fisherman wanted to talk about himself, not the 'fucking Nazi'. There were four big fishing companies in San Antonio at the time of the Coup, he explained: *Contiki*, *Sopesa*, *Arauco* and *Harling*, and the DINA took over all of them. Silva worked for *Harling*. A month after the Coup, he was arrested for being a member of MIR. He was twenty-one.

'I was taken in a refrigerated van to Tejas Verdes, then held underground, in the cafeteria.' He knew the place from military service. 'I was interrogated and tortured. I wore a hood, so didn't see anyone.' He heard Brazilian, French and German accents.

Released after six months, Silva didn't return to *Harling*, as the

DINA had taken over. Some detained comrades were released, others were dropped in the ocean from a helicopter, he believed, or were disappeared by other means. A few chose exile abroad. A year on, Silva was re-arrested, and taken to the cabins at the old holiday camp on the beach at Santo Domingo, south of San Antonio. He remembered the Chevrolet C-10 van, the snub-nosed front, the fabric over the back. I showed him a picture, he nodded.

He was at Santo Domingo for thirty-four days, hands tied, eyes blindfolded, with sixty or seventy other detainees. 'Santo Domingo was terrible, even worse than the first time.' As Silva spoke, he clenched his hands, like Anatolio Zárate. Each shed had four rooms with bunk beds. 'One shed was used to torture, another as a waiting room.' During the day they heard children on the beach, in the evening just silence. 'Over time the voices of the detainees fell silent. This increased our fear, as we didn't know if they'd been released or killed.'

In April 1975 he was taken to Santiago, to the Villa Grimaldi, then Tres and Cuatro Álamos. A month later he was released and taken to a place north of Valparaíso, returning to San Antonio in June. 'My *compañeros* were gone, I was alone and frightened. After three months I started work again at the *Pesquera Chile*, taking the tails off langoustines.'

'The fishery was used as a place of torture. I saw him where the nets were repaired, the bald guy. I didn't know his name, but that is where I would see him. Twice in a week. With an accent, wearing a suit, so he stood out immediately.' He remembered the guttural voice. 'It was the only German accent.'

How old was the man?

'I know you think I don't remember,' said Jorge Silva, 'but I do.'

Do you want to see a video of Rauff, or hear his voice? I asked.

Silva looked at me and shook his head. 'No, I don't want to see it. It brings bad memories, like talking about Contreras.' Terrible memories, so terrible, that a few years ago Jorge Silva tried to kill himself by jumping off the new bridge that crossed the Maipu River.

He was not happy about the exchanges with the German journalist who made the radio programme a few months earlier, he told me. 'They wanted me to make connections about this German man. Of course I remember him, I didn't know the name, but I would see him, in a suit, a strong impression, at the *Pesquera*. He was the right-hand man of the people in the fishing company.'

Silva was unhappy that the broadcast caused a judge in Santiago to contact him. 'If I speak to you, the judge will call me again,' he said, which he didn't want. He answered Judge Guillermo del Barra's questions for ten minutes, over a Zoom call. 'I wasn't shown a photo of Rauff. He never asked about the vans, or what happened to me. All he wanted to know about was Rauff.'

Will you go to the Memorial at Santo Domingo? Silva asked me.

In the afternoon, I said.

'I'll go with you,' he said.

I'm not alone, I explained. I'm here with others.

'Who?'

Jorgelino Vergara, *El Mocito*.

'Go without me,' said Jorge Silva. 'You write your book, it's important, because judges don't look at these cases, but I have no interest in Rauff. What I want is for the people who did these things to us to go to prison.'

He didn't wish to spend time with Vergara. The conversation was over.

## 130

After leaving Jorge Silva, I drove with Fuenzalida, Vergara and Monserrat to the port of San Antonio. Extensively rebuilt after the earthquake of 1985, it is today dominated by the vast and garish Arauco San Antonio shopping mall. Opened in 2009, its name honours the Chilean real-estate company that runs it. There is no suggestion that the company has any connection with the *Pesquera Arauco*.

The *Pesquera Arauco*'s facilities were on the south side of the port, off Bernardo O'Higgins street. The buildings and plant were gone, today there are just barren spaces occupied by a few colourful shipping containers. The site was well located, the Tejas Verdes barracks just five minutes away, the cabins at Santo Domingo a few minutes further south. The Bahía Hotel in Cartagena, to the north, mentioned by Vergara, was a fifteen-minute drive.

We went to the site of the cabins at Santo Domingo. It's a bucolic spot, this former concentration camp by the sea, the sound of waves and gulls, and children shouting as they weaved their way around the parasols on the beach. This was where Jorge Silva was held, and Vergara ran barefoot, impressing Manuel Contreras's daughter.

There's not much left today. Bright-blue signs mark the National Monument, the 'former Detention Centre of the Popular Beach at Rocas de Santo Domingo'. A large black and white photograph shows how it was, buildings and dunes to the horizon. The holiday cabins put up by Allende, and later used for torture, were gone. What remained were ghostly posts on which the huts once rested, steps that led nowhere, a few scattered remnants of porcelain toilet bowls, and the concrete bases for the toilets. 'This was where I walked the Contreras family dog, a German shepherd called "Kazán", my favourite,' said Vergara. 'At the same time, many people died here, prisoners who were tortured, then . . . goodbye.'

That was long ago. Today, the beach has a simple café, on an elevated wooden platform with a fine view of the ocean, the beach and the remnants of the cabins. We ate ice cream. Contreras lived on the hill behind us, Vergara said, a few minutes away. He took us there, to a building that had been rebuilt. 'This man Rauff, who was called *El Chacal*, came here to visit Manuel Contreras. Back then it was in the forest, very secluded. This was where he came, where I saw him, more than once. And at La Bahía hotel. Let's go and find it.'

\*\*\*

We drove to Cartagena, back through San Antonio, on the coast road. We passed the Punta Panal lighthouse, a police recreational centre, and a sign for the tomb of the avant-garde writer Vicente Huidobro, whose nephew Miguel Serrano offered a Nazi salute and greeting at Walther Rauff's funeral in 1984. Recognised as one of Chile's four great poets, Huidobro lived his last years in the seaside town, fashionable among the literati. Long ago, Cartagena must have been magical.

Vergara had mentioned a meeting between Rauff and Contreras at a hotel called La Bahía, near San Antonio. I found one establishment with that name, on the Avenida Playa Chica in Cartagena, overlooking the beach. This couldn't be it, Vergara thought. His memory was of a place up in the hills. In the 1970s, the hotel was owned by Benito Tricio. His name turned up in a 1970s newspaper, about a case at the Supreme Court, reporting that in 1975 Tricio 'collected several payments from the DINA in cheques signed by Manuel Contreras'. The hotel La Bahía was a place where money was exchanged and deals were done. Not long after, Tricio became Spain's Honorary Consul in San Antonio.

Vergara told us about a car journey he once took. 'I was in Santiago and travelled back to Santo Domingo with Mamo,' he said:

Usually I went with the family, but this time it was just the two of us. Another car followed, with guards. Mamo wanted to drive, as it was a new car, a Ford Mercury, given to him by his friend Pinochet. That's why he wasn't with a driver, it was just Mamo and me. While we were driving he called this man in the photograph on the radio phone. Well, he called someone, and said he wanted to meet this man. It was arranged. We stopped at a hotel, I think it was the Bahía.

The photograph he spoke of was the one I had shown him first, Rauff in Kissinger-style glasses, sitting with Nena as she leaned in, boats bobbing on the sea behind them, a kind of paradise. 'There, at La Bahía Hotel, this man in the picture was waiting for us, with a cigarette, he was a heavy smoker.'

Vergara remembered the man. 'He looked exactly the same, I saw him on several occasions, a sinister man.' He paused. 'That photograph wasn't taken at the Hotel La Bahía, which was further from the sea, it would be a different place.'

'We got to the hotel,' he continued. 'I went to the restroom, then came down to the table where they were sitting in a large room, the two of them. They gave me a soda, told me to go out and wait in the car. I didn't sit with them. I drank the soda, went back to the car. This was 1974, in the summer.'

We arrived at the hotel. Like the town, it had seen better days, was shuttered. 'Yes, this was it,' said Vergara. 'Funny thing, I was sure it was in the hills, but this was it, where I saw Rauff.'

Even though the place was shuttered, there was a telephone number above the door. Vergara called, someone picked up, he made up a story, that he was passing through, might want to hire the place for a party, a book party. I'll meet you at six, the owner said, later in the afternoon. We hung around, ate more ice cream, walked along the sea front. The town was filled with fine buildings and mansions, old and new, now dilapidated. In the 1970s, the social scene would have been exhilarating.

At the northern end of the beach, on a modest promontory, up a few steps, on a pedestal, we stood and admired the statue of the *Virgen del Suspiro* (the Virgin of the Sighs). I sat there for a bit, as Fuenzalida and Vergara wandered around. It was a long day, a heavy day, they never stopped talking.

A man approached me. 'Where are you from?' he enquired. We

got to talking. 'I'm Sergio, from Baltimore, but I was born here in 1961, I'm visiting my mother.'

He noticed me admiring a modernist building carved into the rocks, just above us. 'It was a night club, owned by a leftist, they took him away after 11 September.' Sergio said this pointedly. 'I'm very pro-Pinochet,' he added. 'And yes, I knew the owner of the hotel, Tricio. And yes, Contreras used to go there, he was a friend of Tricio's, and of my father. I was friendly with Contreras's son. Many important people would go there, it was a big place, especially in the holidays, at New Year.' He laughed. 'Maybe even Michael Townley came! He lives in Ohio now.'

I wasn't sure how Sergio knew this, but he wasn't about to say more.

Six o'clock came and went, the hotel owner didn't show. Vergara called him. I'll come later, he said. We didn't want to wait, so headed back to the car, parked in front of the hotel La Bahía. At that moment, on the roof terrace, a man emerged. We shouted up. He was the caretaker, he came down and let us in.

'Yes, this is the place, I remember everything'. Vergara said this in hushed tones. 'I was here three times, and twice Rauff was here, in this room. They drank together, Rauff smoked.'

Do you know what they talked about?

'They spent an hour and a half together. I don't know what it was about.'

He overheard some words though. 'They spoke of "packages", to be eliminated, no trace.' Rauff's role was 'to make them disappear forever'.

I mentioned Jorge Silva's conversation with the German journalist, who Vergara had also spoken with. They talked about the *perrera*, the incinerator in a Santiago park used to exterminate stray dogs, in the Quinta Normal district, now the Park of the Kings.

'The incinerator was used to disappear bodies, more than three hundred,' said Vergara.

Fuenzalida had heard rumours that Rauff went to the *perrera*, that he was part of the 'Final Solution' group.

Could this be true?

Jorgelino Vergara looked out towards the sea and the sun. He nodded. Yes, he'd heard about it but from others, he hadn't seen the place himself. 'It's not like this room. Rauff sat here, with Contreras.'

He pointed to the windows. 'I saw them, I was with them. It was work, it was not a social meeting.'

He had no doubt that Rauff worked with Contreras.

'That's what I told the judge,' he said.

# THE JUDGE

## 131

The day in and around San Antonio was long, and it left many impressions and thoughts to digest. We drove back in near silence, me and Monserrat and two men who had either witnessed or participated in terrible crimes, who gave testimony that caused many to be prosecuted and imprisoned, and who faced threats because of what they'd done. I thought about Jorge Silva, and his brief, unsatisfactory interview with a judge. I thought too about Anatolio Zárate, and Walther Rauff's distinct voice and German accent.

Back in Santiago, I met with another judge, one about whom many spoke with great respect, reverence even. The name was familiar: Mario Carroza, who opened the investigation into the *Pesquera Arauco*, whose work was then taken up by Judge Paola Plaza, and then by Judge De la Barra. 'No judge has played a more significant role in the investigation of Pinochet-era crimes than Mario Carroza,' a distinguished journalist told me. He was involved in many of the biggest cases, including those of Carmelo Soria and Alfonso Chanfreau, and the 'Caravan of Death' and Operation Condor cases. In 2015, as investigating judge at the Court of Appeal, it was Carroza who opened the two cases about the *Pesquera Arauco*. He had recently been promoted to the Supreme Court.

We spoke first by Zoom, then Carroza invited me to meet him at the Supreme Court, in Santiago, a fabulously gothic building that his legal assistant showed us around. We visited the courtroom where Pinochet's lawyers lost their argument on immunity and, in the basement, portraits of Supreme Court presidents whose names were familiar, for refusing to extradite Contreras, for convicting Contreras, for limiting the application of the Amnesty Law, and for the decisions on Carmelo Soria and on Pinochet.

Mario Carroza took me to a small office. He came to the law after taking a degree in philosophy, he explained, and obtained his legal qualifications at night school. From the outset he always wanted to be a judge. In Chile, like other continental legal systems, that is a professional career path.

He wanted to talk about Rauff. He knew about his past, although the name had not emerged in his *Pesquera Arauco* investigations. I told him what information I had.

No documents could confirm or refute that Rauff worked for the DINA.

No one actually saw him at Colonia Dignidad or on Dawson Island, although there were many rumours.

A prisoner who recognised the voice of Rauff as his interrogator and torturer at Tejas Verdes. Anatolio Zárate.

A DINA agent who saw Rauff at the DINA headquarters in Santiago, and was told he worked for the *Pesquera Arauco* in San Antonio, but did not know his name. Samuel Fuenzalida.

A junior waiter who saw Rauff with Manuel Contreras in Santo Domingo and in Cartagena, near San Antonio, but did not know his name. Jorgelino Vergara.

A nephew (of Rauff's 'carer' Nena) who saw him in Punta Arenas, and knew that he took military flights between there and Santiago. Raúl Donoso.

A fisherman who saw Rauff at one of the San Antonio fisheries. Jorge Silva.

A grandson in whose room Rauff stayed, in Santiago, who saw Rauff leave each day, in a suit and tie, looking for work. Walther III.

A prisoner who recognised Rauff as his interrogator at Londres 38, in Santiago. León Gómez.

'I know León Gómez,' Judge Carroza interrupted. 'He was a witness in many cases, and a cousin of mine married him, when he was a history teacher.' He knew of his detention at Londres 38, and his books and testimony in many cases. 'I cannot say that everything León Gómez writes is accurate, but he accurately described many facts that occurred. In essence, the facts are as he describes them. He is credible. Many investigations began with his accounts, and many members of the armed forces have been convicted on the basis of his testimony.'

He was not in a position to know how credible was León Gómez's recognition of Rauff at Londres 38. However, Gómez had recognised others who tortured him and his evidence proved to be reliable. 'He provided accurate identifications of Miguel Krassnoff at Londres 38.' Judge Carroza was not sceptical about León Gómez's claim to have been interrogated by Rauff. 'If there were Germans there, it would be easy to identify them. The place was very small, so you could hear everything, the voices and their conversation.'

Judge Carroza did not immediately recall the affidavit that was said to have mentioned Rauff. The link between Londres 38 and Colonia Dignidad was, however, well established. The testimony of Samuel Fuenzalida confirmed it, and investigations into the connection were continuing. 'León gave many affidavits, so there could be one where he mentions Walther Rauff, but I'm not sure.' They were kept at the Museo Histórico Nacional.

A man of obvious diligence, Judge Carroza raised one issue that had always troubled him about León Gómez:

> You never know why someone would be released from detention, while others were disappeared. If you cooperated, you had better chances. For example, León Gómez did not go to Villa Grimaldi, but directly to Cuatro Álamos. These were places where people were held incommunicado, often before being expelled from Chile. I never knew the circumstances of the release of León Gómez, but throughout the years I had much contact with him in different cases.

## 132

Do you think there was a relationship between Rauff and the DINA? 'I would not be surprised,' replied Judge Carroza. 'There was a very strong link between Londres 38 and Colonia Dignidad, with frequent prisoner exchanges, and cooperation on methods of torture.' Carroza had visited Londres 38 many times, it was a small place. 'León was there when it was the only torture centre,' he explained:

> When Londres 38 was exposed internationally, revealed to be a torture centre, the DINA had to open other facilities, like Villa Grimaldi and José Domingo Cañas. Many people held at Londres

38 were transported to other locations. For this they would use the *Pesquera* vans, which were refrigerated. However, there is great uncertainty, because there is no one who was transported and then set free. So, it is very likely that those transported in the vans were being taken to a final destination.

For this, he thought, the *Pesquera* played a central role.

'The vans went to San Antonio or Valparaíso,' Carroza said. 'It has not been proven, but there are two theses. The first is that the destination was the fishing company, where they could be disposed as fishmeal, but I never got a technical explanation of this. The second is that they were dropped into the sea, using rails.' This was what happened to Marta Ugarte, whose body washed up on a beach near Valparaíso. 'When I left the investigation, that was where things were: the fishing company, or disposal at sea.'

As an experienced investigating judge, did he have an instinct about the rumours of the fishmeal?

'The use of *Pesquera Arauco* refrigerated vans is confirmed. They were used to transport people, living and dead. They were used to carry dead bodies to Patio 29, in the Cementerio General.' This was a plot I had visited in Santiago's main cemetery, where many detainees were secretly buried, or where those killed – like the singer-songwriter Víctor Jara – for whom no body was found, are memorialised.

'It is clear that the refrigerated vans were used to dispose of bodies.' This was confirmed in the 'Patio 29' case, investigated by Paola Plaza, where the aim was mainly to locate the bodies and try to identify them, not to prosecute people.

Your instinct?

Several elements gave credence to the fishmeal story, he thought. 'The DINA was keen to find a way to dispose of bodies. They buried them, but finding traces of human remains became problematic. That was why they worked with Colonia Dignidad, to exhume and dispose of bodies, without leaving a trace.'

The judge paused. 'There is another element that makes me think the fishmeal theory could be true. It is what happened with the Hornos de Lonquén, where they used an oven as a crematorium to dispose of bodies.' This was a reference to the cremation of fifteen men, arrested within weeks of the Coup, whose remains were found in locations between Santiago and San Antonio. 'They used the same system that was used in Germany,' Carroza explained. 'That was one of the reasons we always thought these ideas came from foreigners, not from Chileans. It makes sense.'

'I opened the case about the *Pesquera* that was filed by Londres 38,' he continued. 'We focused on the transports, the use of the vans, but there were some investigations about the production of fishmeal.'

The investigations produced several witness statements, which I had read. I told Carroza they gave the impression of having been prepared with a degree of coordination, giving rise to more questions than answers.

Judge Carroza smiled and nodded. 'That part of the investigation was like that. The police struggled to find concrete answers. We know about the DINA's connection with the *Pesquera*. We know about the use of vans. However, no one has said anything related to the arrival of bodies.'

Because people are frightened to speak?

He shrugged, silently.

Should it be looked into?

'This is what we are investigating now, and the link with Colonia Dignidad. Rauff could well be the "grey mind", the point of connection between the DINA, the *Pesquera* and Colonia Dignidad.' Later Carroza returned to this theme. 'You know, Contreras and Rauff would spend a lot of time together in Colonia Dignidad, they would go hunting there together, when they were nearby.' This I had not heard.

Did Rauff's name come up during investigations about Colonia Dignidad?

'Yes, but not as a strong or permanent presence, only someone who would come sporadically. There is one witness that Paola Plaza has recently questioned, a younger one, who referred to other Germans, including Rauff.'

I asked Carroza about Fuenzalida, the former DINA agent.

Samuel has cooperated a great deal, and thanks to him many disappeared have been found. He was a killer, he was in charge of 'finishing' people. He knows we will be kinder to him if he cooperates, and he's one of the few from the Army who is collaborating. Because of this, not everything he says may be entirely reliable. But if he says he recognises the man in the photograph, that he saw him in Marcoleta, that he was connected with the *Pesquera Arauco*, I would have no doubts that is true. No doubts.

And *El Mocito*?
Vergara was careful what he said, Carroza explained, limiting himself to details of things he saw before he was eighteen. The judge had interviewed him:

I think that everything he told me, and the prosecuting judge who first found him, was true and helpful. Many people were convicted because of his testimony. He gave details that were precise and proved to be accurate. He was the one who unveiled information about what happened at the Simón Bolívar centre, which was not known before he spoke. He has more information than what he is willing to share.

I told him of other details I had come across. Pinochet brought Rauff to Chile from Ecuador, and they stayed in touch. Under his regime, Rauff felt like 'a protected national monument'. General Mendoza visited the *Pesquera Camelio* within a few months of the Coup, and a few weeks later sent police officers to work for the *Pesquera Arauco* to protect the vans. Rauff's grandson told me that his father was with Pinochet in 1984.
Judge Carroza cleared his throat:

Having investigated these matters for more than twenty years, I can say that you have more than enough elements to establish a legal presumption as to the involvement of Rauff in the work of the DINA. The connection between the DINA and the *Pesquera Arauco* is clear. The connection between San Antonio and Londres 38 is clear, with trips back and forth. DINA agents, like the Army, had no training to operate the *Pesquera Arauco*. Rauff managed another fishery. These elements all point to a single conclusion.

And of course, Rauff had a history on the use of vans to disappear people.
Going forward?

'There needs to be an investigation into the role of civilians and businesses in the repression. The investigation of the *Pesquera Arauco* has not yet been possible. It remains to be done.'

Carroza paused:

There is a new National Search Plan, to find and identify the remains of the disappeared. Perhaps this will throw light on the role of the *Pesquera Arauco*, and on Walther Rauff. Fifty years have passed, but there is a momentum to move forward in these matters. It all depends on the will of the investigator. I had the will. Now it will depend on the will of others. Share all the information you have with Plaza and De la Barra.

As the conversation drew to a close, I mentioned a phone call I recently had with Sebastian Rauff, the brother of Walther III, who spoke of his father's relationship with the General, and of his grandfather's notebooks. The notebooks were passed to Rauff's son, and were probably now in the possession of his widow, Beatriz Vázquez. I tried to find her, without success. Carroza then said:

If Paola Plaza had knowledge of this, she could interview Mrs Vázquez and ask about the notebooks. Alternatively, she could order the police to go to her house, enquire about the notebooks, take them into their possession, for the *Pesquera Arauco* case. Erika Hennings could also request this, through the lawyers. You need to prove three elements: that Beatriz Vázquez exists, that the notebooks exist, and that she has possession of them.

I mentioned Rauff's personal correspondence. Rauff was careful what he wrote, but he mentioned elements that suggested a relationship with the DINA. An attentive reader could glean something from the correspondence.

'It always depends on the perspective from which you read a text,' said Mario Carroza. 'A policeman, a judge and a researcher could read the same letter, and each might find something different.'

He slowed. 'The questions are endless, the interest remains. It is very good that someone is focusing on this character, Walther Rauff, unveiling new aspects of his life. The whole story of *El Mocito* started in exactly the same way.' Until 2007, Judge Carroza explained, no one knew anything about this man Vergara, or his role, or what he knew. No one had heard of him. Then, once the door was opened, it never closed.

We circled back to Pinochet, and some of the facts I had come across that he did not know of.

He was involved in the 'Caravan of Death' case, for several years, yet Judge Carroza never saw an order that bore the signature of Pinochet. I mentioned the document that Cristián Toloza had given to Jonathan Powell, to buttress the claim that Pinochet could lose his immunity when he returned home.

'It is very likely that more documents exist that have not yet emerged,' said Carroza, 'held by the Army or the Ministry of Defence. It is possible too that the intelligence service may have destroyed them.'

To protect people?

Judge Carroza nodded.

Was it possible that the President of the Supreme Court and the President of Chile reached an understanding, to facilitate Pinochet's return?

'I think yes, it is credible that President Frei spoke with the President of the Supreme Court.'

Was it likely that Rauff assisted Pinochet in facilitating the disappearances?

Judge Carroza nodded. 'With your account, various elements have come together that I feel able to verify as accurate.'

Why did the legal system and the judges await the return of Pinochet to start to function as they should?

'In the early years of the DINA, the judiciary in Chile failed completely. That failure continued into and through the 1990s, even with the arrival of democracy. The judges looked the other way. There were investigations, yes, but no trials, and no convictions, not until Pinochet returned.'

So his return was positive, in that sense?

'The arrest of Augusto Pinochet in London had a significant effect. The judges began to feel more empowered. We felt we had competence, and that feeling was supported by the Supreme Court.'

But impunity remains?

'For civilians and corporations there has been, and there continues to be, total impunity.'

Judge Carroza turned to me. Why was I interested in this story, and Rauff's role in the crimes of Augusto Pinochet?

It was a decent question. It began with the law, how the crimes invented for Nuremberg were taken forward, the interplay between immunity and impunity. There was too a personal connection, my involvement in Pinochet's case in London, my feelings about the outcome and the circumstances of his return, and the discovery of a family connection through my wife, with the killing of Carmelo Soria. Then another personal connection, as I discovered, along the way, that one of the many murdered in Rauff's vans in Poland was Herta Gruber. She was twelve years old, my mother's older cousin.

Mario Carroza listened attentively.

'I knew a detainee at Londres 38,' he said. 'He was with me at university, *El Pedagócico*, we studied philosophy together.' This was a reference to the Pedagogical Institute at the University of Chile. 'His name was Alfonso Chanfreau.'

Our eyes met.

'It is a fine thing to investigate for a personal reason,' said Judge Carroza. 'A very fine thing.'

# EPILOGUE

# TWO MEN, TWO FACES

The arrest of Augusto Pinochet, on the evening of 16 October 1998, had many consequences.

It was the first time a former head of state of one country had been arrested in another country, for committing an international crime. It caused others to reflect on their own immunities.

In late 1999, during the Pinochet proceedings, it was said that the President of Croatia, Franjo Tuđman, opted not to take a trip to Germany for important medical treatment, fearing a secret indictment for crimes committed during the Yugoslavia conflict. He died in December of that year.

In March 2002, Henry Kissinger cancelled a trip to Brazil. This followed reports he might be questioned for his role in the Chilean Coup, after publishing an article against universal jurisdiction and the arrest of Pinochet.

In February 2011, George W. Bush aborted a visit to Switzerland. This was said to be due to concerns he could be interviewed for his authorisation of waterboarding, an act of torture and an international crime.

In August 2023, President Vladimir Putin decided not to travel to South Africa. Indicted by the International Criminal Court in The Hague, for his role in deporting children from Ukraine, an arrest warrant had been issued against him.

\*\*\*

The consequences in Britain were varied.

Tony Blair's government replaced the Appellate Committee of the House of Lords with a new Supreme Court. 'I regretted the change, and the contribution of the Hoffmann episode to it,' said James

Vallance White. 'Without Hoffmann, Goff would have sat, the case would have gone the other way, and Pinochet would have been home in November 1998.'

Nico Browne-Wilkinson was deeply affected by the saga. He retired early from the Appellate Committee of the House of Lords, and the 'froideur' with his fellow judge, Hoffmann, ended a long friendship.

Michael Caplan was appointed a Queen's Counsel, a rare honour for a solicitor. 'I received a very nice, hand-written letter from the General, in Spanish', and a medal from the Pinochet Foundation. The case was a 'career highlight', he said. 'I met interesting people and we made legal history, for which much credit goes to the human rights groups.'

Jack Straw regretted his decision to allow Pinochet to return, and the fact he was never tried and convicted in Chile. 'I kept this bloke locked up for sixteen months, and that changed the face of . . .' he said wistfully. 'I could have decided he was fit to travel and left it to the Spanish courts. I wish I had, but there you go.'

Jean Pateras continues to interpret for the Metropolitan Police, and still marvels about the evening of 16 October 1998 and everything that followed.

Clare Montgomery left the barristers' chambers she shared with Alun Jones and joined with other colleagues, myself included, to establish a new barristers' chambers. We hoped that the interplay between English, European and international laws, so emblematic in the Pinochet case, might offer a new path.

My friendship with James Cameron became even stronger, and a quarter of a century on he is my closest friend. He left the law and moved on to climate change and other vital issues. 'Funny thing,' he mused, 'how different my life could have been if the UK Attorney General or Spain tried to hire me before the Pinochet team, rather than after.'

***

In Spain too there were consequences.

The government curtailed universal jurisdiction, to stop future Pinochet-like cases. Today, with few exceptions, Spanish courts cannot exercise jurisdiction for international crimes committed abroad.

Juan Garcés continues his fight for accountability for Pinochet's crimes. Incensed that Pinochet returned home early, he nevertheless believes the case was important, that it 'breached a wall of impunity in Santiago'.

Baltasar Garzón generated controversy for his efforts to investigate the crimes of the Franco era, and other crimes in Spain. These caused him to be removed from his position as a judge, an act the UN Human Rights Committee considered to be unlawful. The Pinochet case 'changed Chile and the world', he believes.

Carlos Castresana continues to work as a prosecutor, and was a candidate to serve as Prosecutor at the International Criminal Court. He too is sanguine about Pinochet's return. 'The statue at the Moneda Palace is Allende, not Pinochet.'

*\*\**

In Chile, Pinochet and his arrest remain divisive issues.

His return changed the course of criminal proceedings. Although the Amnesty Law of 1978 remains in force, hundreds of cases have been brought against those who perpetrated crimes authorised by Pinochet or in his name. Those convicted of crimes against humanity include individuals involved in the murder of Carmelo Soria and the torture and disappearance of Alfonso Chanfreau. Manuel Contreras died in prison in 2015, while his deputy Pedro Espinoza, Miguel Krassnoff and Christoph Willeke remain incarcerated.

In August 2023, President Boric published a national plan to discover the fate of at least 1,469 disappeared individuals, to end the torture of their families and friends. He publicly thanked those responsible for Pinochet's arrest. 'What you did gave hope not only to Chileans but to everyone, that there can be justice, and it is always worth continuing to fight for it.'

In June 2024, the Chilean government announced that Colonia Dignidad would be expropriated and turned into a site of national memory, with the support of the German government. The Colony 'offends the conscience of humanity', said Justice Minister Luis Cordero, a place where slavery and sexual crimes were perpetrated, and where 'disappearances, torture and political executions were committed by the police and intelligence services of the dictatorship'. Yet justice has been limited. Those convicted served the military or the DINA. Others who were responsible or complicit – those who worked for private companies, or newspapers, and even the judges – have generally avoided justice and accountability. No civilian associated with the crimes of the *Pesquera Arauco*, including Walther Rauff, has been investigated or charged.

For the crimes of the Pinochet era, as for those perpetrated by British, German and Spanish settlers in earlier times, impunity reigns.

\*\*\*

Should Pinochet have returned to Chile or been sent to Spain? Feelings are mixed on this question.

Some, like José Miguel Insulza, thought it right that he returned to Chile, even if they regret that he was not tried and convicted. Cristián Toloza, who negotiated the return, with consummate professionalism, had regrets. 'I am not proud of my role in bringing him home.'

Hernán Felipe Errázuriz welcomed the outcome, but won't be writing about the experience. 'I cannot because I have the trauma of the human rights violations, because what happened was awful.'

To the end, Miguel Schweitzer was a true believer in the Pinochet project. 'The country was fortunate to have his government', even as the arrest allowed 'human rights issues to come alive in Chile and internationally', which was perhaps not a bad thing. 'I learned a lot and it made me somebody in Chile,' he said, 'even if being involved caused me to lose work opportunities.'

'A final anecdote,' he said, a letter the Pinochet Foundation received from the British government. 'It contained a cheque for £980,000, if I remember correctly, made out to Pinochet personally, to cover expenses in London.'

'£980,000!' he said again.

'Crazy!' said José Miguel Insulza.

'I am stunned,' said Jack Straw. Not unreasonably, given the passage of time, he didn't recall a statement he made to the House of Commons, after Pinochet's return.

The Law Lords decided that Pinochet should be reimbursed out of public funds for costs incurred for hearings before the Divisional Court and the first two cases at the House of Lords, 'in the unusual circumstances of the case'.

'That's the system,' said Michael Caplan. 'There was an application for legal costs, after he left, and it did cause a bit of outrage.'

Do you have any regrets? I asked Schweitzer.

The question elicited a throaty chuckle.

'I would do it all over again,' he said. Yes, the murders of Carmelo Soria and Orlando Letelier were 'unfortunate', and yes, there were 'things about the General's government' which he didn't like. 'Knowing what I know now . . .'

Was an expression of regret coming?

'Knowing what I know now, I would not have done it for free.'

What you know now, but didn't know in London, was that Pinochet squirrelled millions away illegally, in America?

'I should have said "Yes, I will defend you, but you must pay my fees."'

Miguel Schweitzer was silent for another moment, then added: 'There was a fee, but in another form.' Two days after they got back, Pinochet's emissaries came to his house.

'"The General sends you this, in appreciation of all you have done." They gave me his walking stick, as he had promised.'

You must come and see it, he said. I never did, as Miguel Schweitzer died soon after that conversation.

His wife sent a photograph.

When I mentioned the story of the fee and the walking stick to Paola Plaza, the judge, she smiled and said: 'Let me surprise you.'

Surprise me, I said, and she did.

'I wanted to ask Miguel Schweitzer if he knew about the *boinas negras*, the black berets who protected Pinochet. I called him on a Friday, to set up a meeting. On the Sunday I learned that he had died.'

\*\*\*

For the families of those killed or disappeared, who have spent decades fighting for justice, Pinochet's return was a bitter moment, as was Schweitzer's role.

'I feel nothing about Miguel Schweitzer,' said Laura González-Vera, Carmelo Soria's widow. 'I knew him as a child, and that he was right-wing. I did not see him again until he was in the Supreme Court, during Carmelo's case. We looked at each other. We did not speak. There was nothing else.'

'I felt disgusted when Pinochet returned,' said her daughter Carmen Soria. 'Disgusted with the political parties of the Concertatión, disgusted with Insulza, disgusted with all who brought Pinochet home. Twenty-five years later, I am still on the same page. Disgusted.'

Yet her commitment to accountability is strong. She and her mother continue to press for Michael Townley's extradition from the United States to face justice in Chile. They are supported by the Chilean government but opposed by successive US administrations, who are able to rely on the deal negotiated by Miguel Schweitzer.

Laura González-Vera successfully sued Townley in the American courts, which ordered him to pay her US $7 million in damages, but refused to disclose his new identity or location. Townley has made modest payments, but Laura González-Vera has directed these to be received elsewhere.

Carmen Soria took her father's case to the Inter-American Commission of Human Rights. While Pinochet was in London, the Commission ruled that the torture and murder of Carmelo Soria was an international crime, subject to universal jurisdiction, that Chile violated his rights, must prosecute those responsible, pay compensation to the family, and repeal the 1978 Amnesty Law.

Three years after Pinochet returned, the Chilean government agreed to pay the Soria family an *ex gratia* payment of US$1.5 million. It took another four years for the Senate to ratify the agreement, and when it did the vote was only passed by a narrow majority.

When Pinochet was back, the Chilean courts reopened the Soria case, which moved from investigation to prosecution. Jorgelino Vergara confirmed the DINA's involvement in the murder, through the Lautaro Brigade. Michael Townley provided details on what happened at the house on the Vía Naranja on that July night in 1976. Mariana Callejas confirmed her husband's presence, Pedro Espinoza's role, and her memory of the 'laughter and noises' as Soria pleaded for his life.

In August 2023, forty-seven years after the killing, the Supreme Court confirmed the convictions of Pedro Espinoza and five other men for their involvement in the murder of Carmelo Soria. Espinoza, incarcerated at Punta Peuco prison in Tiltil, declined my request for an interview. Three of those convicted went on the run, their whereabouts unknown.

\*\*\*

Interest in Walther Rauff persists.

He features as a character in novels.

He is the protagonist in a collection of poems.

He is the subject of newspaper articles in Milan, based on CIA documents that describe his time in the city. 'Newspapers, Spies and a Luxury Hotel', runs the headline, a tale of crime and collaboration.

A radio station in Germany broadcasts an hour-long programme on Rauff, Pinochet and the DINA, which is then made available in Spanish.

The Chilean Senate takes care, in adopting a resolution on Nazis in Chile, to avoid expressing regret for the failure to extradite Rauff to West Germany, decades earlier.

An antique shop in Santiago sells a porcelain dining service said to have been owned by him. 'Each piece bears the initials of the owners of the set: W.R.', the shop announces. 'I've never seen that dining service,' Walter Rauff's sceptical grandson told me.

In May 2024, Chilean television marked the fortieth anniversary of his death with a special report, and several newspapers published articles.

And on it goes.

\*\*\*

León Gómez offered to accompany me to Londres 38. We meet outside the building, on the cobblestones over which the *Pesquera Arauco*'s refrigerated vans once passed. Cigarette in hand, he's with Horacio, his son, and Miguel Ángel Rebolledo, a fellow detainee.

We walk over the black and white tiles of the entrance, as the bells of San Francisco ring. 'We knew where we were when they rang,' says Miguel Angel.

'This was where we sat, waiting to go up to the second floor, to be interrogated,' says León, in the large room on the ground floor.

They reminisce about the visit in 1992, with Erika Hennings and others, when they identified their torturers, in the case of Alfonso Chanfreau.

'I recognised Krassnoff from a photograph in *El Mercurio*, in October 1973,' says León, just as he recognised Rauff from the photograph in December 1962. His evidence was treated as reliable by the judge, and helped to convict Krassnoff and two others.

'I found a picture of Rauff,' he says. 'I meant to bring it, sorry, I forgot.'

On the first floor, the interrogators softened León up, then it got worse. 'Someone in the room typed, an old machine, a big, tall, old one, not the flat type.' Loud. 'Tip, tip, tip, tap, tap, tap'. Rauff liked a decent typewriter.

'If we screamed too much, they turned on the music,' says Miguel Angel, 'but it was worse to hear the screaming of others.'

'Rauff watched and listened, sometimes his hands would point,' says León, 'as if to say, "More electricity!", or "Cut the electricity!" Mainly he would listen, this German man, who spoke in German.'

Miguel Angel isn't so sure about the details. 'You are so tense as you prepare to be tortured, you can't recall the details.'

'My father first talked of this only recently,' says Horacio, before León Gómez suffered a stroke. 'He didn't talk much, but when I asked him about foreigners he said: "There was a German man." The first time he didn't say Rauff's name, it was a short conversation, *a la pasada*, in passing.'

'Guatón Romo was the main torturer,' says Miguel Angel. Really brutal.

'I remember the scent,' León says.

'*Flaño*,' says Miguel Angel.

*Flaño?*

'Romo wore a strong, terrible perfume, very cheap. We knew what the smell of *Flaño* meant was coming, before he came into the room.'

\*\*\*

A few days later, at a dinner in Santiago, I mention my visit to Londres 38, seated next to a lady who did not seem to be antagonistic towards Pinochet. 'I love the smell of *Flaño* on young men,' she tells those assembled, who are slightly surprised.

'I remember the sounds, not the smells,' says Erika Hennings, when I mention this moment at the dinner. Like Laura González-Vera and Carmen Soria, she has been litigating for years, including on the *Pesquera Arauco*. Erika wants to know what I have picked up from Samuel Fuenzalida, who she knows – 'a man in limbo' – and Jorgelino Vergara, who she doesn't.

With the wife of a disappeared man I find it difficult to talk about the *Pesquera Arauco*'s refrigerated vans and facilities, and the connection with Rauff.

'Tell me,' Erika insists.

I tell her what I know.

'I know about San Antonio and Rocas de Santo Domingo,' she says. 'Many believe it to be a place of final destination.' She knows too of the *Pesquera Arauco* stories. 'We have heard rumours about the fishmeal plant, but there has never been testimony in court,' she says. 'Maybe because of the horror.'

Silence.

'There is testimony on the use of the boats, to disappear people,' she says.

Silence.

'I am suspicious about the fish food story.'

Her voice is soft and beautiful. She loved her husband Alfonso, she loves him still, she won't stop, she won't give up.

In many ways, the Chanfreau case is intertwined with the Soria case, and the two families know each other.

'You know what Carmen Soria is like!' Erika says. 'I will never forget how she came to me and said: "Erika! How did you do it?" By always being there, I told her, by persisting.'

Like the Soria case, Erika's cases before the Chilean judges went nowhere, so she left, for France, within days of Pinochet being arrested in London. A decade later, the Cour d'Assises in Paris handed down two judgements, one criminal, the other civil. Thirteen men were convicted for the kidnap and torture of Alfonso Chanfreau, including Contreras and Espinoza. In France they got life imprisonment, and Miguel Krassnoff got thirty years.

Everything is connected.

After Pinochet returned to Chile, the Chanfreau case finally kicked off. In 2015 the Supreme Court convicted Krassnoff, Basclay Zapata and others for the kidnapping of Alfonso Chanfreau, a crime against humanity. The Court sentenced them to lengthy prison terms and awarded the family US $400,000 in damages. In April 2023, the courts convicted the third man who Erika and León Gómez had identified in the parade, so many years before.

Zapata apologised to Hennings before he died in 2017 in Punta Peuco prison, but wouldn't disclose the whereabouts of her husband's remains. Krassnoff, who has more than eighty convictions for crimes that include the murders of Soria and Chanfreau, and is serving sentences of over a thousand years, remains unrepentant. He has powerful supporters, including José Antonio Kast, who was defeated by Gabriel Boric in the 2021 presidential election and remains a supporter of Pinochet. Kast has a German father, who joined the Nazi Party in 1942. After visiting Krassnoff in Punta Peuco, Kast called for him to be pardoned.

'Pinochet's arrest made the struggle for justice and accountability more visible,' Erika Hennings says, but emphasises that the struggle for justice pre-dated events in London, and that she wanted him judged.

'In the end he wasn't judged here in Chile either, despite the proceedings brought by Jaime Guzmán, but pffff . . .'

Should he have been judged in Spain?

'I would have preferred that he be judged, period. He wasn't judged. He was only arrested. The impunity went on.' The courts were slow, the focus mostly on the DINA, the private companies got off, she mused. 'There are descendants to protect, I suppose.'

She welcomes the *Programa Nacional de Búsqueda*, the national plan to gather information about the disappeared.

'It recognises the importance of the disappeared.'

Will you ever learn what happened to Alfonso?

'I don't think so. Occasionally I want to abdicate my work, but I won't, because of my grandson.'

Does Krassnoff know what happened to Alfonso?

'Yes, he does.'

\*\*\*

I meet Judge Guillermo De la Barra in Santiago in March 2024. He took over the *Pesquera Arauco* file from Judge Paola Plaza, who succeeded Judge Mario Carroza. De la Barra is affable and open, but I can't work out how much he really cares about the case.

'When we were first in touch,' he says, 'there were no investigations on the role of Walther Rauff in the *Pesquera Arauco* case, and now there are.'

He has spoken with numerous witnesses who have 'situated Rauff as an advisor of the DINA,' he says. 'I have interviewed Jorge Silva, Samuel Fuenzalida and *El Mocito*, and also Christoph Willeke.' The last, a DINA agent, told him that he knew of Rauff but never saw him.

Did you show him a photograph of Rauff?

'I didn't, because he said he knew what he looked like.'

What is your sense about Rauff's role in the *Pesquera Arauco*?

'I have no doubt Rauff was involved in the disappeared,' says Judge de la Barra. He is up to speed on Rauff's past, including his connections with Pinochet.

\*\*\*

I return to Londres street, for a last look. There are newly planted trees and, on the walls of several buildings, porcelain plaques and other objects to mark places of interest.

There's a bust of a nineteenth-century historian, who wrote about Chile's colonial history. There's a hotel, a parking garage, the head-quarters of a political party. There's a shop that sells large sheets of plastic, big enough in which to wrap a corpse.

It is a most ordinary street, but one with a history.

There's a sign for the Galería Bolt, the art gallery that Neruda spent time at, in collaboration with Marina Latorre, the founder of *Portal*, a poetry magazine. She was born in Punta Arenas and ended up living on Londres street. Together they once walked on the cobble-stones of a street over which the vans he wrote about would pass.

On the corner, where Londres street meets Libertador Bernardo O'Higgins avenue, stands the Church of San Francisco. On one wall someone has sprayed a few words, *No quiero tus golpes*, 'I don't want your coups'.

On another wall of the church a porcelain sign announces that a hermitage was once here, that it was founded by Pedro de Valdivia, conquistador and first governor of Chile. The plaque says he came from Spain with a painting, *Our Lady of Succour*, a fact recorded by Alonso de Ercilla y Zúñiga in his epic poem *La Araucana*. The plaque does not say that the poem was beloved by Pinochet, or that he set up a torture centre just a few steps away.

I go into the Church, make my way to the famed painting, which hangs above the High Altar. Nearby is an elegant glass-fronted cabinet, which holds a gold medal given to the Chilean poet Gab-riela Mistral. It came with the Nobel Prize for Literature she was awarded in December 1945, as Courtroom 600 in Nuremberg heard arguments about crimes against humanity and genocide.

The Nobel committee commended the lyrical power of Mistral's words, which reflected 'the idealistic aspirations of the entire Latin American world'. I came to know her work only recently, in Val-paraíso, the city where Pinochet was born and Rauff celebrated his seventieth birthday.

I was in Valparaíso for a literary festival, invited to talk about my books on Lviv and the Ratline, and to introduce my research on Pinochet and Rauff. I hoped someone might attend who knew a thing or two about the two men. As the session ended, a lady raised her hand.

'My name is Proserpina Fierro,' she said. She'd read about the event and seen the publicity photograph of Rauff.

'I knew Walther Rauff in the 1970s.' Many in the theatre felt a frisson. She didn't say much more, and didn't mention in her public comments how she first came across him, at the *Pesquera Camelio* building at Tres Puentes, back in 1975.

I visit Proserpina Fierro that evening, at her home in nearby Quilpué. She tells me she was the first woman in Chile to obtain a doctorate in electrical engineering. It was shortly after the Coup, and she was offered a job in Brazil, but then Pinochet intervened and ordered her not to leave. 'By order of the General,' she was informed by one of Pinochet's ministers, Herman Brady, 'your work is too important to our country.'

Fierro got a job in Punta Arenas, working at ASMAR, the state-owned naval construction and repair company at Tres Puentes, next to the *Pesquera Camelio*. As the only woman, fellow workers asked her to visit the cannery to see whether she might obtain some scallop shells, to decorate the office party. Off she went, to see the *jefe*, the boss, in the vast building next door.

She was directed to the upper floor, to the vast room, with a large desk at one end on which sat a large typewriter, the desk guarded on either side by two men and two rottweilers. Walther Rauff sat at the desk.

'I never forgot the accent or the formality. I knew nothing of his past, only learned about it after he died. He was a man attached to management, process and order. He was an organiser, he coordinated many things simultaneously.'

Over time, she learned of Rauff's closeness to the Camelio family, of his appreciation for Pinochet and the regime. Yes, she said, he travelled, but she did know where. 'Maybe to Argentina? Or Porvenir, where he had a house.' She saw it once, but never went, no one did, not without an appointment.

I share what I have learned about the man who gave her some scallop shells. Proserpina Fierro shows no surprise.

'He was a man with two faces. A dominant face, of absolute control over the space he occupied at a particular moment. Another face, that of a kind, good man, the one I usually saw, which was why I liked him.'

She holds my eye as she speaks. 'I imagined your three faces: writer, lawyer, and someone personally touched by the horrors that afflicted your own family. Could you separate these faces? I wondered which would prevail when you spoke. That's why I came to the event at the festival.'

She is not surprised that Rauff harmed people, long ago and more recently. 'It was his character, his approach. He was given a job, he did it.'

She is not surprised he may have had a second life, once more using vans to disappear people, first gas, then refrigerated.

'If they told me this when I met him, I would have believed it, as I believe it now.' She reflects, thinking with precision, speaking with precision.

'When you were in his presence, there were moments when his face reflected the capacity for such actions. It was not hatred. It was an absolute coldness, a desire for absolute control. Even in moments of joy, or laughter, you sensed that every impression he gave was controlled, that it was absolutely, tightly controlled . . .'

I hope you will write 'a rounded portrait' of Walther Rauff, she says, and of Pinochet. Do I sense in her a certain affection for both men?

'I like physics, so precision and accuracy are important to me, as are the perspectives of time and age, in offering colours on this story.'

And the story interests you because . . . ?

'Pinochet and Rauff? They were alike. Each had two faces. One gentle, the other hard. They were joined.'

And they both got away with it.

'Yes,' she says.

Sort of.

one day we found king crab skeletons
from the main house we saw
red stains on the peat
the legs had inside them
a flexible and transparent cartilage


Mariana Camelio, 'Laguna Grande', *Isla Riesco*, 2019

# ACKNOWLEDGEMENTS

This book is a consequence of an invitation to visit Lviv, in Ukraine, back in 2010, and may be considered the third in an *East West Street Trilogy*. I conducted a first interview in 2015, and since then have benefited from the assistance and support of a great number of individuals and institutions in Britain, Chile, Germany and Spain, and also beyond. Sometimes the assistance has been substantial and sustained over time, in other cases the input was informal, even limited to a reminiscence or two. I am deeply grateful to everyone who has contributed. If errors or omissions have crept in, they are my responsibility alone.

I have benefited greatly from the intelligence and energy of a superb group of research assistants. Monserrat Madariaga Gómez has been my main assistant on this journey, as fine a researcher as I have ever had the privilege of working with. My thanks also to: Jessie Barnett-Cox, Joao Bofill Rodrigues, Josefina del Rosario Lago, Alvaro Galindo, Grega Grobovsek, Lea Main-Klingst, Camilo Martín Muriel, Yaara Mordecai, Aleix Pérez i Pitarch, Samuel Rehberger, A.J. Solovy, Lieta Vivaldi and Luis Viveros.

Louise Rands† provided wonderful assistance on typing and transcriptions in the early years, after which Karen Carter took over, indefatigably attentive and wonderful.

At University College London, Deans Piet Eekhout and Eloise Scotford have been unstintingly supportive, as have all my colleagues, as has Maureen Worth at Harvard Law School. At Matrix Chambers and now 11 KBW, colleagues have been generous in bearing with my inattentions, in particular Mark Dann, Lee Cutler, Tori Eastwick and Kian Daniels.

I have benefited greatly from conversations and information from around the world.

Particular thanks are due to family members of some of the principal characters in the book, in particular Carmen Soria and Laura González-Vera, my new Chilean family; Mariana Camelio and Pablo Ojeda in Punta Arenas; Erika Hennings in Santiago and Paris; Paula Polanco in Santiago; Walther Rauff III in Santiago; and Miguel Schweitzer III in Punta Arenas.

In Chile, Rodrigo Rojas and Morgana Rodríguez Larraín went far beyond friendship, offering hospitality and door openings and so much more, all because of that first Bolaño lecture. León Gómez, Erika Hennings and Miguel Angel and Margarita Rebolledo offered time and more. My thanks also to: José Agüero Nuñez, Margarita Alegría, Adelia Andrade, Emma Barrientos, Carlos Basso, Sergio Bitar, Juan Pablo Bohoslavsky, Eduardo Camelio, Mario Carroza, Ascanio Cavallo, Cath Collins, Luis Cordero, Guillermo de la Barra, Raul Donoso, Ariel Dorfman, Hernán Felipe Errázuriz, Hernán Fernández, Karinna Fernández, Alejandro Ferrer, Moritz Fried the ice-cream guy, Ximena Fuentes, Samuel Fuenzalida, Galo Ghigliotto, Eugenio Gligo Viel, Baldovino Gomez, Monica Gonzalez, Claudio Grossman, Gustavo Guzmán, Dominique Herve, José Miguel Insulza, Andrea Jeftanovic, Ximena Katz, Albert van Klaveren, Benjamin Labatut, Harald Lindemann, Loreta Lopez, Andrés López Awad, Arturo Majlis, Cecilia Medina, Gloria Miqueles, Juan Carlos Muñoz Alegría, Francisco Orrego Vicuña†, Aldo Perán, Andrea Pivcevic, Paola Plaza, Paula Polanco, Vladimiro Poll, Manuela Portales, Sebastian Rauff, Cristián Rigo Ramirez, Benjamin Salas Kantor, Horst Schaffrick, Miguel Schweitzer, Monika Sears, Chantal Signorio, Cristián Toloza, Juan Torres, Javier Urbina, Jorgelino Vergara, Paola Vezzani, María Vivat, Pastor Ricardo Wagner, Yael Zaliasnik and the staff and coffee-makers at Hotel Maison Italia 1029.

In Germany: Martin Cüppers, Niklas Frank, Gerd Heidemann, Rainer Huhle, Wilfried Huismann, Dieter Maier, Anna Richter and Nina Sillem.

In Spain: Mario Boero Vargas, Carlos Castresana, Ernesto Ekaizer, Juan Garcés and Baltasar Garzón.

In the United Kingdom, a special thank you to my colleagues on various aspects of the Pinochet case, in particular Reed Brody, and also: Andrew Clapham, Helen Duffy, Ed Fitzgerald, Jonathan Marks, Nigel Pleming, Ken Roth, Urmi Shah, Rabinder Singh, Richard Stein, Wilder Taylor, José Miguel Vivanco, as well as pro bono counsel Paul Hoffman, William Aceves, Susan Benesch, William Gravitt and Dian Orentlicher.

And also: Lucy Bailey, Susie Bascon, Simon Brown, Simon Browne-Wilkinson, Michael Caplan, Susanna Clapp, Dave Clark, Lawrence Collins, Sherard Cowper-Coles, Peter Dean, John Dew, Nicholas Evans, Vincent Fean, Matthew Gould, Jeremy Hayes, Leonard Hoffmann, Kerstin Hoge, James Holland, David Hope, Robert Howard, Alun Jones, Nick Kent, Christina Lamb, Daniel Lee, David Milliband, Clare Montgomery, Andrew Patrick, Jean Pateras, Jonathan Powell, Angus Reilly, Nicholas Shakespeare, Gordon Slynn, Amy St Johnson, Jack Straw, David Sugarman, Jonathan Sumption, James Vallance White, Essi Viding, and Simon Wessely.

Elsewhere: Natalia Barbero, Uki Goni, Luis Moreno Ocampo (Argentina); Linda Erker, Cristina Fuentes, Kerstin von Lingen, Friderica Wächter, Horst Wächter, Erich Zott (Austria); Pierre Klein (Belgium); Hernán Escudero Álvarez, Alvaro Galindo (Ecuador); William Bourdon, Beatrice and Serge Klarsfeld, Gwen Strauss (France); Maurice Apprey, Fui Tsikata (Ghana); Yossi Chen, Yuval Shany (Israel); Eric Lerner (Italy); Herman Bennett, Charles Brower, Suzanne Browne-Fleming, Jeremy Eichler, Joseph Finnegan, Gonzalo Flores, Linda Kinstler, Peter Kornbluh, Jennifer Morgan, Cullen Murphy, Amy Rao, Lucy Reed and Ken Silverstein (United States).

I have benefited from the assistance of generous archivists: Richard Ovenden (Bodleian, Oxford), Matthew Butson (Getty Images), Katharine Friedla (Stanford University) and María del Carmen Elizalde (Central University of Ecuador).

Vickie Taylor produced the usual wonderful maps, with support from Scott Edmonds, and photographic assistance was provided by my dear friends Jonathan Klein and Diana Matar.

My generous, marvellous, comforting agents, who are so very patient: Georgia Garrett, Laurence Laluyaux and Stephen Edwards at Rogers, Coleridge & White in London, and Melanie Jackson in New York.

My wonderful editors: Jenny Lord at Weidenfeld & Nicolson, who has taken the lead, supported by a fine team, including Leanne Oliver, Georgia Goodall, Natalie Dawkins, copyeditor Richard Mason, and picture researcher Susannah Jayes; Todd Portnowitz and Victoria Wilson at Alfred A. Knopf; Isabel Obiols and Silvia Sese at Anagrama, and Lorena Fuentes in Santiago; and Hélène Monsacré at Albin Michel and Tanja Hommen at Fischer.

My dear friends: James Cameron, with whom this particular journey began; Javier Cercas, James Crawford†, James Daunt (on titles and such matters), Adriana Fabra, David Kennedy, Hisham Matar, Mariana Montoya, Gerry Simpson, Alia Trabucco Zerán and Juan Gabriel Vásquez.

My dear family: my late father, Allan, who was always there; my mother Ruth, who is more than always there; Marc, the best brother anyone could ever hope for; nephew Emil, for stepping in at short notice with a painting of the *Walter*; Annie, my valued aunt; and Leina, my fabulously Spanish mother-in-law who opened some vital doors.

And even closer to home: Leo, on history; Lara, on family tales; and Katya, on seeing and design.

And Natalia, she who keeps us all ticking, with feet on the ground, the embodiment of all that is great in life and love, who opened some doors – including Chile and Spain – and closed others, always in that principled, robust and generous way.

Thank you, thank you, thank you.

# SOURCES

'The connection among proofs, truth and history cannot easily be dismissed'

Carlo Ginzburg, *Threads and Traces*, 2012

Over the past eight years working on this book I have benefited from many works of fiction and non-fiction on the lives of Augusto Pinochet and Walther Rauff, events in Chile and matters of international law, as well as documentary and drama films, and radio programmes.

## Archives

I have made use of several archives, in particular:

CIA Reading Room (online), Special Collection, Walter Rauff
See e.g. /specialCollection/nwcda7/164/RAUFF, WALTER/RAUFF, WALTER_0106.pdf
Hoover Institution Library & Archives, Gerd Heidemann Collection, [Boxes 92, 93 and 94]
Bodleian Oxford, Bodleian Libraries, Archive of (Charles) Bruce Chatwin
Politisches Archiv des Auswärtigen Amtes Berlin
Bundesarchiv Berlin
The letters of Walther Rauff (1946–1982): made available by Martin Cüppers (from the private collection of Hans-Jochen Emsmann)
Documents relating to Walther Rauff: made available by Dieter Maier

# Books

The writings of Bruce Chatwin and Roberto Bolaño have offered guidance and inspiration:

Roberto Bolaño, *By Night in Chile* (Vintage, 2009, tr. Chris Andrews)

Roberto Bolaño, *Nazi Literature in the Americas* (Picador, 2010, tr. Chris Andrews)

Roberto Bolaño, *Between Parentheses* (New Directions, 2004, tr. Natasha Wimmer)

Bruce Chatwin, *In Patagonia* (Jonathan Cape, 1977)

Bruce Chatwin and Paul Theroux, *Patagonia Revisited* (Jonathan Cape, 1985)

Elizabeth Chatwin and Nicholas Shakespeare, *Under the Sun: The Letters of Bruce Chatwin* (Jonathan Cape, 2010)

Susanna Clapp, *With Chatwin: Portrait of a Writer* (Vintage, 1998)

Numerous works of contemporary fiction and poetry, which relate to actual events, have provided a rich source of inspiration:

Isabel Allende, *The House of the Spirits* (Alfred Knopf, 1985)

Pascual Brodsky, *Años de fascinación* (Hueders, 2017)

Roberto Brodsky, 'Amores que matan', in Mili Rodríguez Villouta (ed.), *Compasión* (Planeta, 2000)

Mariana Callejas, *La larga noche* (Lo Curro, 1987)

Mariana Camelio, *Isla Riesco* (jampstér libros, 2019)

Ariel Dorfman, *Death and the Maiden* (Nick Hern Books, 1991)

Gloria Dunkler, *Spandau* (Ediciones Tácitas, 2012)

Nona Fernández, *El taller* (2012, a play)

Nona Fernández, *Space Invaders* (Graywolf Press, 2013, tr. Natasha Wimmer)

Nona Fernández, *Twilight Zone* (Daunt Books, 2016, tr. Natasha Wimmer)

Galo Ghighliotto, *El museo de la bruma* (Laurel, 2019)

Carlos Iturra, *Crimen y perdón* (Catalonia, 2008)

Andrea Jeftanovic, *Theatre of War* (Charco, 2020, tr. Frances Riddle)

Pedro Lemebel, *My Tender Matador* (Grove Press, 2003, tr. Katharine Silver)

Pedro Lemebel, *De perlas y cicatrices* (LOM, 1998)

Lina Meruane, *Nervous System* (Atlantic, 2021, tr. Megan McDowell)

Pavel Oyzarzun, *Será el paraíso* (LOM, 2019)

Muriel Rukeyser, *El Libro de Los Muertos* (Usach, 2021)

Luis Sepúlveda, *The Shadow of What We Were* (Europa, 2011, tr. Howard Curtis)

Alia Trabucco Zerán, *The Remainder* (Other Books, 2018, tr. Sophie Hughes)

Mario Vargas Llosa, *The Feast of the Goat* (Faber & Faber, 2012, tr. Edith Grossman)

Alejandro Zambra, *Ways of Going Home* (Granta, 2013, tr. Megan McDowell)

Raúl Zurita, *INRI* (New York Review Books, 2018)

As to non-fiction, I wish to pay particular tribute to Professor Martin Cüppers, whose *Walther Rauff – In deutschen Diensten* (WBG, 2013) is the leading work on which I have placed great reliance. The other books on which I have drawn, and sit on the shelves above my writing desks – on memoir, crime, law, photography, politics, history – include:

Mario Amorós, *Pinochet: Biografía Militar y Política* (Penguin Random House, 2019)

Dietrich Angerstein, *Los años bajo fuego* (Memoria Creativa, 2019)

Luz Arce, *The Inferno: A Story of Terror and Survival in Chile* (University of Wisconsin, 2004)

Andrés López Awad and Camilo Pérez Alveal, *Carmelo: matar dos veces a un mismo hombre* (CEIBO, 2023)

Ronald Bartle, *Bow Street Beak* (Barry Rose, 2000)

Carlos Basso, *Chile Top Secret: El submundo clandestino de la CIA, la KGB, la DINA y los nazis* (Aguilar, 2017)

Carlos Basso, *República nazi de Chile* (Aguilar, 2020)

Carlos Basso, *La secta perfecta: Los secretos más oscuros de Colonia Dignidad* (Aguilar, 2022)

Sergio Bitar, *Prisoner of Pinochet: My Year in a Chilean Concentration Camp* (University of Wisconsin, 2017)

Roberto Bolaño, *Between Parentheses: Essays, Articles and Speeches 1998–2003* (New Directions, 2016)

Robert Borgel, *Étoile jaune et croix gammée: les juifs de Tunisie face aux nazis* (Le Manuscrit, 2007)

Werner Brockdorff, *Flucht von Nürnberg* (Welsermühl, 1969)

Reed Brody and Michael Ratner (eds.), *The Pinochet Papers* (Kluwer, 2000)

Mariana Callejas, *Siembra Vientos: Memorias* (CESOC, 1995)

Ascanio Cavallo and Rocío Montes, *La historia oculta de la década socialista* (Uqbar, 2022)

Cath Collins, *Post-Transitional Justice: Human Rights Trials in Chile and El Salvador* (Penn State University Press, 2015)

Cath Collins, Katherine Hite and Alfredo Joignant (eds.), *The Politics of Memory in Chile from Pinochet to Bachelet* (Rienner, 2013)

Madeline Davis, *The Pinochet Case: Origins, Progress, Implications* (Institute of Latin American Studies, 2003)

John Dinges, *The Condor Years: How Pinochet and His Allies Brought Terrorism to Three Continents* (New Press, 2004)

John Dinges and Saul Landau, *Assassination on Embassy Row* (Pantheon, 1980)

Ernesto Ekaizer, *Yo, Augusto* (Aguilar, 2003)

Michel Faure, *Augusto Pinochet* (Perrin, 2020)

Andrew Feinstein, *Pablo Neruda: A Passion for Life* (Bloomsbury, 2004)

Gabriel García Márquez, *Clandestine in Chile* (New York Review Books, 1987)

Baltasar Garzón, *No a la impunidad* (2019, Debate)

Paul Ghez, *Six mois sous la botte* (Le Manuscrit, 2009)

León Gómez Araneda, *Que el pueblo juzgue: Historia del golpe* (Terranova, 1988)

León Gómez Araneda, *Tras la huella de los desaparecidos* (Caleuche, 1990)

Juan Guzmán, *Au bord du monde: Les mémoires du juge de Pinochet* (Les Arènes, 2005)

David Hope, *House of Lords 1996–2009: Lord Hope's Diaries* (Avizandum, 2018)

Joan Jara, *Victor: An Unfinished Song* (Bloomsbury, 1998)

Ernst Klee, Willi Dressen and Volker Riess (eds.), *The Good Old*

*Days: The Holocaust as Seen by its Perpetrators and Bystanders* (Free Press, 1991)

Peter Kornbluh, *The Pinochet File: A Declassified Dossier on Atrocity and Accountability* (New Press, 2013)

Dieter Maier, *Colonia Dignidad: Auf den Spuren eines deutschen Verbrechens in Chile* (Schmetterling, 2017)

Cristóbal Marín, *Huesos Sin Descanso: Fueguinos en Londres* (Debate, 2019)

Gladys Marín, *Regreso a la esperanza: Derrota de la Operación Cóndor* (Instituto de Ciencias Alejandro Lipschutz, 1999)

Peter Mason, *The Lives of Images* (Reaktion Books, 2001)

Claude Nataf, *Les juifs de Tunisie sous le joug nazi* (Le Manuscrit, 2012)

Ángel Parra, *Manos en la nuca* (Tabla Rasa, 2005)

Leith Passmore, *The Wars Inside Chile's Barracks* (University of Wisconsin, 2017)

Juan Cristóbal Peña, *La secreta vida literaria de Augusto Pinochet* (Debate, 2013)

Mónica Pérez and Felipe Gerdtzen, *Augusto Pinochet: 503 días atrapado en Londres* (Los Andes, 2000)

Augusto Pinochet, *The Crucial Day: September 11, 1973* (Renacimiento, 1982)

Augusto Pinochet, *Camino recorrido* (1990, self-published)

Patricia Politzer, *Fear: Lives under Pinochet* (New Press, 2001)

Javier Rebolledo, *La danza de los cuervos: el destino final de los detenidos desaparecidos* (CEIBO, 2012)

Jan Stehle, *Der Fall Colonia Dignidad: Zum Umgang bundesdeutscher Außenpolitik und Justiz mit Menschenrechtsverletzungen 1961–2020* (Transcript, 2021)

Steve J. Stern, *Remembering Pinochet's Chile: On the Eve of London 1998* (Duke University Press, 2004)

Steve J. Stern, *The Memory Box of Pinochet's Chile* (Duke University Press, 2004–10)

Steve J. Stern, *Battling for Hearts and Minds: Memory Struggles in Pinochet's Chile, 1973–1988* (Duke University Press, 2006)

Steve J. Stern, *Reckoning with Pinochet: The Memory Question in Democratic Chile, 1989–2006* (Duke University Press, 2010)

Jack Straw, *Last Man Standing: Memoirs of a Political Survivor* (Macmillan, 2012)

Hernán Valdés, *Diary of a Chilean Concentration Camp* (Victor Gollancz, 1975)

Luis Vega, *Estado militar y transición democrática en Chile* (El Dorado,1991)

## Other media

On the visual side – films and series – that address subjects touched on in this book, I have benefited greatly from:

*The Battle for Chile I: The Insurrection of the Bourgeoisie* (Patricio Guzmán, 1975)

*The Battle for Chile II: The Coup* (Patricio Guzmán, 1977)

*The Battle for Chile III: Popular Power* (Patricio Guzmán, 1979)

*Missing* (Costa Gavras, 1982)

*Death and the Maiden* (Roman Polanski, 1994)

*The Pinochet Case* (dir. Patricio Guzmán, 2001)

*Machuca* (Andrés Wood, 2005)

*Tony Manero* (Pablo Larraín, 2009)

*Dawson Isla 10* (Miguel Littin, 2009)

*Post mortem* (Pablo Larraín, 2010)

*No* (Pablo Larraín, 2013)

*The Quispe Girls* (Sebastian Sepúlveda, 2014)

*Colonia* (Florian Gallenberger, 2016)

*Santiago, Italia* (Nanni Moretti, 2018)

*A Sinister Sect: Colonia Dignidad* (Netflix, 2020)

*1976* (Manuela Martelli, 2022)

*El Conde* (Pablo Larraín, 2023)

*Los colonos* (Felipe Gálvez Haberle, 2023)

## Epigraphs

Finally, each section of the book is introduced with an epigraph, a line or more that is emblematic of what follows. These are the sources:

*Page*

vii   Jean Bodin (1576) and Richard Knolles (1606). *The Six Bookes of a Common-Weale. Written by I. Bodin a famous Lawyer, and a man of great Experience in matters of State. Out of the French and Latine copies, done into English, by Richard Knolles* (London: G. Bishop)

vii   Walther Rauff, conversation with Gerd Heidemann, June 1979, Heidemann Archive.

vii   Augusto Pinochet, interview with Maria Elvira Salazar, Canal 22, Miami, November 2003.

1     Cesare Beccaria, *Des délits et des peines* (1764), chap. XXXV, French transl. (1773) (Institut Coppet, 2011)

85    Roberto Bolaño, 'Entre Pinochet y el culo del mundo', *Ajoblanco*, Vol. 113, November 1998, 35

163   Bruce Chatwin, *In Patagonia* (Jonathan Cape, 1977)

219   Leonard Cohen, 'Everybody Knows', *I'm Your Man* (Columbia Records, 1988)

297   Pablo Neruda, 'A heroic deed in the name of freedom', *El Siglo*, 2 July 1965

380   Mariana Camelio, *Isla Riesco* (jampstér libros, 2019)

385   Carlo Ginzburg, *Threads and Trace* (University of California Press, 2012)

# ILLUSTRATION CREDITS

151 Pinochet legal team, London, December 1998 (Miguel Schweitzer Walters)
166 Bombera Alemana, Punta Arenas, 6 November 2022 (Philippe Sands)
173 Rauff cabin, Punta Arenas, 15 January 2024 (Philippe Sands)
181 South Pacific Corretaje Marítimo Limitada flag, Santiago (courtesy of www.crwflags.com)
183 Viña Linderos wine label (Hoover Institution Library & Archives, Gerd Heidemann Collection)
185 Walther Rauff and Karl Wolff, Munich Restaurant, Santiago, June 1979 (Hoover Institution Library & Archives, Gerd Heidemann Collection)
188 Rauff house, Santiago (Yossi Chen, Yad Vashem archives)
206 House of Lords, Law Lords deliberation room, London, 21 February 2024 (Philippe Sands)
214 Augusto and Lucía Pinochet, Margaret Thatcher, London, 26 March 1999 (Ian Jones/Stringer/Getty)
225 *Lord Lonsdale*, Punta Arenas, by Bruce Chatwin, 1975 (Bodleian Libraries, Archive of (Charles) Bruce Chatwin)
234 Dawson Island, February 1899 (Alberto M. De Agostini, Museo Maggiorino Borgatello, Biblioteca Nacional de Chile)
235 Selk'nam archers (Martin Gusinde/Anthropos Institut)
248 Rauff (1966), Rauff (1976), Lindes (undated) (*Ercilla* magazine, Martin Cüppers, Carlos Basso)
259 León Gómez, Santiago, 2 December 2021 (Philippe Sands)
278 Samuel Fuenzalida, Santiago, 14 December 2021 (Philippe Sands)
282 Henry Kissinger with glasses (Bettman/Getty)
287 DINA headquarters, Santiago, Marcoleta Street, 1 November 2022 (Philippe Sands)
312 Augusto Pinochet, RAF Waddington, 2 March 2000 (Jean Pateras)
325 Jorgelino Vergara, Teno, 9 November 2022 (Philippe Sands)
329 Walther Rauff, Porvenir, November 1964 (*Ercilla* magazine)
333 Hake, *Pesquera Arauco*, San Antonio 1976 (Zig-Zag Quimantú Archive, Museo Histórico Nacional)
343 Chevrolet C30 advertisement (Veoautos.cl)
347 Jorge Silva, San Antonio, 8 March 2024 (Philippe Sands)
350 Hotel La Bahía, Cartagena, 1960s (*La Gaceta de Los Clásicos*)
353 Hotel La Bahía, Cartagena, 8 March 2024 (Philippe Sands)
369 Augusto Pinochet, walking stick, 2020 (Miguel Schweitzer Walters)
379 Centolla Camelio package, 1970s (Hoover Institution Library & Archives, Gerd Heidemann Collection)

# NOTES

xxiv  like a pig on a spit: Patricio Rivas, 'Setenta y dos horas en Londres 38', 25 *Revista de Estudios Sociales* (2006), 49–51.

3  request of a Spanish judge: 'Pinochet Arrested in London', *BBC News*, 17 October 1998; 'Chileans React with Disbelief', *BBC News*, 18 October 1998.

3  Things will never go back to the way they were.': Roberto Bolaño, 'Entre Pinochet y el culo del mundo', *Ajoblanco*, vol. 113, November 1998, 35.

3  said one minister: 'Pinochet Decision for Straw', *The Guardian*, 19 October 1998.

4  'ending their days in a Spanish prison': Hansard, House of Lords, 6 July 1999, column 801 (Margaret Thatcher, Statement on General Pinochet); Ros Taylor, 'Augusto Pinochet', *The Guardian*, 19 January 1999.

4  good, brave and honourable soldier': Ros Taylor, 'Pinochet's Friends Go on the Offensive', *The Guardian*, 19 January 1999.

4  with his wife Lucía Hiriart: See also Alejandra Matus, *Doña Lucía: La biografía no autorizada* (Ediciones B, 2013).

5  expropriating their assets: Decree Law 77, 8 October 1973.

5  moved prisoners in and out: Statement of Samuel Fuenzalida, Court of Appeal, case of Operación Colombo, case of Jorge Grez Aburto, judgement of 7 May 2014, at p. 29 (on file).

5  finance its secret activities and repression: Pablo Seguel, *Los soldados de la represión* (Ediciones UAH, 2022).

6  'A country occupied': Daniel Borzutzky, 'Today or a Million Years Ago: An Interview with Raúl Zurita', *Poetry Foundation*, 24 March 2015.

6  tour of assassinations: *Ibid.*; and Javier Rebolledo, *El despertar de los cuervos: Tejas verdes, el origen del exterminador en Chile* (Planeta, 2016), and *A la sombra de los cuervos* (Planeta, 2017).

6  'I always felt affection for him.': Augusto Pinochet, *The Crucial Day* (Editorial Renacimiento, 1982), 52.

7  many others injured: 'Participé en el atentado a Pinochet: Patricio Manns y una confesión inesperada', *La Cuarta*, 25 September 2021.

7    murdered or disappeared: *Report of the National Commission on Truth and Reconciliation*, February 1991 (Rettig Report) (English translation available at: https://www.usip.org/sites/default/files/resources/collections/truth_commissions/Chile90-Report/Chile90-Report.pdf).

8    Wasn't it only four million?: Felix Jiménez Botta, 'From Antifascism to Human Rights: Politics of Memory in the West German Campaigns Against the Chilean and Argentinean Military Regimes, 1973–1990', *Zeithistorische Forschungen/Studies in Contemporary History* 17, no. 1 (2020); Norbert Blüm and Ludger Reuber, *Politik als Balanceakt. 'Unverblümtes' aus der Werkstatt Bonn* (Universitas, 1993), 22; Olivier Guez, *La disparition de Josef Mengele* (Livre de Poche, 2017), 89–90.

8    accounts of communist crimes: Juan Cristóbal Peña, *La secreta vida literaria de Augusto Pinochet* (Random House Mondadori, 2013), 207.

8    the poet recorded: Alonso de Ercilla y Zuñiga, *La Araucana* (Vanderbilt University Press, 1945, reprinted 2014, tr. Charles Lancaster and Paul Manchester), Canto XXXII, 26.

8    in Washington two years before: Decree Law No. 2191 grants amnesty to the persons indicted for the referred offences, *Diario Oficial*, 18 April 1978; *see also* Investigating Judge Adolfo Bañados, 12 November 1993, Case No. 192-1978, para. 18; Supreme Court of Chile, 30 May 1995, Case No. 192-1978, para. 8.

8    at the time of his murder: Herbert Mitgang, 'Publishing: The Letelier Case', *The New York Times*, 18 July 1980.

9    the Spanish Civil War: U.S. Department of State Secret Memorandum of Conversation between Henry Kissinger and Augusto Pinochet, 'US Chilean Relations' (8 June 1976), in Peter Kornbluh, *The Pinochet File*, 2nd edn. (The New Press, 2013), 264.

9    that's the rumour: Entrevista a Orlando Letelier (grabación Sonora), Archivo Audiovisual, Biblioteca Nacional Digital de Chile, https://www.bibliotecanacionaldigital.gob.cl/bnd/625/w3-article-625617.html.

9    to deal with Letelier: Kornbluh, *The Pinochet File*, 350.

10   Chanel No. 5 perfume: 'Berríos: Los casetes secretos del "químico de Pinochet", Chapter 1: Armas químicas', *Vergara 240* (2023).

10   a Nobel Prize for Borges: Peña, *La secreta vida literaria de Augusto Pinochet*, 118; Christopher Hitchens, 'Jorge Luis Borges', *The Spectator*, 21 June 1986.

10   or CNI: 'Interview with Manuel Contreras: "La DINA no se manejaba sola"', *Terrorismo de estado en Chile* (19 October 2011).

10   four years of criminality: John Dinges and Saul Landau, *Assassination on Embassy Row* (Pantheon, 1980), 299, 307.

10   Minister of Justice in Chile: 'Telegram from the Department of State to the Embassy in Chile', *Foreign Relations of the United States, 1977–1980*, vol. XXIV, South America, Latin America Region. Doc. 211 (14 March 1978).

10   Contreras and Espinoza: Dinges and Landau (1980), 336.

11   (he'd later recant, claiming duress): *Ibid.*, 332; 'Interview with Manuel Contreras: "La DINA no se manejaba sola"', *Terrorismo de estado en Chile* (19 October 2011); 'Affidavit of Pedro Espinoza Bravo sworn before notary Arturo Carvajal Escobar', (Santiago, 2 May 1978).

11   reveal them if necessary: Kornbluh, *The Pinochet File*, 407; Manuel Salazar Salvo, 'Contreras: Historia de un Intocable. Los años 80 y el camino a la cárcel', *Interferencia*, 26 April 2021.

11   other DINA activities: 'Telegram from the Department of State to the Embassy in Chile', *Foreign Relations of the United States, 1977–1980*, vol. XXIV, South America, Latin America Region. Doc. 212 (14 April 1978); Kornbluh, *The Pinochet File*, 405.

11   Pinochet had played no role: Dinges and Landau (1980), 337–8, 391.

11   for the crimes committed: CIA Intelligence Report, 'Strategy of Chilean Government with Respect to Letelier Case, and Impact of Case on Stability of President Pinochet', 23 June 1978, in Kornbluh, *The Pinochet File*, 440–1.

11   was his line: *Ibid.*, CIA Directorate of Intelligence, 'Pinochet's Role in the Letelier Assassination and Subsequent Coverup' (1 May 1987).

11   not details or the means: Christina Lamb, 'Tea with Pinochet', *New Statesman*, 26 July 1999.

11   if not the crime: Kornbluh, *The Pinochet File*, 406–9.

11   Israel Borquez duly confirmed: *Ibid.*, 405–9; CIA Directorate of Intelligence, 'Pinochet's Role in the Letelier Assassination and Subsequent Coverup' (1 May 1987).

11   any risk of extradition: CIA Directorate of Intelligence, 'Pinochet's Role in the Letelier Assassination and Subsequent Coverup' (1 May 1987).

12   modest presidential salary: Ascanio Cavallo and Rocío Montes, *La historia oculta de la década socialista* (Uqbar, 2022), 288.

12   'to the best of my ability': David Burnham, 'American Testifies He Has No Regrets About Assassinating Letelier', *The New York Times*, 23 January 1979.

12   not to implicate Pinochet: Kenneth Brademeier, 'Silbert Agreed with Chile to Curtail Information', *The Washington Post*, 24 January 1979.

12   charges for other crimes: 'US Won't Extradite Figure in Letelier Case', *The New York Times*, 26 July 1983; Ali Beydoun, 'The U.S. Should Expedite Extradition for Chilean Diplomat's Assassin', *The Washington Post*, 23 September 2016.

12   crimes committed abroad: Erika Harding, 'Chile: Former Officials Contreras & Espinoza Found Guilty in Letelier Assassination', *NotiSur*, 9 November 1993.

13   would protect him abroad: In ordering Chile to pay compensation of US $2.5 million to the Letelier and Moffitt families, a US-Chile Commission respected Chile's sovereign immunity: *Dispute Concerning Responsibility for the Deaths of Letelier and Moffitt* (United States, Chile), Award, XXV *RIAA* (1992), 3–19.

13   they were committed: Nigel Rodley, *The Treatment of Prisoners under International Law* (Oxford, 1987), 101–7.

13   arrested in the past: Author interview with Miguel Schweitzer, 4 September 2020.

13   he told Thatcher over tea: David Sugarman, 'The Hidden Histories of the Pinochet Case' *Journal of Law and Society*, vol. 51 (2024), x, at xx.

13   Hatchards on Piccadilly: Cavallo and Montes, *La historia oculta de la década socialista*, 15.

14   to match his eyes: Jon Lee Anderson, 'The Dictator', *The New Yorker*, 11 October 1998.

15   Chilean exiles sought him out: 'The Lawyer Who Wouldn't Forget', *The Guardian*, 2 February 1999.

17   'the criminal code only in 1971.': Law 44/1971 amending the Criminal Code, Article 137 bis, 16 November 1971, Boletín Oficial del Estado [BOE] 274 (Spain); Aleix Pérez i Pitarch, 'Spain, 1996: the origins of the Pinochet case: the initial legal framework (and why words matter)', Paper submitted in fulfilment of LLM Degree (Harvard Law School, May 2022), 17.

18   (wide central avenue): Ivan Boileau, 'La Ciudad Lineal: A Critical Study of the Linear Suburb of Madrid' (1959), 230.

18   find the perpetrators: Aleix Pérez i Pitarch, 'Spain, 1996', 10.

19   because of the Amnesty Law: Supreme Court of Chile, 4 June 1996, Case No. 1-1993; a final appeal to the Supreme Court was dismissed on 23 August 1996; Aleix Pérez i Pitarch, 'Spain, 1996', 10.

21   'because she was always so busy': 'Arturo Soria y su hermano Carmelo, hacia 1940, cuando llegaron a Chile', *El Mercurio*, 31 August 1980.

27   Pedro Lemebel called it: Pedro Lemebel, 'Carmen Soria (O la eterna lucha de un ético mirar)', in *Zanjón de la Aguada* (Editorial Planeta Chilena, 2003).

28 killed by DINA agents: Rettig Report (1991), vol. 1, 779.
29 Human Rights: Inter-American Commission on Human Rights, Report No. 133/99, Case 11.725: Carmelo Soria Espinoza (19 November 1999).
29 'the writer Mariana Callejas.': Andrés López Awad and Camilo Pérez Alveal, *Carmelo: matar dos veces a un mismo hombre* (CEIBO, 2023); Nelson Jofré, *La implacable verdad policial: La apasionante investigación del detective que descubrió al grupo más secreto y letal de la Dina* (Catalonia, 2023).
30 torture and disappearances: Victoria Dannemann, 'Garcés: "Como testigo de crimen, debía evitar la impunidad"', *DW*, 15 October 2018.
30 to stop both cases: Alejandra Matus, 'Torres Silva, el fiscal favorito de Pinochet', *Los Casos de la Vicaria* (undated); Silva appeared before the Court on 3 October 1997, and Garcés filed a motion to dismiss Silva's requests on 27 October 1997 (*see* Doc. 1997-10-27 JG au JCI num. 6 – Réponse au Général Torres Silva.pdf); *see also* 'General Torres Silva comparaît devant le JCI n° 6', *El País*, 18 October 1997 (on file).
31 were also in touch: Open Democracy, *Justice in the World's Light* (2001) (Geoffrey Bindman: 'Augusto Pinochet visited London on several occasions. On two of them I tried to have him arrested. I was representing Amnesty International UK. On one occasion we went to Bow Street to ask for a warrant for Pinochet's arrest – he was attending an arms fair in Birmingham. The magistrate was reluctant, and adjourned the case. The following day Pinochet returned to Chile'; on another occasion 'he was visiting London for shopping and to see his friend, Margaret Thatcher. We asked the Attorney General to prosecute. Eventually, he referred the matter to the Metropolitan Police who were interested. They asked us for more evidence of tortures that had taken place after November 1988, when the 1984 International Convention against Torture was brought into English law.')
32 tortured and disappeared: Rettig Report (1991), vol. 2, 847.
34 and decided to act: Ernesto Ekaizer, *Yo, Augusto* (Aguilar, 2003), 494.
34 'the moment of his statement': 'Spanish Request to Question General Pinochet', 14 October 1998, in Reed Brody and Steven Ratner, *The Pinochet Papers* (Springer, 2000), 55.
34 (Bogota and north Oxford): https://www.johndew.uk/prints1
34 frolics of their own: Author interview with Dave Clark, 17 November 2023, special adviser to Robin Cook.
35 Operation Condor and Pinochet: Doc. 1998-10-16 Plainte et demande au JCI num. 5 d'arrêter Pinochet, à 13-10 heures.pdf, by which time

Enrique Santiago filed the criminal complaint against Pinochet.

35    Pinochet's extradition to Spain: John Hooper, 'Move to Question Pinochet in the UK', *The Guardian*, 14 October 1998; Note by Jessie Barnett-Cox, 1 March 2017.

35    'so far I do not have it.': Lourdes Gómez and Ramón Lobo, 'Amnistía pide al Gobierno británico que retenga al ex dictador Pinochet', *El País*, 16 October 1998.

39    'disappearances, helped us.': 'Un français serait mort à la suite des tortures', *Le Monde*, 30 October 1975.

39    personally signed by Pinochet: Decreto traspaso de Londres 38 al Instituto O'Higginiano, 29 November 1978 (on file).

40    29 September 1992: Transcript, 29 September 1992, Santiago (on file).

43    a first-hand account: *Hansard*, House of Commons, 9 February 1999, column 143.

49    told Pinochet of his rights: Ekaizer, *Yo, Augusto*, 535.

49    It was nearly midnight: 'The service of the arrest warrant is an operational matter for the Metropolitan Police', Straw told Parliament. 'The first provisional arrest warrant for Senator Pinochet was served by two officers of the Metropolitan Police Extradition Squad at 11.45pm on 16 October 1998. In attendance were the head of the Metropolitan Police Extradition Unit and another officer; a civilian interpreter; a doctor; and two nurses. There was no armed backup', *Hansard*, House of Commons, 9 February 1999, column 143.

50    'this was happening to him': Email, Nicholas Blake to author, 23 August 2022.

52    'mediocrities on right and left': Roberto Bolaño, 'Entre Pinochet y el culo del mundo', *Ajoblanco*, vol. 113, November 1998, 35.

52    cavorted with the dictator: Roberto Bolaño, 'El pasillo sin salida aparente', *Ajoblanco*, vol. 116, May 1999, 54–7.

52    'branching out into other areas.': Roberto Bolaño, *By Night in Chile* (Vintage, 2009), 65.

53    'they are prepared to go': *Ibid.*, 86, 100.

54    'World Cup in West Germany': *Ibid.*, 100.

55    'Spanish UNESCO official.': *Ibid.*, 106–7, 120, 122, 124, 126.

55    'more or less everybody knows.': Roberto Bolaño, *Between Parentheses* (Picador, 2016), 82.

55    published in 1994: Lemebel, *De perlas y cicatrices* (Lom, 1998).

55    offered by *El Mercurio*: Gloria Esquivel, 'Literatura en tiempos de tortura', *Semana*, 28 February 2010; Michael Lazzara, 'Writing Complicity: The Ideological Adventures of Mariana Callejas', *Radical History Review* 124 (2016), 141; Roberto Brodsky, 'Amores que matan', in Mili Rodriguez Villouta (ed.), *Compasión* (Planeta, 2000).

55 eliminate Pinochet's opponents: 'Berríos: Los casetes secretos del "químico de Pinochet", Chapter 1: Armas químicas', *Vergara 240* (undated).

55 the killing of Letelier: *Ibid.* (NELSON JOFRÉ: 'Look, Carmelo Soria . . . there is one of the people who lived inside, eh, he says that he was sprayed with sarin. A single person says it, but there is a confessed author who killed him with punches, right?, fracture, they made him a key, they put a leg on the ladder, they fractured him, in short. In other words, it was the most stormy thing how they eliminated it, but they say that they also applied it . . . they sprayed sarin on it.')

56 her American husband excelled: Mariana Callejas, *La larga noche* (Editorial Lo Curro, 1981), 69.

56 other private functions: Mónica González, 'Lujos y caprichos de un dictador', *Revista Anfibia*, 23 August 2017.

59 'magical realism' of the area: Bolaño, *Between Parentheses*, 275–6.

59 fine observer of legal detail: Sybille Bedford, 'On the Go', *The New York Review of Books*, 9 November 1978.

59 between travel and violence: Laurence Piercy, 'Bruce Chatwin, W. G. Sebald, and the Red-Brown Skin', in Jenni Adams and Sue Vice, *Representing Perpetrators in Holocaust Literature and Film* (Valentine Mitchell, 2013), 251 at 255.

60 'climb back up the ladder': Letter, Rauff to Wächter, 25 May 1949 (on file).

60 in the garbage: Martin Cüppers, *Walther Rauff, in deutschen Diensten: vom Naziverbrecher zum BND-Spion* (WBG Academic, 2013), 381.

60 'mobile German vans': Bodleian Archives and Manuscripts, *Archive of (Charles) Bruce Chatwin*, MS.Eng.e.3688.

61 decades later: Heidemann Archive, 48.

61 As a cadet: Cüppers, *Walther Rauff*, 40.

61 on a friendship tour: *Ibid.*, 49.

62 he would say: Rauff Testimony, Santiago (BAL, B 162/3637, Bl. 87), 28 June 1972, on file; Cüppers, *Walther Rauff*, 69.

62 his Nazi file recorded: Walther Rauff, *Fragenbogen und Lebenslauf, Personal-Bericht*, NS file, 1938 (on file).

62 the Protestant Church: *Ibid.*

62 naval officers in 1928: Letter, Rauff to Barbara W, 16 March 1979 (on file); Heidemann Archive, 108.

62 'from a technical standpoint.': Heidemann Collection, 139.

63 'their bodies then cremated': Cüppers, *Walther Rauff*, 119.

63 Willy Just, a technician: Eugene Kogon, Hermann Langbein and

Adalbert Rückerl (eds.), *Nazi Mass Murder: A Documentary History of the Use of Poison Gas* (Yale University Press, 1993).

63   in the public interest: Rauff Testimony, Santiago, 28 June 1972, on file.

63   'where the gas was distributed.': Deposition by H. Wentritt, 2 February 1961, StA Hannover, AZ.2 Js 299/60 (ZSL, Az.415 Ar-Z 220/59, Bl. 260b).

63   between Berlin and Warsaw: Cüppers, *Walther Rauff*, 119.

63   ('We connect people'): German Register of Patents and Trademarks, Reg.No.30201822312.https://register.dpma.de/DPMAregister/marke/register/3020182231210/DE

63   before the van's arrival: Kogon et al., *Nazi Mass Murder*, 182.

63   Rauff received regular updates: Note RSHA/IID 3a of 27.4.1942, AOD, R 58/871; Cf. Vern. Anton Sukkel of 8.2.1961, BAL, B 162/5066, Bl. 260 m-s; *Ibid.*, Willy Just of 18.2.1961, op. cit., Bl. 260 t-y; Memo Staw Hannover of 1.3.1965, op. cit., pp. 316–19 (on file).

63   disguised as ambulances: Letter, Becker to Rauff, 16 May 1942, IMG, vol. 26, Doc. PS-501, 103 *et seq.*

64   'less time needed to clean up': *Ibid.*

64   'with no major incidents': Letter, Just to Rauff, 5 June 1942, *Nazism: A History in Documents and Eyewitness Accounts, 1919–1945*. Vol. II, J. Noakes and G. Pridham (eds.) (Schocken, 1988), (vol. 1), (vol. 2). Doc. 913.

64   'use of the gas vans.': Rauff Testimony, Santiago, 28 June 1972 (on file).

65   'interior of the van': Testimony of Walter Burmeister, gas-van driver, in E. Klee, W. Dressen and V. Riess, *The Good Old Days* (Free Press, 1988), 219–20.

65   dark-grey vans: Cüppers, *Walther Rauff*, 133, citing RSHA/IID 3a to Group Leader IID v. 5.6.1942, AOD, R 58/871; *see also* Kogon et al., *Nazi Mass Murder*.

66   ridding the country of Jews: Claude Nataf, *Les juifs de Tunisie sous le joug nazi, 9 November 1942 to 8 May 1943* (Le Manuscrit, 2012), 10.

66   'red with anger' when agitated: *Ibid.*, 253.

66   'extermination of the Jews': *Ibid.*, 43.

66   168 avenue de Paris in Tunis: Robert Borgel, *Étoile jaune et croix gammée: les juifs de Tunisie face aux nazis* (Le Manuscrit, 2007), 93.

66   he'd take 10,000: *Ibid.*, 110.

66   'what you can expect': Nir Cohen, 'Inside the Diary of SS Officer Known as Gas Chamber "Mastermind"', Y *Net News: Jewish World*, 17 April 2015.

66 'Jew dogs, swine': Borgel, *Étoile jaune et croix gammée*, 138.

66 brandished a short stick: *Ibid.*, 108.

66 'take their responsibilities': *Ibid.*, 109.

66 levied on the community: *Ibid.*, 267; Paul Ghez, *Six mois sous la botte* (Le Manuscrit, 2009), 217.

66 'To be able to make lists,' he said: Borgel, *Étoile jaune et croix gammée*, 64.

66 'ordered to carry out.': Nataf, *Les juifs de Tunisie sous le joug nazi*, 48–9.

67 'ever happening to them.': Rauff Testimony, Santiago, 28 June 1972 (on file).

67 a German Cross, in silver: Rahn an HöSSPF Italy of 15.4.1944, BAB, R 70 Italien/20; Letter to the Liaison Officer of the Personal Staff of the Reichsführer-SS, from General Karl Wolff (with attachments) (8 June 1944): https://northafricanjews-ww2.org.il/sites/default/files/ybz_item_files/8%281%29.pdf

67 on 12 September: 'Les archives secrètes de la CIA en Corse', *Corse Matin*, 23 February 2016; Jean-Pierre Girolami, '1943–1946: contre les "profiteurs de guerre" une "épuration molle" des condamnations pour collaboration', *Corse Matin*, 22 October 2023.

67 Wagner, Mozart and Beethoven: teatroallascala.org, 1943/44 season.

67 Italian Jews to Auschwitz: Luigi Borgomaneri, *Hitler a Milano* (Datanews Editrice, 1997), 103.

67 destruction of numerous homes: *Ibid.*, 117; detailed interrogation report, Milan, 4 June 1945, signed H. T. Shergold, Major I.O., O.C. Army Section, CSDIC, CMF, Public Record Office of Kew, Wo, 204/13006.

67 'innocent people will be affected.': Borgomaneri, *Hitler a Milano*, 120, citing Rauff to Parini, letter, 25 July 1944, Prefect of Milan, ASM, Gp., II, c. 365.

67 corpses openly mutilated: Cüppers, *Walther Rauff*, 193.

67 (under international law.): *Questions of Jurisdictional Immunities of the State and Measures of Constraint against State-Owned Property (Germany v. Italy)*, Application instituting proceedings containing a request for provisional measures, [2022] ICJ General List No. 183, paras 29–48; *see also Jurisdictional Immunities of the State (Germany v Italy, Greece Intervening)* [2012] ICJ Reports 179, para. 139.

68 this time in gold: Awarded on 25 February 1945, Cüppers, *Walther Rauff*, 108.

68 he would say: Cüppers, *Walther Rauff*, 199.

68 Rauff met Mussolini: Heidemann Archive, 65, 108.

68　(and served in Litzmannstadt): Protocol of Interrogation of Ms Emilie Hermine Finnegan, née Lukasch, 4 September 1968 (High Court of Berlin, proceedings against Friedrich Boßhammer) (on file).

68　'They thought we were Americans.': CIA Doc. 0022, 22 May 1945.

68　(Rauff would say): Heidemann Archive, 89.

69　the rest of his life: Cüppers, *Walther Rauff*, 207.

69　and then Ancona: *Ibid.*, 211, 213, 265; Letter, Rauff to Hans-Jochen Emsmann, 26 August, 22 September, 17 November 1946.

69　'an approximate figure,' he stated: Office of the United States Chief Counsel for Prosecution of Axis Criminality, 'Statement of Standarten Fuehrer Walther Rauff of 19 October 1945', *Nazi Conspiracy and Aggression*, vol. IV, document No. 2348-PS.

69　and his affidavit: *Trial of the Major War Criminals Before the International Military Tribunal* (Nuremberg, 20 December 1945), 4: 235.

69　crimes against humanity: Gerald Steinacher, *Nazis on the Run* (Oxford University Press, 2011), 206; Philippe Sands, *The Ratline* (Weidenfeld & Nicolson, 2020), 290.

69　he wrote to his nephew: Letter, Rauff to Hans-Jochen Emsmann, 22 September 1946.

69　way to Rome: Cüppers, *Walther Rauff*, 216.

70　the Soviet threat: Niall Ferguson, *Kissinger: 1923–1968, The Idealist* (Penguin, 2015), 198.

70　decent and trustworthy: Cüppers, *Walther Rauff*, 218.

70　'helped a lot': Heidemann Archive, 105.

70　and then Syria: *Ibid.*

70　'along Gestapo Lines': CIA Doc. 0096, 11 May 1949.

70　'Wonderful!': Cüppers, *Walther Rauff*, 233.

70　by personal gain: CIA Doc. 0083, 11 October 1950.

71　was expelled from Syria: CIA Doc. 0096, August 1949; Chern Chen, 'Former Nazi Officers in the Near East: German Military Advisors in Syria, 1949–56' (2018), 732–51.

71　(because of his time in Tunis): Heidemann Collection (Archive Stanford), 64, 109, 112, 114.

71　knowing nothing of Rauff's past: Yosef (Yossi) Chen, *The Mossad's Pursuit of Nazi War Criminals* (Mossad History Department, 2007), 153–96.

71　he'd find work in Quito: Cüppers, *Walther Rauff*, 236. A colleague in Ecuador informed me that Hanz Karste married Beatriz Peña, from Cuenca, and the couple had three children (Elizabeth, Hans and Susana). Ms. Peña's parents were said to be anxious about the identity of Karste's stepfather, Rauff, a matter discussed with the priest before the marriage.

71  dealership in Quito: Cüppers, *Walther Rauff*, 239; CIA Doc. 0077, 13 June 1950; CIA Doc. 0079, 7 July 1950.

72  birthday did not dim: Cüppers, *Walther Rauff*, 243, 244, 251, 258.

72  Carlos Prats provided references: Interview with Walther Rauff III, 3 December 2021 (Santiago).

72  War Academy in Santiago: Alejandro Matus, *Doña Lucia: La biografía no autorizada* (Ediciones B, 2014); Augusto Pinochet, *Camino Recorrido* (1990), 55–155.

72  Pablo Pinochet: Letter, María del Carmen Elizalde P, Responsable del Archivo General, Universidad Central del Ecuador, with records attached, 26 January 2023 (on file).

72  Rauff would later say: Cüppers, *Walther Rauff*, 259; Heidemann Collection, 13.

73  'you should move there.': *Ibid.*

73  to be eliminated: Interview with Walther Rauff III, 3 December 2021 (Santiago).

73  which liked Germans: Henry Löschner 'got me the job down there': Heidemann Archive, 61, 327; Löschner, a German who had lived in Ecuador for many years, was believed to have spied for Germany during the war; *see* Jacob McIntosh, 'The Forgotten Story of Montreat: The Special War Problems Division's Detention of Axis Citizens During World War II', *Proceedings of the National Conference on Undergraduate Research, Montana State University* (26 March 2020), 466.

73  reside permanently in Chile: Decree, 26 November 1959 (on file).

73  intelligence service: Cüppers, *Walther Rauff*, 275.

73  'special outlook on life': *Ibid.*, 281, 283.

73  Chile, Ecuador and Peru: *Ibid.*, 279.

74  search for laboratory equipment: Cüppers, *Walther Rauff*, 284; Miguel Schweitzer and Stitchkin were among those recognised as prominent members of the Jewish community; Gustavo Guzmán, *Attitudes of the Chilean Right Towards Jews* (Brill, 2022), 142.

74  surveillance techniques: Cüppers, *Walther Rauff*, 284.

74  Rauff in Milan: *Der Spiegel*, 1 June 1960; Cüppers, *Walther Rauff*, 287.

74  West German marks: Cüppers, *Walther Rauff*, 289.

74  'Eichmann trial situation', they said: *Ibid.*, 294.

74  he needed more training: Heidemann Archive, 329; Cüppers, *Walther Rauff*, 300–1.

74  decline any further: Cüppers, *Walther Rauff*, 298–304.

75 agent from East Germany: *See* https://agora.sub.uni-hamburg.de//
subhh-adress/cntmng;jsessionid=E4926DB339D14EEC105FBE79
0941AE92.agora13?type=pdf&did=c1:1028107; German Ministry for
State Security (Stasi) Records Archive, MfS-Lexikon: 'Kreusel, Karl',
https://www.stasi-unterlagen-archiv.de/mfs-lexikon/detail/kreusel-
karl; Boletín No. 5.047-07, Informe de la Comisión de Derechos Humanos, Nacionalidad y Ciudadania, recaído en el proyecto de ley,
en primer trámite constitucional, que concede, por especial gracia,
la nacionalidad chilena al señor Dietrich Paul Friedrich Angerstein
Brink, 26 June 1007.

75 a boat that Rauff sailed: Dietrich Angerstein, 'Silvester auf der Sand-
bank', *Cóndor*, 30 December 2020.

76 'sea life in the cans.': Heidemann Archive, 343.

76 knock on the front door: Telex No. 127, 5 December 1962, Ambassador Strack, Santiago, to Foreign Office (on file).

76 'Eichmann's Office Arrested in Our City': *La Prensa Austral*, 6 December 1962.

77 'the killing of any Jews': 'Ex-Nazi Colonel Arrested in Chile Denies
Killing 90,000 Jews', *Bulletin no. 236, Jewish Telegraph Agency*, 10
December 1962.

77 Belgrade, Yugoslavia: Cüppers, *Walther Rauff*, 266.

77 investigate Rauff any further: *Ibid.*, 267–8.

77 'a distant corner': *Ibid.*, 272.

78 aiding and abetting murder: *Ibid.*, 273.

78 as early as April 1961: *Ibid.*, 274, 291.

78 who happened to be Jewish: Guzmán, *Attitudes of the Chilean Right
Towards Jews*, 142.

78 Punishment of Genocide: Cüppers, *Walther Rauff*, 307–8.

79 sentenced to death: *Ibid.*, 316.

79 'any killing of Jews.': *Ibid.*, 314.

79 like Eichmann, or assassinated: *Ibid.*, 320.

79 'I'd have everyone against me.': Heidemann Archive, 116 (advice of
Colonel Schaffhauser).

79 ('prisoners of history'): Robert Servatius, 'Defender of a Nazi', *The
New York Times*, 18 April 1961.

80 German diplomatic staff: Heidemann Archive, 69–70.

80 in Punta Arenas: Schäfer to West German Embassy, letter, Santiago,
12 June 1963, cited in Ingo Kletten, 'Eine lange Nachgeschichte – Der
Fall des SS-Standartenführers Walther Rauff nach 1945 in Chile',
*Nürnberger Menschenrechtszentrum*, 3 June 2008.

80 reported around the world: 'Bonn Regime Bids Chile Extradite
Former Nazi', *The New York Times*, 6 December 1962.

80  surrounded by reporters: 'In Santiago, a Nazi S.S. General is apprehended and held for extradition to West Germany. Walter Rauff has been charged by the West German Government with complicity in the wartime killing of 90,000 Jews', *AP Archive*, https://www.youtube.com/watch?v=niT-S7bEYp0

80  enhancement of the gas vans: '97 mil judíos muertos con gases lo condenan', *La Tercera*, 27 April 1963.

80  'he does not dispute them.': *Ibid.*

81  Esmeralda regiment: Letter, FRG Consulate, Antofagasta, to FRG Ambassador, Santiago, 4 March 1963 (on file); Mario Amorós, *Pinochet: Biografía Militar y Política* (Ediciones B, 2019), 129.

81  the gravest crimes: Cüppers, *Walther Rauff*, 326.

81  a serving BND agent: *Ibid.*, 327.

81  BND documents: Heidemann Archive, 69.

81  his role as a BND agent: Cüppers, *Walther Rauff*, 329.

81  it time-barred the case: Corte Suprema, 26 April 1963, Rauff, Walther (extradición pasiva), in *Revista de Derecho, Jurisprudencia y Ciencias Sociales*, Secunda Parte, Tomo LX, enero–abril 1963, 112 *et seq.* See also Gustavo Guzman, 'Chile y el Holocausto: A cincuenta años de la captura de Walther Rauff', *El Mostrador*, 6 December 2012.

82  barely reported the ruling: Guzmán, *Attitudes of the Chilean Right Towards Jews*, 161.

82  'nothing to be afraid of': Walther Rauff interview, Huntley-Brinkley Report, NBC-TV, *Historia Channel*, interviewed by Tom Streithorst, *Radio TV Monitoring Service*, 25 April 1966 (on file); https://www.youtube.com/watch?v=dsdSMLKvLN0

82  30,000 Jews to death: *Ibid.*, *Radio TV Monitoring Service*, 2 May 1966 (on file).

82  an exceptional occurrence: Author interview with Miguel Schweitzer Walters, 4 September 2020.

87  politically engaged: Guzmán, *Attitudes of the Chilean Right Towards Jews*, 200.

87  Pinochet and Nixon supporter: John Bartlett, 'Files Reveal Nixon Role in Plot to Block Allende from Chilean Presidency', *The Guardian*, 8 August 2023.

90  not involved in its occurrence: Author interviews with David Clark, 19 November 2023; Sherard Cowper-Coles, 9 January 2024; John Dew, 9 January 202; email, Andrew Patrick, 10 January 2024.

93  case and other crimes: Audiencia Nacional de España, Sala de lo Penal, Pleno, Rollo de Apelación 173/98 – Sección Primera – Sumario 1/98, 5 November 1998.

94  Pinochet's extradition: José Yoldi, 'La fiscalía se opone a que se pida

la extradición de Pinochet', *El País*, 24 October 1998.

94 independently and expeditiously: Anne Swardson, 'Pinochet Case Tries Spanish Legal Establishment', *The Washington Post*, 22 October 1998.

95 a few months earlier: Cavallo and Montes, *La historia oculta de la década socialista*, 22.

95 to commit these acts: Brody and Ratner, *The Pinochet Papers*, 67.

96 the sixteenth century: Joanne Foakes, *The Position of Heads of State and Senior Officials in International Law* (Oxford University Press, 2014), 13.

96 crimes to go unpunished: C. Beccaria, *Des délits et des peines* (1764), ch. XXXV, French transl. (Institut Coppet, 54).

96 its leader or diplomats: *The Parliament Belge*, UK Court of Appeal (1880) LR 5 PD 197.

97 'the dignity of his nation': *The Schooner Exchange v McFaddon*, U.S. Supreme Court (1812) 7 *Cranch* 116.

97 'the sanctity of treaties': Treaty of Peace with Germany (Treaty of Versailles) (28 June 1919), 2 Bevans 43, Article 227.

97 as head of state: Agreement for the Prosecution and Punishment of the Major War Criminals of the European Axis, and Establishing the Charter of the International Military Tribunal (8 August 1945), 82 *UNTS* 279-84 (annex), Art. 7.

97 the same rule: International Military Tribunal of the Far East (19 January 1946), *TIAS* 1589, Art. 6.

97 'or private individuals': Convention on the Prevention and Punishment of Genocide, 9 December 1948, Paris ('Persons committing genocide or any of the other acts enumerated in article III shall be punished, whether they are constitutionally responsible rulers, public officials or private individuals').

97 or war crimes: Statute of the International Criminal Tribunal for the former Yugoslavia (as amended 2009) (UN Doc. S/RES/827) UNSC 1993, Article 7; Statute of the International Criminal Tribunal for Rwanda (UN Doc. S/RES/955) UNSC 1994, Article 6.

98 before national courts: Arthur Watts, 'The Legal Position in International Law of Heads of States, Heads of Governments and Foreign Ministers' (1994), 247 *Recueil des Cours de l'Académie de Droit International*, 82–4.

100 'the greatest judge of our time': Maev Kennedy, 'Tributes to Lord Bingham, "The greatest judge of our time"', *The Guardian*, 12 September 2010.

101 gave its judgement: *Re Augusto Pinochet Ugarte* [1998] 38 ILM 68 (QB), 74.

102 'falsity of the accusations.': *Ibid.*, para. 58.

104 on its front page: Joanna Bale, Roland Watson and Michael Evans, 'Pinochet Wins First Battle on Extradition', *The Times*, 29 October 1998; Jamie Wilson and Amelia Gentleman, 'Pinochet Wins his High Court Battle', *The Guardian*, 29 October 1998; Warren Hoge, 'English Court Rules Pinochet Should Be Free', *The New York Times*, 29 October 1998.

104 'dictators and former dictators': *Ibid.*

104 'engaged in the conduct': Michael Binyon and Frances Gibb, 'Experts Say Pinochet Ruling "not the end"', *The Times*, 29 October 1998.

104 'international law aspects': Open Democracy, *Justice in the World's Light* (2001) (Geoffrey Bindman).

106 'will escape justice.': François Sergent, 'Première victoire de Pinochet à Londres', *Libération*, 29 October 1998.

108 their loved ones: Norberto Bermúdez, '"Esto, Señorías, fue un genocidio"', *Página 12*, 30 October 1998.

108 'as never again.': *Ibid.*

109 jurisdiction over Pinochet: Audiencia Nacional, Criminal Division, Plenary Session, 5 November 1998, presiding Judge Siro Francisco García Pérez, translation, 22–28 (on file); and Brody and Ratner, *The Pinochet Papers*, 95.

109 'missions to be carried out': Garzón Doc., 199–200 (on file).

109 wrote Garzón: *Ibid.*, 270, 291–2, 301.

110 'Senator Pinochet has immunity.': House of Lords, excerpts from legal submissions, in Brody and Ratner, *The Pinochet Papers*, 109.

110 English or international law: *Ibid.*, 115.

110 'public international law': *Ibid.*, 126.

110 the Chanfreau story: *Pauline Jaccard-Veloso and Others v United Kingdom* (Request for the indication of interim measures pursuant to rule 36, 4 November 1998), Application No. 44191/98 (ECtHR) (on file).

113 'oozing confidence': *The Financial Times*, 22 September 1998, 1.

113 published after retirement: David Hope, *House of Lords 1996–2009: Lord Hope's Diaries* (Avizandum, 2018), 64.

113 reason for the exasperation: *Ibid.*, 67–9.

114 'proceedings against him': Ekaizer, *Yo, Augusto*, 628.

115 supported the argument: Case for the Respondent, para. 52, in Brody and Ratner, *The Pinochet Papers*, 120.

115 among the judges: Hope, *House of Lords 1996–2009*, 67.

116 one of the guests: Bolaño, *Between Parentheses*, 73.

118 the Palace walls: Hope, *House of Lords 1996–2009*, 68.

122 protesters in tow: Warren Hoge, 'Pinochet Is Shown the Door by a

Vexed London Hospital', *The New York Times*, 2 December 1998.

122 Margaret Thatcher: Christina Lamb, 'Tea with Pinochet', *New Statesman*, 26 July 1999.

126 German Club was terminated: Kletten, 'Eine lange Nachgeschichte'; author interview with Eduardo Lehmann, 29 July 2023.

126 will lose interest: Cüppers, *Walther Rauff*, 333.

126 ('the business came to an end'): Heidemann Archive, 337.

129 'more tender and faithful.': Jorge Barbarovic, 'Refugiado in Porvenir', *Ercilla*, 18 November 1964.

130 'the use of vans.': Pablo Neruda, 'A Heroic Deed in the Name of Freedom', *El Siglo*, 3 July 1965.

130 the judge reported: Cüppers, *Walther Rauff*, 346.

130 3,832 human beings: Judgement of 6 June 1966; Cüppers, *Walther Rauff*, 346.

131 My memory has gone, he said: Cüppers, *Walther Rauff*, 347.

131 'They can't even listen to the radio!': *Ibid.*, 340.

131 delighted to work with him: Heidemann Archive, 339.

131 'as a single older man?': *Ibid.*, 341.

131 'I've totally secluded myself.': *Ibid.*, 344.

131 'and we lived together.': *Ibid.*, 341.

131 'she devours communists': *Ibid.*, 342.

131 'able to get me,' he'd say: *Jewish Observer and Middle East Review*, 15 April 1966, cited by Kletten, 'Eine lange Nachgeschichte'.

131 expected time of return: Cüppers, *Walther Rauff*, 347.

132 Olympia typewriter: Mario Guisande Pelic, 'El magallánico que fue secretario del Nazi Walter Rauff', *La Prensa Austral*, 4 October 2019.

132 hit-squad rumours: Cüppers, *Walther Rauff*, 342–3.

132 one fisherman recalled: Leonidas Bustamente, *Relatos de vida en los mares australes* (Ediciones Kultrún, 2017), 28–9.

132 ('Chile's Exporter of the Year'): https://issuu.com/cameliochile/docs/portafolio_camelio_optimizado

133 (minister in Pinochet's government.): Stephen Kinzer, 'Two New Political Antagonists Emerging in Chile', *The New York Times*, 15 September 1983.

134 disappeared for a few days: *Ercilla*, 18 November 1964.

135 'emigrating to Argentina.': Letter, Rauff to Ilse Emsmann, 7 October 1970.

135 'to the officers.': Letter, Rauff to Hans-Jochen Emsmann, 10 September 1971.

135 who would embrace him publicly: Cüppers, *Walther Rauff*; Letter, Rauff to Ilse Emsmann, 25 October 1964.

135 for international crimes: Convention on the Non-Applicability of Statutory Limitations to War Crimes and Crimes Against Humanity, 26 November 1968, in force 11 November 1970.

135 to end Rauff's impunity: Letter, Wiesenthal to Allende, 21 August 1972 (on file); Simon Wiesenthal, *Justice Not Vengeance* (Weidenfeld & Nicolson, 1988), 63.

135 'socialists, communists and whatever else.': Heidemann Archive, 114.

135 getting Rauff back: Letter, Allende to Wiesenthal, 21 September 1972 (on file); Letter, Wiesenthal to Dr Adalbert Rückerl, 24 October 1972 (on file); Cüppers, *Walther Rauff*, 349, note 79.

136 a leading Chilean actor: Rene Sepúlveda, *PEC*, 14 July 1972, no. 462, pp. 14–15.

136 'but they won't let me.': Letter, Rauff to Hans-Jochen Emsmann, 16 August 1972.

136 the details of a coup: Carlos Lopez, *Allende and the Military* (Council for Inter-American Security Educational Institute, 1978), 15; Letter, Rauff to Ilse Emsmann, 1964.

136 had infected the country: Decree Law No. 1, 11 September 1973, Constitutive Act of the Military Junta, *Diario Oficial*, Chile.

137 'protect national security': Decree Law No. 521, 18 June 1974, Creates Dirección Nacional de Inteligencia (DINA), *Diario Oficial*.

137 682 men and women: León Gómez, *Tras la huella de los desaparecidos* (Caleuche, 1990), 456–96.

138 31,856 were tortured: *Una Política Pública Permanente: Garantía de No Repetición*, powerpoint prepared by Luis Cordero, Minister of Justice and Human Rights, September 2023.

138 in full public view: Inger Agger and Søren Buss Jensen, *Trauma and Healing Under State Terrorism* (Zed, 1996), 170.

138 'all the Marxists rounded up': Bruce Chatwin, *In Patagonia* (Vintage, 2009), 187.

138 the Third Naval Zone: Edicto, Fiscalia Naval de Magallanes, 14 February 1974 (Luis Vera and Carlos Oyarzo), signed by Salvador Camelio Lopez (Secretario) and Jorge Beyta Valenzuela (Fiscal Naval Magallanes) (on file); Edward Snyder, 'The Dirty Legal War: Human Rights and the Rule of Law in Chile 1973–1995', *Tulsa Journal of Comparative and International Law* 2 (1994), 254 at 265–8.

138 would disappear: Rettig Report (1991), vol. 1, 591.

138 the Pudeto Regiment: *Ibid.*, p. 592.

138 'what was happening.': Agger and Jensen, *Trauma and Healing Under State Terrorism*, 171.

138 Straits of Magellan: Agrupación Hijas/os y Nietas/os por la Memoria, *Cartografía, Sitios de Memoria: Región de Magallanes y de la*

*Antártica Chilena* (Imprenta La Prensa Austral, 2020), 34.

138　in Punta Arenas: Rettig Report (1991), vol. 1, 593.

139　aged twenty-three: https://memoria.bienes.cl/sitios/memorial-de-los-derechos-humanos-de-punta-arenas

139　'Small town, big hell.': The three victims were: Carlos Raúl Baigorri Hernandez, aged 31; Germán Simón Carcamo Carrasco, aged 24; and Ramón Domingo Gonzalez Ortega, aged 37, Rettig Report (1991), vol. 1, 594.

139　he wrote to his nephew: Cüppers, *Walther Rauff*, 354; Letter, Rauff to Hans-Jochen Emsmann, 30 June 1980.

139　'a very good job.': *Ibid.*, 355.

140　home in Quito: *Ibid.*, 354.

140　'that is worth a lot': *Ibid.*

140　Rauff reported to Ilse: Letter, Rauff to Ilse Emsmann, 4 March 1974.

140　he told Ilse: Letter, Rauff to Ilse Emsmann and Wulff, 11 January 1976.

140　(Rauff in the 1972 stage play): Inter-American Commission of Human Rights, Annual Report 1985–6, Chapter 4, 'Chile', Section 3.

140　Pinochet's office: 'Hoy se realiza cambio de mando en la intendencia', *La Prensa Austral*, 4 March 1974.

141　'achievements in this industry.': Letter, Rauff to Hans-Jochen Emsmann, 6 August 1977.

141　said the reporter: Letter, Rauff to Ilse and Hans-Jochen Emsmann, 11 January 1976.

141　but be discreet: Letter, Rauff to Ilse Emsmann, 4 March 1974.

141　in a Communist regime: Letter, Rauff to Hans-Jochen Emsmann, 21 May 1977.

141　(used by senior Nazis): 'They tell me that there were thousands and thousands of those flat-footed primitives in this city once upon a time', Hans Frank, the Governor General of Nazi-occupied Poland, declared on 1 August 1942, in Lviv, announcing the elimination of Jews: Philippe Sands, *East West Street* (Weidenfeld & Nicolson, 2016), 239.

141　of Santiago: Letter, Rauff to Ilse Emsmann and Wolff, 12 June 1976.

141　from Punta Arenas: Letter, Rauff to Ilse and Hans-Jochen Emsmann, 11 January 1976.

141　('live by ourselves'): Interview, Monserrat Madariaga and Raúl Donoso, 31 January 2022.

141　the family's Aryan roots: Letter, Rauff to Hans-Jochen Emsmann, 6 August 1977.

141　weren't much better: Heidemann Archive, 340.

141　'eighteen-hour days': Letter, Rauff to Ilse and Hans-Jochen Emsmann,

11 January 1976; 12 June 1976.

142 as unpersuasive: Rol. 37.829-4, Primer Juzgado del Crimen (case of Manuel Ruben Fernandez Torres and Mario Barria Diaz), opened on 9 December 1975; also Juzgado del Trabajo, Adolfo Martinez Uribe v. Pesquera Camelio Ltda, represented by Walter Rauff, opened on 5 April 1977).

142 contacts with the Navy: Author interview with Mariana Camelio, 4 July 2023.

142 'not to be released to *Die Welt*.': Letter, Rauff to Hans-Jochen Emsmann, 21 May 1977; 6 August 1977.

142 'state-certified war criminal': Letter, Rauff to Hans-Jochen Emsmann, 20 December 1974.

144 *Le Monde*: 'L'ancien "SS" Walter Rauff est placé à la tête des Services de Renseignements', *Le Monde*, 3 July 1974; CIA Doc. 0106 and 0107 7, 10 July 1974.

144 the government as 'fascist': 'Le gouvernement dément que l'ancien "SS" Rauff dirige des Services de Renseignements', *Le Monde*, 4 July 1974.

145 'plucked out of thin air': CIA Doc. 0103, July 1974.

145 Chilean government's denial: CIA Doc. 0105, July 1974.

145 performed in Santiago: Cüppers, *Walther Rauff*, 357, citing DB Santiago an AAv. 14.10.1974, PAAA, AV 12777.

145 'offer to work for DINA.': *Ibid.*, note 121.

145 was cited in support: Marcus Klein, 'Walther Rauff und die chilenische Militärdiktatur unter Augusto Pinochet', *Vierteljahrshefte für Zeitgeschichte* 67 (2019), 235, 246.

145 near San Antonio: *Ibid.*, 248.

145 Pinochet's government: *Ibid.*

145 treated as credible: Cüppers, *Walther Rauff*, 357, citing letter, Wiesenthal to John R.C., 11 November 1974; to John F., 10 and 26 March 1975.

145 a DINA 'advisor': Kletten, 'Eine lange Nachgeschichte', citing Simon Wiesenthal, *Gerechtigkeit, nicht Rache* (Frankfurt am Main 1995).

146 to be unsubstantiated: Rose Styron, 'Special Report on Chile, Amnesty International, Report on Torture' (New York, 1975), 243–82, cited in Klein, 'Walther Rauff und die chilenische Militärdiktatur unter Augusto Pinochet', 256.

146 the paper reported: Jonathan Kandell, 'Nazis Safer in South America Today', *The New York Times*, 18 May 1975.

146 support the bold assertion: Eric M. Breindel, 'A New Life', *The Harvard Crimson*, 26 October 1974.

146 emulated the Gestapo: Klein 'Walther Rauff und die chilenische

Militärdiktatur unter Augusto Pinochet', 254.

146 'involvement in the DINA': *Ibid.*, 255.

146 'Chilean military government': CIA Doc. 0109, 13 April 1976.

146 which he declined to do: Klein 'Walther Rauff und die chilenische Militärdiktatur unter Augusto Pinochet', 257, citing the Vienna Wiesenthal Centre, Archive, Akt Rauff 1, Wiesenthal an Kissinger, Wien, 1.4.1975, und Isaacs an Wiesenthal, Washington, D.C., 17 April 1975.

146 advising the DINA: CIA Doc., 0110, 8 July 1977.

146 'as an advisor': *Ibid.*

147 through the fax machine: Hope, *House of Lords 1996–2009*, 68.

147 'a truly great satisfaction': *BBC Worldwide Monitoring*, 25 November 1998, source RNE, Radio 1, Madrid, 1449 GMT.

147 Augusto junior: *Daily Mail*, 26 November 1998, 9.

147 a muted reaction: *The Chattanooga Times* (Tennessee), 26 November 1998, 354.

147 reported *The Financial Times*: 'LordsRuling a Landmark in Human Rights Law', *The Financial Times*, 26 November 1998, 6.

147 'seen as a milestone': *The Guardian*, 26 November 1998, 24.

147 'waffling barristers': *The Guardian*, 26 November 1998, 4.

148 participated in the case: Ekaizer, *Yo, Augusto*, 655.

155 he heard about Caplan's call: Hope, *House of Lords 1996–2009*, 69.

156 let him leave the country: Diana Woodhouse, *The Pinochet Case: A Legal and Constitutional Analysis* (Bloomsbury, 2000), 95–6.

156 thought David Hope: Hope, *House of Lords 1996–2009*, 69.

156 judgement under challenge: *Ibid.*, 71.

156 Hope wrote in his diary: *Ibid.*

156 'rather shocking': *Ibid.*, 72.

157 the main opinion: *R v. Bow Street Metropolitan Stipendiary Magistrate, Ex Parte Pinochet Ugarte* (No. 2) [1999] UKHL 52.

158 'pushing at an open door': Hope, *House of Lords 1996–2009*, 72.

158 the directorship was not: *Ibid.*, 70.

158 'ensure that this does not happen again': Woodhouse, *The Pinochet Case*, 95–6.

158 'remote and improbable argument': Open Democracy, *Justice in the World's Light* (2001) (Geoffrey Bindman).

159 but no crescendo: Clare Dyer, 'Law Lords Condemn Hoffmann', *The Guardian*, 16 January 1999.

159 he must decide what to do: Hope, *House of Lords 1996–2009*, 74.

159 supported the decision: Burrell, 'Hoffmann Given Boost by Lord Irvine', *The Independent*, 9 February 1999.

159 words I paraphrased: Hope, *House of Lords 1996–2009*, 69.

161 after we'd spoken: *British Library, Sounds Archive*, 'Lord Hoffmann

interviewed by Louise Brodie', Part 7 (2011).

165 to write *In Patagonia*: Chatwin, *In Patagonia*, 178.

167 than the Austrian technique: 'El viaje histórico de esquiadores a grandes centros de Francia', *La Prensa Austral*, 24 January 1971.

168 is long gone: 'Treinta años sin el cine Gran Palace', *La Prensa Austral*, 4 October 2022.

168 he would say: Heidemann Archive, 342.

169 'Menéndez Braun, Asesinos': 'En Punta Arenas derribaron un busto de Menéndez y en su lugar colocaron el de un cazador selk'nam', *CriticaSur*, 7 November 2019.

169 done the feet: 'Elemento destacado del mes de septiembre: "Escena de Gansos" de José Ruiz Blasco', *Museo Regional de Magallanes*, 1 September 2014.

169 a measure of justice: http://www.dawson2000.com/sreyes.htm (accessed 21 March 2000, link no longer available).

170 'Cousin Charley': Bruce Chatwin, 'The Making of a Writer: I Always Wanted to Go to Patagonia', *The New York Times*, 27 February 1983.

170 'our prayers were offered.': Chatwin, *In Patagonia*, 187.

170 the paper reported: *La Prensa Austral*, 15 May 1984.

171 in southern France: Bruce Chatwin to Elizabeth Chatwin, letter, 10 February and 1 March 1975, in Elizabeth Chatwin and Nicholas Shakespeare (eds.), *Under the Sun: The Letters of Bruce Chatwin* (Vintage, 2011), 242, 246.

171 12 Rue Droite, Bonnieux: *Ibid.*, Chatwin to Derek Hill, 12 January 1976; Chatwin to Charles Chatwin, letter, 2 December 1975; Chatwin to John Kasmin, letter, 12 January 1976, 252, 254.

178 Nazi sympathies: Christopher Jerez Pinto, '¿Quiénes son los Von Appen?: La familia de origen nazi y dueña de Ultramar que tiene en jaque a los trabajadores portuarios', *El Desconcierto*, 18 December 2018.

181 'for the industry I created.': Cüppers, *Walther Rauff*, 340, 360; Letter, Rauff to Hans-Jochen Emsmann, 6 August 1977.

181 surgery on his stomach: Cüppers, *Walther Rauff*, 360.

181 believed to be Jewish: Heidemann Archive, 343–4.

181 and the grandchildren: Cüppers, *Walther Rauff*, 370.

181 'with everything made up': *Ibid.*; Heidemann Archive, 147.

181 'From Adolf Hitler to Sara Braun': Heidemann Archive, 146.

182 It was: Cüppers, *Walther Rauff*, 364, 365; Email, Gustavo Guzmán, 30 May 2024.

182 'a Negro': Cüppers, *Walther Rauff*, 367, 368.

182 arrest was too great: *Ibid.*, 364.

182 'and would change nothing.': *Ibid.*, 379, 380.

182 'placement with the DINA': Marie José Chombert de Lauwe, 'Le néo-nazisme aujourd'hui', *Le Monde*, 10 November 1978.

182 unproven 'calumny': Julio Retamal Favereau, 'Walter Rauff et le régime du général Pinochet', *Le Monde*, 24 November 1978.

183 grounds of ill health: Cüppers, *Walther Rauff*, 374.

183 Frau Himmler and her daughter: Heidemann Archive, 59.

183 once Wolff was done: *Ibid.*, 117, 145, 146, 154.

183 from around the world: *Ibid.*, 56, 70, 155, 156.

184 'In Chile it comes in cannisters.': *Ibid.*, 80.

184 Rauff retorted: *Ibid.*, 56, 59, 68, 90, 99, 106, 114, 139, 156, 159, 232.

184 he didn't even look inside: *Ibid.*, 180–4.

184 Chilean Generals and Pinochet: *Ibid.*, 70, 118, 119, 120, 142, 157, 184.

185 'friends with intelligence people.': *Ibid.*, 68, 157.

185 the Israeli intelligence agency: Chen, *The Mossad's Pursuit of Nazi War Criminals*, 153; see Danny Orbach, *Fugitives: A History of Nazi Mercenaries during the Cold War* (Hurst, 2022).

186 in gas-van operations: Chen, *The Mossad's Pursuit of Nazi War Criminals*, 155.

186 'Rauff camouflaged as an ambulance': *Ibid.*, 158

186 extra protection: *Ibid.*, 166.

186 'that is a fact.': *Ibid.*, 165.

186 to kill him: Yossi Melman and Dan Raviv, 'Why the Mossad Failed to Capture or Kill So Many Fugitive Nazis', *The Washington Post*, 22 September 2017.

187 research a story: Chen, *The Mossad's Pursuit of Nazi War Criminals*, 170.

192 sent to West Germany: Cüppers, *Walther Rauff*, 380.

192 calling for the extradition: *Ibid.*, 384.

192 expelled from Chile: *Ibid.*, 383–4.

192 she told Parliament: *Hansard*, House of Lords, 23 February 1984, column 583 (Margaret Thatcher, 'Nazi War Criminals').

192 soon followed suit: Cüppers, *Walther Rauff*, 387.

192 Walther Rauff junior: Author interview with Sebastian Rauff, 13 February 2023.

192 Foreign Minister declared: Cüppers, *Walther Rauff*, 388.

193 he said tetchily: Patricia Sethi, 'Pinochet on Chile', XV, *Latin American Studies Association* XV, no. 2 (1984), 11–15.

194 connection to Pinochet: Robert McFadden, 'Walter Rauff, 77, Ex-Nazi, Dead; Was an Accused War Criminal', *The New York Times*, 15 May 1984.

194 in Punta Arenas: 'Murio Rauff', *La Prensa Austral*, 15 May 1984, 1.

194 said a man in Porvenir: 'Vida tranquila y trabajo, Walter Rauff a

Porvenir', *La Prensa Austral*, 16 May 1984.

195 'has or has not done': Cüppers, *Walther Rauff*, 390.

198 'unspecified, unofficial capacity': CIA Doc. 0001, March 1984.

198 never personally killed: 'Den Schreibtischtätern auf der Spur. Noch zwei jahre bis zur Verjährung von NS-Gewaltverbrechen', 17 March 1967, *Frankfurter Allgemeine Zeitung* (said to be the first use of the word).

198 'lung and abdominal pain.': Cüppers, *Walther Rauff*, 356, citing *Kölner Stadt-Anzeiger*, 16/17 June 1984.

198 'Walther Rauff's Last Concentration Camp': *Análisis*, 11 September 1984.

198 torturers at Londres 38: Kletten, 'Eine lange Nachgeschichte', citing Schraga Elam and Dennis Whitehead, 'In the Service of the Jewish State', *Haaretz*, 29 March 2007, and Klaus Schnellenkamp, *Geboren im Schatten der Angst* (Munich, 2007), 67.

199 'official advisor': Cüppers, *Walther Rauff*, 356, 358.

199 Colonia Dignidad: Carlos Basso, *Chile Top Secret: El submundo clandestino de la CIA, la LGB, la DINA y los nazis* (Aguilar, 2017), 91 *et seq.*

199 cause them problems?: Marcus Klein, 'Walther Rauff und die chilenische Militärdiktatur unter Augusto Pinochet', 240, 249, 259, 261.

200 'onto the Bench.': Hope, *House of Lords 1996–2009*, 70.

200 'in paragraphs': *Ibid.*, 75.

201 *The Times* reported: *The Times*, 18 January 1999.

203 former head of state: Sugarman, 'The Hidden Histories of the Pinochet Case', confirming the important contribution of Susan Benesch.

203 with the Convention: Brody and Ratner, *The Pinochet Papers*, 220–2.

203 turn to me and smile: Clare Dyer, 'Pinochet's Future May Hang on a Date', *The Guardian*, 20 January 1999.

204 only a domestic court: Brody and Ratner, *The Pinochet Papers*, 231 *et seq.*

206 'his own inclinations': Hope, *House of Lords 1996–2009*, 78–9.

206 after he left office?: *The Times*, 22 January 1999.

206 Hope thought: Hope, *House of Lords 1996–2009*, 76.

207 remain in post: Clare Dyer, 'Pinochet Judge is Forgiven', *The Guardian*, 9 February 1999.

207 national reconciliation: Clare Dyer, 'Shock at Pope's Pinochet Plea', *The Guardian*, 20 February 1999.

207 return of the General: 'Impactó el deceso de Roberto Dávila', *El Sur*, 28 January 2000.

207 in 1973 and 1974: *The Times*, 22 March 1999.

207 inconclusively: Hope, *House of Lords 1996–2009*, 80.

207 Browne-Wilkinson stood: Ekaizer, *Yo Augusto*, 724.

209 to spread the news: Hope, *House of Lords 1996–2009*, 76.

209 decide what to do: *Ibid.*

209 the written judgements: *R v. Bow Street Metropolitan Stipendiary Magistrate, Ex Parte Pinochet Ugarte* (No. 3) [2000] 1 AC 147.

209 an end to immunity: *Ibid.*, 278, citing Sheldon Glueck, 'The Nuremberg Trial and Aggressive War', *Harvard Law Journal 59*, (1946), 396, 398.

210 Marcos Quesada Yáñez: Geoffrey Robertson, 'Bad News for Torturers', *The Independent*, 25 March 1999.

210 in his diary: Hope, *House of Lords 1996–2009*, 76–7.

211 he wrote: *Ibid.*, 77.

211 would be ridiculous: *Ibid.*, 78.

211 'to defeat justice.': 'Blair on Bombing Serbia', *The Guardian*, 26 March 1999.

211 the front pages: Frances Clines, 'NATO Opens Broad Barrage Against Serbs', *The New York Times*, 25 March 1999.

211 in *The New York Times*: *The New York Times*, 2 July 1999, A16.

212 'universal application.': Open Democracy, *Justice in the World's Light* (2001).

213 to express solidarity: Amelia Gentleman, 'Thatcher Takes Elevenses with Old Ally', *The Guardian*, 26 March 1999.

213 over two decades: Garzón submitted new materials on 26 March and 5 April 1999 (on file).

214 was established: *Velásquez Rodríguez v Honduras (Merits)* (IACtHR, 29 July 1988), Series C No. 4, paras 150, 155–8.

214 international agreements: UN General Assembly Resolution 47/133: 'Declaration on the Protection of all Persons from Enforced Disappearance', 18 December 1992.

214 European Court of Human Rights: *Janoweic and Others v Russia (Merits and Just Satisfaction) (Grand Chamber)*, Applications No. 55508/07 and 29520/09 (ECtHR, 21 October 2013), paras 177–8; *Varnava and Others v Turkey (Merits and Just Satisfaction) (Grand Chamber)*, Applications No. 16064/90, 16065/90, 16066/90, 16068/90, 16069/90, 16070/90, 16071/90, 16072/90 and 16073/90 (ECtHR, 18 September 2009), para. 200.

215 path of democracy: Anabel Díez, 'Aznar cree que un juicio a Pinochet impedirá que otros dictadores se vayan', *El País*, 21 October 1998.

221 women with flags: Galo Ghigliotto, *Museo de la Bruma* (Laurel, 2019), Items 1, 2, 3, 4, 5, 11, 31, 32, 35, 37, 41,43, 51, 131, 176, 205, 218, 219, 248, 257, 258, 308.

221 Popper was a genocidaire: *Ibid.*, 13.

225 the small plane: Chatwin, *In Patagonia*, 228.

226 Bitar recalled: Sergio Bitar, *Prisoner of Pinochet: My Year in a Chilean Concentration Camp* (University of Wisconsin Press, 2017, trans. Erin Goodman), 17.

226 the Coup: Rettig Report (1991), vol. 1, 156, 181, 592.

226 modern Spanish usage: Bitar, *Prisoner of Pinochet*, 46–7.

226 Strait's icy waters: *Ibid.*, 59–61.

227 or I-10: *Ibid.*, 75–6.

227 'on the project.': *Ibid.*, 77.

227 'don't you?': *Dawson Isla 10* (dir. Miguel Littin, 2009), at 41.17". David Marcial Pérez, 'García Márquez, objetivo de la policía política del PRI', *El País*, 23 January 2022.

227 in Punta Arenas: Wilfried Huismann and Raul Sohr (dir.), 'A Sangre fría – Pinochet y el "Plan Z"' (2003), 13', https://www.youtube.com/watch?v=f090422kGCk

227 the camp's 'designer': 'Isla Dawson', *Memoria Viva* (undated), https://memoriaviva.com/nuevaweb/centros-de-detencion/xii-region/isla-dawson

227 in a remote archipelago: Gloria Dunkler, *Spandau* (Ediciones Tácitas, 2012); Juan Manuel Vial, 'Un nazi en el sur', *La Tercera*, 5 January 2013.

228 protected by the military: Luis Vega Contreras, *La caída de Allende: anatomía de un golpe de estado* (La Semana Publicaciones, 1983).

228 plans for Dawson: Luis Vega, *Estado Militar y Transición Democrática en Chile* (El Dorado, 1991), 130; Mario Boero Vargas, 'Chile: memoria y antecedentes', *Claves de Razón Práctica* 283 (2022), 82.

228 (DINA's excesses): 'General Lutz was Killed', *La Nación*, 2 December 2007.

228 'Walther Rauff.': https://archivo.laprensaaustral.cl/cronica/los-caminos-de-la-vida-que-llevaron-a-un-ex-preso-politico-a-convertirse-en-miembro-clave-de-amnistia-internacional-en-dinamarca (accessed, 19 November 2021, link no longer working).

229 Salvador Allende: Eva Vergara, 'Mass Grave Is Grim Chapter in Chilean Village', *Los Angeles Times*, 29 July 1990.

231 'played this role.': 'Levantamiento Técnico y Arquitectónico del Campamento de Prisioneros de Río Chico – Río Chico, Isla Dawson, Punta Arenas, Región de Magallanes' (Agrupación Cultural y de Derechos Humanos Orlando Letelier del Solar y Subsecretaría de Derechos Humanos de Chile, December 2019), 80 (Libio Pérez: 'The myth says that he supervised this and that he was seen there and I don't think that happened at all, I just think that these are the specifications of any prison camp').

232 while exiled in Denmark: Miguel Lawner, *Two Years in Chilean Concentration Camps* (Husets, 1976); Hugo Behm Rosas, *Estelas de la Memoria: Compañerismo entre presos políticos de Chile* (2023).

232 '"a Nazi concentration camp."': Report of the Economic and Social Council, 'Protection of Human Rights in Chile', A/10285, 7 October 1975, 63, para. 188 ('Although most of the places of detention are located in Santiago, the Group received evidence showing that ill-treatment took place in other parts of Chile. [. . .] The following locations were mentioned as detention centres: [. . .] (6) Dawson Island (in the province of Magallanes').

233 European colonisers: Marianne Christensen and Flavia Morello, 'Una encrucijada de caminos: el poblamiento de la Isla Dawson', *Magallania* 39, no. 2 (2011), 137–52.

234 recently reported: Informe de la Comisión Verdad Histórica y Nuevo Trato con los Pueblos Indígenas (2008), 42.

234 lawyers in London: 'Federico Marcos del Rosario Errázuriz Zañartu', *Genealog.cl* (undated), https://www.genealog.cl/Chile/E/Errazuriz/#ErrazurizEchaurren,Federico

234 'absolute necessity.': E. Lucas Bridges, *Uttermost Part of the Earth* (Hodder & Stoughton, 1948), 265–7.

235 'the better': *Ibid.*, 268–9; Nicolás Gómez Baeza, 'Scottish Settlers in Patagonia and Tierra del Fuego: Sheep Farming Capitalisms in a South American Frontier', *Scottish Centre for Global History*, 15 September 2020.

235 and a tie pin: 'The British Presence in Patagonia', *Patbrig.org* (undated), https://patbrit.org/bil/supp/c0278-memorabilia.htm.

235 a Selk'nam: Philippe Sands, 'The Glass Arrowhead', in Caroline Charco (ed.), *Explorers, Dreamers and Thieves* (2024, Charco).

235 indigenous community: 'Pueblo selk'nam es reconocido entre las principales etnias indígenas', *La Prensa Austral*, 11 August 2023.

235 the United Kingdom have not: 'Representante Selk'nam en la Convención Constituyente: "Este Estado no nos reconoce"', *Radio Universidad de Chile*, 13 August 2021, https://www.youtube.com/watch?v=NpR5YB09avM.

238 many thought: Hope, *House of Lords 1996–2009*, 82.

238 protecting Pinochet: Andrew Hewett, Witness Statement, 16 April 1999.

239 'a fully informed manner': 'Pinochet Lawyers' Court Challenge Dismissed', *The Guardian*, 27 May 1999.

240 ('like being on a wheel'): Christina Lamb, 'Tea with Pinochet', *New Statesman*, 26 July 1999.

240 torture cases to London: Judge Garzón, Orders, 27, 30 April 1999; 26 May 1999; 2 June 1999 (on file).

241 *The New York Times* reported: Warren Hoge, 'Trial Opens for Pinochet with Listing of 35 Crimes', *The New York Times*, 28 September 1999.

242 and incontinence: Ewan MacAskill, 'Pinochet Kidnapped, Says Thatcher', *The Guardian*, 7 October 1999.

243 'a peaceful retirement.': OHCHR, 'High Commissioner for Human Rights Welcomes Latest Decision in Pinochet Case', 8 October 1999.

243 'I am accused.': Jamie Wilson, Clare Dyer and Jonathan Franklin, 'Cheers and Tears as Court Rules Pinochet Can Be Extradited for Torture Trial', *The Guardian*, 9 October 1999.

245 William Branham: Carlos Basso, *La secta perfecta* (Aguilar, 2022), 53.

245 chose for the Colony: Bruce Falconer, 'The Torture Colony', *The American Scholar*, 1 September 2008.

246 killed or disappeared: 'Report of the Ad-Hoc-Working Group to Inquire into the Present Situation of Human Rights in Chile' (4 February 1976), ECOSOC Commission on Human Rights, E/CN.4/1188, para. 129; UN Secretary-General, 'Report of the Ad Hoc Working Group, submitted in accordance with General Assembly resolution 3448(XXX)' (8 October 1976), A/31/253, para. 321.

246 Luis Peebles: Amnesty International, *Colonia Dignidad: Deutsches Mustergut in Chile – ein Folterlager der DINA* (Amnesty International Publications, March 1977).

246 recognised as Schäfer: Bruce Falconer, 'The Torture Colony', *The American Scholar*, 1 September 2008.

246 reliable on torture: Jorge Escalante, 'Las confesiones de Gerhard Mücke, uno de los jerarcas nazis de Colonia Dignidad', *La Nación*, 12 August 2005; I, León Gómez and Miguel Ángel Rebolledo, 13 November 2021.

246 presence at the Colony: Kletten, 'Eine lange Nachgeschichte' ('Rauff was a visitor to the German sect settlement Colonia Dignidad used by the DINA [Schnellenkamp 2007, p. 67]. When he was due to visit, sect leader Paul Schäfer would say: "I'm going to pull my hair out today". The settlement's hospital once referred him to a clinic in Santiago' [Heller 1993, p. 185]).

247 drugs and electricity: Falconer, 'The Torture Colony'.

249 Gestapo methods: Colonia Dignidad, Interrogation Techniques Document (21973), 11 (on file).

249 'never a real agent': *Ibid.*, 10.

250 in October 1973: 'Für Chile Immer Engagiert', *Lateinamerika Nachrichten*, no. 450, December 2011.

250 the Netflix series: *Colonia Dignidad: Eine deutsche Sekte in Chile* (2021).

251 ('help if needed'): *MoritzEis*, https://pedidos.moritz.cl

252 a lifetime of horror: Voice of America, 'Survivors of Nazi Commune in Chile: Germany's Compensation Not Enough', *Voice of America*, 18 May 2019.

254 'heard of him again': 'Carabineros negó ayuda a otro prófugo de Dignidad', *Fortin Mapocho*, 28 April 1988.

255 immunity was not absolute: Chilean Supreme Court, 19 July 1988, *Szurgelies and Szurgelies v Spohn*, reprinted in *International Law Reports* 89 (1988), 44, 45.

255 'conflict with immunities': Francisco Orrego Vicuña, 'Diplomatic and Consular Immunities and Human Rights', *International and Comparative Law Quarterly* 40, no. 1 (1991), 34, 47–8.

255 Pinochet's immunity: 'Celebrating the Life and Legacy of Francisco Orrego Vicuña', *LSE Law School*, 2 October 2019, 28 minutes in, https://www.youtube.com/watch?v=egrjgBw7m3w

256 (prosecutor of Nazis): Cüppers, *Walther Rauff*, 356, note 115; Kletten, 'Eine lange Nachgeschichte'.

256 'Walther Rauff': León Gómez Araneda, 'Libro Proyecto de Investigación: "En la huella de los detenidos-desaparecidos"', Archivo Museo de la Memoria (1988), 2.

256 said the researcher: Emails, Dominique Hervé to author, 2 April 2019; Lieta Vivaldi to author, 14 May 2019, 27 June 2019, 6 October 2019; León Gómez to Lieta Vivaldi, 17 July 2019.

257 Rauff's 'office': Cüppers, *Walther Rauff*, 356.

257 Dieter Maier: Email, Dieter Maier to author, 21 and 24 March 2021.

257 a book by Heller: Kletten, 'Eine lange Nachgeschichte'; Cüppers, *Walther Rauff*, 356, note 116; 368, 127.

257 'the original source': *Military and Paramilitary Activities in and against Nicaragua (Nicaragua v United States) (Merits)* [1986] ICJ Reports 14, para. 63.

257 'in Santiago,' he said: Email, Dieter Maier to author, 21 March 2021.

258 'his torture session.': *Ibid.*

258 'additional confirmation.': Email, Dieter Maier to Lea Main-Klingst (c.c. author), 29 April 2021.

258 'the last time I saw him.': 'Chanfreau Oyarce Alfonso René', *Memoria Viva* (undated), https://memoriaviva.com/nuevaweb/detenidos-desaparecidos/desaparecidos-c/chanfreau-oyarce-alfonso-rene

258 she reportedly observed: Cerutti, 'Les nazis et le cône sud-américain'

(2011), 101 ('affirme que plusieurs détenus ont remarqué chez l'un des tortionnaires un très net accent allemand. Il s'agirait selon toute vraisemblance de Walter Rauff').

258 was happy to meet: Email, Monserrat Madariaga to author, 4 May 2021.

260 a DINA informant: Michael Lazzara (ed.), *Luz Arce and Pinochet's Chile: Testimony in the Aftermath of State Violence* (Palgrave Macmillan, 2011).

260 Alfonso Chanfreau: 'A la caza del "Guatón Romo"', *The Clinic*, 1 November 2018.

260 human rights violations: Supreme Court Chile, Case No. 469-98, September 1998, paras. 9–10 (disappearance of Pedro Enrique Poblete Córdova).

260 Romo died in 2007: 'La escabrosa entrevista que concedió Romo a Univisión', *La Tercera*, 4 July 2007.

263 'then buried on land.': Alfonso René Chanfreau Oyarce, Procesamiento, 14 July 2011, 266, 297, 1328 (on file).

263 where the affidavit was: 'Pablo Neruda did not die of cancer but may have been poisoned', *Novinite.com*, 21 October 2017.

266 'at risk of death': 'Pinochet en peligro de muerte', *Panamá América*, 29 July 1999.

266 in June 1215: Ekaizer, *Yo, Augusto*, 840.

266 King's College London: *Ibid.*, 841.

266 assassination attempt: Xavier Montanyà, *La gran evasión* (Pepitas de Calabaza, 2008), 13.

266 was not acceptable: Ekaizer, *Yo, Augusto*, 277, 503, 841.

267 Toloza reportedly told Frei: *Ibid.*, 842, 846, 851–2, 855.

267 his Spanish counterpart: *Ibid.*, 854, 858.

267 handing down of the judgement: *Ibid.*, 858, 859, 876.

267 too frail: *Ibid.*, 898–9.

268 to return to Chile: *Ibid.*, 893.

268 to be prosecuted: *Ibid.*, 896.

268 Toloza replied: *Ibid.*, 897.

268 medical issues: *Ibid.*, 901.

269 he was assured: Home Office to Pinochet, letter, 5 November 2000 (cited in *R., ex parte Belgium v Secretary of State for the Home Department*, ILDC 227, Judgement of 15 February 2000, at para. 9).

269 (extradited to Spain): Pinochet to Home Office, letter, 29 November 2000 (*ibid.*, para. 11).

270 right-wing candidate: Ekaizer, *Yo, Augusto*, 916.

270 (*¡Cómo se le occurre!*): Mónica Pérez y Felipe Gerdtzen, *Augusto Pinochet: 503 Días Atrapado en Londres* (Catalonia, 2016) 282.

270 'see him in the back!': Author interview with Peter Dean, 3 October 2023; 'La acusación presenta un escrito para aclarar las irregularidades del informe médico', *El Mundo*, 24 January 2001.

270 present throughout: *Ibid.*, *El Mundo*.

271 reportedly concluded: I, Jean Pateras, 3 October 2023.

271 could not be feigned: Ekaizer, *Yo, Augusto*, 924.

272 in his condition: Cited in *R., ex parte Belgium v Secretary of State for the Home Department*, ILDC 227, Judgement of 15 February 2000, at para. 13.

272 in Parliament: Hansard, House of Commons, 12 January 2000, column 277.

272 when he returned to Chile: Ekaizer, *Yo, Augusto*, 926.

274 of the DINA: Eugenia Palieraki, *¡La revolución ya viene!: El MIR chileno en los años sesenta* (Editorial LOM, 2014).

274 on suspicion of terrorism: 'Dance Card', in Roberto Bolaño, *Last Evenings on Earth and Other Stories* (New Directions, 2006).

274 'its literary value': Larry Rohter, 'A Chilean Writer's Fictions Might Include His Own Colorful Past', *The New York Times*, 8 February 2009.

275 near San Antonio: 'Ricardo Ernesto Lagos Salinas', *Memoria Viva* (undated), http://www.memoriaviva.com/English/victims/lagos-salinas.htm

275 no hard proof: Basso, *Chile Top Secret*.

275 said Basso: Ken Silverstein, *Private Warriors* (Verso, 2000), 125.

275 arms deals for Pinochet: Maria Soledad de la Cerda, *Chile y los hombres del Tercer Reich* (Sudamericana, 2000).

277 ninety-eight disappearances: Pablo Seguel Gutiérrez, 'La Brigada de Inteligencia Metropolitana de la Dirección de Inteligencia Nacional: Desafíos para la investigación en torno a sus recintos de detención, organización interna y racionalidad del servicio de inteligencia de la dictadura militar en Chile 1973–1976', *IX Jornadas de Trabajo sobre Historia Reciente, 1–3 August 2018* (2021), 685–706.

278 tortures and disappearances: 'Informe del experto sobre la cuestión de la suerte de las personas desaparecidas en Chile', Commission on Human Rights, E/CN.4/1363, 2 February 1980.

278 were convicted: See e.g. Rol No. 2.18298 (Tejas Verdes case), Judgement of 9 August 2010 (at p. 9); Rol. No. 33.340-2003 (Alfonso Chanfreau case), Judgement of 22 May 2003 (at p. 9).

278 occurred in 1975: 'Corte Suprema condena a 31 agentes de la DINA por secuestro calificado de Juan Carlos Perelman', *El Clarin*, 27 October 2021.

278 in August 1974: 'Operación Colombo: Corte Suprema condena a

exagentes de la DINA por secuestro calificado de fotógrafo', *Diario Constitucional*, 21 September 2023.

279 Chile and France: 'Historic Decision on the Crimes of the Chilean Dictatorship', *FIDH*, 17 December 2010; https://memoriaviva.com/nuevaweb/criminales/criminales-m/moren-brito-marcelo-luis-manuel

280 (died in 2022): Jorge Escalante, 'Las confesiones de Gerhard Mücke, uno de los jerarcas nazis de Colonia Dignidad', *La Nación*, 12 August 2005.

280 'obvious they knew each other.': 'El agente que llevó a Álvaro Vallejos a Colonia Dignidad: La palabra de un ex DINA contra Schaefer', *El Mercurio*, 24 July 2005.

280 a Chilean judge: Author interview with Samuel Fuenzalida, 14 December 2021.

280 ten years in prison: Rol 2.182-1998, Villa Baviera, episode Álvaro Modesto Vallejos Villagrán, first instance verdict, 7 May 2015; Santiago Appeals Court, Rol 1.051-2015, 10 April 2017; Supreme Court, Rol 19.127-2017, 7 August 2018; 'Condenan a 22 agentes de la DINA a 15 años de presidio por secuestro a militantes del MIR en la Operación Colombo', *CNN Chile*, 7 August 2018.

288 legal proceedings: Paul Kelso and Jamie Wilson, 'Belgian Challenge to Pinochet Ruling', *The Guardian*, 24 January 2000.

288 the judge asked: Investigating Judge Damian Vandermeersch, request for letters rogatory, 19 January 2000 (on file).

288 Extradition Convention: The obligations that Belgium alleged to have been violated included the 1984 Convention, the 1957 Extradition Convention, the 1959 European Convention on Mutual Assistance in Criminal Matters, and the general obligation of cooperation and good faith in international law.

289 (Second World War crimes.): *Certain Property (Liechtenstein v Germany) (Preliminary Objections)* [2005] ICJ Reports 6; *Jurisdictional Immunities of the State (Germany v Italy, Greece Intervening)* [2012] ICJ Reports 99.

289 no standing to sue: *R., ex parte Belgium v Secretary of State for the Home Department*, ILDC 227, Judgement of 15 February 2000, para. 3.

289 who expedited the case: 'Pinochet Opponents Win Legal Point', *BBC*, 8 February 2000.

289 Pinochet's legal situation: *R., ex parte Belgium v Secretary of State for the Home Department*, ILDC 227, Judgement of 15 February 2000, para. 3.

289 'and prosecution': *Demjanjuk v Petrovsky* (1985), 603 F.Supp. 1468.

290 on the web: Marlise Simons, 'Spanish Newspapers Disclose Secret

Pinochet Health Reports', *The New York Times*, 17 February 2000.

291 could stand trial: 'Comments', 'Spanish Doctors on British Medical Report', 18 February 2000, in Brody and Ratner, *The Pinochet Papers*, 461.

291 same conclusion: Jamie Wilson and Ian Black, 'Pinochet Fit for Trial, Says Belgium', *The Guardian*, 23 February 2000.

294 statement to Parliament: Hansard, House of Commons, 2 March 2000, column 664.

295 'sent to Spain.': Open Democracy, *Justice in the World's Light* (2001) (Geoffrey Bindman).

299 Britain, Chile and Spain: Hugh O'Shaughnessy, 'Secret UK Deal Freed Pinochet', *The Observer*, 7 January 2001.

299 'difficult to manage': Manuel Délano, 'Blair negoció con Frei en secreto el regreso de Pinochet a Chile', *El País*, 17 October 2000.

299 in March 2000: Mónica Pérez and Felipe Gerdtzen, *Augusto Pinochet: 503 Días Atrapado en Londres* (Catalonia, 2016), 274; O'Shaughnessy, 'Secret UK Deal Freed Pinochet'.

299 told an interviewer: *British Library, Sounds Archive*, 'Lord Hoffmann Interviewed by Louise Brodie', Part 7 (2011).

301 Izurieta served: Francesc Relea, 'El ejército chileno recibe la decisión de los lores con "frustración, indignación e inquietud"', *El País*, 26 November 1998.

301 Pinochet's health: 'Pinochet en peligro de muerte', *Panamá América*, 29 July 1999.

301 Frei's government: Ekaizer, *Yo, Augusto*, 800.

301 lawyers in Spain: 'El general Salgado se reúne hoy con autoridades de Defensa y con los abogados de Pinochet en España', *El País*, 10 August 1999.

302 Pinochet or Chile: Tony Blair, *A Journey* (Hutchinson, 2010).

304 'Secretary-General.': Raúl Troncoso Castillo, died 28 November 2004; see 'El Ministro del Interior chileno dice que el fallo de la Audiencia provocará "una tembladera mundial"', *El País*, 2 November 1998.

308 to stand trial: Ekaizer, *Yo, Augusto*, 901.

309 was now recognised: 'Belgium: Pinochet Case Won't Go to International Court', *AP Archive*, 2 March 2000, https://www.youtube.com/watch?v=3whZFmusLpQ

313 'have taken place': Margaret Thatcher, *Statecraft: Strategies for a Changing World* (HarperCollins, 2003), 269, 271.

314 Pinochet's favourite tune: Ekaizer, *Yo, Augusto*, 971.

314 newscaster reported: 'Pinochet, le retour', *ina.fr*, 3 March 2000.

315 María Isabel Allende: *Ibid.*

315 prospects at the time: 'Chilean Leftists Sue Pinochet', *The New York Times*, 13 January 1998.

315 slowly it progressed: Juan Guzmán, *Au bord du monde* (Les Arènes, 2005), 239.

315 'Caravan of Death' case: Judgement, Santiago Court of Appeal, 5 June 2000.

316 located and identified: Judgement, Supreme Court, 9 August 2000.

316 'the same document.': *Ibid.*, p. 539, paras. 8/9.

316 a door had opened: Cath Collins, 'Human Rights Trials in Chile During and After the "Pinochet Years"', *International Journal of Transitional Justice* 4 (2010), 67–86.

316 a limitation period: 'Condenan a represores de la dictadura militar', *El Mostrador*, 16 March 2010.

318 health was too fragile: Sophie Arie, 'Doctors Concerned over Pinochet Verdict', 323 (7305), *BMJ* 130 (2021).

318 if not in practice: Guzmán, *Au bord du monde*, 224, 241, 243, 265, 268, 269, 280.

318 resignation letter: Kornbluh, *The Pinochet File*, 490.

319 Orlando Letelier: Dinges and Landau, *Assassination on Embassy Row*, 369.

319 decades earlier: Permanent Subcommittee on Investigations, Minority Staff, 'Disguised Pinochet Account Names', https://nsarchive2.gwu.edu/NSAEBB/NSAEBB149/names.pdf

319 to avoid scrutiny: Kornbluh, *The Pinochet File*, 491.

319 froze his assets: *Ibid.*, 490; US Senate, Permanent Subcommittee on Investigations, 'Money Laundering and Foreign Corruption, Supplemental Staff Report on U.S. Accounts Used by Augusto Pinochet', 16 March 2005.

319 'the General's return.': 'The Secret Pinochet Portfolio: Former Dictator's Corruption Scandal Broadens', National Security Archive Electronic Briefing Book No. 149, *National Security Archive*, https://nsarchive2.gwu.edu/NSAEBB/NSAEBB149/index.htm

319 embezzlement and bribery: Kornbluh, *The Pinochet File*, 492.

319 network in Miami: Maria Elvira Salazar, 'Entrevista a Pinochet', 10 November 2010, https://www.youtube.com/watch?v=nKeLy5HmUZ0

320 'because of me': EastSouthWestNorth, citing article by Oscar Corral, *Miami Herald*, 18 March 2005, http://www.zonaeuropa.com/20050320_1.htm

320 the Valech Report: Larry Rohter, 'A Torture Report Compels Chile to Reassess Its Past', *The New York Times*, 28 November 2004.

320 'one homicide': Kornbluh, *The Pinochet File*, 494.

320 the Villa Grimaldi: *Ibid.*, 495.

321 under Allende: Associated Press, 'Pinochet Takes "Political Responsibility" for Actions of Chilean Dictatorship', *The Washington Post*, 25 November 2006.

321 'had escaped judgment.': Ariel Dorfman, 'Spitting on a Dead Man', *Los Angeles Times*, 17 December 2006.

321 celebrated his demise: Jonathan Franklin, 'Chilean Government Rejects State Funeral for Pinochet as Thousands Queue to Pay Respects', *The Guardian*, 12 December 2006.

321 tens of thousands of supporters: 'Pinochet's Funeral Draws 60,000', *CBC News*, 12 December 2006.

322 the streets of Santiago: 'Texto íntegro de la carta póstuma de Pinochet', *El Mundo*, 24 December 2006.

323 four disappeared individuals: Michael Lazzara, 'Complicity and Responsibility in the Aftermath of the Pinochet Regime: The Case of *El Mocito*', *Rúbrica Contemporánea* 5, no. 9 (2016), 59, 61.

323 *El Mocito*: Javier Rebolledo, *Danza de los cuervos: El 'Mocito' y el destino final de los detenidos desaparecidos*, 2nd edn. (CEIBO, 2012); Marcela Said and Jean de Certeau (dirs.), 'El Mocito', *The Clinic*, 19 March 2018, https://www.youtube.com/watch?v=1xNHzCLQIMc

324 assisted in disappearances: Rebolledo, *Danza de los cuervos*; Rodrigo Alvarado, 'La historia íntima del secreto mejor guardado de la Dictadura', *The Clinic*, 3 July 2012.

324 Carmelo Soria: Chilean Supreme Court, 13 March 2019, Case No. 1-1993, para. 91.

324 hiding in Australia: Ben Doherty, '"We Demand Justice": The Retired Sydney Nanny and the Chilean Families Still Looking for Answers', *The Guardian*, 23 June 2021.

326 DINA agents and activities: 'Clarín, la DINA, la Casona de Volpone y un abogado del Banco Central', *El Mostrador*, 3 January 2013.

326 Demolished in 2013: Macarena Segovia, 'Con oposición del Ejército cuartel donde partió la DINA es declarado Monumento Nacional', *El Mostrador*, 12 November 2014; 'Memorial Rocas AR', *Docubase MIT Documentary Lab*, 2021, https://docubase.mit.edu/project/memorial-rocas-ar

330 the Italian Embassy: 'Asesinato de Lumi Videla: El "Guatón" Romo contó que el general Garín le pagó por su silencio', *La Nación*, 25 July 2007.

331 'other people, Peruvians.': 'Brigada Lautaro de la DINA habría usado gas sarín para eliminar a peruanos', *El Mostrador*, 18 June 2007.

333 fishmeal each day: Francisca Espinosa Muñoz, '"La batalla de la merluza": Política y consumo alimenticio en el Chile de la Unidad Popular (1970–1973)', *Historia (Santiago)* 51, no. 1 (2018), 31–54.

334 held for several months: Author interview with Anatolio Zárate, 7 March 2024.

334 with the Americans: Author interview with Judge Paola Plaza, 14 November 2022; 'Regimiento No. 2 de Ingenieros "Tejas Verdes"', *Memoria Viva* (undated), https://memoriaviva.com/nuevaweb/centros-de-detencion/v-region/regimiento-no-2-de-ingenieros-tejas-verdes; 'Anatolio Zárate: "A Labbé yo lo vi cuando me estaban torturando"', *Soychile.cl*, 20 October 2014.

334 Samuel Fuenzalida: Jonathan Franklin, 'Augusto Pinochet's Former Bodyguard Detained at Santiago Military Base', *The Guardian*, 21 October 2014.

334 Espinoza as his deputy: Karinna Fernández and Magdalena Garcés Fuentes, 'Los casos de la Pesquera Arauco y Colonia Dignidad', in Juan Pablo Bohoslavsky, Karinna Fernández and Sebastián Smart (eds.), *Complicidad económica con la dictadura chilena. Un país desigual a la fuerza* (LOM Ediciones, 2019), 391 *et seq.*; *Pinochet's Economic Accomplices* (Lexington, 2020), 345.

334 the Letelier killing: Nelson Jofré, *La implacable verdad policial: La apasionante investigación del detective que descubrió al grupo más secreto y letal de la Dina* (Catalonia, 2023), 54–5.

334 run by Contreras: *Ibid.*, 345.

334 Tejas Verdes barracks: Santiago Court of Appeals, Chilean Supreme Court, 7 May 2014, Case No. 2.182-98, 31.

334 including Londres 38: Statement of Jorge Manuel Silva Huerta (p. 32), section 74, In case 2182-98 (Tejas Verdes), 9 August 2010 (on file).

334 fishmeal the other: Case 2182-98 (Tejas Verdes), Judgement of 9 August 2010, 37 (citing testimony of Patricio Eduardo Gutiérrez Fernández (fojas 3338), driver of Pesquera Arauco van, https://expedientesdelarepresion.cl/wp-content/uploads/2018/09/sentencia-caso-tejas-verdes-torturas.pdf).

334 used the vans: Case 2182-98 (Operation Colombo, episode Jorge Grez Aburto), Court of Appeal of Santiago, Judgement of 7 May 2014, 244 (on file).

334 'carry out inspections': Case 2182-98 (Tejas Verdes, episode Felix Varga), Judgement of 4 March 2009, at 36 (on file); *Pinochet's Economic Accomplices*, 345.

334 the *Pesquera*'s facility: Case 202-2015 file, testimony of Anatolio Zárate ('. . . around 1976, he [Arnoldo Aravena Contreras, RIP] confided me that one of the freezers of the Pesquera Arauco, specifically the one located in the southern part of the offices, had been used to store corpses until the *Kiwi* boat would take them to the sea for disposal'), p. 422 (on file).

334 female prostitutes: Email, Carlos Basso to author, 11 December 2021.

335 and met Rauff: Case 202-2015 file, p. 651, and Ministry of the Interior Decree 450 of 30 August 1974 (Art. 1: 'Authorizes Pesquera Arauco S.A. . . . to establish a service of private vigilantes for a two year period . . .'; Art. 2 restricts it to the Pesquera's facilities at Lo Valledor (where the 310 Chevrolet vans are kept, since 1973); Art. 3 limits number of firearms for each vigilante to three, with a stock of four loads of ammunition per arm).

335 around San Antonio: *Pinochet's Economic Accomplices*, 345.

335 drugged and strangled: JUDGEMENT: 'Condenan a 18 ex agentes de la dictadura por el asesinato de la profesora Marta Ugarte', *El Desconcierto*, 29 November 2021.

335 dropped into the Pacific Ocean: 'Operación Kiwi: enterrados en el mar', *La Nación*, 12 September 2004.

335 (the following year.): Case 202-2015, pp. 5895–5906 (on file); *Pinochet's Economic Accomplices*, 345.

336 witness testimony: Case 202-2015, pp. 15396–8, 15652–8 (on file).

336 bodies at sea: See Report of the Economic and Social Council, 'Protection of Human Rights in Chile', A/10285, 7 October 1975.

336 said to be involved: Statement of Anatolio Zárate, 13 October 2014, in Case 202-2015 file, at 515393 (on file).

336 *Pesquera Arauco*: Judge Hernan Crisoto Greisse, in Operación Colombo Aedo and others, proceedings in Case 2182–98, p. 16275, 12 June 2015, investigation later incorporated into Case 202–2015, p. 442.

336 'in San Antonio.': Case 202-2015 file; I: Samuel Fuenzalida, 8 March 2024.

338 Londres 38: 'Londres 38 interpone querella contra pesquera colaboradora de la DINA', 3 October 2017, https://www.londres38.cl/1937/w3-article-99099.html

338 of the disappeared: *Pinochet's Economic Accomplices*, p. 346.

338 man-made toxin: Gideon Long, 'Pablo Neruda: Chilean Poet's Death Still Shrouded in Mystery', *BBC*, 24 September 2023; see generally Andrew Feinstein, *Pablo Neruda: A Passion for Life* (Bloomsbury, 2004).

340 kidnapping and torture: Jorge Escalante, 'Las confesiones de Gerhard Mücke, uno de los jerarcas nazis de Colonia Dignidad', *La Nación*, 12 August 2005; 'Chile Sentences Two Germans for Pinochet-Era Crimes', *DW*, 20 October 2015; 'Muere Gerhard Mücke, criminal de la dictadura y líder de Colonia Dignidad', *SwissInfo*, 18 September 2022.

340  disappeared at sea: 'Y hasta que la Corte Suprema se dio cuenta: Verdad judicial, Pinochet sabía todo sobre operación para lanzar desaparecidos al mar', *The Clinic*, 16 August 2009.

343  (about US \$250): Tom Burgis, 'Chile's Torture Victims to Get Life Pensions', *The Guardian*, 30 November 2004.

343  and disappeared them: *Parque Arauco*: https://www.parauco.com/parque-arauco-corporativo-en/nuestra-empresa/identificacion-de-la-compania

349  'then . . . goodbye.': 'Vor 50 Jahren: Putsch in Chile – Pinochets deutsche Paten', *ARD Audiothek*, 3 September 2023.

350  deals were done: Jorge Escalante, 'El hijo del dictador chileno Augusto Pinochet fue un agente de la DINA', *El Mundo*, 11 September 2010.

351  said Vergara: 'Vor 50 Jahren'.

354  the Supreme Court: Noemi Arcos, 'La trayectoria judicial de Mario Carroza, nominado por quinta vez a la Corte Suprema', *El Dinamo*, 14 August 2019.

365  the Yugoslavia conflict: Ian Traynor, 'Franjo Tudjman', *The Guardian*, 13 December 1999.

365  the arrest of Pinochet: Daniel Marans, 'Henry Kissinger Just Turned 92, Here's Why He's Careful About Where He Travels', *Huffington Post*, 28 May 2015; Henry Kissinger, 'The Pitfall of Universal Jurisdiction', *Foreign Affairs*, July/August 2001.

365  an international crime: 'Bush Cancels Geneva Speech "Fearing" Possible Torture Charges', *France 24*, 5 February 2011.

365  issued against him: 'Putin Won't Attend a South Africa Summit Next Month, Avoiding Possible Arrest', *NPR*, 19 July 2023.

366  ended a long friendship: Hoffmann told me he wrote to Browne-Wilkinson, but received a 'pompous' response with an 'unappealing' tone that might have come from a school prefect. 'Poor old Browne-Wilkinson, I think he had something of a nervous breakdown,' Hoffmann recalled. 'Whether this contributed to it in any way I don't know, but he went into a depression, found it impossible to write judgements, then retired.' Hoffmann, Leonard (7 of 10), National Life Story Collection: Legal Lives C736/010.

367  crimes committed abroad: Rosa Ana Alija Fernández, 'The 2014 Reform of Universal Jurisdiction in Spain: From All to Nothing', 13 *Zeitschrift für Internationale Strafrechtsdogmatik* 717 (2014).

367  to be unlawful: UM OHCHR, 'Baltasar Garzón trials were arbitrary and failed to comply with principles of judicial independence and impartiality', 26 August 2021.

367  'to fight for it.': Canciller van Klaveren por Pinochet: "La jurisdicción

chilena en esa época no estuvo a la altura"', *La Mostrador*, 16 July 2023.

367 German government: 'Chile Begins Expropriation of Land from Colonia Dignidad', *DW*, 2 June 2024.

368 'services of the dictatorship': 'Expropiación de Colonia Dignidad es decisión del Estado, dice ministro de Justicia chileno Cordero', *DW Espana*, 8 June 2024.

369 'circumstances of the case': 'Senator Pinochet', Legal Fees, *Hansard*, vol. 357, 20 November 2000, Col. 99W. The total was £1,209,775.05 (£270,935.89 for the first House of Lords hearing; £151,361.30 for the application to set aside the first judgement; and £787,477.86 for the cost of Divisional Court hearings).

370 'Disgusted.': Carmen Soria, Foreword, in Awad and Pérez Alveal, *Carmelo*.

370 Miguel Schweitzer: 'Chile Asks U.S. to Extradite Suspects in 1976 Murder of Diplomat', Reuters, 17 May 2016.

370 received elsewhere: *Civil Action 02-02240, Laura González-Vera et al v. Henry Alfred Kissinger et al*, Order for Default Judgment against Defendant Michael Townley, 23 November 2005; https://www. elclarin.cl/fpa/pdf/p_231105_en.pdf; Laura González-Vera and Ali Abed Beydoun, as Personal Representative of the Estate of Carmelo Soria Espinoza, Deceased, Appellants v. Michael Vernon Townley, et al., Appellees, United States Court of Appeals, District of Columbia Circuit, 23 February 2010, *595 F.3d 379* (2010); Adam Klasfeld, 'Court Won't Help Find Pinochet's Former Goon', Courthouse News Service, 20 March 2010; message from Carmen Soria, 22 June 2024.

370 1978 Amnesty Law:*Carmelo Soria Espinoza v. Chile*, Case 11.725, Report No. 133/99, OEA/Ser.L/V/II.106 Doc. 3 rev. at 494, 19 November 1999, paras. 110 and 149.

371 a narrow majority: Senate, Republic of Chile, 'Proyecto de ley que declara la nulidad del Decreto Ley N° 2.191, de 1978', 21 April 2006; after two failed attempts, on 18 July 2007 the Senate (presided by Eduardo Frei) passed the Law by 16 votes to 14: 'Senado aprobó indemnización para familia de Carmelo Soria', *cooperativa.cl*, 18 July 2007.

371 the Lautaro Brigade: Case I-1993, Townley Testimony, 13 July 2006, p. 61 (on file).

371 July night in 1976: 'Townley afirmó haber visto a Carmelo Soria secuestrado en casa de Lo Curro', *El Mostrador*, 21 August 2006.

371 pleaded for his life: Report of Testimony, 3 September 1992, from Rafael Castillo to Osvaldo Carmona (on file); *see also* 'Informe Especial: Michael Townley – Confesiones de un asesino', 24 Horas TVN

Chile, https://www.youtube.com/watch?v=yg_WUmIv3LA (at 60'); Case I-1993, Testimony of Michael Townley, 13 July 2006 (on file).

371 whereabouts unknown: Supreme Court, Case No. 1-1993, Carmelo Soria Espinoza, 22 August 2023; Lun Lee, Prófugos y millonarios: ex DINA condenados por asesinat o de Carmelo Soria cobran pensión siendo fugitivos de la justicia, *Interferencia.cl*, 21 March 2024.

371 a character in novels: Pavel Oyarzún, *Será el paraíso* (LOM, 2019).

371 a collection of poems: Dunkler, *Spandau*; Juan Manuel Vial, 'Un nazi en el sur', *La Tercera*, 5 January 2013.

371 crime and collaboration: 'Giornale, spie e hotel di lusso', *Corriere della Sera*, 18 August 2023.

371 available in Spanish: Wilfried Huismann, 'Vor 50 Jahren: Putsch in Chile – Pinochets deutsche Paten', *WDR*, 3 September 2023.

371 decades earlier: República de Chile, *Diario de Sesión del Senado*, Legislatura 355, Sesión 82, 15 January 2008, 54 *et seq.*

371 sceptical grandson told me: *Lamesavintage*, March 2023 (Instagram).

372 published articles: 'El jerarca nazi que murió impune en Chile', *24 Horas*, 10 May 2024; Victor Hernández, 'A 40 años de la muerte de Walter Rauff', *El Magallanes*, 12 May 2024, 37–41.

374 thirty years: Cour d'Assises de Paris, 3ème Section, Case 07/2007, Arrêt Criminel, 17 December 2010; Case 07/2007, Arrêt Civil, 17 December 2010; Paulo Paranagua, 'La justice française condamne les accusés jugés pour la disparition de Français au Chili', *Le Monde*, 18 December 2010.

374 in damages: Supreme Court, judgement of 29 April 2015, confirming ruling of the Visiting Minister Jorge Zepeda Arancibia in case N° 33.340-2003 of the Court of Appeal.

374 so many years before: 'Corte de Apelaciones confirma condenas contra exagentes DINA por secuestro de Alfonso Chanfreau', *El Mostrador*, 27 April 2023.

374 her husband's remains: 'Murió el ex agente de la DINA Basclay Zapata', *cooperativa.cl*, 3 December 2017.

374 to be pardoned: Maite Fernandez Simon, 'Wartime ID Card Suggests Father of Chilean Presidential Candidate was Nazi', *The Washington Post*, 9 December 2021; Alberto González, 'Abogado Meza revela gestiones de Kast para indultar a reos de Punta Peuco: "Ha sido muy consecuente"', *Bibliochile.cl*, 16 December 2021.

375 about the disappeared: 'Atención: Chile anuncia un plan nacional para que el Estado asuma la búsqueda de unas 1.100 víctimas por la dictadura', *Semana*, 8 July 2023.

# INDEX

Priebke, Erich, 69
Project Andrea, 55
Project Colombo, 320
Pudeto Regiment, 11, 138, 167
Puerto Montt, 139, 263, 279, 343
Punta Arenas, 165–170, 261, 285, 376,
377; maps, *124*, *125*; barracks, 138,
167, 168, 169; Braun-Menéndez
Palace, 169; cemetery, 139, 168; in
Chatwin's book, 59; Club Andino,
168, 173; Club de la Unión, 75, 168;
detention and torture after Coup,
138, 170, 226; football stadium, 138,
168; German community, 61, 75, 126,
165, 166, 168; Grand Palace cinema,
74, 76, 168; history, 61, 165, 167–168;
indigenous inhabitants, 165, 169;
Rauff's office, 131, 168; museum, 166,
168, 173, 234; 'Palace of Smiles' *see*
Old Naval Hospital; Plaza de Armas,
61, 75, 165, 166, 169, 234–235; Rauff's
homes, 74, 131, 168, 173; Sara Braun
company, 61, 73, 134, 194; Sara Braun
Palace, 166, 169; Sotito's restaurant,
168; University, 167
Punta Peuco prison, 326, 371, 374
Putin, Vladimir, 365

Quesada Yáñez, Marcos, 109, 210
Quilpué, 377
Quito, 71–72, 74, 140, 175, 178, 249, 250

Ratline, xv, xxvi, 59–60
*The Ratline* (Philippe Sands), 16, 59, 251
Rauff, Alf (son), 63, 69, 70, 72, 74, 79,
126, 141
Rauff, Edith (née Richter), 62, 69, 70, 72,
73, 74, 195
Rauff, Ilse (sister), 60, 72, 135, 139–141,
182
Rauff, Sebastian (grandson), 360
Rauff, Walther: appearance, 53, 66,
81, 82, 128, 141, 144, 172, 179,
183, 187, 188, 191, 194, 262, 282;
photographs of, *53*, *79*, 172, *185*, *248*,
262, 282–283, 284, *329*, 330, 351;
character, 62, 63, 66, 68–69, 70, 73,
81, 82, 129, 130, 132, 133, 134, 141,
174, 175, 178, 184, 194, 261, 377–378;
voice and accent, 66, 82, 327, 344,

347, 377; early life, 61; naval career,
61–62, 74, 184; first trip to Chile, 61;
marriages and children, 62; joins Nazi
Party, 62; SS career, 62–68; designs
gas vans, 63–64, 186; posted to
Tunisia, 66–67, 82, 144, 184; operates
in Italy, 67–68; awarded German
Cross, 67, 68; imprisoned in Italy,
68–69, *68*; at Nuremberg trials, 69; in
Syria and Lebanon, xxv, 59, 70–71;
fugitive in Italy, 69–70, 71; works
for Israeli intelligence, 71, 186; lives
in Ecuador, 71–73; meets Pinochet,
72–73, 178; settles in Patagonia, 73;
works for West German intelligence,
73–74, 75, 77, 78, 81, 184; visits
West Germany, 73–74; manages
Pesquera Bonacic, 75–76, 126–127,
131; moves in with Nena Zúñiga,
131; arrested for murder, 76, 77, 79,
168, 170, 186; extradition attempt
by West Germany, 76–83, 87, 112,
146, 176–177, 186, 240, 284, 316,
371; testifies against other Nazis,
130–131; manages Pesquera Camelio,
131, 136, 171–172, 181, 194, 284, 377;
quiet life in Patagonia, 126, 131, 132,
140, 170, 231; extradition request
by Wiesenthal, 135, 192; welcomes
coup, 136, 138, 139; visits Santiago
regularly after coup, 141, 179, 228;
Mossad assassination attempt, 189;
avoids expulsion, 192–193; retirement
in Santiago, 72, 179, 181–182, 192;
declining health, 181, 193; does not
attend Nena's funeral, 192; death
and funeral, 194–198, 350; link to
author's family, 362; link to Chilean
intelligence, 184–185 *see also*
Dirección de Inteligencia Nacional
(DINA); links to Chilean military,
135, 138, 141, 142, 176, 195, 355;
links to Eichmann, 76–77, 126; links
to Pinochet, 60, 81, 136, 140, 175,
184–185, 194, 196, 227–228, 237, 275;
links to Camelio family, 171–174;
anti-communist, 66, 72, 76, 133, 140,
141, 174, 175, 182; anti-democratic,
136, 141; anti-Semitic, 66, 72, 79,
141, 175, 179, 181, 182, 194; dislikes